FROMMER'S

COMPREHENSIVE TRAVEL GUIDE

TORONTO '93-'94

by Marilyn Wood

PRENTICE HALL TRAVEL

NEW YORK • LONDON • TORONTO • SYDNEY • TOKYO • SINGAPORE

FROMMER BOOKS

Published by Prentice Hall General Reference
A division of Simon & Schuster Inc.
15 Columbus Circle
New York, NY 10023

ISBN 0-671-84707-4
ISSN 1047-7853

Design by Robert Bull Design
Maps by Geografix Inc.

FROMMER'S EDITORIAL STAFF
Editor-in-Chief/Editorial Director: Marilyn Wood
Editorial Manager/Senior Editor: Alice Fellows
Senior Editor: Lisa Renaud
Editors: Charlotte Allstrom, Thomas F. Hirsch, Peter Katucki, Sara Hinsey Raveret, Theodore Stavrou
Assistant Editors: Margaret Bowen, Lee Gray, Chris Hollander, Ian Wilker
Editorial Assistants: Gretchen Henderson, Bethany Jewett
Managing Editor: Leanne Coupe

Special Sales
Bulk purchases of Frommer's Travel Guides are available at special discounts. The publishers are happy to custom-make publications for corporate clients who wish to use them as premiums or sales promotions. We can excerpt the contents, provide covers with corporate imprints, or create books to meet specific needs. For more information write to Special Sales, Prentice Hall Travel, Paramount Communications Building, 15 Columbus Circle, New York, NY 10023

Manufactured in the United States of America

CONTENTS

LIST OF MAPS

TORONTO

TORONTO WALKING TOURS

EXCURSION AREAS

INVITATION TO THE READERS

In researching this book, I have come across many wonderful establishments, the best of which I have included here. I am sure that many of you will also come across special hotels, inns, restaurants, guesthouses, shops, and attractions. Please don't keep them to yourself. Share your experiences, especially if you want to comment on places that have been included in this edition that have changed for the worse. You can address your letters to:

Marilyn Wood
Frommer's Toronto '93–'94
c/o Prentice Hall Travel
15 Columbus Circle
New York, NY 10023

A DISCLAIMER

Readers are advised that prices fluctuate in the course of time and travel information changes under the impact of the varied and volatile factors that affect the travel industry. Neither the author nor the publisher can be held responsible for the experiences of readers while traveling. Readers are invited to write to the publisher with ideas, comments, and suggestions for future editions.

SAFETY ADVISORY

Whenever you're traveling in an unfamiliar city or country, stay alert. Be aware of your immediate surroundings. Wear a moneybelt and keep a close eye on your possessions. Be particularly careful with cameras, purses, and wallets, all favorite targets of thieves and pickpockets.

CHAPTER 1

INTRODUCING TORONTO

- **WHAT'S SPECIAL ABOUT TORONTO**

1. HISTORY & BACKGROUND

- **DATELINE**
- **FAMOUS TORONTONIANS**

2. RECOMMENDED BOOKS

Once lampooned as dull and ugly, a city whose inhabitants fled to Buffalo for a good time and where the blinds were drawn on Sunday at the main department store (Eaton's) to stop anyone from sinfully window-shopping, Toronto, now with a population of over three million, has burst forth during the last three decades from its stodgy past and grabbed attention as one of the most exciting cities on the North American continent.

How did it happen? Unlike most cities, Toronto got a chance to change its image with a substantial blood transfusion from other cultures. Once a quiet, conservative community dominated by sedate Anglo-Saxons, who entertained either at home or in their clubs, Toronto was given a huge infusion of energy by the post–World War II influx of large numbers of Italians, Chinese, and Portuguese, as well as Germans, Jews, Hungarians, Greeks, East Indians, West Indians, and French Canadians. Now the city, a multicultural patchwork quilt, throbs with life as people flock to Harbourfront and the Ontario Science Centre, crowd aboard the ferries to the Islands in summer, gather at street cafés and restaurants, shop the boutiques and shopping centers, attend the theaters and concert halls, and generally fill the city with life and movement—ad infinitum.

And somehow, although some Torontonians would disagree, the city has become a model city where conservative traditions have managed to temper the often runaway impulse of developers and businesspeople to destroy the old in order to create the new. In Toronto progress has not inevitably brought in the wrecker's ball. Much has survived. When you see Holy Trinity Church and the Scadding House, one of the oldest residences in the city, standing proudly against the glass-galleried Eaton Centre, preserved because the people demanded it, you know that certain values and a great deal of thoughtful debate have gone into the making of this city.

A model city. Indeed, Jane Jacobs, the urban planner, historian, and sociologist, chose to live here to watch her theories actually working on the downtown streets—where people walk to work from their restored Victorian town houses, where no developer can erect downtown commercial space without including living space, where the subway positively gleams and the streets are safe, where old buildings are saved and converted to other uses, where the architects design around the contours of nature instead of just bulldozing the

WHAT'S SPECIAL ABOUT TORONTO

Beaches
- ☐ Wards Island and Centre Island beaches and the boardwalk and lakefront at The Beaches.

Architectural Highlights
- ☐ Royal Bank Tower (1972–76), a shimmering shaft of gold.
- ☐ City Hall (1965), by Viljo Revell, symbol of Toronto's rebirth.
- ☐ SkyDome (1989), the world's first stadium with a fully retractable roof.
- ☐ Roy Thomson Hall (1981), glass and mirrors outside, acoustic high-tech inside.
- ☐ Underground City, five miles of interconnecting tunnels lined with 1,000 stores.
- ☐ Flatiron Building (1892), as photogenic as ever at Church and Front.
- ☐ Provincial Parliament Buildings, great Romanesque architecture in pink sandstone.

Museums
- ☐ The Royal Ontario Museum, known especially for its Chinese and Canadiana collections.
- ☐ The Art Museum, with the world's largest collection of Henry Moore works.
- ☐ Ontario Science Centre, with hundreds of engaging interactive exhibits that wow kids and adults alike.

Events/Festivals
- ☐ Canadian National Exhibition, the world's largest annual fair.
- ☐ Caribana, carnival Toronto style.
- ☐ Royal Agricultural Show, a serious "State Fair" plus a horse show attended by royals.

For the Kids
- ☐ Ontario Science Centre, Harbourfront, Ontario Place, and Metro Zoo are the top hits.

Shopping
- ☐ The Eaton Centre, 300-plus stores in attractive glass-domed marble-and-fountain ambience.
- ☐ Honest Ed's, the original launching pad for Ed Mirvish's meteoric rise to wealth and fame.

Streets/Neighborhoods
- ☐ Chinatown, a large bustling community with great shopping, browsing, and dining.
- ☐ Bloor/Yorkville, whose designer boutiques, art galleries, and cafés make it prime strolling territory.
- ☐ Queen Street West, youthful, funky, and fun with lots of reasonably priced, sophisticated dining.

A Zoo
- ☐ Metro Zoo, great for the animals and great for the visitors.

Natural Spectacles
- ☐ The Toronto Islands, a great escape from the urban landscape that's only a short ferry trip away.

After Dark
- ☐ 40-plus theaters make Toronto the second-largest theater center in North America.

trees, where 200 parks invite you to PLEASE WALK ON THE GRASS, and where over three million people live harmoniously for the most part in an exciting, vibrant city that has retained the traditional Canadian values of peace, order, and good government.

1. HISTORY & BACKGROUND

HISTORY

FROM FUR TRADING POST TO MUDDY YORK As with most cities, geography, trade, and communications are the influences that have shaped Toronto and its history. Although the city today possesses a downtown core, it also sprawls across a large area—a gift (or drawback, depending how you look at it) of geography, for there are no physical barriers to stop it. Initially, the flat broad plain rising from Lake Ontario to an inland ridge of hills (around St. Clair Avenue today) and stretching between the Don River in the east and the Humber in the west made an ideal location for a settlement.

Native Canadians had long stopped here at the entrance to the Toronto Trail—a short route between the Lower and Upper Lakes—which they traveled, from Lake Ontario via the Humber and Holland rivers to Lake Simcoe and finally via other water routes to Georgian Bay. French fur trader Etienne Brûlé was the first European to travel this trail in 1615, but it wasn't until 1720 that the first trading post, known as Fort Toronto, was established by the French to intercept the furs that were being taken across Lake Ontario to New York State by English rivals. This trading post was replaced in 1751 by Fort Rouille, which was built on the site of today's CNE grounds. When the 1763 Treaty of Paris ended the Anglo-French War after the fall of Québec, French rule in North America was effectively ended and the city's French antecedents were all but forgotten.

Only 20 miles across the lake from the U.S. border, Toronto has always been affected by what happens south of the border. When the American Revolution established a powerful and potentially hostile new nation, Toronto's location became strategically more important, or it certainly seemed so to John Graves Simcoe, lieutenant-governor of

DATELINE

- **1615** Etienne Brûlé travels the Toronto Trail.
- **1720** France establishes post at Toronto.
- **1751** Fort Rouille built.
- **1763** Treaty of Paris effectively ends French rule in Canada.
- **1787** Lord Dorchester, British governor at Québec, purchases land from Scarborough to Etobicoke from the Mississauga tribe.
- **1791** British colony of Upper Canada formed.
- **1793** Governor of Upper Canada, Col. John Simcoe, arrives and names settlement York.
- **1796** Yonge Street laid out, a 33-mile ox-cart trail.
- **1797** Center of government transferred from Niagara to York.
- **1813** War of 1812: Americans invade, blow up Fort York, and burn Parliament buildings.
- **1820s** Immigration of Nonconformists and Irish Catholics

(continues)

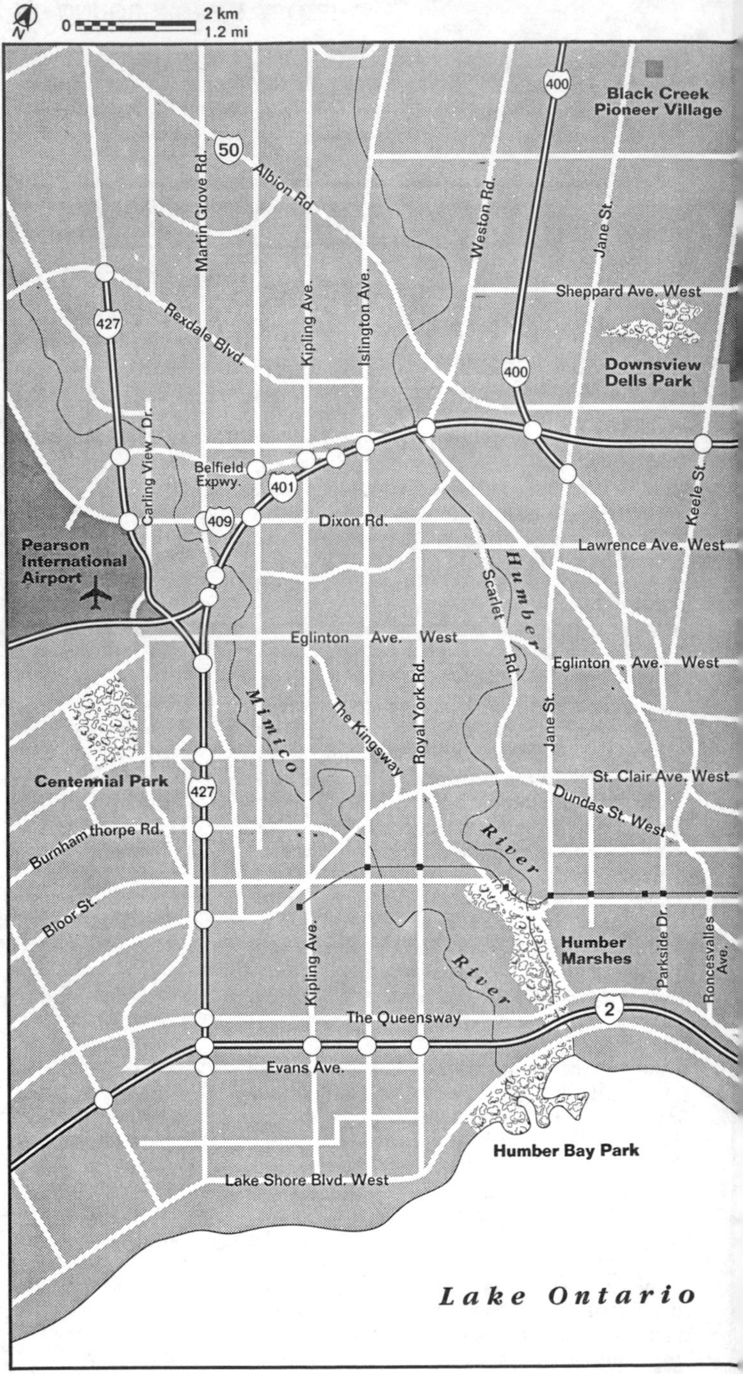
2 km
1.2 mi
N
Black Creek Pioneer Village
Downsview Dells Park
Pearson International Airport
Centennial Park
Humber Marshes
Humber Bay Park
Lake Ontario
Albion Rd.
Martin Grove Rd.
Weston Rd.
Jane St.
Sheppard Ave. West
Rexdale Blvd.
Kipling Ave.
Islington Ave.
Carling View Dr.
Belfield Expwy.
Dixon Rd.
Keele St.
Lawrence Ave. West
Scarlet Rd.
Humber
Eglinton Ave. West
Eglinton Ave. West
Mimico
The Kingsway
Royal York Rd.
St. Clair Ave. West
Dundas St. West
Burnhamthorpe Rd.
River
Bloor St.
River
Parkside Dr.
Roncesvalles Ave.
The Queensway
Evans Ave.
Lake Shore Blvd. West
50
400
427
401
409
2

METROPOLITAN TORONTO

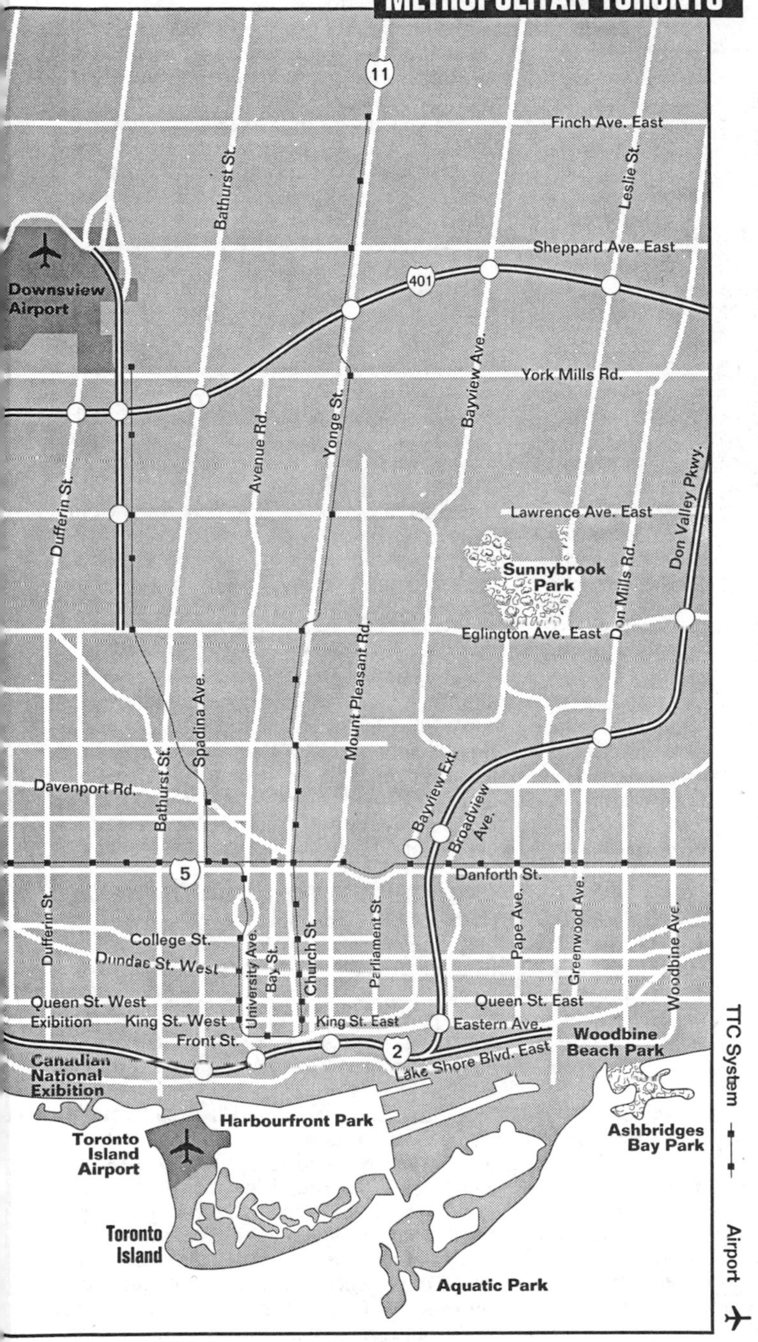

11
Finch Ave. East
Leslie St.
Bathurst St.
Sheppard Ave. East
401
Downsview Airport
York Mills Rd.
Bayview Ave.
Yonge St.
Avenue Rd.
Dufferin St.
Don Valley Pkwy.
Lawrence Ave. East
Sunnybrook Park
Don Mills Rd.
Eglington Ave. East
Mount Pleasant Rd.
Spadina Ave.
Bathurst St.
Davenport Rd.
Bayview Ext.
Broadview Ave.
5
Danforth St.
Dufferin St.
Parliament St.
Pape Ave.
Greenwood Ave.
Woodbine Ave.
College St.
Dundas St. West
University Ave.
Bay St.
Church St.
Queen St. West
Queen St. East
Exibition
King St. West
King St. East
Eastern Ave.
Front St.
Woodbine Beach Park
Canadian National Exibition
2
Lake Shore Blvd. East
Harbourfront Park
Toronto Island Airport
Ashbridges Bay Park
Toronto Island
Aquatic Park
TTC System
Airport

DATELINE

fosters reform politics.

- **1821** Bank of Upper Canada chartered.
- **1824** William Lyon Mackenzie starts the *Colonial Advocate*.
- **1828** Erie Canal extended to Oswego on Lake Ontario.
- **1830** Upper Canada College opens.
- **1830s** Orange Order becomes prominent influence in politics.
- **1832–34** Cholera epidemics.
- **1834** City named Toronto; City Council replaces magistrates; William Lyon Mackenzie becomes first mayor.
- **1837** Rebellion led by former mayor William Lyon Mackenzie, sparked by bad economic times.
- **1841** Act of Union establishes the United Province of Canada, with Kingston as ruling seat; Toronto loses status as a capital.
- **1842** Streets are gas lit.
- **1843** The university, King's College, opens.
- **1844** City hall built; George Brown founds the *Globe*.
- **1847** Electrical telegraph service opened to Montréal and New York.
- **1840s–'50s** Mass Irish immigration.

(continues)

the newly formed province of Upper Canada, which had been established in 1791 to administer the frontiers—from Kingston and Quinte's Isle to Windsor and beyond—settled largely by Loyalists fleeing the Revolution. To Simcoe Toronto was more defensible than Fort Niagara and a natural arsenal for Lake Ontario, which also afforded easy access to Lake Huron and the interior.

The governor had already purchased a vast tract of land from the Mississauga tribe for the paltry sum of 1,700 pounds plus such baubles as blankets, guns, rum, and tobacco, and in 1793 Lieutenant-Governor Simcoe, his wife, Elizabeth, and the Queen's Rangers arrived to build a settlement. Simcoe ordered a garrison built, renamed the settlement York, and laid it out in a 10-block rectangle around King, Front, George, Duke, and Berkeley streets. Beyond stretched a series of 100-acre lots from Queen to Bloor, which were granted to government officials to mollify their resentment about having to move to this mosquito-plagued, marshy, muddy outpost. Its muddiness was indeed prodigious, and in fact there is a story told of a fellow who saw a hat lying in the middle of a street, went to pick it up, and found the head of a live man submerged below it! In three short years a small hamlet had grown and Simcoe had laid out Yonge Street—then a 33-mile oxcart trail—and four years later the first Parliament meeting confirmed York as the capital of Upper Canada.

FROM MUDDY YORK TO THE FAMILY COMPACT The officials were a more demanding and finicky lot than the sturdy frontier farmers, and businesses sprang up to serve them, so that by 1812 the population had grown to 703 and included a brewer-baker, a blacksmith, a watchmaker, a chairmaker, an apothecary, a hatter, and a tailor.

During the War of 1812, despite initial victories at Queenston and Detroit, Canada was under siege, and in April 1813, 14 ships carrying 1,700 American troops invaded York, blew up the uncompleted fort, burned the Parliament Buildings, and carried off the mace (which was not returned until 1934). The British general burned the 30-gun warship the *Sir Isaac Brock,* which was being built, and retreated, leaving young John Strachan to negotiate the capitulation. This event did much to reinforce the town's pro-British, anti-American attitude—an attitude that persists to some extent to this day. In retaliation for the burning of Fort York, some Canadians went down and torched the American president's residence. (The Americans later whitewashed it to hide the charred wood—hence, the White House.)

A conservative pro-British outlook permeated the official political oligarchy that dominated York, and this group was dubbed the Family Compact. Many of the names that visitors will see on street signs, subway stops, and maps are derived from this august group of early government officers and their families. Among them were William Jarvis, a New England Loyalist who became provincial secretary; English-born Thomas Ridout and William Chewett, who served in the surveyor-general's office; John Beverley Robinson, son of a Virginia Loyalist, who at age 22 became attorney-general and later chief justice of Upper Canada; Scottish army-surgeon Dr. James Macaulay; Anglo-Irish Peter Russell, Simcoe's receiver-general and later provincial administrator; Scottish-educated Dr. John Strachan, who rose from being a schoolmaster to an Anglican rector and the most powerful figure in York; Anglo-Irish Dr. William Warren Baldwin, doctor, lawyer, architect, judge, and parliamentarian, who laid out Spadina Avenue as a thoroughfare leading to his house of that name in the country; Scots magistrates Alexander Wood and William Allan; and the Boultons, prominent lawyers, judges, and politicians—Judge D'Arcy Boulton built a mansion, The Grange, which later became the core of the art museum and still stands today.

These men were extremely conscious of rank, conformist, conservative, pro-British, Tory, and Anglican. Their power would be broken only later in the 19th century as a larger and more diverse population gave reformers a chance to challenge their control, but even today their influence still lingers in the corporate world where a handful of companies on and individuals control 80% of the companies on the Toronto Stock Exchange.

THE EARLY 19TH CENTURY—CANAL, RAILROAD & IMMIGRATION The changes that would eventually

DATELINE

- **1849** Great fire destroys much of city; Anglican King's College converts to secular University of Toronto.
- **1850** Public School Board established.
- **1851** Population 30,000 (33% Irish); Anglican Trinity College founded; Northern Railway begins construction; St. Lawrence Hall built.
- **1852** Toronto Stock Exchange opens; Grand Trunk Railroad charted, linking Québec-Montréal-Toronto-Guelph-Sarnia.
- **1853** St. James Cathedral completed at King and Church.
- **1855** Railway links to Collingwood on Georgian Bay and to Hamilton-London line; Detroit and New York accessible.
- **1858** Storm creates the Toronto Islands.
- **1861** Population 44,000; horse-powered street railway runs along Yonge to Yorkville.
- **1862** Allan Gardens developed.
- **1867** Canadian Confederation; Toronto becomes capital of new province of Ontario; Canadian Bank of Commerce founded.
- **1868** Canada First Movement begins.

(continues)

dilute their control began in the early 19th century, especially during the 1820s, '30s, and '40s, when immigrants—Irish Protestants and Catholics, Scots, Presbyterians, Methodists, and other Nonconformists—poured in to settle the frontier farmlands. By 1832 York had become the largest urban community in the province, with a population of 1,600. Already well established commercially as a supply center, York was given another boost when the Erie Canal was extended to Oswego on Lake Ontario, giving it direct access to New York, and the Welland Canal was built across the Niagara Peninsula, giving it access to Lake Erie and points beyond. In 1834 the city was incorporated and York became Toronto, a city bounded by Parliament Street to the east, Bathurst to the west, the lakefront to the south, and 400 yards north of current Queen Street (then called Lot) to the north. Outside this area—stretching west to Dufferin Street, east to the Don River, and north to Bloor Street—lay the "liberties," out of which new wards would later be carved. North of Bloor, local brewer Joseph Bloor and Sheriff Jarvis were already drawing up plans for the village of Yorkville.

Among the city's more successful merchants were William Allan, Alexander Wood, and Laurent Quetton de St. George, and as they and others prospered and more immigrants arrived, the society became more diverse and demands for democracy and reform were voiced. Among the reformers were such leaders as Francis Collins, who launched the radical paper *Canadian Freeman* in 1825; stationer James Lesslie; lawyer William Draper; and perhaps most famous of all, fiery William Lyon Mackenzie, who was elected Toronto's first mayor in 1834.

Mackenzie had started his *Colonial Advocate* to crusade against the narrow-minded Family Compact, calling for reform and challenging their power to such an extent that some of them dumped his presses into the lake. Mackenzie was undaunted and by 1837 was calling for open rebellion.

A severe depression, financial turmoil, and the failure of some banks all contributed to the 1837 Rebellion, one of the most dramatic events in the city's history. On December 5 the rebels, a scruffy bunch of about 700, gathered at Montgomery's Tav-

DATELINE

- **1869** Eaton's opens.
- **1871** Population 56,000.
- **1872** Simpson's opens.
- **1876** John Ross Robertson starts *Evening Telegram*, which wields influence for next 90 years.
- **1879** Massey Company moves to Toronto.
- **1884** Streets electrically lit.
- **1886** Provincial parliament buildings erected in Queen's Park.
- **1891** Population 181,000.
- **1893** First Stanley Cup played.
- **1894** Massey Hall opens.
- **1896** *MacLean's* magazine started.
- **1901** Population 208,000.
- **1904** Great Fire burns much of downtown.
- **1906** First autos produced by Canada Cycle and Motor Company; Toronto Symphony founded.
- **1907** Bell strike broken; Royal Alexandra opens.
- **1911** Population 376,538.
- **1912** Garment workers' strike broken; Royal Ontario Museum founded.
- **1914** New Union Station built.
- **1914–18** World War 1; 70,000 Torontonians enlist, 13,000 die.

(continues)

ern outside the city (near modern-day Eglinton Avenue). From here, led by mackenzie on a white mare, they marched on the city. Two days later the city's militia, called out by Sheriff Jarvis, scattered the rebels at Carlton Street. Both sides then turned and ran. Reinforcements arrived and pursued the rebels and bombarded the tavern with cannon balls. Mackenzie fled to the United States and two other leaders—Lount and Matthews—were hanged. Their graves can be visited in the Necropolis cemetery.

Between 1834 and 1884 the foundations of an industrial city were laid: Water works, gas, and later electrical lighting were installed, and public transportation was organized. Many municipal facilities were built, including a City Hall, the Royal Lyceum Theatre (1848) on King near Bay, the Toronto Stock Exchange (1852), St. Lawrence Hall (1851), an asylum, and a jail.

During the '50s building of the railroads accelerated the economic pace. By 1860 Toronto was at the center of a railroad web that linked the city north, south, east, and west—the *Great Western* to Hamilton, London, Windsor, and beyond; the *Grand Trunk* to Québec and Sarnia on Lake Huron; and the *Northern Railway* to Georgian Bay.

Toronto became the trading hub for the region, for imports and exports of lumber and grain. Merchant empires were founded; railroad magnates emerged; and institutions like the Bank of Toronto and the Canada Permanent Building and Savings Society were established.

Despite its growth and wealth Toronto still lagged behind Montréal—its population being only half of Montréal's in 1861—but increasingly Toronto took advantage of its superior links to the south, an advantage that would eventually help it overtake its rival. Under the Confederation of 1867 the city was guaranteed another advantage when it was made the capital of the newly created Ontario, which, in effect, gave it control over the minerals and timber of the north.

As the city grew it gobbled up the countryside and so, to compensate for this loss, recreational areas were developed. In 1857 G. W. Allan donated five acres (later enlarged to 10) for the laying out of a garden. In 1860 Queen's Park was laid out. But the

DATELINE

- **1920** Group of Seven exhibited.
- **1921** Population 521,893.
- **1923** Chinese Exclusion Act.
- **1930s** Depression; thousands go on relief or ride the box cars.
- **1931** Maple Leaf Gardens built.
- **1939** Canada enters World War II; thousands of troops leave from Union Station.
- **1940–45** Toronto functions as war supplier.
- **1947** Cocktail lounges approved.
- **1950** Sunday sports allowed.
- **1951** Population 31% foreign-born.
- **1953** Metro created.
- **1954** Yonge subway opens.
- **1960** O'Keefe Centre opens.
- **1961** Population 42% foreign-born.
- **1965** New city hall built.
- **1966** Bloor-Danforth subway opens.
- **1971** Ontario Place built.
- **1972** Harbourfront under development.
- **1974** Metro Zoo and Ontario Science Centre open.
- **1975** CN Tower opens for business.
- **1984** City's 150th anniversary.
- **1989** SkyDome opens.

real gem was donated by architect John Howard in 1873 when he gave to the citizens of the west end High Park. Riverdale park and zoo were developed in the 1890s.

During this same mid-Victorian period the growth of a more diverse population continued. In 1847 Irish famine victims flooded into Toronto, and by 1851 and 1852 the Irish-born were the largest single ethnic group in Toronto. While many of them were Ulster Irish Protestants who did not threaten the Anglo-Protestant ascendancy, these newcomers were not always welcomed—a pattern that was to be repeated whenever a new immigrant group threatened to change the shape and order of society. As the gap between the number of Anglicans and Catholics closed, sectarian tensions increased and the old-country Orange and Green conflicts flared into mob violence.

LATE & HIGH VICTORIAN TORONTO Between 1871 and 1891 the city's population more than tripled, shooting from 56,000 to 181,000. This increasingly large urban market helped spawn two great Toronto retailers—Timothy Eaton and Robert Simpson—who both moved to Toronto from Ontario towns to open stores at Queen and Yonge streets in 1869 and 1872, respectively. Eaton developed his reputation on fixed prices, cash sales only, and promises of refunds if the customer wasn't satisfied, all unique gambits at the time. Simpson copied Eaton and also competed by providing better service, such as two telephones to take orders instead of one. Both developed into full-fledged department stores and both entered mail order, conquering the country with their catalogs.

The business of the city was business, and amassing wealth the pastime of such figures as Henry Pellatt, stockbroker and president of the Electrical Development Company and builder of Casa Loma; E. B. Osler; George Albertus Cox; and A. R. Ames. Although these men were self-made entrepreneurs, not Family Compact officials, they still formed a traditional socially conservative elite linked by money, taste, investments, and religious affiliation, who were still British to a tee. They and the rest of the citizens celebrated the Queen's Jubilee in 1897 with gusto and gave Toronto boys a rousing send-off to fight in the Boer War in 1899. They also, like the British, had a fondness for clubs—the Albany Club for the Conservatives and the National Club for the Liberals. As in England, too, their sports clubs carried a certain cachet—notably the Royal Yacht Club, the Toronto Cricket Club, the Toronto Golf Club, and the Lawn Tennis Club.

As the city's financial power increased, many leading companies and organizations moved their headquarters to the city, and it became a cultural-intellectual powerhouse. The Canadian Institute, the Ontario Society of Artists, the Toronto Philharmonic Society, the Toronto Arts Students League, and the Mendelssohn Choir were all founded in the 1870s or '80s. On the sports front, the first Queen's Plate was run at Woodbine in 1883; the Stanley Cup competition was begun in 1893; baseball overtook cricket; and rowing was a red-hot sport, with Ned Hanlan holding the world title from 1880 to 1884.

The boom also spurred new commercial and residential construction, such as the first steel-frame building—the Board of Trade

Building (1889) at Yonge and Front; George Gooderham's Romanesque-style mansion (1890) at St. George and Bloor (now the York Club); the provincial Parliament Buildings in Queen's Park (1886–92); and the city hall (1899) at Queen and Bay. Public transit was improved, and by 1891 people were traveling the 68 miles of horse-drawn tracks. Electric lights, telephones, and electrical streetcars also appeared in the 1890s.

FROM 1900 TO 1933 Between 1901 and 1921 the population more than doubled, climbing from 208,000 to 521,893, and the economy continued to expand, fueled by the lumber, mining, wholesale, and agricultural machinery industries (Massey-Harris was the city's largest single factory in 1895), and after 1911 by hydroelectric power. Toronto began to seriously challenge Montréal. Much of the new wealth went into construction, and three marvelous buildings from this era can still be seen today: the Horticultural Building at the Exhibition Grounds (1907), the King Edward Hotel (1903), and Union Station (1914–19). Most of the earlier wooden constructions had been destroyed in the Great Fire of 1904, which wiped out 14 acres of downtown.

The booming economy and its factories attracted a wave of new immigrants—mostly Italians and Jews from Russia and Eastern Europe—who were very different from the British and Irish who had come earlier. They settled in the city's emerging ethnic enclaves. By 1912 Kensington Market was well established, and the garment center and Jewish community were firmly ensconced around King and Spadina. Little Italy clustered around College and Grace. By 1911 more than 30,000 Torontonians were foreign-born, and the slow march to change the English character of the city had begun.

✪ By 1911 more than 30,000 Torontonians were foreign-born, and the slow march to change the English character of the city had begun.

It was still a city of churches worthy of the name "Toronto the Good," with a population of staunch religious conservatives, who barely voted for Sunday streetcar service in 1897 and banned tobogganing on Sunday in 1912. As late as 1936, 30 men were arrested at the lakeshore resort of Sunnyside because they exposed their chests—even though the temperature was 105°F! In 1947 cocktail lounges were approved, but it wasn't until 1950 that commercialized sports could be played on Sunday.

Increased industrialization brought social problems, largely concentrated in Cabbagetown and the Ward, a large area that stretched west of Yonge and north of Queen. Here, poor people lived in crowded, wretched conditions: Housing was inadequate, health conditions were poor, and rag-picking or sweatshop labor was the only employment.

As industry grew unionism also increased, but the movement, as in the United States, failed to organize politically. Two major strikes—at Bell in 1907 and in the garment industry in 1912—were easily broken.

As the city became larger and wealthier it also became an intellectual and cultural magnet. Artists like Charles Jefferys, J. H.

MacDonald, Arthur Lismer, Tom Thomson, Lawren Harris, Frederick Varley, and A. Y. Jackson, most associated with the Group of Seven, set up studios in Toronto, their first and now-famous group show opening in 1920. Toronto also became the English-language publishing center of the nation. A number of Canadian references were compiled, like *The Canadian Encyclopaedia, Chronicles of Canada,* and *The Makers of Canada,* and national magazines like *MacLean's* (started in 1896) and *Saturday Night* were launched. The art museum, the Royal Ontario Museum, the Toronto Symphony Orchestra, and the Royal Alexandra Theatre all opened before 1914.

Women advanced, too, at the turn of the century. In 1880 Emily Jennings Stowe became the first Canadian woman authorized to practice medicine. In 1886 women were admitted to the university. Clara Brett Martin was the first woman admitted to the law courts, and the women's suffragist movement gained strength, led by Dr. Stowe, Flora McDonald Denison, and the Women's Christian Temperance Union.

During World War I, Toronto sent 70,000 men to the trenches; about 13,000 were killed. At home, the war had a great impact economically and socially: Toronto became Canada's chief aviation center; factories, shipyards, and power facilities expanded to meet the needs of war; and women entered the work force in great numbers.

After the war the city took on much more of the aspect and tone that is still recognizable today. Automobiles appeared on the streets—the Canadian Cycle and Motor Company had begun manufacturing them in 1906 (the first parking ticket was given in 1908); one or two skyscrapers appeared; and although 80% of the population still boasted British origin, ethnic enclaves were clearly defined.

The 1920s roared along, fueled by a mining boom, which saw Bay Street turned into a veritable gold-rush alley where everyone was pushing something hot. The Great Depression followed, racking up 30% unemployment in 1933. The only distraction from its bleakness was the opening of Maple Leaf Gardens in 1931, which besides being an ice hockey center also hosted large protest rallies during the Depression and later such diverse groups and personalities as the Jehovah's Witnesses, Billy Graham, the Ringling Bros. Circus, and the Metropolitan Opera.

As in the United States, hostility toward new immigrants was rife during the twenties, and it reached one of its peaks in 1923, when the Chinese Exclusion Act was passed, banning Chinese immigration. In the '30s antagonism to the Jews intensified. Signs such as NO JEWS,

IMPRESSIONS

Oh for a half-hour of Europe after this sanctimonious icebox.
—WYNDHAM LEWIS, *THE LETTERS OF WYNDHAM LEWIS*

Toronto is known as Toronto the Good, because of its alleged piety. My guess is that there's more polygamy in Toronto than Baghdad, only it's not called that in Toronto.
—AUSTIN F. CROSS, *CROSS ROADS* (1936)

NIGGERS, OR DOGS were posted occasionally at Balmy and Kew beaches, and in August 1933, the display of a swastika at Christie Pits caused a battle between Nazis and Jews.

AFTER WORLD WAR II In 1939 Torontonians again rallied to the British cause, sending thousands to fight in Europe. At home, plants turned out fighter bombers and Bren guns, and people endured rationing—one bottle of liquor a month and ration books for sugar and other staples—while they listened to the war-front news delivered by Lorne Greene. Already prosperous by World War II, Toronto continued to expand during the '40s. The suburbs alone added more than 200,000 to the population between 1940 and 1953. By the '50s the urban area had grown so large, disputes between city and suburbs were so frequent, and the need for social and other services were so great that an effective administrative solution was needed. In 1953 the Metro Council was established, composed of equal numbers of representatives from the city and the suburbs (the mayor, two controllers, and nine aldermen from the city and the mayors and reeves from the suburbs). Metro was responsible for power plants, sewage-treatment plants, pumping stations, expressways, and the TTC. It also assessed property taxes, which were collected by the local municipalities.

Toronto became a major city in the '50s, with Metro providing a structure for planning and growth. The Yonge subway opened, and a network of highways was constructed, linking the city to the affluent suburbs, which were populated by families who were buying cars, TVs, barbecues, refrigerators, and washing machines—all the modern conveniences associated with house-and-backyard suburbia. Don Mills, the first new town, was built between 1952 and 1962; Yorkdale Center, a mammoth shopping center, followed in 1964. Much of this growth was also fueled by the location of branch plants by American companies that were attracted to the area because of its access to a large market and efficient transportation, including an airport.

The city also began to loosen up, and while the old social elite (still traditionally educated at Upper Canada College, Ridley, and Trinity College) continued to dominate the boardrooms, politics, at least, had become more accessible and fluid. In 1954 Nathan Phillips became the first Jewish mayor, a symbol of how much the city's population had changed in the '50s when the real flood of immigration began. Initially immigration was European—primarily British, then American and French, and then relatives of the Europeans who were already here—but in 1947 the Chinese Exclusion Act of 1923 was repealed, opening the door to the relatives of Toronto's then-small Chinese community. After 1950 Germans and Italians were allowed to enter, adding to the communities that were already established, and then, under United Nations pressure, Poles, Ukrainians, Central European and Russian Jews, Yugoslavs, Estonians, Latvians, and other East Europeans poured in. Most arrived at Union Station, having journeyed from the ports of Halifax, Québec City, and Montréal. At the beginning of the '50s the foreign-born were 31% of the population; by 1961 they were 42%, and the number of people claiming British descent had fallen from 73% to 59%. The '60s were to bring an even richer mix of people—Portuguese,

Greeks, West Indians, South Asians, and Chinese, Vietnamese, and Chilean refugees—changing the city's character forever.

In the '60s the focus shifted from the suburbs to the city as people moved back downtown, renovating the handsome brick Victorians so characteristic of today's downtown. Yorkville emerged briefly as the hippie capital—the Haight-Ashbury of Canada. Gordon Lightfoot and Joni Mitchell sang in the coffeehouses, and anti-Vietnam protests took over the streets. It was shortlived, and perhaps the failure of the experimental alternative Rochdale College in 1968 marked the beginning of the end of that era. By the mid-'70s Yorkville had been transformed into a village of elegant boutiques and galleries and high-rent restaurants, and the funky village had moved to Queen Street West.

In the '70s Toronto became the fastest-growing city in North America. For years the city had competed with Montréal for first-city status, and now the separatist issue and the election of the Parti Québécois in 1976 hastened Toronto's dash to the tape. It overtook Montréal as a financial/investment banking center and for the number of corporate headquarters. Its stock market was more important, and it was also the country's prime publishing center. A dramatically different new city hall opened in 1965, symbol of the city's equally new dynamism; the Bloor-Danforth subway line opened in 1966; skyscrapers went up at Bloor and Yonge in the early '70s; and Eglinton and St. Clair became mini-city hubs on the subway line north. Toronto also began reclaiming its waterfront and developing Harbourfront. New skyscrapers and civic buildings reflected the city's new power and wealth—the Toronto Dominion, the 72-story First Canadian Place, Royal Bank Plaza, Roy Thomson Hall, the Eaton Centre, the CN Tower—all of which transformed the old '30s skyline into an urban landscape worthy of world attention.

Unlike the rapid building of highways and other developments completed in the '50s, these developments were achieved with some balance and attention to the city's heritage. From the late '60s through the early '80s the citizens fought to ensure that the city's heritage was saved and that development was not allowed to continue as wildly as it had done in the '50s. The best examples of the success of this reform movement were the stopping of the proposed Spadina Expressway in 1971 and the fight against several urban renewal plans, including Trefann Court.

During the '70s the provincial government also helped develop attractions that would polish Toronto's patina and attract visitors:

IMPRESSIONS

Returning to Toronto was like finding a Jaguar parked in front of the vicarage and the padre inside with a pitcher of vodka martinis reading Lolita.

—Article in MacLean's, January 1959

Toronto does not have to devote all its energies and resources to seeking remedies for yesterday's problems—slums, ghettos and unemployment. Free of these major constraints, it can be a truly future-oriented protypic city.

—Buckminster Fuller (1968)

Ontario Place in 1971, Harbourfront in 1972, and the Metro Zoo and the Ontario Science Centre in 1974. Government financing also supported the arts and helped turn Toronto from a city with 4 theaters in 1965 to one boasting 22 in 1976 and more than 40 today. And the growth continues with the 1989 opening of SkyDome—the first stadium in the world with a fully retractable roof—innovatively located, would you believe, right downtown.

FAMOUS TORONTONIANS

Margaret Atwood (b. 1939) Poet/novelist, satirist, and feminist, considered the high priestess of Canadian literature (read *Survival*). One of her recent novels, *The Handmaid's Tale,* was made into a movie starring Robert Duvall and Faye Dunaway (1989).

The Band A Toronto sextet that performed as backup for Bob Dylan in the '70s.

Drs. Frederick Banting (1891–1941) and **Charles Best** (1899–1978) Inventors of insulin at the University of Toronto in 1921.

Blue Rodeo Rock group formed in 1984 that achieved big success with the single "Try" and the album *Outskirts,* both in 1987.

Jack Bush (1909–77) Member of the Painters Eleven, a group of Canadian abstract expressionists based in Toronto in the '50s. He became internationally known for "drawing with color."

Morley Callaghan (1903–90) Novelist who met Hemingway while working on the *Toronto Daily Star* and later in Paris along with other members of the Lost Generation, a period that he recalled in *That Summer in Paris.* He wrote for the *New Yorker* and authored many novels, including *The Loved and the Lost,* which won the Governor-General's Award.

John Candy (b. 1950) A former star of "SCTV," Candy graduated to such movies as *Planes, Trains, and Automobiles* and *Uncle Buck*.

Austin Clarke (b. 1932) Novelist born in Barbados who attended the University of Toronto. *The Meeting Point* was the first novel in a trilogy recording Caribbean life in Toronto.

Cowboy Junkies Four-person group formed in 1987 that scored American success and a big hit with their 1988 album *The Trinity Session.* More recent recordings have included *Black Eyed Man.*

Robertson Davies (b. 1913) Playwright, novelist, journalist, professor, and former Master of Massey College at the University of Toronto, famous for his *Deptford Trilogy* and for the creation of Samuel Marchbanks. His many novels often reflect a Jungian approach.

Timothy Eaton (1834–1907) Retail magnate who migrated from St. Mary's, Ontario, in 1869 to a city that he felt was ready for his merchandising ideas.

Marian Engel (1933–85) Novelist. Many of her novels are set in Toronto. *Bear* won the Governor-General's Award in 1976.

Glenn Gould (1932–82) Pianist and great Bach interpreter who lived as a recluse in Toronto, rarely performing except in a recording studio.

Group of Seven Famous Canadian painters, including Tom Thomson, Lawren Harris, Arthur Lismer, A. Y. Jackson, Frederick

Varley, and J. E. H. MacDonald, who were first exhibited in Toronto in 1920.

Dan Hill (b. 1954) Singer-songwriter who scored his first big hit with "Sometimes When We Touch" (1977).

Jane Jacobs (b. 1916) Urban planner and sociologist, author of *The Death and Life of the Great American Cities,* who moved from New York to Toronto to observe her ideas in action.

Norman Jewison (b. 1926) Film director. Among his films are *Fiddler on the Roof* and *Moonstruck,* for which he was nominated for an Academy Award as best director. He grew up in the Beaches.

Paul Kane (1810–71) Irish-born painter who lived in Toronto, famous for his landscapes and portraits of Native Canadians.

William Lyon Mackenzie (1795–1861) Urban journalist/reformer, publisher of the *Colonial Advocate,* first city mayor, and leader of the Rebellion of 1837.

Raymond Massey (1896–1983) Actor and member of the influential Toronto family of Massey-Ferguson fame. He played opposite Cary Grant in *Arsenic and Old Lace.*

Marshall McLuhan (1911–80) University of Toronto professor who gave us "The medium is the message." Author of *The Mechanical Bride* (1951).

Honest Ed Mirvish (b. 1914) A Toronto legend who rose from running the city's ultimate bargain-basement store to wealth and position. Savior of Toronto's Royal Alexandra Theatre and most recently the Old Vic in London.

Raymond Moriyama (b. 1929) Architect who designed the Ontario Science Centre, Metro Toronto Library, and Scarborough Civic Centre.

Northern Dancer Winner of two-thirds of the Triple Crown. He once commanded $1 million stud fees.

Michael Ondaatje (b. 1943) Novelist and poet who was born in Ceylon but now lives in Toronto. *In the Skin of the Lion* is set in Toronto in the 1920s and '30s.

Sir Henry Pellatt (1859–1939) Stockbroker and utility magnate who built Casa Loma and whose family fortunes collapsed in the 1913 crash.

Mary Pickford (1893–1979) America's silent-film sweetheart, she lived on University Avenue where Sick Children's Hospital stands today.

Joe Shuster (1914–92) Creator of Superman, who modeled the *Daily Planet* after the *Toronto Daily Star.* He moved to Cleveland as a young man.

Jane Siberry (b. 1955) Singer-songwriter made famous by her album *The Speckless Sky* (1985).

John Strachan (1778–1867) One of the founders of Toronto, he negotiated with the invading Americans in 1813. A staunch Anglican and Anglophile, first bishop of Toronto, he dubbed Thomas Jefferson "a mischief maker."

Harold Town (b. 1924) Member of the Painters Eleven, known for his collages and "fat paint" paintings.

Wayne and Shuster (b. 1918; 1916–90) The two comics who appeared regularly on "The Ed Sullivan Show."

Neil Young (b. 1945) Singer-songwriter and one-time member of Crosby, Stills, Nash & Young, famous for his album *After the Goldrush* (1970).

2. RECOMMENDED BOOKS

GENERAL There are plenty of books that deal with all aspects of Canada's history and society. Anything by Pierre Berton is great reading; George Woodcock's *The Canadians* (Harvard University Press, 1979) is a lively, honest appraisal of his fellow nationals and national culture; Edmund Wilson's *O Canada: An American's Notes on Canadian Culture* (Noonday Press, 1965) provides an outsider's vision of what the culture's about. Donald Creighton has written many books about specific issues in Canadian history as well as his *Canada's First Century* (Macmillan, 1976).

For a general sociological history of the growth of Toronto, complete with statistics and historical photographs, there's the two-volume *Toronto: An Illustrated History* (Lorimer & Company, 1985). The first volume (to 1918) is by J. M. S. Careless; the second volume (after 1918) is by James Lemon.

William Kilbourn's *Toronto Remembered* (Stoddart, 1984) is, as the subtitle states, "a celebration of the city" by the author himself and many other fine writers, all of whom provide insights into the city's life and history. It's made even livelier by the quotations and illustrations that accompany the text—a delightful read.

Other general city and provincial histories include G. P. de T. Glazebrook's *The Story of Toronto* (Toronto, 1971) and Robert Bothwell's *A Short History of Ontario* (Hurtig, 1986).

ART & ARCHITECTURE *A Concise History of Canadian Painting* by Dennis Reid (Oxford University Press, 1988) is a well-written, well-illustrated, and informative history that has chapters on significant periods of art in Toronto, including the Group of Seven and the Painters Eleven. Entertaining and anecdotal, too.

David Burnett and Marilyn Schiff's *Contemporary Canadian Art* (Hurtig, 1983) is a well-written, concise, and liberally illustrated history of Canadian art from the 1940s to the 1980s.

Edith G. Firth's *Toronto in Art* (Fitzhenry & Whiteside, 1983) provides a pictorial history of the city as viewed by artists from the early 19th century through the 1980s. It contains more than 170 delightful illustrations.

The book on Toronto's architecture is Eric Arthur's *Toronto, No Mean City,* which, in its 1986 edition by University of Toronto Press, has been revised by Stephen Otto. Arthur conveys his great love for the city and the history of its buildings, many of which he helped to save.

Toronto Observed by William Dendy and William Kilbourn (Oxford University Press, 1986) focuses on the many architectural treasures that still stand in the city. It's a large-format volume with elegant black-and-white photographs of each of the 77 buildings and architectural groupings discussed.

For more of a walking-tour approach complete with maps

referenced to the text, there's Patricia McHugh's *Toronto Architecture* (McClelland & Stewart, 1989).

William Dendy's *Lost Toronto* (Toronto, 1978) recovers in words and pictures the great buildings that have been demolished.

Lucy Martyn's *Toronto: A Hundred Years of Grandeur—The Inside Story of Toronto's Great Homes* (Toronto, 1978) gives a glimpse into the lives of the wealthy—the era of millionaires and Toronto aristocrats. The life of one such self-made man is described in Carlie Oreskovich's *Sir Henry Pellatt: The King of Casa Loma* (McGraw-Hill Ryerson, 1982). Other titles to look for are A. S. Thompson's *Spadina: A Story of Old Toronto* (Paguarian Press, 1988) and *Jarvis Street* (Toronto, 1980).

FICTION Many of Margaret Atwood's novels are set in Toronto, including *Life Before Man* (1980), which examines the redefinition of sexual roles that occurred in the '60s and '70s, and *Cat's Eye* (1989), in which an artist returns to the city for an exhibition of her work and recalls her years as a child in Toronto.

Austin Clarke's trilogy—*The Meeting Point* (1967), *Storm of Fortune* (1971), and *The Bigger Light* (1975)—portrays the life of a family of Caribbean immigrants in Toronto.

Marian Engel's *The Year of the Child* (1981) portrays the life of a family on one particular street in Toronto. Other novels include *Honeyman Festival* and *No Clouds of Glory*.

Hugh Garner's *Cabbagetown* (1950) paints what the author described as an Anglo-Saxon slum. *The Silence on the Shore* (1962) and *The Intruders* (1978) are also set in Toronto, as are several of the mysteries he wrote.

Katherine Govier's stories, *Fables of Brunswick Avenue* (1985), for example, depict the era and social scene of Toronto's young urban professionals.

Joyce Marshal's *Lovers and Strangers* (1957) is set in Toronto in the 1940s.

CHAPTER 2

PLANNING A TRIP TO TORONTO

This chapter is devoted to the where, when, and how of your trip—the advance-planning issues required to get it together and take it on the road.

After deciding where to go, most people have two fundamental questions: What will it cost? and How do I get there? This chapter will answer both of these questions and also resolve other important issues, such as when to go, what pretrip health precautions to take, what insurance coverage is necessary, and where to obtain more information about Toronto.

1. INFORMATION, ENTRY REQUIREMENTS & MONEY

SOURCES OF INFORMATION

IN THE UNITED STATES General information on travel in Canada can be obtained from the following offices in the United States:

Atlanta—Canadian Consulate General, 400 South Tower, One CNN Center, Atlanta, GA 30303-2705 (tel. 404/577-6810).
Boston—Canadian Consulate General, Three Copley Place, Suite 400, Boston, MA 02116 (tel. 617/536-1731).
Buffalo—Canadian Consulate, 3000 Marine Midland Center, Buffalo, NY 14203-2884 (tel. 716/852-1345).
Chicago—Canadian Consulate General, 2 Prudential Plaza, 180 N. Stetson Ave., Chicago, IL 60601 (tel. 312/616-1860).
Cleveland—Canadian Consulate, 55 Public Square, Suite 1008, Cleveland, OH 44113 (tel. 216/771-0150).
Dallas—Canadian Consulate General, 750 North St. Paul, Suite 1700, Dallas, TX 75201 (tel. 214/922-9806).

Detroit—Canadian Consulate General, 600 Renaissance Center, Suite 1100, Detroit, MI 48243-1704 (tel. 313/567-2086).
Los Angeles—Canadian Consulate General, 300 South Grand Ave., Suite 1000, Los Angeles, CA 90071 (tel. 213/687-7432).
Minneapolis—Canadian Consulate General, 701 Fourth Ave., Suite 900, Minneapolis, MN 55415-1899 (tel. 612/333-4641).
New York—Canadian Consulate General, Exxon Building, 16th floor, 1251 Avenue of the Americas, New York, NY 10020-1175 (tel. 212/768-2400).
San Francisco—Canadian Consulate General, 50 Fremont St., Suite 2100, San Francisco, CA 94105 (tel. 415/495-6021).
Seattle—Canadian Consulate General, 412 Plaza 600, Sixth and Stewart, Seattle, WA 98101-1286 (tel. 206/443-1777).
Washington, D.C.—Canadian Embassy, Tourism Section, 501 Pennsylvania Ave. NW, Washington, DC 20001 (tel. 202/682-1740).

IN CANADA The best source for information specific to Toronto is the **Metropolitan Toronto Convention & Visitors Association,** Queen's Quay Terminal at Harbourfront, 207 Queen's Quay West (P.O. Box 126), Toronto, ON, M5J 1A7 (tel. 416/368-9821, or toll free 800/363-1990 from the continental U.S.). Write or call them before you leave and request the kind of information you want.

For information about Ontario, contact **Ontario Travel,** Queen's Park, Toronto, ON, M7A 2E5 (tel. 416/965-4008, or toll free 800/ONTARIO).

ENTRY REQUIREMENTS

DOCUMENTS Every person under 19 years of age is required to produce a letter from a parent or guardian granting him or her permission to travel to Canada. The letter must state the traveler's name and the duration of the trip. It is therefore essential that teenagers carry proof of identity; otherwise their letter is useless at the border.

U.S. citizens and permanent residents of the United States require neither passports nor visas to enter Canada. You will need some proof of citizenship, such as a passport, a birth or baptismal certificate, or a voter's registration card. Permanent U.S. residents who are not U.S. citizens must have their Alien Registration Cards (Green Cards) with them.

Citizens of Australia, New Zealand, the United Kingdom, and Ireland must have valid passports. Citizens of many other countries will need visas, which must be applied for in advance at the local Canadian embassy or consulate. For detailed information, write the **Canadian Immigration Division,** Department of Employment and Immigration, Ottawa, ON, K1A 0J9; or call your local Canadian consulate or embassy.

CUSTOMS Customs regulations are generous in most respects, but they get pretty complicated when it comes to firearms, plants, meats, and pets. Fishing tackle poses no problem, but the bearer must possess a nonresident license for the province or territory where he or she plans to use it. You can bring in free of duty up to 50 cigars, 200 cigarettes, and 2.2 pounds (1kg) of tobacco, providing you're over 16 years of age. You are also allowed 40 ounces (1.14l) of liquor or wine as long as you're over the minimum drinking age of the province you're visiting (19 in Ontario).

For more detailed information about Customs regulations, write to **Customs and Excise,** Connaught Building, Sussex Drive, Ottawa, ON, K1A 0L5.

MONEY

Canadian money figures in dollars and cents, but with a distinct advantage for U.S. visitors, for the Canadian dollar is worth around 82¢ in U.S. money (give or take a couple of points' daily variation). So, in effect, you'll receive about 20% more the moment you change your American traveler's checks into local currency. That makes quite a difference in your budget, and since the prices of many goods are roughly on a par with those in the United States, the difference is real, not imaginary. You can bring in or take out any amount of money, but if you are importing or exporting sums of $5,000 or more, you must file a report of the transaction with U.S. Customs. Most tourist establishments in Canada will take U.S. cash, but you can often get a better rate by changing your funds at a bank.

If you do spend American money at Canadian establishments, you should understand how the conversion is calculated. Often there will be a sign at the cash register that reads "U.S. Currency 20%." This 20% is the "premium," which means that for every U.S. greenback you hand over, the cashier will consider it $1.20 in Canadian dollars. For example, for a $7.30 tab you need pay only $6.08 U.S.

Great, isn't it? But remember that the premium figures make it easy on cashiers, and many times you'll do better at a bank. Below is a table showing premium rates and the amount of money you're actually paying for each Canadian dollar. As you can see, if the exchange rate at a bank is 82¢ U.S. for $1 Canadian, you are entitled to a premium rate of 22%. If someone offers you 20%, you're losing money—go to a bank instead.

Major credit cards are accepted throughout Canada.

PREMIUM RATES & U.S. DOLLAR EQUIVALENTS

Premium Rates	U.S. Equivalents
10%	.91
15	.87
20	.83
25	.80
30	.77
35	.74
40	.71

As we go to press the premium rate is 22%, which means that the Canadian dollar is worth 82¢ U.S. Below is a table of equivalence calculated at that premium rate. Remember that this rate fluctuates from time to time and may not be the same when you travel to Toronto. Therefore the following table should be used only as a guide.

CANADIAN & U.S. DOLLAR EQUIVALENTS

Canadian	U.S.	Canadian	U.S.
.25	.21	15	12.30
.50	.41	20	16.40
.75	.62	25	20.50
1	.82	30	24.60
2	1.64	35	28.70
3	2.46	40	32.80
4	3.28	45	36.90
5	4.10	50	41.00
6	4.92	75	61.50
7	5.74	100	82.00
8	6.56	125	102.50
9	7.38	150	123.00
10	8.20	175	143.50

TRAVELER'S CHECKS Before leaving home, purchase traveler's checks and arrange to carry some ready cash (usually about $200).

American Express (tel. toll free 800/221-7282 in the U.S. and Canada) is the most widely recognized traveler's check; the agency imposes a 1% commission. Checks are free to members of the American Automobile Association.

Bank of America (tel. toll free 800/227-3460 in the U.S., or 415/624-5400, collect, in Canada) also issues checks in U.S. dollars for 1% commission everywhere but California.

Citicorp (tel. toll free 800/645-6556 in the U.S., or 813/623-1709, collect, in Canada) issues checks in U.S. dollars or British pounds.

MasterCard International (tel. toll free 800/223-9920 in the U.S., or 212/974-5696, collect, in Canada) issues checks in about a dozen currencies.

Barclays Bank (tel. toll free 800/221-2426 in the U.S. and Canada) issues checks in both U.S. and Canadian dollars.

Thomas Cook (tel. toll free in the U.S. 800/223-7373, or 212/974-5696, collect, in Canada) issues checks in U.S. or Canadian dollars. It's affiliated with MasterCard.

WHAT THINGS COST IN TORONTO	U.S. $
Taxi from the airport to downtown	28.70
Subway/bus from the airport to downtown	6.15
Local telephone call	.23
Double at the Four Seasons (expensive)	189.00
Double at Bond Place (moderate)	66.00
Double at Victoria University (budget)	51.00
Two-course lunch for one at Arlequin (moderate)*	16.00
Two-course lunch for one at Kensington (budget)*	10.00
Three-course dinner for one at Scaramouche (expensive)*	47.00

	U.S. $
Three-course dinner for one at Grano (moderate)*	21.00
Three-course dinner for one at Ginsberg & Wong (budget)*	15.00
Pint of beer	3.50
Coca-Cola	.87
Cup of coffee	.87
Roll of ASA 100 Kodacolor film, 36 exposures	5.42
Admission to the ROM	5.00
Movie ticket	6.14
Theater ticket at the Royal Alex	13.33–70.00

*Includes tax and tip but not wine.

Note: Prices are listed here in U.S. dollars; **all other prices in the book are quoted in Canadian dollars.**

2. WHEN TO GO — CLIMATE, HOLIDAYS & EVENTS

CLIMATE

As a general rule, you can say that spring runs from late March to mid-May (though occasionally there'll be snow in mid-April); summer, from mid-May to mid-September; fall, from mid-September to mid-November; and winter, from mid-November to late March. The highest recorded temperature was 105°F; the lowest, −27°F. The average date of first frost is October 29; the average date of last frost is April 20.

The blasts from Lake Ontario can sometimes be fierce, even in June. Bring a windbreaker or something similar.

Toronto's Average Temperatures (°F)

	Jan	Feb	Mar	Apr	May	June	July	Aug	Sept	Oct	Nov	Dec
High	30	31	39	53	64	75	80	79	71	59	46	34
Low	18	19	27	38	48	57	62	61	54	45	35	23

HOLIDAYS

Toronto celebrates the following holidays: New Year's Day (January 1), Good Friday and/or Easter Monday (variable; in March or April),

Victoria Day (last Monday in May), Canada Day (July 1), Civic Holiday (first Monday in August), Labour Day (first Monday in September), Thanksgiving (second Monday in October), Remembrance Day (November 11), Christmas Day (December 25), and Boxing Day (December 26).

On Good Friday and Easter Monday, both schools and government offices are closed; most corporations are closed on one or the other, and some are closed on both. Only banks and government offices close on Remembrance Day (November 11).

TORONTO CALENDAR OF EVENTS

MAY

- ☐ **Milk International Children's Festival.** A nine-day celebration of the arts for kids—from theater and music to dance, comedy, and storytelling. Usually starts on Mother's Day.

JUNE

✪ ***METRO TORONTO CARAVAN*** *Celebrates the city's ethnic diversity (42 foreign-language newspapers alone are published in the city) as more than 100 cultural groups take to the streets and the stages at more than 40 pavilions. The entertainment is complemented by authentic ethnic foods.*

Where: *Citywide.* ***When:*** *10 days, usually 3rd and 4th weekends.* ***How:*** *Go, but make city hotel reservations in advance.*

- ☐ **DuMaurier Jazz Festival.** The world's top jazz names of modern, traditional, avant-garde, African, and fusion appear in a 10-day festival. Usually the last 10 days in June.
- ☐ **Mariposa Music Festival.** A major musical celebration of traditional folk, neofolk, R & B, and blues, featuring more than 200 top performers. Craft show, too. At Ontario Place and other venues. Usually the third weekend in June.
- ☐ **Fringe Festival.** A 10-day theatrical event with as many as 65 performing artists/groups in one-hour-maximum performances. Shows are given on several different stages and ticket prices are low. Usually the last week in June and the first in July. For information write or call the Fringe Festival, 296 Brunswick Ave., Suite 214, Toronto M5S 2M7 (tel. 416/927-0245).

JULY

- ☐ **Player's Ltd. International.** An important stop on the pro-tennis tour that attracts stars like Becker, Lendl, and McEnroe. National Tennis Centre at York University. Usually 3rd to 4th weekend in July. Call 416/665-9777.
- ☐ **Molson Indy.** At the Exhibition Place Street circuit. Usually 3rd weekend in July. Call 416/869-8538.

✪ ***CARIBANA*** *A West Indian calypso beat takes over the city when three-quarters of a million people dance, sway, and watch the colorful parade. Toronto's version of carnival, complete with traditional foods from the Caribbean and Latin America, ferry cruises, island picnics, concerts, and arts-and-crafts exhibits.*

Where: *Citywide.* ***When:*** *Last two weeks in July.* ***How:*** *Go, but make hotel reservations in advance. Call 416/925-5435 for more information.*

AUGUST

☐ **W.O.M.A.D.** It stands for World of Music, Arts, and Dance, and features groups from around the world for a weekend of concerts, workshops, arts, crafts, lectures, food, film, and more at the Harbourfront. Usually the first or second weekend. For information call 416/973-3000.

✪ ***CANADIAN NATIONAL EXHIBITION*** *The world's largest exhibition, featuring midway rides, display buildings, free shows, and grandstand performers. The Canadian International Air Show is an added bonus. It was first staged, by the way, in 1878.*

Where: *Exhibition Place.* ***When:*** *20 days, from mid-August to Labor Day.* ***How:*** *Contact Canadian National Exhibition, Exhibition Place, Toronto, ON, M6K 3C3 (tel. 416/393-6000).*

SEPTEMBER

☐ **Festival of Festivals.** Second-largest film festival in the world, showing more than 250 films. 10 days in early September. For information, contact the Toronto Convention and Tourist Office or call 416/967-7371.

☐ **Metro Toronto Wang Marathon.** The route passes through the city's Greek, Portuguese, and Italian neighborhoods. For information, call 416/495-4311.

OCTOBER

☐ **Oktoberfest,** in Kitchener-Waterloo, about one hour (60 miles) from Toronto. Usually first and second weekends. For information, contact Kitchener-Waterloo Oktoberfest, P.O. Box 1053, Kitchener, ON, N2G 4G1 (tel. 519/576-0571).

☐ **International Festival of Authors.** A prestigious nine-day literary festival at the Harbourfront that draws some of the finest authors from all over the world to readings and other events, such as the Lives and Times presentations (biography) and on-stage interviews. Usually starts the third weekend.

NOVEMBER

✪ ***ROYAL AGRICULTURAL WINTER FAIR AND ROYAL HORSE SHOW*** *A major event that has been celebrated since 1922. At this show, the largest indoor agricultural and* *equestrian competition in the world, vegetables and fruits are on display, along with crafts, farm machinery, livestock, and more. And it's all accompanied by a horse show that is traditionally attended by a member of the British royal family.*

Where: *Exhibition Place.* ***When:*** *12 days, usually second and third weekends.* ***How:*** *Write or call the Convention and Tourist Office for more information, or call 416/393-6400.*

3. INSURANCE

Before leaving home, always check with your health-insurance company to make sure that your coverage extends to Canada. If it does, fine; if it doesn't, or if the coverage is inadequate, you may want to contact an agent to purchase a short-term insurance policy that covers medical costs and emergencies during your trip.

Do the same with home-owner's insurance. Make sure that your home-insurance policy covers off-premises theft and loss wherever it occurs. Find out what procedures you need to follow to make a claim. Again, if you are not adequately covered you may want to purchase an insurance policy that will cover any loss.

Also check your auto insurance to see what it covers. And don't forget the insurance that you may have gratis from your credit-card companies.

If you have signed up for a tour or have prepaid many of your vacation expenses, you may also want to purchase insurance that covers you in the event that you have to cancel your trip for some reason.

Assess the coverage that you already have and determine any additional coverage you may need to purchase. Your best bet will probably be to purchase a comprehensive travel policy that covers all contingencies—cancellation, health, emergency assistance, and loss. These are obtainable from travel agents, or you can contact the following companies directly for information: **International Underwriters/Brokers, Inc.,** 243 Church St. West, Middleburg, VA 22117 (tel. toll free 800/237-6615); or **Wallach & Company,** 107C W. Federal St., Suite 13, Middleburg, VA 22117-0480 (tel. 703/687-3166).

4. WHAT TO PACK

Travel light. Never bring more luggage than you yourself can carry without assistance for at least several city blocks. Porters aren't always on hand and luggage carts are often not available. The ideal travel kit consists of one suitcase and a shoulder bag.

Your wardrobe will obviously depend on the season in which you travel. In winter you'll need a really good Gortex or down jacket or coat and woolen clothing to accompany it. Try the layering approach to dressing—it works. In summer, too, you'll need a sweater or windbreaker to protect you against the winds from the lake.

Although Canadians are casual about dress they're not quite as casual as Americans, and a man should bring along a jacket and tie in case he runs into one of the few restaurants that still refuse to serve men without them. Everyone should also pack at least one pair of sturdy, no-nonsense walking shoes.

There are a few items to take along that I recommend in all our travel books—the result of wisdom acquired in many years of globetrotting.

1. A travel alarm clock, which renders you independent of hotel wake-up calls
2. A small flashlight, especially if you're driving
3. A very small screwdriver or a Swiss army knife
4. A telescopic umbrella

Since Canada uses the same current and the same plugs as the United States, you can bring along any electrical gadgets you wish.

5. TIPS FOR THE DISABLED, SENIORS & STUDENTS

FOR THE DISABLED Toronto is a very accessible city. Curb cuts are well made and common throughout the downtown area; special parking privileges are extended to disabled visitors who have disabled plates or a special pass from the city where you're a resident that allows you to park in "No Parking" zones. The subway and trolleys are, unfortunately, not accessible, but the city operates a special service for the disabled, called **Wheel-Trans.** For information call 416/393-4111.

For more information contact **Disabled Information on Community Services,** Community Information Centre of Metropolitan Toronto, 590 Jarvis St., Toronto, ON, M4Y 2J4 (tel. 416/392-0505).

FOR SENIORS Bring some form of photo ID, as many city attractions grant special senior discounts. Some hotels, too, will offer special discounted rates.

If you haven't already done so, think about joining the **American Association of Retired Persons (AARP),** 1909 K St. NW, Washington, DC 20049 (tel. 202/872-4700).

Also look into the fun courses that are offered at incredibly low prices by **Elderhostel,** 75 Federal St., Boston, MA 02110 (tel. 617/426-7788).

FOR STUDENTS The key to securing discounts and other special favors is the **International Student Identity Card (ISIC),** available to any bona fide full-time high school or university student. Contact the **Council on International Educational Exchange**

(CIEE), 205 E. 42nd St., New York, NY 10017 (tel. 212/661-1414). The card is available from all Council Travel offices in the United States. To find the office nearest you, call toll free 800/GETANID.

6. GETTING THERE

BY PLANE

THE MAJOR AIRLINES Both **Air Canada** (tel. toll free 800/776-3000) and **Canadian Airlines International** (tel. toll free 800/426-7000) offer service from various points around the globe. The latter operates flights twice weekly from Sydney, Australia, and Auckland, New Zealand; 10 times weekly from Tokyo; 5 times weekly from Hong Kong; twice weekly from Bangkok; and weekly from the People's Republic of China. From South America there's twice-weekly service from Rio de Janeiro and São Paulo.

Direct flights to Canada leave from the following major U.S. cities: Boston, Chicago, Cleveland, Dallas, Honolulu, Houston, Los Angeles, Miami, New York, and San Francisco. Currently, the following airlines fly to Toronto from the United States:

Air Canada operates the most flights to Toronto, from Boston, Chicago, Cleveland, Hartford, New York, Newark, San Francisco, Los Angeles, Miami, Portland, Seattle, Tampa, and Washington.

Canadian Airlines International has flights from Dayton, Daytona, Harrisburg, Indianapolis, and Pittsburgh. Its subsidiary, **Canadian Holidays,** flies from most Florida cities.

American (tel. toll free 800/433-7300) has frequent daily flights from Chicago, Dallas, Nashville, and New York. **United** (tel. toll free 800/241-6522) has flights from several U.S. cities via Chicago. **Northwest** (tel. toll free 800/225-2525) has flights from several U.S. cities via Detroit or Milwaukee. **USAir** (tel. toll free 842-5374) flies from Atlanta, Buffalo, Charlotte, and several other major U.S. cities. **Delta** (tel. toll free 800/239-0700) flies direct from Atlanta, Cincinnati, and Syracuse.

You'll arrive at **Pearson International Airport,** 17 miles northwest of downtown, although certain flights land at the Toronto Island Airport, which will require a short ferry ride to downtown. Always confirm with the airline which airport they're using.

Note: As we go to press, negotiations for the merger of Air Canada and Canadian Airlines International have broken down, and it is not known whether both airlines will be operating independently. Therefore, the information above may have changed by the time you plan to travel.

FARES Wherever you're traveling from, always shop the different airlines and ask for the lowest fare. Check the newspaper ads in the travel sections of the local/national newspapers, too, for special promotional fares or packages that you can take advantage of.

In general, the following are the least-expensive options. Currently the cheapest direct-flight option is the **APEX (Advance Purchase Excursion)** fare, which is usually valid from 7 to 60 days and must be purchased at least 21 days in advance. These requirements do vary, not only from airline to airline but also from one part of the world to another.

The **Excursion** fare is another option. It usually requires a minimum stay of 7 days and a maximum of 60. It often allows a limited number of stopovers, at a surcharge generally ranging from $25 to $50 each. There are no advance-purchase requirements.

BY TRAIN

Amtrak's *Maple Leaf* links New York City and Toronto via Albany, Buffalo, and Niagara Falls, departing daily from Penn Station. The journey takes 11¾ hours. From Chicago, the *International* carries passengers to Toronto via Port Huron, Michigan (a 12½-hour trip).

From Buffalo's Exchange Street Station you can also make the trip to Toronto on the Toronto/Hamilton/Buffalo Railway (THB). Connecting services are also available from other major cities along the border.

Always ask about the availability of discounted fares. Meanwhile, here are a couple of sample fares for use as guidelines only: New York to Toronto, $96 one way, $153 round-trip excursion; from Chicago, $90 and $126, respectively. Meals are not included in these prices. You'll arrive downtown at Union Station.

Call **Amtrak** (tel. toll free 800/USA-RAIL or 800/872-7245) or write Amtrak, Union Station, 60 Massachusetts Ave. NE, Washington, DC 20002 (tel. 202/906-3000), for further information.

BY BUS

Greyhound/Trailways is the only bus company that crosses the border into Canada from the United States. You can travel from almost anywhere in the United States, changing buses along the way until you finally reach Toronto. The bus may be faster and cheaper than the train, and its routes may be more flexible if you want to stop along the way, but it's also more cramped, toilet facilities are meager, and meals are taken at somewhat depressing rest stops along the way.

Depending on where you are coming from you should check into Greyhound/Trailways' special unlimited-travel passes as well as into any discount fares that might be offered. Here are a couple of sample fares: New York to Toronto, $57 one way, $114 round trip; Chicago to Toronto, $87 one way, $174 round trip; San Francisco to Toronto, $228 one way, $325 round trip.

You'll arrive at the Bus Terminal downtown at 610 Bay St., near the corner of Dundas Street. Call **Greyhound/Trailways** at 212/971-6363 for East Coast routes or 213/620-1200 for West Coast service.

BY CAR

Hopping across the border by car is no problem as the U.S. highway system leads directly into Canada at 13 points. Most people driving to Toronto from the United States will enter from Michigan at Detroit-Windsor via I-75 and the Ambassador Bridge or Port Huron–Sarnia via I-94 and the Bluewater Bridge; from New York via I-190 at Buffalo–Fort Erie, at Niagara Falls, N.Y.–Niagara Falls, Ont., or Niagara Falls, N.Y.–Lewiston; via I-81 crossing at Hill Island, or via Rte. 37 at Ogdensburg-Johnstown or Rooseveltown-Cornwall.

CHAPTER 3

GETTING TO KNOW TORONTO

This chapter sets out to answer all your travel questions, furnishing you with all the practical information you'll need during your stay in Toronto to handle any and every experience—from city layout and transportation to emergencies and women's bookstores.

1. ORIENTATION

ARRIVING

BY PLANE More than 20 major airlines serve Toronto with regularly scheduled flights departing from and arriving at **Pearson International Airport,** located in the northwest corner of Metro Toronto about 30 minutes (17 miles) from downtown.

Three terminals, serviced by more than 50 airlines, cater to the traveler and offer the full services expected at international airports. The most spectacular is the new Trillum Terminal 3 used by American, Canadian Airlines, British Airways, KLM, Lufthansa, and Air France, among others. This is a supermodern facility with moving walkways; a huge food court; and hundreds of stores, including North America's very first branch of Harrods.

Facilities at the airport include the exceptionally useful **Transport Canada Information Centres** in all terminals, where a staff fluent in 10 languages will answer queries about the airport, airline information, transportation services, and tourist attractions (tel. 416/676-3506).

The most convenient way to get into the city from the airport, of course, is **by taxi,** which will cost about $35 to downtown.

Also very convenient is the **Airport Express bus** (tel. 416/351-3311), which travels between the airport and downtown hotels—Harbour Castle Westin, the Royal York, L'Hôtel, the Sheraton Centre, the Holiday Inn, and the Chelsea Inn—every 20 minutes from early morning until late at night. Fare is $10.75 for adults, free for one child under 11 accompanied by an adult; additional children pay $8.50. It takes from 35 minutes to 1¼ hours depending on the traffic.

The cheapest way to go is **by bus and subway,** which will take about an hour. Buses travel between the airport and the Islington

IMPRESSIONS

There is a Yankee look about the place . . . a pushing, thrusting, business-like, smart appearance.

—Charles Mackay, *Life and Liberty in America* (1857–58)

The houses and stores at Toronto are not to be compared with those of the American towns opposite. But the Englishman has built according to his means— the American according to his expectations.

—Capt. Frederick Marryat, *A Diary in America* (1839)

---

subway stop about every 30 minutes for a fare of $6. Buses also travel between the airport and the Yorkdale and York Mills subway stations about every 40 minutes for a fare of $6.50 to Yorkdale, $7.50 to York Mills. On both routes one child under 11 travels free if accompanied by an adult. For information, call 416/393-7911 from 7am to 11pm.

In addition, most first-class hotels inside and outside the downtown area run their own **hotel limousine services,** so check when you make your reservation.

If you're **driving to the airport,** take the Gardiner Expressway and Queen Elizabeth Way to Hwy. 427 North; then follow the Airport Expressway signs.

BY TRAIN All VIA Rail passenger trains pull into the massive, classically proportioned **Union Station** on Front Street, one block west of Yonge Street, opposite the Royal York Hotel. The station has direct access to the subway, so you can easily reach any Toronto destination from here (for VIA Rail information, call 416/366-8411; in the United States, call Amtrak toll free at 800/USA-RAIL or 800/872-7245).

BY BUS Out-of-town buses arrive and depart from the **Bus Terminal,** 610 Bay St. at Dundas Street, and provide fast, cheap, and efficient service to Canadian and American destinations. Gray Coach Lines (tel. 416/393-7911), Greyhound/Trailways, and Voyageur Colonial operate from here. For information and schedules, call 416/393-7911.

BY CAR From the United States you are most likely to enter Toronto via either Hwy. 401 or Hwy. 2 and the Queen Elizabeth Way if you come from the west. If you come from the east via Montréal, you'll also use Hwys. 401 and 2. Here are a few approximate driving distances in miles to Toronto: from Atlanta, 977; from Boston, 566; from Buffalo, 96; from Chicago, 534; from Cincinnati, 501; from Dallas, 1,452; from Detroit, 236; from Minneapolis, 972; and from New York, 495.

TOURIST INFORMATION

For information go to or write to the **Metropolitan Toronto Convention & Visitors Association,** 207 Queens Quay West, Suite 590, in the Queens Quay Terminal at Harbourfront (P.O. Box 126), Toronto, ON, M5J 1A7 (tel. 416/368-9821), open Monday through Friday from 8:30am to 5pm. Take the LRT from Union Station to the York Street stop.

More conveniently located, the **Visitor Information Centre** outside the Eaton Centre, on Yonge Street at Dundas Street stays open year round Monday through Saturday from 9am to 6pm and Sunday from 9:30am to 6pm (9:30am to 5:30pm off-season).

Six **summer-only information centers** are found at several locations: Bloor Street East at Yonge Street, outside the Royal Bank; Nathan Phillips Square, in front of City Hall at Queen Street West and Bay Street; the Ferry Docks, beside the Hilton Harbour Castle hotel; the CN Tower on Front Street West; the Metro Zoo; and the Royal Ontario Museum, on the southwest corner of Bloor Street and Avenue Road. These are open Monday through Saturday from 9am to 7pm and Sunday from 9:30am to 6pm.

The **Community Information Centre,** 590 Jarvis St., 5th floor (tel. 416/392-0505), specializes in social and health service information but will try to answer any question, and if they can't, they will direct you to someone who can.

CITY LAYOUT

Toronto is laid out in a grid system. **Yonge** (pronounced Young) **Street** is the main north-south street, stretching from Lake Ontario in the south well beyond Hwy. 401 in the north; the main east-west artery is **Bloor Street,** which cuts right through the heart of downtown. Yonge Street divides western cross streets from eastern cross streets.

"Downtown" usually refers to the area stretching south from Eglinton Avenue to the lake between Spadina Avenue in the west and Jarvis Street in the east. Because this is such a large area, for the purposes of this book I have divided it into **downtown** (from the lake north to College/Carlton Street), **midtown** (College/Carlton Street north to Davenport Road), and **uptown** (north from Davenport Road). In the first area you'll find all the lakeshore attractions—Harbourfront, Ontario Place, Fort York, Exhibition Place, the Toronto Islands, plus the CN Tower, City Hall, SkyDome, Chinatown, the Art Gallery, and the Eaton Centre. Midtown includes the Royal Ontario Museum; the University of Toronto; Markham Village; and ultrachic Yorkville, a prime area for browsing and dining al fresco. Uptown is primarily a fast-growing singles' and young couples' residential and entertainment area.

Metropolitan Toronto is spread over 634 square kilometers and includes East York and the cities of (from west to east) Etobicoke, York, North York, and Scarborough. Some of its primary attractions exist outside the core, such as the Ontario Science Centre, the Metropolitan Zoo, and Canada's Wonderland. Be prepared to journey somewhat.

UNDERGROUND TORONTO It is not enough to know the streets of Toronto; you also need to know the warren of subterranean walkways that enable you to go from Union Station in the south to City Hall. Currently, you can walk from the Queen Street subway station west to the Sheraton Centre, then south through the Richmond-Adelaide Centre and First Canadian Place, all the way (through the dramatic Royal Bank Plaza) to Union Station. En route, branches lead off into the Toronto Dominion Centre and Stock Exchange. Other walkways exist around Bloor Street and Yonge Street and elsewhere in the city (ask for a map of these at the tourist

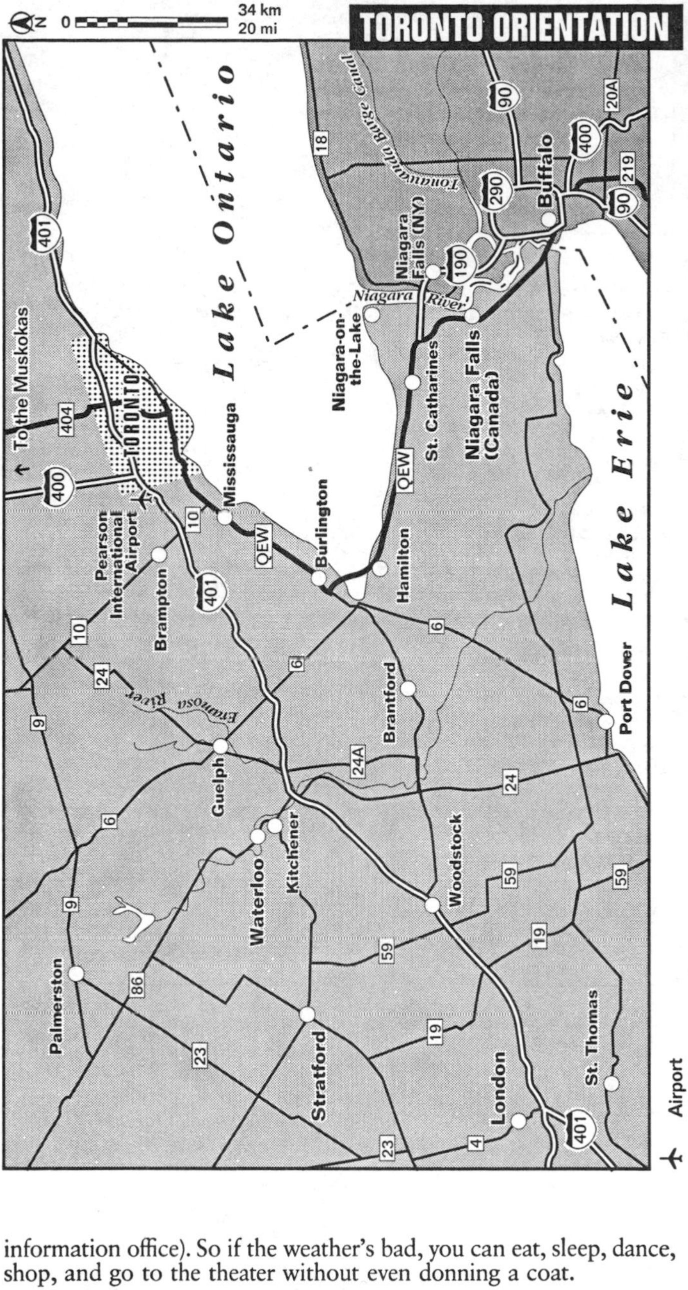
TORONTO ORIENTATION
0
34 km
20 mi
Lake Ontario
Lake Erie
To the Muskokas
TORONTO
Mississauga
Pearson International Airport
Brampton
Burlington
Hamilton
Niagara-on-the-Lake
St. Catharines
Niagara Falls (Canada)
Niagara Falls (NY)
Buffalo
Niagara River
Tonawanda Barge Canal
Port Dover
Brantford
Guelph
Eramosa River
Kitchener
Waterloo
Woodstock
Palmerston
Stratford
London
St. Thomas
Airport
401
400
404
10
QEW
18
90
190
290
20A
219
6
24
24A
9
59
19
86
23
4

information office). So if the weather's bad, you can eat, sleep, dance, shop, and go to the theater without even donning a coat.

NEIGHBORHOODS IN BRIEF Metropolitan Toronto consists of five cities and one borough under one administrative umbrella. What follows, with a few exceptions, are in the downtown city center:

TORONTO
Downtown Toronto

Allan Gardens 2
Art Gallery of Toronto 4
Bus Station 3
Campbell House 6
City Hall 7
CN Tower 17
Convention Centre 18
Toronto Dominion Centre 12
Eaton Centre 9
The Grange 5
Harbourfront Antiques Market 20
Maple Leaf Gardens 1
O'Keefe Centre 14
Old City Hall 8
Royal Alexandra Theatre 10
Royal Bank Plaza 13
Roy Thomson Hall 11
St. Lawrence Market 15
SkyDome 19
Union Station 16

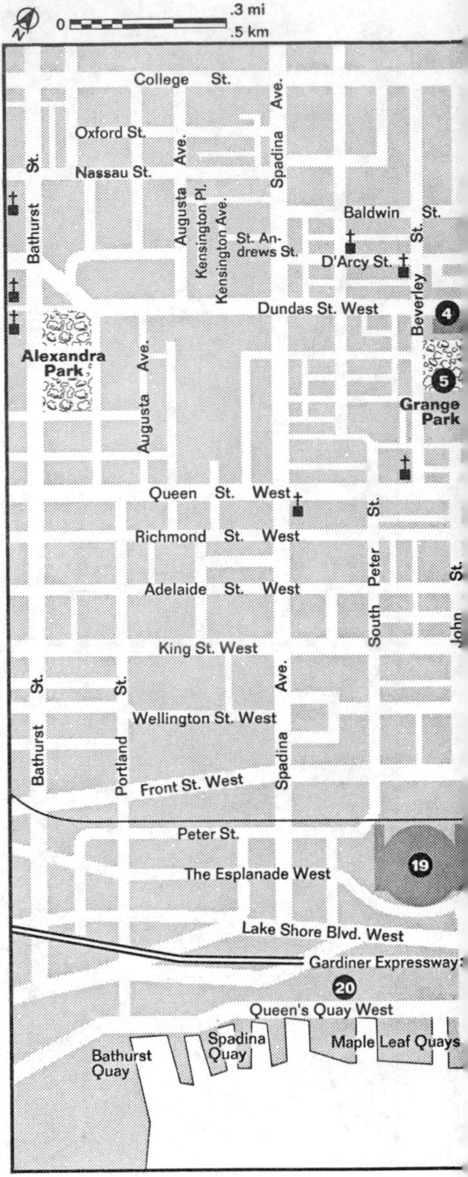
N
0
.3 mi
.5 km
College St.
Oxford St.
Nassau St.
Bathurst St.
Augusta Ave.
Kensington Pl.
Kensington Ave.
Spadina Ave.
Baldwin St.
St. Andrews St.
D'Arcy St.
Beverley St.
Dundas St. West
4
Alexandra Park
Augusta Ave.
5
Grange Park
Queen St. West
Richmond St. West
Adelaide St. West
South Peter St.
John St.
King St. West
Bathurst St.
Portland St.
Spadina Ave.
Wellington St. West
Front St. West
Peter St.
19
The Esplanade West
Lake Shore Blvd. West
Gardiner Expressway
20
Queen's Quay West
Spadina Quay
Bathurst Quay
Maple Leaf Quays

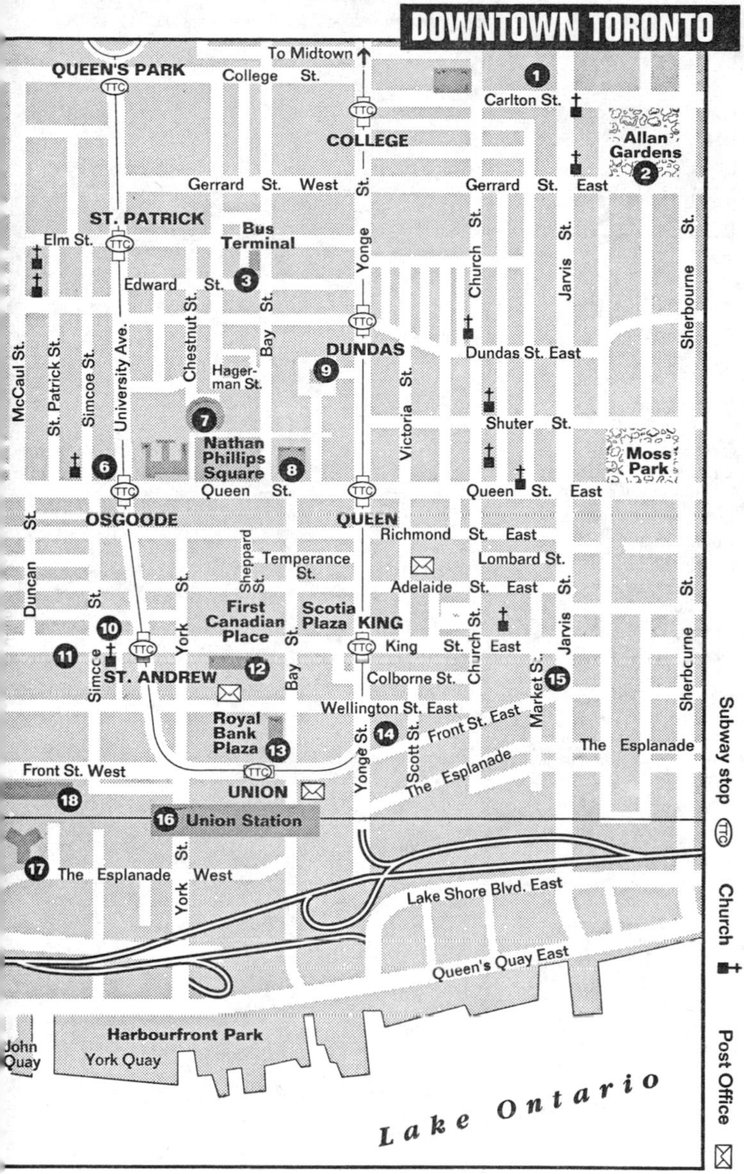
DOWNTOWN TORONTO
To Midtown
QUEEN'S PARK
College St.
Carlton St.
COLLEGE
Allan Gardens
Gerrard St. West
Gerrard St. East
ST. PATRICK
Bus Terminal
Elm St.
Edward St.
Yonge St.
Church St.
Jarvis St.
Sherbourne St.
Chestnut St.
Bay St.
DUNDAS
Dundas St. East
Hagerman St.
McCaul St.
St. Patrick St.
Simcoe St.
University Ave.
Victoria St.
Shuter St.
Nathan Phillips Square
Moss Park
Queen St.
Queen St. East
OSGOODE
QUEEN
Richmond St. East
Duncan St.
Sheppard St.
Temperance St.
Lombard St.
York St.
Adelaide St. East
First Canadian Place
Scotia Plaza
KING
King St. East
ST. ANDREW
Colborne St.
Market St.
Wellington St. East
Royal Bank Plaza
Scott St.
Front St. East
The Esplanade
Front St. West
UNION
Union Station
The Esplanade West
Lake Shore Blvd. East
Queen's Quay East
Harbourfront Park
John Quay
York Quay
Lake Ontario
1
2
3
6
7
8
9
10
11
12
13
14
15
16
17
18
Subway stop
TTC
Church
Post Office

TORONTO
Midtown

Allan Gardens 11
Gardiner Museum of Ceramic Art 3
Maple Leaf Gardens 10
McLaughlin Planetarium 5
Metro Library 1
Ontario Parliament Building 9
Queen's Park 7
Royal Ontario Museum (ROM) 2
Sigmund Samuel Building 6
University of Toronto 8
Varsity Stadium 4

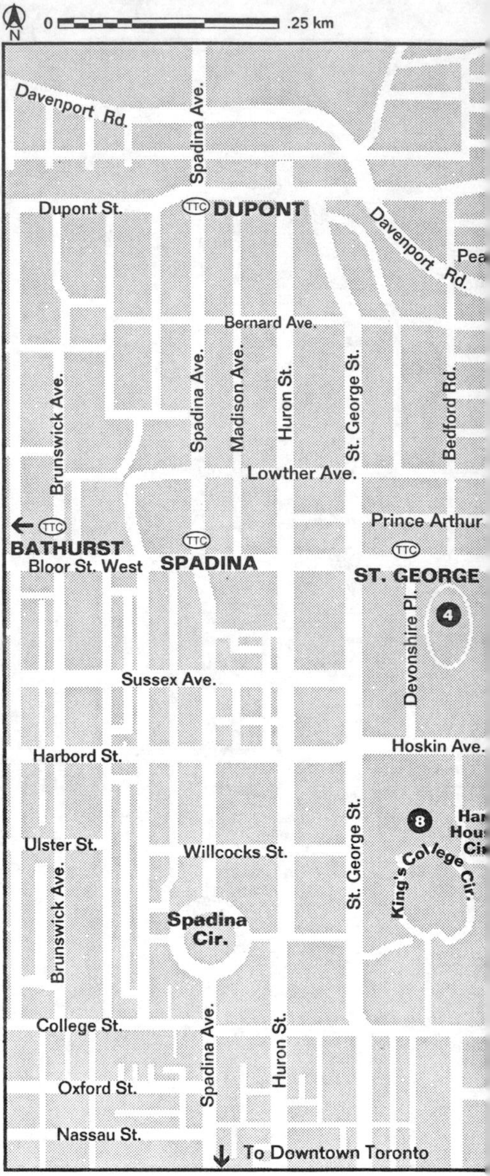
N
0
.25 km
Davenport Rd.
Spadina Ave.
Dupont St.
TTC DUPONT
Davenport Rd.
Bernard Ave.
Brunswick Ave.
Madison Ave.
Huron St.
St. George St.
Bedford Rd.
Lowther Ave.
Prince Arthur
TTC
BATHURST
Bloor St. West
TTC
SPADINA
TTC
ST. GEORGE
Devonshire Pl.
4
Sussex Ave.
Hoskin Ave.
Harbord St.
8
Ulster St.
Willcocks St.
King's College Cir.
Spadina Cir.
College St.
Oxford St.
Nassau St.
To Downtown Toronto

MIDTOWN TORONTO

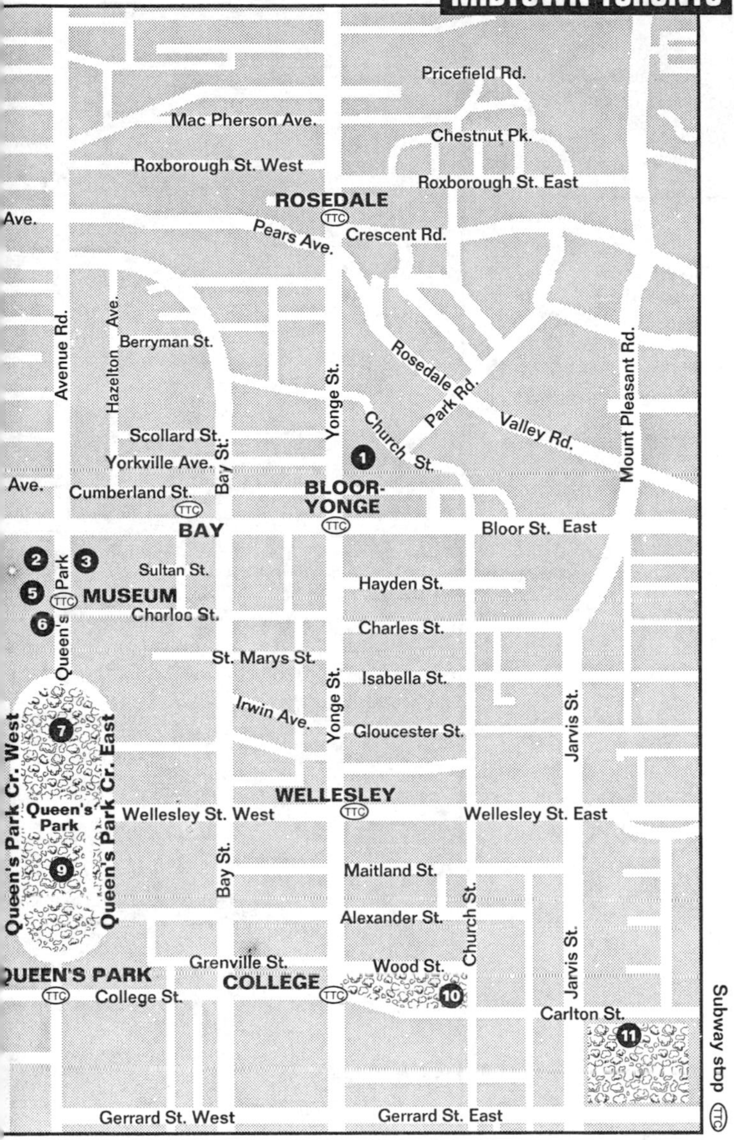

Pricefield Rd.
Mac Pherson Ave.
Chestnut Pk.
Roxborough St. West
Roxborough St. East
ROSEDALE
TTC
Ave.
Pears Ave.
Crescent Rd.
Avenue Rd.
Hazelton Ave.
Berryman St.
Rosedale Park Rd.
Yonge St.
Church St.
Valley Rd.
Mount Pleasant Rd.
Scollard St.
Yorkville Ave.
Bay St.
1
Ave.
Cumberland St.
BLOOR-YONGE
BAY
Bloor St. East
2
3
Queen's Park
Sultan St.
5
MUSEUM
Hayden St.
Charles St.
6
St. Marys St.
Isabella St.
Irwin Ave.
Gloucester St.
Jarvis St.
7
Queen's Park Cr. West
Queen's Park Cr. East
WELLESLEY
Queen's Park
Wellesley St. West
Wellesley St. East
9
Maitland St.
Alexander St.
Grenville St.
Wood St.
QUEEN'S PARK
COLLEGE
10
College St.
Carlton St.
11
Gerrard St. West
Gerrard St. East
TTC Subway stop

TORONTO
Uptown

Balfour Park ❸
Chorley Park ❺
Craigleigh Gardens ❻
Moore Park Ravine ❹
Mount Pleasant Cemetery ❶
Upper Canada College ❷

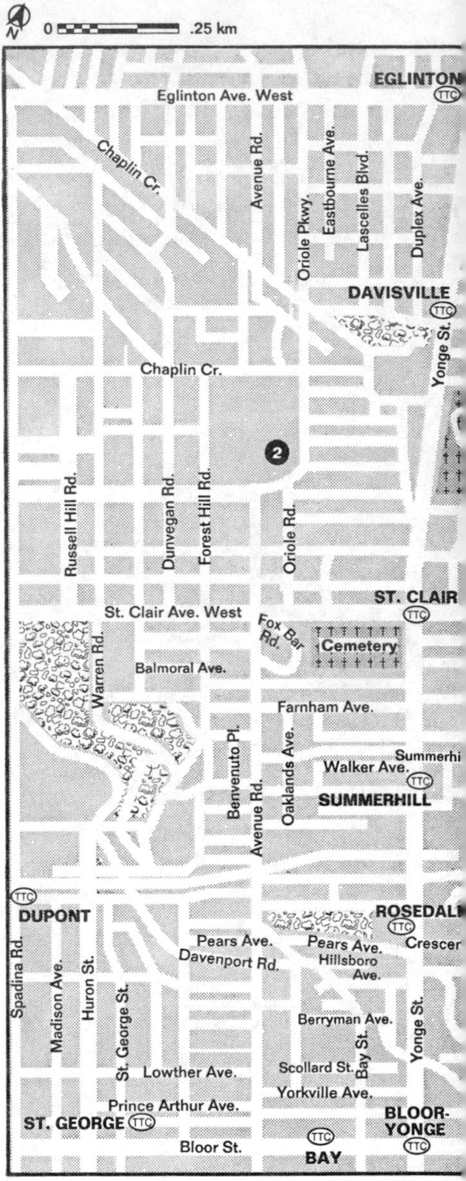
N
0 .25 km
EGLINTON
TTC
Eglinton Ave. West
Chaplin Cr.
Avenue Rd.
Oriole Pkwy.
Eastbourne Ave.
Lascelles Blvd.
Duplex Ave.
DAVISVILLE
TTC
Yonge St.
Chaplin Cr.
2
Russell Hill Rd.
Dunvegan Rd.
Forest Hill Rd.
Oriole Rd.
ST. CLAIR
TTC
St. Clair Ave. West
Fox Bar Rd.
Cemetery
Warren Rd.
Balmoral Ave.
Farnham Ave.
Benvenuto Pl.
Oaklands Ave.
Avenue Rd.
Walker Ave.
Summerhi
TTC
SUMMERHILL
TTC
DUPONT
ROSEDAL
TTC
Crescer
Pears Ave.
Pears Ave.
Davenport Rd.
Hillsboro Ave.
Spadina Rd.
Madison Ave.
Huron St.
St. George St.
Berryman Ave.
Bay St.
Yonge St.
Scollard St.
Lowther Ave.
Yorkville Ave.
Prince Arthur Ave.
ST. GEORGE
TTC
BLOOR-YONGE
TTC
Bloor St.
TTC
BAY

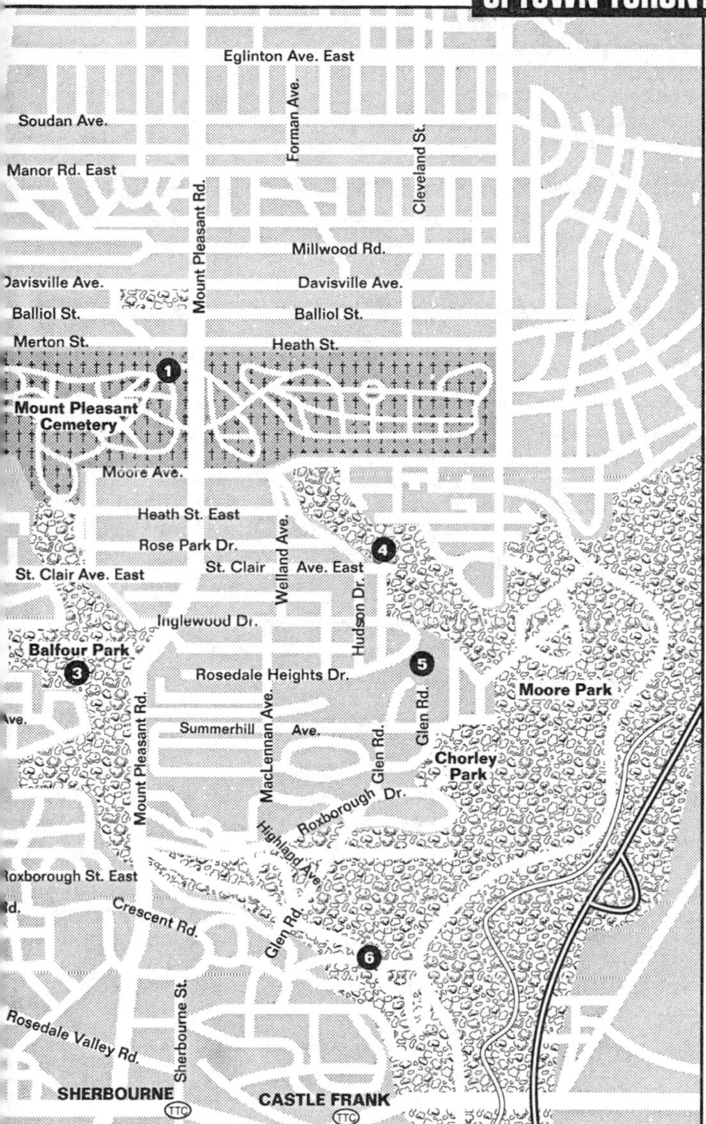
Eglinton Ave. East
Soudan Ave.
Forman Ave.
Cleveland St.
Manor Rd. East
Mount Pleasant Rd.
Millwood Rd.
Davisville Ave.
Davisville Ave.
Balliol St.
Balliol St.
Merton St.
Heath St.
1
Mount Pleasant Cemetery
Moore Ave.
Heath St. East
Welland Ave.
4
Rose Park Dr.
St. Clair Ave. East
St. Clair Ave. East
Hudson Dr.
Inglewood Dr.
Balfour Park
3
5
Rosedale Heights Dr.
Moore Park
Mount Pleasant Rd.
MacLennan Ave.
Glen Rd.
Summerhill Ave.
Glen Rd.
Chorley Park
Roxborough Dr.
Highland Ave.
Roxborough St. East
Crescent Rd.
Glen Rd.
6
Sherbourne St.
Rosedale Valley Rd.
SHERBOURNE
TTC
CASTLE FRANK
TTC

Subway stops TTC

Harbourfront/Lakefront The landfill on which the railroad yards and dock facilities were built. Now a glorious playground opening onto the lake.

Financial District Home to the banks and the trust and insurance companies and birthplace of Toronto's first skyscrapers. From Front Street north to Queen Street, between Yonge Street and York Street.

Old Town/St. Lawrence Market During the 19th century this was the focal point of the community. Today the market's still going strong and a stroll around the surrounding area will recapture an earlier era. East of Yonge Street between the Esplanade and Adelaide Street.

New Town/King Street West Theater District An area of dense cultural development, it contains the Royal Alex, Roy Thomson Hall, the CBC building, the Convention Centre, and the CN Tower. From Front Street north to Queen Street and from Bay Street west to Bathurst Street.

Chinatown As the Chinese community has grown, Chinatown has extended along Dundas Street and north along Spadina Avenue. A fascinating mixture of old and new—tiny hole-in-the-wall restaurants contrast with glitzy shopping centers built with new Hong Kong money. Dundas Street West from University Avenue to Spadina Avenue and north to College Street.

Yonge Street Toronto's main drag. Lined with stores and restaurants of all sorts. Seedy in places, with a small section of strip and porno joints, especially around College and Dundas streets.

Queen Street Village Youthful and funky. The old has not been entirely driven out by the new. The street offers an exciting mix—antiques stores, secondhand bookshops, reasonably priced dining, and more. Queen Street from University Avenue to Bathurst Street.

Queen's Park and the University Home to the Ontario Legislature and many of the colleges and buildings that make up the University of Toronto. From College Street to Bloor Street between Spadina Avenue and Queen's Park Crescent.

Cabbagetown Once described by writer Hugh Garner as the largest Anglo-Saxon slum in North America, this area stretching east of Parliament Street to the Don Valley between Gerrard Street and Bloor Street has been gentrified and is now home to such celebrities as dancer Karen Kain.

Yorkville Originally a village outside the city. In the '60s it

---

IMPRESSIONS

[On Toronto in 1927] Drear but pompous . . . It looked more or less like a bit of Birmingham straightened out, drained of bawdy and homogenized—"a nest," suggested the local writer Jesse Edgar Middleton cosily, or perhaps despairingly, "of British-thinking, British-acting people."
—JAN MORRIS, *TRAVELS* (1976)

The wild and rabid toryism of Toronto is, I speak seriously, appalling.
—CHARLES DICKENS, LETTER TO JOHN FORSTER (1842)

became Toronto's Haight-Ashbury but is now a fashionable enclave of designer boutiques, galleries, cafés, and restaurants. North and west of Bloor Street and Yonge Street.

The Annex An architecturally unique residential community, which led the fight against the Spadina Expressway. From Bedford Road to Bathurst Street and from Bloor Street to Bernard Street.

Rosedale Named after Sheriff Jarvis's residence. Curving tree-lined streets and elegant homes are the hallmarks of this leafy suburb. Northeast of Yonge Street and Bloor Street to Castle Frank and the Moore Park Ravine. Synonymous with the wealthy elite.

Forest Hill The second prime residential area and home to Upper Canada College and Bishop Strachan School for girls. Stretches west of Avenue Road between St. Clair Avenue and Eglinton Avenue.

The Beaches Communal, youthful, and cozy. The Boardwalk and beach make it a relaxing casual neighborhood. Only 15 minutes from downtown at the end of the Queen Street East streetcar (trolley) line.

The East End—the Danforth Largely a Greek and Indian community. Here you'll find a number of restaurants, shops, and cafés catering to both communities. A continuation of Bloor Street across the Don Valley Viaduct.

North York Recent redevelopment of this community about eight miles north of Toronto's Queen Street has made this one of the hottest real estate markets in the country.

2. GETTING AROUND

BY PUBLIC TRANSPORTATION

Public transit is operated by the **Toronto Transit Commission (TTC)** (tel. 416/393-4636 daily from 7am to 11:30pm for information), which provides an overall interconnecting subway, bus, and streetcar system.

Fares (including transfers to buses or streetcars) are $2 (or ten tickets for $13) for adults, $1 (ten tickets for $6.50) for students 19 and under and seniors, and 50¢ (eight tickets for $2.50) for children under 12. You can purchase from any subway collector a special $5 day pass good for unlimited travel Monday to Friday after 9:30am and all day Saturday. On Sundays or holidays (except Labor Day), a similar $5 pass may be used by up to six people (maximum of two adults).

For surface transportation you need a ticket, a token, or exact change. Tickets and tokens may be obtained at subway entrances or authorized stores that display the sign TTC TICKETS MAY BE PURCHASED HERE. Always obtain a transfer, just in case you need it. They are obtainable free of charge in the subways from a push-button machine just inside the entrance or directly from drivers on streetcars and buses.

THE SUBWAY It's a joy to ride—fast, quiet, and sparkling clean. It's a very simple system to use, too, consisting of two lines—Bloor-Danforth and Yonge-University-Spadina—designed basically in the form of a cross: The Bloor Street east-west line runs from Kipling

Avenue in the west to Kennedy Road in the east, where it connects with Scarborough Rapid Transit traveling from Scarborough Centre to McCowan Road. The Yonge Street north-south line runs from Finch Avenue in the north to Union Station (Front Street) in the south. From here, it loops north along University Avenue and connects with the Bloor line at the St. George station. A Spadina extension runs north from St. George to Wilson Avenue.

A new transportation link connects downtown to Harbourfront, running from Union Station along Queens Quay to Spadina with stops at Queens Quay ferry docks, York Street, Simcoe Street, and Rees Street. No transfer is needed from subway to LRT and vice versa.

The subway operates Monday through Friday from 6am to 1:30am and Sunday from 9am to 1:30am. From 1am to 5:30am a Blue Night Network operates on basic surface routes running about every 30 minutes. For route information, pick up a Ride Guide at subway entrances or call 416/393-4636.

Smart commuters (and visitors) park their cars for a low all-day parking fee at subway terminal stations at Kipling, Islington, Finch, Wilson, Warden, Kennedy, and McCowan; or at smaller lots at Sheppard, York Mills, Eglinton, Victoria Park, and Keele. You'll have to get there very early, though.

BUSES & STREETCARS Where the subway leaves off, buses and streetcars take over to carry you east-west or north-south along the city's arteries. When you pay your fare (on bus, streetcar, or subway), always pick up a transfer, so that if you want to transfer to another mode of transportation, you won't have to pay another fare. For complete TTC information, call 416/393-4636.

BY TAXI

As usual, this is an expensive mode of transportation: $2.20 the minute you step in and then $1.40 for every additional mile. There's also a 10¢ charge for each bag. As you can see, cab fares can mount up, especially in rush hours. Nevertheless, if you need a cab you can hail one on the street (they also line up in front of the big hotels) or call one of the major companies: **Diamond** (tel. 416/366-6868), **Yellow** (tel. 416/363-4141), or **Metro** (tel. 416/364-1111 or 363-5611).

BY CAR

CAR RENTALS Prices on car rentals change so frequently and vary so widely that probably your best bet is to shop around using the *Yellow Pages*. Still, just to give you some idea, here are a couple of companies and their rates: **Budget,** 171 Bay St. (tel. 416/364-7104), charges $40 (including 200 free kilometers) per day plus 12¢ per kilometer, or $200 per week (including 1,400 free kilometers), for a subcompact car. **Tilden,** 930 Yonge St. (tel. 416/925-4551), charges $30 per day (including 200 free kilometers) plus 15¢ per kilometer, or $189 per week, for a small car; there are 10 Metro locations. Always ask about special weekend rates and other discounts.

Note: If you're under 25, check with the company—many will rent on a cash-only basis, some only if you have a credit card, and others will not rent to you at all.

THE TTC SYSTEM

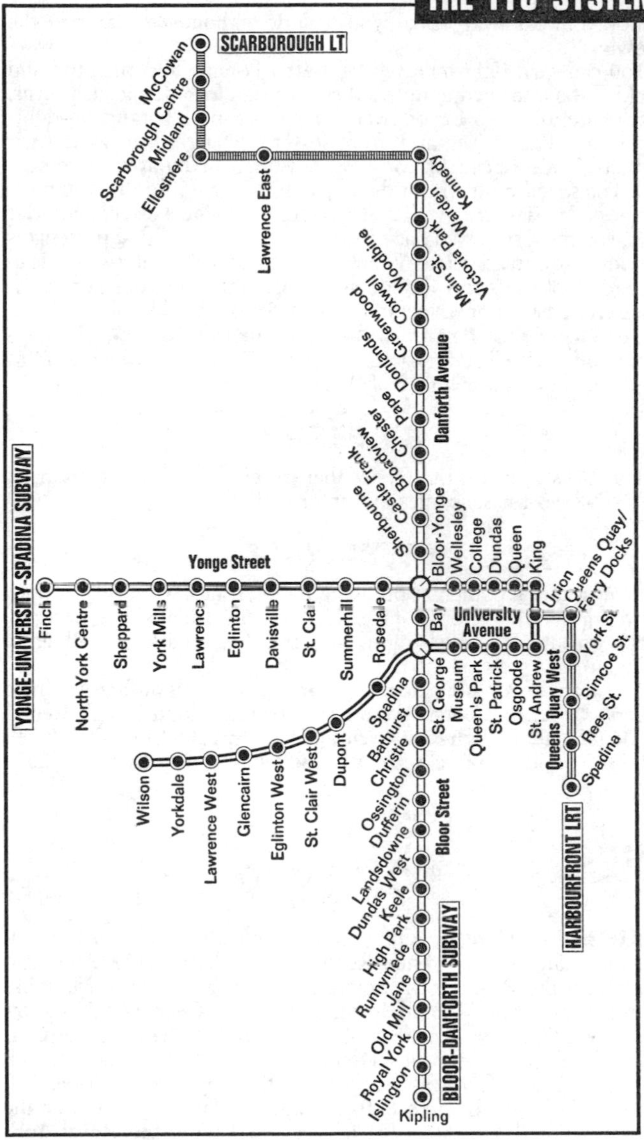
SCARBOROUGH LT
McCowan
Scarborough Centre
Midland
Ellesmere
Lawrence East
Kennedy
Warden
Victoria Park
Main St.
Woodbine
Coxwell
Greenwood
Donlands
Pape
Chester
Broadview
Castle Frank
Sherbourne
Danforth Avenue
Bloor-Yonge
Wellesley
College
Dundas
Queen
King
Union
Queens Quay/
Ferry Docks
York St.
Simcoe St.
Rees St.
Spadina
Queens Quay West
HARBOURFRONT LRT
YONGE-UNIVERSITY-SPADINA SUBWAY
Yonge Street
Finch
North York Centre
Sheppard
York Mills
Lawrence
Eglinton
Davisville
St. Clair
Summerhill
Rosedale
Bay
University
Avenue
St. George
Museum
Queen's Park
St. Patrick
Osgoode
St. Andrew
Spadina
Dupont
St. Clair West
Eglinton West
Glencairn
Lawrence West
Yorkdale
Wilson
Bathurst
Christie
Ossington
Dufferin
Landsdowne
Dundas West
Keele
High Park
Runnymede
Jane
Old Mill
Royal York
Islington
Kipling
Bloor Street
BLOOR-DANFORTH SUBWAY

DRIVING & PARKING Driving and parking in the city can be very frustrating because the traffic moves slowly downtown and parking costs are extremely high.

Parking downtown runs about $4 per half hour, with a $15 to $17 maximum. After 6pm and on Sunday, rates go down to around $6. Generally the city-owned lots, marked with a big green "P," are slightly cheaper. Observe the parking restrictions—otherwise the city will tow your car away. Still, if you can't do without your car, note the following:

You can turn right on a red light after coming to a full stop and checking the intersection unless there is a sign forbidding such turns. Watch carefully also for one-way streets and no-left- and no-right-turn signs. The driver and front-seat passenger must wear their seatbelts (if you're caught not wearing yours, you'll pay a substantial fine). The speed limit within the city is 30 m.p.h. (50kmh). You must stop at pedestrian crosswalks. If you are following a streetcar and it stops, you must stop well back from the rear doors so that passengers can exit easily and safely. (Where there are concrete safety islands in the middle of the street for streetcar stops, this rule does not apply, but exercise care nonetheless.) Radar detectors are illegal.

The **Canadian Automobile Association (CAA),** 60 Commerce Valley Dr. E., Markham (tel. 416/771-3111), provides aid to any driver who is a member of AAA.

BY FERRY

Metro Parks operates the ferries that travel to the Toronto Islands. Call 392-8193 for schedules and information.

BY BICYCLE

You can secure a pamphlet outlining biking routes from the Toronto Convention and Visitor's Office. The Toronto Islands, the Beaches, Harbourfront/Lakefront/Sunnyside, and High Park are all great biking areas.

You can **rent bicycles** at Harbourfront right across from Queen's Quay; on Center Island from Toronto Island Bicycle Rental (tel. 365-7901); at High Park Cycle and Sports, 1168 Bloor St. W. (tel. 532-7300); and at Bicycle Transit, 2348 Lakeshore Blvd. (tel. 252-1393).

FAST FACTS: TORONTO

Airlines Here are a few useful airline addresses: Air Canada, 130 Bloor St. W., at Avenue Road (tel. 416/925-2311); American Airlines, in the Royal York Hotel, 100 Front St. W., the Manulife Center, 55 Bloor St. W., and Toronto Dominion Centre, 69 Yonge St. (tel. 416/283-2243); Canadian Airlines International, on the concourse level of the Toronto Dominion Centre, 69 Yonge St. (tel. 416/675-2211); Northwest Airlines, in the Royal York Hotel, 100 Front St. W. (tel. toll free 800/225-2525); United Airlines, at the airport (tel. toll free 800/241-6522); and USAir, the Royal York Hotel, 100 Front St. W. (tel. 416/361-1560).

Airport See "Orientation," earlier in this chapter.

Area Code Toronto's area code is 416.

Auto Rentals See "Getting Around," earlier in this chapter.

Buses See "Getting Around," earlier in this chapter.

Business Hours Banks are generally open Monday through Thursday from 10am to 3pm and Friday from 10am to 6pm. To get the most advantageous rate of exchange, go to a bank. Most government and corporate offices are open Monday through Friday from 9am to 5pm. Stores are generally open Monday through Wednesday from 9:30 or 10am to 6pm and Saturday and Sunday from 10am to 5pm, with extended hours (until 8 to 9:30pm) on Thursday and usually Friday.

Car Rentals See "Getting Around," earlier in this chapter.

Climate See "When to Go" in Chapter 2.

Currency See "Information, Entry Requirements & Money" in Chapter 2.

Currency Exchange The best place to change your currency is at a bank. Currency can also be conveniently exchanged at the airport.

Dentist The Royal College of Dental Surgeons (tel. 961-6555) offers emergency after-hours dental care. Otherwise, ask at the front desk or the concierge at your hotel. (See also "Medical Services," below.)

Doctor The College of Physicians and Surgeons, 80 College St. (tel. 961-1711), operates a referral service from 9am to 5pm.

Documents Required See "Information, Entry Requirements & Money" in Chapter 2.

Driving Rules See "Getting Around," earlier in this chapter.

Drugstores Look under "Pharmacies" in the *Yellow Pages*. Shoppers Drug Mart, at 360 Bloor St. W., at Spadina Avenue, stays open Monday through Friday until midnight. They operate many other branches downtown. The other big chain is Pharma Plus, with a store at 68 Wellesley St., at Church Street (tel. 924-7760), which is open daily from 8am to midnight.

Electricity Same as in the United States—110 volts, 50 cycles, AC.

Embassies/Consulates All embassies are in Ottawa, the national capital. However, many nations maintain consulates in Toronto, including the following: Australian Consulate-General, 175 Bloor St. E. (tel. 323-1155 or 323-3919); British Consulate-General, 777 Bay St. (tel. 593-1267); Irish Trade Board, 160 Bloor St. E. (tel. 929-7394); and the United States Consulate, 360 University Ave. (tel. 595-1700).

Emergencies Call 911 for fire, police, and ambulance.

Etiquette At Confederation, Canadians opted for peace, order, and good government (as opposed to life, liberty, and the pursuit of happiness)—and it shows. You'll see respect for the individual expressed in terms of consideration for others and the community as a whole. Canadians will appreciate you more if you behave with decorum in public. Don't litter; don't push and shove; don't cause a ruckus. Although they will probably not initiate a conversation, being naturally reserved, they will welcome it if you do. I have always found Canadians very helpful. On a recent visit to Toronto with a wheelchair-bound friend, I never once had to ask for help. It was always offered before I could ask, and often people would retrace their steps to assist me in carrying the chair up a flight of steps.

Eyeglasses Two offices of A-1 Public Optical, 69 Queen St. E., at Church Street (tel. 364-0740), and at 750 Dundas St. W., at Bathurst Street (tel. 860-1550), offer one-hour service, depending on the prescription.

Hairdressers/Barbers For expensive coiffuring, try the Vidal Sassoon Salon, 37 Avenue Rd. (tel. 920-1333), or Choppers Hair Design, 89 Bloor St. W. (tel. 928-9199). There are, of course, plenty of more modest salons like the small one in Village by the Grange. Ask at your hotel for a recommendation.

Holidays See "When to Go" in Chapter 2.

Hospitals Try Toronto General Hospital, 200 Elizabeth St. (emergency tel. 340-3948).

Hotlines Help is available from the following: rape crisis (tel. 597-8808), assault victims (tel. 863-0511), drug/alcohol crisis (tel. 595-6128), and suicide prevention (tel. 285-7779).

Information See "Information, Entry Requirements & Money" in Chapter 2 and also, "Orientation," earlier in this chapter.

Laundry/Dry Cleaning The following are conveniently located self-service Laundromats: Bloor Laundromat, 598 Bloor St. W., at Bathurst Street (tel. 588-6600); and Speedy Automatic Coin Wash, 568 Church St., at Wellesley Street (tel. 922-1147).

For one-hour dry cleaning, try Best Serve–One Hour Cleaners, 531 Yonge St., at Wellesley Street (tel. 416/921-9016), which gives this service until 10am. It's open from 7am to 6pm Monday through Saturday. One-hour dry cleaning is also available at Parliament One-Hour Cleaning, 436 Parliament St., at Spruce Street, near Carlton Street (tel. 923-5276).

Libraries Metro Library is at 789 Yonge St. (tel. 393-7000).

Liquor/Liquor Laws Liquor is sold at Liquor Control Board of Ontario (LCBO) stores, open Monday through Saturday. Most are open from 10am to 6pm (some stay open evenings). Call 365-5900 or 963-1915 for locations. These stores sell liquor, wine, and some beers. Check the *White Pages* under "Liquor Control Board" for locations.

True wine lovers, though will want to check out Vintages stores (also operated by the LCBO), which carry a more extensive and more specialized selection of wines. The most convenient downtown location is in the lower-level concourse of Hazelton Lanes (tel. 924-9463).

Beer is sold at Brewers Retail Stores, most of which are open Monday through Friday from 10am to 10pm and Saturday from 10am to 8pm. Check the *Yellow Pages* under "Beer and Ale" for locations.

Some quiddities of the local law: Drinking hours are 11am to 1am Monday through Saturday and noon to 11pm Sunday (cocktail lounges are not usually licensed to sell liquor on Sunday; dining lounges are). The minimum drinking age is 19.

Lost Property The TTC Lost Articles Office is at the Bay Street subway station (tel. 416/393-4100), open Monday through Friday from 8am to 5:30pm.

Luggage Storage/Lockers Lockers are available at Union Station.

Mail Postage for letters and postcards to the United States costs 48¢; to overseas, 84¢. Mailing letters and postcards within Canada costs 42¢.

Maps Try Canada Map Company, 211 Yonge St., north of Queen Street (tel. 362-9297), or Open Air Books and Maps, 25 Toronto St., near Yonge and Adelaide streets (tel. 363-0719).

Medical Services For medical or dental problems, the Toronto General Hospital, with an entrance at 150 Gerrard St. W., provides 24-hour emergency service (tel. 416/340-3948).

Money See "Information, Entry Requirements & Money" in Chapter 2.

Newspapers/Magazines The three daily newspapers are the *Globe and Mail,* the *Toronto Star,* and the *Toronto Sun. Eye* and *Now* are the arts-and-entertainment weeklies of the moment. In addition, there are many English-language ethnic Toronto newspapers serving the Portuguese, Hungarian, Italian, East Indian, Korean, and Chinese communities. *Toronto Life* is the major monthly city magazine. *Where Toronto* is usually provided free in your hotel room.

Some of the best newsmagazine selections can be found at the Book Cellar and Maison de Presse, both in Yorkville; Coles the World's Biggest Bookstore and Pages on Queen Street West; and Lichtman's News and Books, at Yonge and Bloor streets, Yonge and Richmond streets, the Atrium on Bay Street, Yonge Street and Eglinton Avenue, and 1430 Yonge Street.

Photographic Needs For major repairs there's the Camera Repair Centre, 1162 Yonge St., north of the Rosedale subway station (tel. 923-8143).

Convenient downtown photo stores include Black's Camera, in the Eaton Centre (tel. 598-1596), the Manulife Centre, 55 Bloor St. W. (tel. 922-8475) and at many other locations; Japan Camera Centre, in the Eaton Centre (tel. 598-1474), College Park (tel. 598-1133), First Canadian Place (tel. 366-1207), and other locations.

Police In a life-threatening emergency, call 911. For all other matters you can reach the Metro police at 324-2222.

Post Office The main post office is at 17 Front St. W., between Yonge Street and Bay Street (tel. 416/973-2433), open Monday through Friday from 8am to 5:45pm. Other offices are also open from 8am to 5:45pm Monday through Friday only. For a list of postal stations, look in the blue pages of the telephone directory under "Government of Canada."

Radio The programming of the Canadian Broadcasting Corporation is one of the joys, as far as I'm concerned, of traveling in Canada. It offers a great mix of intelligent discussion and commentary as well as drama and music. In Toronto the CBC broadcasts on 740 AM and 94.1 FM.

CHIN, at 1540 AM and 100.7 FM, will get you in touch with the ethnic/multicultural scene in the city. Other stations include the following: 680 AM (CFTR), contemporary hits; 1010 AM (CFRB), news and information; 1050 AM (CHUM), soft rock/oldies; 91.1 FM (CJRT), classical and jazz; 98 FM (CHFI), adult contemporary music; 99.9 FM (CKFM), adult contemporary music; 104.5 FM (CHUM), adult contemporary music; and 107 FM (CILQ), the hottest rock albums.

Religious Services Toronto has houses of worship for all major faiths, including the following: St. James Cathedral (Anglican), 65 Church St., at King Street (tel. 364-7865); Rosedale Baptist Church, 877 Yonge St. (tel. 926-0732); Zen Buddhist Temple, 86 Vaughan Rd. (tel. 658-0137); Church of the Mother of God Proussa (Greek Orthodox), 461 Richmond St. E. (tel. 364-8918); Beth Sholom Synagogue, 1445 Eglinton Ave. W. (tel. 783-6103); St. George's Lutheran Church, 410 College St. (tel. 921-2687); St. Andrew's Presbyterian Church, 75 Simcoe St., at King Street (tel. 593-5600); and St. Michael's Cathedral (Roman Catholic), 200 Church St. (tel. 364-0234).

Restrooms Public restrooms are found in major shopping complexes like Eatons, the Manulife Centre, the Holt Renfrew

Centre, the Colonnade, and similar convenient locations. They are invariably clean and well kept. You can also use hotel and restaurant facilities.

Safety As large cities go, Toronto is generally safe. But there are precautions that you should take whenever you're traveling in an unfamiliar city or country. Stay alert and be aware of your immediate surroundings. Wear a moneybelt and keep a close eye on your possessions. Be particularly careful with cameras, purses, and wallets, all favorite targets of thieves and pickpockets. Be especially careful walking on dark streets and in parks after dark. Every society has its criminals. It's your responsibility to be aware and alert even in the most heavily touristed areas.

Shoe Repairs For while-you-wait service, go to Mr. Presto, either at the Bay subway station (tel. 928-9171) or at Royal Bank Plaza (tel. 860-1712); Mastercraft Shoe Rebuilders, in First Canadian Place (tel. 366-6213); Roy's Shoe Repair Bar, in the Manulife Centre at 55 Bloor St. W. on Concourse Level (tel. 923-4696); or Speedy Shoe Repair, 481 University Ave., at Dundas Street (tel. 595-5592).

Taxes The provincial retail sales tax is 8%; there's also a 5% tax on hotel/motel rooms and a national 7% goods and services tax (GST).

In general, nonresidents may apply for a refund of these taxes for nondisposable merchandise that will be exported for use provided they were removed from Canada within 60 days of purchase. Note, though, that the following do not qualify for rebate: meals and restaurant charges, alcohol, tobacco, gas, car rentals, and such services as dry cleaning and shoe repair. For an application form and information, write or call Revenue Canada, Customs and Excise, Visitor Rebate Program, Ottawa, Canada K1A 1J5 (tel. 613/991-3346) *well in advance* of your trip. You can also contact Ontario Travel, 77 Bloor St. W., Queen's Park, Toronto, ON, M7A 2R9 (tel. 416/314-0944, or toll free 800/668-2746).

For information on the new GST, call 416/973-1000.

Taxis See "Getting Around," earlier in this chapter.

Telephone A local call from a telephone booth costs 25¢. Watch out for hotel surcharges on local and long-distance calls; often a local call will cost $1 from a hotel room.

Television If your hotel room has a TV set, it's more than likely tied into the local cable network, on which you'll find the following: Channel 4, a local independent station; Channel 6, CBC (the Canadian Broadcasting Corporation); Channel 7, City TV (a local independent station); Channel 8, CTV Community Station; Channel 11, a local independent station; Channel 12, CBC; Channel 15, NBC; Channel 16, CBS; Channel 14, ABC; Channel 18, PBS; Channel 19, a local independent station; Channel 23, weather station; Channel 44, Sports Network; Channel 46, CNN; and Channel 53, Financial News Network. In regular TV listings 3 and 5 are the CBC; 2 is NBC; 4 is CBS; and 7 is ABC.

Time Toronto is on Eastern standard time. Daylight saving time is in effect April through October.

Tipping Basically it's the same as in the United States: 15% in restaurants, 15% to 20% for taxis, and $1 per bag for porters.

Transit Information For information on the subway, bus, and streetcar system, call 393-4636.

Useful Telephone Numbers Call 283-1010 for the "Talking Yellow Pages," and then enter the following digits for specialized information: 3000, business news; 3005, stock market report; 3010, events calendar; 3130, "What's On for Kids"; 3041, national sports report; 3150, "What's Happening on Campus"; and 8180, weather.

3. NETWORKS & RESOURCES

FOR STUDENTS Toronto has several major colleges as well as the large and sprawling University of Toronto.

George Brown College of Applied Arts and Technology (tel. 867-2000) has several campuses around town, including the St. James campus at 200 King St. E.; the Kensington Campus near the Kensington Market at 21 Nassau St.; the Nightingale Campus at 2 Murray St., near University Avenue and Dundas Street; and the campus at Casa Loma, 160 Kendal Ave., at Davenport Road and Spadina Avenue. Schools include Theatre and Dance Schools. The college bookstores are at 200 King St. E. (tel. 867-2365) and at 160 Kendal Ave. (tel. 944-4440).

Ryerson Polytechnical Institute (tel. 979-5000) is located at 350 Victoria St., at Gould Street. Here are some useful telephone numbers:

Student information (tel. 979-5036)
Bookstore (tel. 979-5116)
CKLN radio, 380 Victoria St. (tel. 595-1477)
The Ryersonian newspaper (tel. 979-5323)
Theater (tel. 977-1055)
Women's center (tel. 598-9838)

The **University of Toronto,** Simcoe Hall, King's College Circle, Toronto ON, M5S 1A1 (tel. 416/978-2011 or 978-4111 for tour information), is the largest university in Canada, with 52,000 students (41,000 full-time). It offers many activities and events year round that any visitor can attend—lectures, seminars, concerts, and more. U of T Day is usually celebrated in the middle of October, when the university holds open house to the community and also celebrates with a Children's Fair and the annual Homecoming football game and parade.

Downtown, the main **St. George Campus** university buildings are located in an area stretching from College Street to Bloor Street and from University Avenue to Spadina Avenue. Composed of several separate colleges, most of which are on the downtown campus, the university also operates **Erindale College** on Mississauga Road North in Mississauga and **Scarborough College** on Military Trail in Scarborough.

Some useful university addresses and telephone numbers include the following:

Libraries: John P. Robarts Research Library (tel. 978-2294); Science and Medicine Library (tel. 978-8617); Sigmund Samuel Library (tel. 978-2280).

Student Affairs: Dental Clinic (tel. 979-4335); information and events (tel. 978-2021); Hart House (tel. 978-4732); International Student Centre, 33 St. George St. (tel. 978-2564); Students Association, 119 St. George St. (tel. 598-3110); U of T Gays and Lesbians, 315 Bloor St. W. (tel. 971-7880); Koffler Student Services Centre, 214 College St.

Theaters and Sports: Athletic tickets (tel. 978-4112); Hart House Theater (tel. 978-8668); Macmillan Theatre and Walter Hall, Faculty of Music (tel. 978-3744); University College Playhouse, University College (tel. 978-4870); Varsity Arena (tel. 978-7388); Varsity Stadium (tel. 978-7389).

Publications and Radio: Bookstore, 214 College St. (tel. 978-7900); *Bulletin,* 45 Willcocks St. (tel. 978-7016); *The Varsity,* 44 St. George St. (tel. 979-2831); *U of T* magazine, 45 Willcocks St. (tel. 978-2102); U of T Radio, 91 St. George St. (tel. 595-0909).

FOR GAY MEN & LESBIANS Any gay man or lesbian will find the following resources useful. First, pick up a copy of *Xtra!,* available free at many bookstores, including the **Gay Liberation Bookstore/Glad Day Bookshop,** 598A Yonge St., 2nd floor (tel. 961-4161), open Monday to Friday from 10am to 9pm, Saturday until 7pm, and Sunday from noon until 6pm.

For information, call the **Gay Phone Line** (tel. 964-6600) or the **Gay Community Calendar,** P.O. Box 8, Adelaide Street Station (tel. 923-4297).

For political and community information, contact **Gay & Lesbian Youth Toronto** (tel. 591-6749) or the **Coalition for Gay Rights,** 736 Bathurst St. (tel. 533-6824).

FOR WOMEN For books and information on the feminist scene, stop by the **Toronto Women's Bookstore,** 73 Harbord St., at Spadina (tel. 922-8744). It's open Monday through Thursday and Saturday from 10:30am to 6pm, Friday until 9pm, and Sunday from noon to 5pm.

If you don't want to stop by Harbord Street, then call the **Women's Information Line** (tel. 598-3714) or secure a copy of the local women's publication, ***VOICE,*** 152 Arlington St. (tel. 656-4949).

CHAPTER 4

TORONTO ACCOMMODATIONS

Although Toronto has many fine hotels, it's not easy to find good-value accommodations downtown. The city is expensive. Most of the top hotels are pricey and cater to a business clientele; at even the more moderate establishments you can expect to pay \$80 to \$100 per day; budget hotels, which are few, charge less than \$80, while nonhotel accommodations, like university dorms, start at \$45 to \$50 per night. Bed-and-breakfasts are a good budget bet, but even they are creeping upward in price.

The situation is not helped by a 5% accommodations tax and the new national 7% GST.

There are some things that you can do to combat the situation. I cannot stress enough how important it is to ask for a discount. Hotel rates move up and down depending on the traffic—in fact, hotels are beginning to apply the same yield management techniques that airlines have been using successfully, so that rates go up and down depending on the occupancy. For example, a single room listed at \$199 could rent for as little as \$130. If a room goes unsold the revenue is lost forever. The management would much prefer to sell a room than not, so don't be ashamed to ask. State what you're prepared to pay and see what happens. If business is slow, it will work; if it's not, it won't.

Take advantage of special discounts. Always ask about discounts for special groups of people—corporate personnel, government employees, the military, seniors, students—whatever group to which you legitimately belong. Also ask about seasonal discounts, especially summer rates and weekend packages, which can help you secure some great bargains even at the most luxurious establishments.

Remember, too, that the prices quoted here are so-called rack rates—the prices quoted to walk-ins. These can be as much as 40% higher than other discounted rates—government, corporate, and so on. Again, ask for the discount.

In addition, always ask about parking charges and surcharges on local and long-distance phone calls. Both can make a big difference in your bill.

Special Note: When these room rates were researched, Canada was in a severe recession that was much worse than that in the United States. I was astonished to find that some hotel prices had actually dropped below those listed in the previous edition of this book. I have changed the prices to reflect that, but if the economic situation improves substantially you can expect the prices to zoom back up.

When you're planning a visit to Toronto, it's wise to reserve in advance. **Accommodation Toronto** (tel. 416/596-7117), a free service of the Hotel Association of Metropolitan Toronto, is available from 8:30am to 5pm Monday to Friday and from 9:30am to 5:30pm Saturday, Sunday, and holidays, to make your booking and provide further information.

In the pages that follow I have categorized my favorites according to price and location. Downtown runs from the lakeshore to College/Carlton Street between Spadina Avenue and Jarvis Street; midtown refers to the area north of College/Carlton Street to where Dupont crosses Yonge Street, also between Spadina and Jarvis; uptown, west, and east designate areas outside the city core. I have included a substantial selection of airport hotels because "The Strip," as it's called, has about 20 hotels and functions as a large entertainment center, not only for visitors but also for natives who think nothing of popping out there to a dance club or dining spot.

AN IMPORTANT NOTE ON PRICES The price brackets for a double room are roughly as follows: very expensive, $200 and up per day; expensive, from $100 to $140; moderate, from $75 to $100; budget, less than $60. I emphasize that these are only very rough categories, and subtle distinctions of taste, clientele, and reputation must also be taken into account.

Unless stated otherwise, *the prices cited in this guide are given in Canadian dollars,* which is good news for you because the Canadian dollar is worth 22% less than the American dollar but buys just about as much. As we go to press, $1 Canadian is worth 82¢ U.S., which means that your $100-a-night hotel room will cost only $82 U.S. a night, your $50 dinner for two will cost only $41 U.S., and your $5 breakfast will cost only $4.10 U.S.

Note: The accommodations tax is 5%, and the goods and services tax is 7%, but both are refunded to nonresidents upon application (see "Taxes" in "Fast Facts: Toronto" in Chapter 3).

BED & BREAKFAST For interesting, truly personal accommodations, contact **Toronto Bed & Breakfast,** 253 College St. (P.O. Box 269), Toronto, ON, M5T 1R5 (tel. 416/588-8800 from 9am to noon and 2 to 7pm), for their list of homes offering bed-and-breakfast accommodations within the city for an average $60 to $70 per night double. The association will reserve for you, or you can choose an establishment and make all the arrangements yourself.

You can also contact **Metropolitan Bed and Breakfast,** 615 Mount Pleasant Rd., Suite 269, Toronto, ON, M4S 3C5 (tel. 416/964-2566), which lists close to 100 lovely bed-and-breakfast accommodations, ranging from $55 and up double. Include $2 for postage and handling when you write requesting a booklet. They will make reservations for you.

Other organizations to try include the **Downtown Toronto Association of Bed and Breakfast Guesthouses,** P.O. Box 190, Station B, Toronto, ON, M5T 2W1 (tel. 416/977-6841 or 690-1724). This association represents about 30 B&Bs and is operated by Susan Oppenheim, an enthusiastic B&B host herself who has a spacious Victorian home where she welcomes guests into her large country kitchen. The best time to call is between 9:30am and 2:30pm. All homes are no-smoking. Room prices range from $45 to $65 single and $55 to $75 double.

Bed & Breakfast Accommodators, 223 Strathmore Blvd.,

Toronto, ON M4J 1P4 (tel. 416/461-7095), offers nine rooms with three shared baths. Facilities include a kitchen and daily maid service. Breakfast is included. It's located off Greenwood Avenue, convenient to the Greenwood subway stop. Rates are $45 single and $55 double. Fully furnished two- and three-bedroom apartments are also available.

Bed and Breakfast Homes of Toronto, P.O. Box 46093, College Park Post Office, 444 Yonge St., ON M5B 2L8 (tel. 416/363-6362), represents about 18 homes with doubles starting at $50.

1. DOWNTOWN

The downtown area runs from the lakefront to College/Carlton Street between Spadina Avenue and Jarvis Street.

VERY EXPENSIVE

CAMBRIDGE SUITES HOTEL, 15 Richmond St. E., Toronto ON M5C 1N2. Tel. 416/368-1990, or toll free 800/463-1990. Fax 416/601-3751. 230 suites. A/C MINIBAR TV TEL **Subway:** Queen.

$ Rates (including continental breakfast): $190 single; $210 double. **Parking:** $12.

Ideally situated downtown, this all-suite hotel features comfortable accommodations and the extra-special conveniences that make all the difference to the traveler. Each large 550-square-foot suite has a refrigerator, a microwave, and dishes, along with a supply of coffee, tea, and cookies. If you like, you can leave a list and your grocery shopping will be done for you. The furnishings are extremely comfortable and include a couch, armchairs, and a coffee table. (In some cases, french doors separate the living area from the bedroom.) There are two TVs and two telephones in each suite, with hookups for conference calls and a computer. There's also a dressing area with a full-length mirror and a marble bathroom, equipped with a hairdryer and a full complement of amenities. The penthouse luxury suites are duplexes that have Jacuzzis.

Dining/Entertainment: Facilities include a small, comfortable bar and a fine dining room that serves reasonably priced entrées at dinner, such as salmon teriyaki or breast of chicken with cilantro and lime beurre blanc.

Services: Daily maid service, valet, concierge.

Facilities: Business center; laundry; convenience store; fitness center, boasting a fine view of the city and equipped with whirlpool; exercise room and sauna.

HILTON INTERNATIONAL, 145 Richmond St. W., Toronto, ON, M5H 3M6. Tel. 416/869-3456, or toll free 800/445-8667. Fax 416/869-1478. 601 rms and suites. A/C TV TEL **Subway:** Osgoode.

$ Rates: $160 single; $180 double. Extra person $20. One child under 18 stays free in parents' room. Weekend packages available. **Parking:** $16 overnight.

TORONTO
Downtown Toronto

Amsterdam Guest House 24
Best Western Primrose Hotel 2
Bond Place Hotel 7
Chestnut Park Hotel 9
Clarion Essex Park 22
Days Inn Carlton Inn 1
Delta Chelsea Inn 4
Hilton International 10
Holiday Inn City Hall 8
Holiday Inn on King 23
Hotel Ibis 5
Hotel Victoria 14
Journey's End 12
King Edward Hotel 13
L'Hôtel 16
Neil Wycik College Hotel 3
Novotel 19
Radisson Plaza Hotel Admiral 18
Royal York 21
Sheraton Centre 11
SkyDome 17
Strathcona 15
Toronto International Hostel 6
Westin Harbor Castle 20

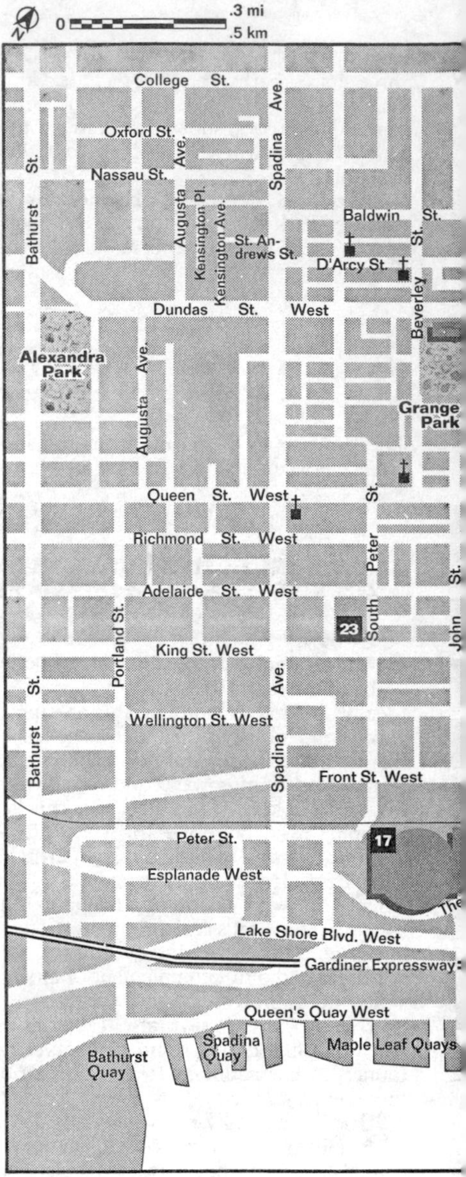
N
0
.3 mi
.5 km
College St.
Oxford St.
Nassau St.
Bathurst St.
Augusta Ave.
Kensington Pl.
Kensington Ave.
Spadina Ave.
Baldwin St.
St. Andrews St.
D'Arcy St.
Beverley St.
Dundas St. West
Alexandra Park
Augusta Ave.
Grange Park
Queen St. West
Richmond St. West
Peter St.
Adelaide St. West
Portland St.
23
South
John St.
King St. West
Bathurst St.
Spadina Ave.
Wellington St. West
Front St. West
Peter St.
17
Esplanade West
The
Lake Shore Blvd. West
Gardiner Expressway
Queen's Quay West
Bathurst Quay
Spadina Quay
Maple Leaf Quays

DOWNTOWN TORONTO ACCOMMODATIONS

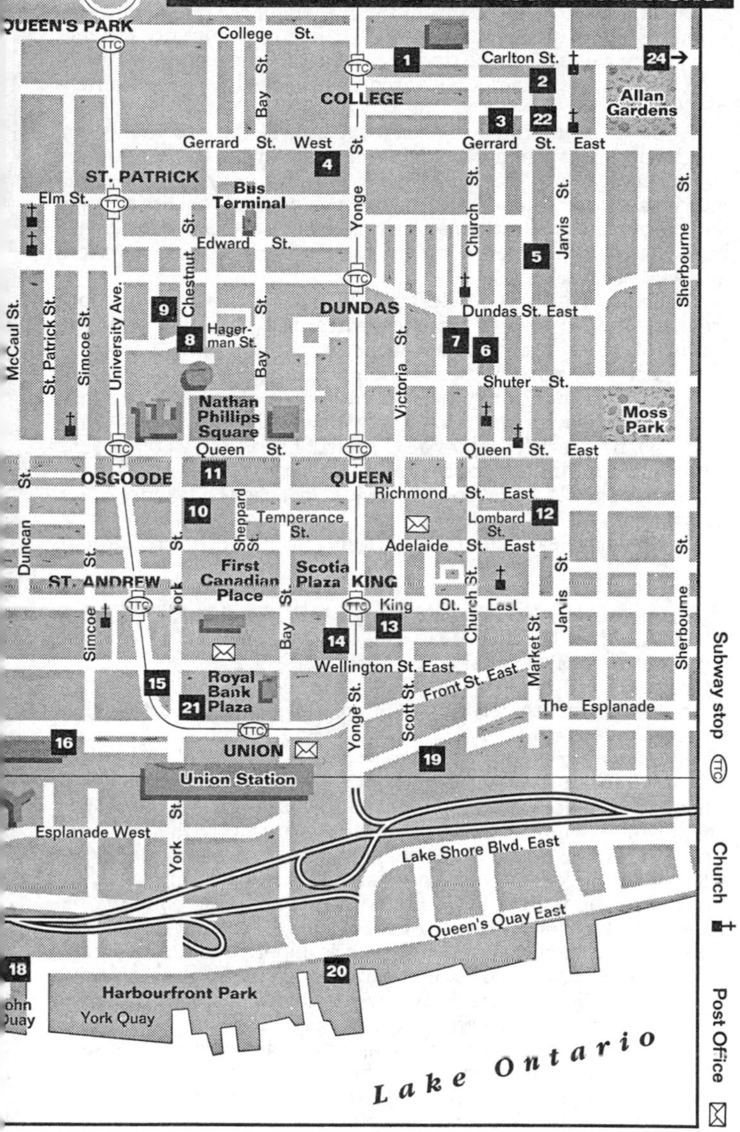

QUEEN'S PARK
College St.
Carlton St.
COLLEGE
Allan Gardens
Gerrard St. West
Gerrard St. East
ST. PATRICK
Elm St.
Bus Terminal
Edward St.
Bay St.
Yonge St.
Church St.
Jarvis St.
Sherbourne St.
DUNDAS
Dundas St. East
Hagerman St.
Chestnut St.
McCaul St.
St. Patrick St.
Simcoe St.
University Ave.
Victoria St.
Shuter St.
Nathan Phillips Square
Moss Park
Queen St.
Queen St. East
OSGOODE
QUEEN
Richmond St. East
Lombard St.
Temperance St.
Sheppard St.
Adelaide St. East
Duncan St.
York St.
First Canadian Place
Scotia Plaza
ST. ANDREW
KING
King St. East
Market St.
Wellington St. East
Front St. East
Scott St.
Royal Bank Plaza
The Esplanade
UNION
Union Station
Esplanade West
Lake Shore Blvd. East
Queen's Quay East
Harbourfront Park
York Quay
Lake Ontario
1
2
3
4
5
6
7
8
9
10
11
12
13
14
15
16
18
19
20
21
22
24
TTC
Subway stop
Church
Post Office

If you approach the Hilton from the rear you'll see the steam rising from this plush hotel's show pool, just one of the luxury facilities available at this stylish, 32-story, $40-million establishment. Part of the Hilton hotels chain, it is conveniently located near the Convention Centre.

If you wish, you can take a glass-enclosed elevator to your room, which will be large and impeccably decorated with all the expected conveniences—push-button phone, color TV, AM/FM radio, and individual temperature control—plus such unusual touches as scales and alarm clocks. Rooms are currently furnished in white French provincial or dark-wood contemporary with blue-green or melon-and-gold color schemes.

Dining/Entertainment: Trees 20 feet tall separate the lobby from the Garden Court restaurant, where you can enjoy breakfast, lunch, afternoon tea, or dinner while seated on a cushioned rattan chair. The hotel also houses the renowned Trader Vic's, featuring Polynesian fare and decor; the adjacent lounge offers over 90 potent exotic drinks, such as the Scorpion (with a fresh gardenia floating in the glass). Barristers, as might be expected, has a clubby atmosphere, with wonderful leather armchairs and couches.

Services: 24-hour room service, concierge, laundry/valet, babysitting.

Facilities: Heated indoor pool, sauna, whirlpool, exercise room, Executive business center.

KING EDWARD HOTEL, 37 King St. E., Toronto, ON, M5C 2E9. Tel. 416/863-9700. Fax 416/367-5515. 315 rms and suites. A/C MINIBAR TV TEL **Subway:** King.

$ Rates: $210–$230 single; $230–$250 double; from $370 suite. Weekend packages $130–$150 per night for room and free parking. **Parking:** $24.

In its heyday the King Edward welcomed the Prince of Wales (later Edward VIII) and attracted such notables as Rudolph Valentino, Charles de Gaulle, Olivia de Havilland, Richard and Liz, the Beatles, and anybody who was anybody in Toronto. During the 1970s the King Edward was a fading relic attempting to survive with dignity but without too much success. Fortunately, the King Eddie (as it was fondly known), built in 1903, did not succumb to the bulldozer but underwent a $40 million refurbishment and reopened in 1981. Today the original elements of the hotel, such as imported marble Corinthian columns and sculpted ceilings, have been restored to their former elegance. The lobby soars 40 feet to a colonnaded rotunda, capped by a glass dome that lets the sun stream in.

The 315 rooms—the small number guaranteeing very personal service—are extremely spacious, beautifully decorated in subtle champagne/beige and apricot/brown hues. Each comes fully equipped with a remote-control color TV; telephones in the bedroom and bathroom; a clock-radio; and such niceties as complimentary newspaper delivery, bathrobes, super-fluffy towels sans monogram, shampoo, perfume, and marble bathtubs.

Dining/Entertainment: The Lobby Lounge offers afternoon tea and cocktail entertainment. The famous old Victoria Room, a refuge for the well-to-do, has been turned into the Café Victoria, where baroque plasterwork and etched glass are combined and a light, airy feel is imparted by many tall shrubs. The Consort Bar, on the main floor, has eight-foot-high windows offering lovely views of

King Street. For formal dining, Chiaro's specializes in fine French and continental cuisine with main dishes priced from $21 to $30.

Services: 24-hour room service, concierge, laundry/valet, complimentary shoeshine and newspaper, nightly turndown, twice-daily chamber service.

Facilities: Health club with masseuse.

L'HOTEL, 225 Front St. W., Toronto, ON, M5V 2X3. Tel. 416/597-1400, or toll free 800/828-7447. Fax 416/597-8128. 549 rms, 38 suites. A/C MINIBAR TV TEL **Subway:** Union.

$ Rates: $230–$275 single; $250–$300 double. Extra person $20. Weekend packages available. **Parking:** $16.

L'Hôtel, attached to the Convention Centre, is ideally located for the CN Tower, SkyDome, Roy Thomson Hall, and the theater district. Rose marble, cherry wood, and polished bronze are used throughout the lobby. The 25-story tower slopes back and upward from the main entrance, creating a garden court, which accommodates a lounge and café.

The rooms, decorated in dusky rose or muted green, are finely appointed, with marble bathroom counters, writing desks, and elegant table lamps, and feature such residential touches as draped tables and matching window valances. All feature color TVs, clock-radios, individual climate control, two telephone lines, and hairdryers. No-smoking rooms are available.

Entrée Gold accommodations offer additional amenities—complimentary breakfast, cocktail canapés, and shoeshine, as well as private check-in and honor bar and nightly turndown.

Dining/Entertainment: The Skylight Lounge, decorated with trees and plants, is well known for its Sunday brunch and after-theater menu. In the elegant Chanterelles, imaginative main courses range from $20 to $29. Luncheon prices range from $11 to $15. A special pretheater menu is offered. The Orchard Café offers casual dining.

Services: 24-hour room service, concierge, laundry/valet.

Facilities: Indoor pool, whirlpool, saunas, well-equipped exercise room, squash courts, sundeck.

NOVOTEL, 45 The Esplanade, Toronto, ON, M5E 1W2. Tel. 416/367-8900, or toll free 800/221-4542. Fax 416/360-8285. 256 rms, 10 suites. A/C MINIBAR TV TEL **Subway:** Union.

$ Rates: $155 single or double. **Parking:** $7.

Located just off Yonge Street near the St. Lawrence Centre and O'Keefe Centre, the Novotel is an ultramodern hotel, built in Renaissance style with a Palladian entrance leading to a marble lobby with oak and Oriental decorative accents.

The rooms are nicely appointed with all the expected conveniences, each including a remote-control TV, two telephones, a hairdryer, a minibar, a radio/TV speaker in the bathroom, and skirt hangers.

Dining/Entertainment: The restaurant/lounge Café Les Arcades serves breakfast, lunch, and dinner. Main courses include chicken with ginger and prime rib, priced from $13 to $17, as well as eggs and pasta. A quick buffet breakfast is available, and free morning coffee is provided.

Services: Room service (available from 6am to midnight), concierge, laundry/valet.

Facilities: Indoor pool, sauna, whirlpool, exercise room.

RADISSON PLAZA HOTEL ADMIRAL, 249 Queen's Quay W., Toronto, ON, M5J 2N5. Tel. 416/364-5444, or toll free 800/333-3333. Fax 416/364-2975. 140 rms, 17 suites. A/C MINIBAR TV TEL **Subway:** Union.

$ Rates: $165–$210 single; $180–$215 double. Extra person $20. Weekend packages available. **Parking:** $11.

As the name and the harborfront location suggest, the Hotel Admiral has a strong nautical flavor. The lobby combines polished woods and downtown Toronto brass with nautical paintings. The horseshoe-shaped roofdeck comes complete with pool and cabana-style bar/terrace.

The rooms are elegantly furnished with Korean-style chests of drawers with brass trimmings, marble-top sidetables, and desks, all set on jade carpets. Extra amenities include two push-button phones, a hairdryer and clothes line in the bathroom, a clock-radio, a minibar, and a complimentary newspaper.

Dining/Entertainment: The Commodore's Dining Room, which looks out onto Lake Ontario and the waterfront, serves classic continental cuisine, with main courses ranging from $20 to $32. The Galley serves a more modest menu, priced from $8 to $16. The adjacent Bosun's Bar also offers light snacks.

Services: 24-hour room service, concierge, complimentary newspaper delivery.

Facilities: Outdoor swimming pool, whirlpool, squash court.

ROYAL YORK, 100 Front St. W., Toronto M5J 1E3. Tel. 416/863-6333, or toll free 800/828-7447, 800/268-9411 in the U.S. 1,337 rms, 71 suites. A/C MINIBAR TV TEL **Subway:** Union.

$ Rates: $210 single; $225 double. Business-class service $20 extra. Many special packages available. **Parking:** $17.

To many citizens and regular visitors, the Royal York *is* Toronto, because in its 35 banquet and meeting rooms many of the city's historical and social events have taken place. It is by any measure a huge enterprise—it's a major convention hotel and, as such, is not to everyone's taste. Still, there is a magnificence to this hotel, which opened in 1929 and has hosted a raft of royalty, heads of state, and celebrities. The lobby itself is vast, impressive, and crowned by an incredible inlay coffered ceiling that is lit by large cast-bronze chandeliers. If you stay here, do go down and look at some of the banquet rooms, several of which have splendid ceiling murals, and the series of provincial meeting rooms, each with a unique decor.

The statistics are mind-boggling—for example, the Royal York can sleep 2,800 guests; it contains ⅛ mile of carpeting; and it can accommodate 10,000 people at one meal sitting. The kitchen bakes 10,000 rolls daily; uses 18,000 eggs per week; and washes 25,000 pieces of china and 45,000 pieces of silverware daily.

The hotel has recently undergone and is still undergoing major renovations. Rooms vary in size, but a standard room will have a king-size bed. The decor varies but tends to staid beiges, golds, and ochres or else a combination of jade and rose with antique reproduction furnishings that always include an armchair and a well-lit desk. Nice features are solid-wood doors, windows that open, and wall moldings. Rooms for the disabled are exceptionally well equipped for wheelchair guests and for the deaf and blind. Business class provides a

FROMMER'S SMART TRAVELER: HOTELS

1. Always remember that a hotel room is a perishable commodity: If it's not sold, the revenue is lost forever. Therefore, it is a fact that rates are linked to the hotel's occupancy level. If it's 90% occupied the price goes up; if it's 50% occupied the price goes down. So always try negotiating by stating *your* price.
2. In summer, ask about seasonal rates. All city hotels—even the most expensive—offer dramatic discounts then.
3. Many hotels offer big discounts or package rates on weekends (Friday to Sunday night). If you're staying on a weekend, always ask about these.
4. Take advantage of downtown university accommodations.
5. Consider the bed-and-breakfast alternative (there are several organizations in the Toronto area).
6. Before selecting a hotel, always ask about parking charges. These can be more than $20 or as little as $7, or if the hotel is outside downtown, free. It can make a difference if you're staying a while.

superior room on a private floor, with private lounge, complimentary breakfast and newspaper, and nightly turndown.

Dining/Entertainment: The Royal York boasts an incredible 12 restaurants and lounges. The Imperial Room is perhaps the best known, with its full stage, floor-to-ceiling drapes, and classical accents. Once the cabaret venue of the city, it now offers fine dining and dancing. The Acadian Room offers continental cuisine in an elegant atmosphere. For a show of Japanese finesse there's a Benihana steakhouse; the Italian Bistro offers pizza along with other traditional Italian food. The Gazebo affords a gardenlike setting for lunch and afternoon tea; Lytes is a luncheon spot, while the Coffeehouse offers all-day dining and a deli provides 24-hour takeout. The Lobby Bar features a sports screen; the Library Bar is a more intimate and cozy meeting spot. Downstairs you'll find the Black Knight Karaoke bar; Dick Turpin's, an English-style pub with sing-along entertainment; and the small York Station bar.

Services: Room service (available from 7am to 1am), concierge.

Facilities: Skylit indoor lap pool with hand-painted trompe-l'oeil murals and potted palms, exercise room, saunas, steam rooms and whirlpool, barbershop and beauty salon, shopping arcade, business center.

THE SHERATON CENTRE, 123 Queen St. W., Toronto, ON, M5H 2M9. Tel. 416/361-1000, or toll free 800/325-3535. Fax 416/947-4883. 1,315 rms, 79 suites. A/C MINIBAR TV TEL **Subway:** Osgood.

$ Rates: $185–$210 single; $195–$235 double. Extra person $20; roll-away bed $10. Two children under 18 stay free in parents' room. Various packages available. **Parking:** $13 a day (more for valet parking).

A city in itself, the Sheraton Centre contains more than 40 shops in the Plaza, 8 restaurants and bars, and 2 movie theaters. It's conveniently located at the heart of the city's underground passageways, right across from City Hall. Behind the lobby, you'll even find two acres of landscaped gardens with a waterfall and summer terrace.

In this 43-story complex there are more than a thousand spacious rooms, all attractively furnished and well equipped. The Towers rooms, which are more expensive, offer additional amenities—bathrobes, additional telephone in the bathroom, a private elevator and reception area, and complimentary continental breakfast and evening hors d'oeuvres. All the rooms have recently been refurbished as part of a $47 million renovation.

Dining/Entertainment: In the shopping concourse you'll find an authentic-looking English pub (shipped from England in sections) called Good Queen Bess, complete with toby jugs, cozy fireplaces, and mugs of Newcastle brown. At the Reunion bar in the lobby, where you'll be served great drinks and snacks, you'll find a dance floor, fooz ball, and 13 thirty-inch video monitors sharing the space with you. The premier restaurant, offering spectacular views from the 43rd floor, is the Winter Palace where the chef turns out classics like duck à l'orange, prime rib, and Dover sole (priced from $20 to $35). Postcards presents cuisine from around the world, with regular special promotions featuring breakfasts, luncheon buffets, and dinners from the country of the moment, along with a regular all-day menu.

Services: 24-hour room service, laundry/valet, babysitting.

Facilities: Indoor and outdoor pools, sauna, games room, hot tub, exercise room, shopping mall, two movie theaters.

SKYDOME, 45 Peter St. S., Toronto, M5V 3B4. Tel. 416/360-7100. Fax 416/341-5090. 346 rms. A/C MINIBAR TV TEL **Subway:** Union.

$ Rates: City view, $130–$210 single or double; field side, $275 standard room, from $400 deluxe room.

For sports fans and baseball fans in particular, this is hotel heaven. Imagine having a room that overlooks the bullpen and the splendid green of the park, as do 70 rooms of this hotel located right inside the SkyDome stadium.

Standard rooms come with a view window, more expensive field-side rooms have raised living areas, and then there are the suites. The city-view rooms are the least expensive. Each unit has modern furnishings and is equipped with telephone in the bathroom and full amenities, including a hairdryer.

Dining/Entertainment: Café on the Green overlooks the field, and, adjacent to the hotel, so do Sightlines and the Hard Rock Café.

Services: 24-hour room service, laundry/valet, concierge.

Facilities: Fitness center with pool, squash courts, sauna, and exercise room.

WESTIN HARBOUR CASTLE, 1 Harbour Square, Toronto, ON, M5J 1A6. Tel. 416/869-1600, or toll free 800/228-3000. Fax 416/869-0573. 922 rms, 56 suites. A/C MINIBAR TV TEL **Subway:** Union; then LRT to the hotel.

$ Rates: $190–$230 single; $210–$250 double. Extra person $20. Children stay free in parents' room. Weekend packages (double occupancy) and special long-term rates available. **Parking:** $16.50.

The Harbour Castle is located right on the lakefront, ideally situated for the Harbourfront and linked to downtown by the LRT. The rooms are located in two towers joined at the base by a five-story podium. Marble, oak, and crystal adorn the spacious lobby, which commands a great harbor view. The hotel has recently undergone a $50 million facelift.

Each room has a view of the lake and is furnished with a remote-control color TV featuring in-room movies, a bathroom telephone, a marble-top desk and night table, a table and floor lamps, and color-coordinated fabrics. There are 442 no-smoking rooms.

Dining/Entertainment: The moderately priced Regatta Restaurant and Terrace overlooking the harbor serves breakfast, lunch, and dinner. The Lighthouse, a revolving restaurant on the 37th floor, reached via a glass-walled elevator, provides fabulous views during lunch, brunch, or dinner. Tea is served in the lobby lounge, along with cocktails and a continental breakfast. Off the main lobby, the Chartroom offers a quiet haven for a drink.

Services: 24-hour room service, concierge, laundry/valet, guest room voice mail, beauty shop.

Facilities: Fitness center with indoor pool, whirlpool, sauna, steamroom, squash courts, jogging track, massage clinic, shopping arcade; Executive Club for business travelers.

EXPENSIVE

BEST WESTERN CHESTNUT PARK HOTEL, 108 Chestnut St., Toronto, ON, M5G 1R3. Tel. 416/977-5000 or toll free 800/668-6600. Fax 416/977-9513. 512 rms, 8 suites. A/C MINIBAR TV TEL **Subway:** St. Patrick.

$ Rates: $140 single; $160 double. Children under 16 stay free in parents' room. **Parking:** $13.

The Chestnut Park is conveniently located two blocks from the Eaton Centre on Chestnut Street, just off Dundas Street between Bay Street and University Avenue. The Canadian Museum of Textiles is connected to the hotel via a walkway. The ambience is modern, with many Oriental decorative furnishings in the lobby and throughout.

The rooms are spiffily furnished and equipped with telephones with computer- and fax-compatible jacks, safes, color TVs, and bathrobes.

Dining/Entertainment: Tapestries is open for breakfast, lunch, and dinner, offering Chinese specialties, pasta, and continental cuisine, including such dishes as loin of lamb with fig sauce, New York steak with shallot sauce, and tiger shrimp with cumin and tomato salsa (from $10 to $20 at dinner). The Gallery Lounge overlooks the lobby.

Services: 24-hour room service, concierge, valet.

Facilities: Indoor swimming pool, health club with sauna and exercise room.

CLARION ESSEX PARK HOTEL, 300 Jarvis St., just south of Carlton, Toronto, ON M5B 2C5. Tel. 416/977-4823, or toll free 800/567-2233. Fax 416/977-4830. 102 rms. A/C MINIBAR TV TEL

$ Rates: $110–$135 single or double. **Parking:** $10.

Everything at the Clarion Essex Park has been transformed in a recent renovation. The lobby is sheathed in marble and accented with Oriental screens and fresh flowers, and the whole place has been turned into a very comfortable moderately priced facility. All rooms are queens or kings, and each is nicely furnished with a sofa, a desk, and a coffee table and fully equipped with a push-button phone, a cable color TV housed in a cabinet, and a fully tiled bathroom with a hairdryer and all the amenities. Closets are large.

Dining/Entertainment: The Clarion has a restaurant/bistro with a bar.

Services: Room service (available from 7am to 10pm).

Facilities: Indoor pool, fitness center.

DAYS INN CARLTON INN, 30 Carlton St., Toronto, ON, M5B 2E9. Tel. 416/977-6655, or toll free 800/268-9076. Fax 416/977-0502. 535 rms and suites. A/C TV TEL **Subway:** College.

$ Rates: $125 single; $135 double. Extra person $15. Children under 18 stay free in parents' room. Summer discounts available. **Parking:** $10.

Nicely furnished rooms with modern conveniences at fair prices are the hallmark of the Carlton Inn, a modern, centrally air-conditioned high-rise. Besides offering reasonably priced (for Toronto) accommodations, the inn is well located, only a few steps from Yonge Street, right next door to Maple Leaf Gardens.

All rooms contain color TVs with in-house movies. Refrigerators are available on request.

Dining/Entertainment: There is a lounge, a sports bar, and a restaurant.

Services: Laundry/valet.

Facilities: Indoor and outdoor pool and saunas.

DELTA CHELSEA INN, 33 Gerrard St. W., Toronto, ON, M5G 1Z4. Tel. 416/595-1975, or toll free 800/268-1133. Fax 416/585-4393. 1,548 rms, 52 suites. A/C TV TEL **Subway:** College.

$ Rates: $165 single; $180 double; from $200 suite. Extra person $15. Children under 18 share parents' room free. Weekend packages available. Seniors $90. **Parking:** $14—but only 300 spaces.

The Delta Chelsea, located between Yonge and Bay streets, is still one of Toronto's best buys—particularly for families and on weekends—although prices have risen considerably in recent years. The crowded scene in the lobby, though, testifies to its continued popularity.

All rooms have color TVs with in-room movies; push-button phones; and bright, modern furnishings. Some rooms have kitchenettes. The new south tower opened in late fall 1990, with 600 rooms featuring dual phones with data jacks, call waiting, and conference-call features. The new tower also contains a penthouse lounge, a business center, and more dining facilities.

Dining/Entertainment: Wittles offers fine, elegant dining. The Express Café is a self-service cafeteria with very reasonable prices. The Kitchen Garden offers an extensive range of items—deli, sandwiches, pizza, and roast chicken, as well as baked items. The restaurants offer a good-value children's menu, and children under 7 eat free. The Chelsea Bun, which serves lunch buffets and Sunday brunch, offers live entertainment daily and Dixieland jazz on Saturday afternoon.

Services: 24-hour room service; babysitting; laundry/valet pickup; Special Signature service including additional amenities like complimentary breakfast and newspaper, minibar, bathrobe.

Facilities: Swimming pool, whirlpool, sauna, exercise room, lounge, games room with pool tables, and—a blessing for parents—a children's creative center where three- to eight-year-olds can play under expert supervision (it's open until 10pm on Friday and Saturday, and there's a nominal charge); beauty salon; business center.

HOLIDAY INN CITY HALL, 89 Chestnut St., Toronto, ON, M5G 1R1. Tel. 416/977-0707. Fax 416/977-1136. 717 rms and suites. A/C TV TEL **Subway:** Dundas or University.

$ Rates: $135 single; $150 double. Extra person $15. Children under 19 stay free in parents' room. **Parking:** $13.

The Holiday Inn City Hall, right behind City Hall, has all the earmarks of the chain, plus a little extra. The rooms have recently been upgraded, with such nice amenities as pants pressers and hairdryers. Each room is large and well furnished, with a console control panel by the bed for the color TV and radio, a vanity mirror or sink outside the bathroom, and individual climate control.

Dining/Entertainment: The Dewey Secombe and Howe Bar serves a luncheon buffet and finger foods in the evening to accompany the piano entertainment. The Chestnut Tree restaurant on the main floor offers all-day dining.

Services: Room service (available from 6am to 11pm), concierge, babysitting.

Facilities: Indoor and outdoor swimming pools, sauna, exercise room, games area, sun terrace, business center.

HOLIDAY INN ON KING, 370 King St. W. (at Peter), Toronto, ON M5V 1J9. Tel. 416/599-4000. 405 rms, 20 suites. A/C TV TEL **Subway:** St. Andrew.

$ Rates: From $110 single or double. Extra person $15. **Parking:** $10.

Housed in an odd-looking Miami-style building, the Holiday Inn is well located for the theater district and the CN Tower. The rooms are pleasantly furnished in pastels, with sage-green carpeting and floral bedspreads; each is fully equipped with a push-button phone, a clock/radio, a TV on a stand, a wet bar, and a decently lit desk. Many have balconies. The bathrooms have a number of amenities, including hairdryers.

Dining/Entertainment: The Holiday Inn offers two restaurants and a lounge.

Facilities: Outdoor pool, sauna, fitness center.

HOTEL IBIS, 240 Jarvis St., Toronto, ON, M5B 2B8. Tel. 416/593-9400, or toll free 800/221-4542. Fax 416/593-8426. 294 rms and suites. A/C TV TEL **Subway:** Dundas.

$ Rates: $105 single; $120 double. Extra person $10. Children under 12 stay free in parents' room. **Parking:** $8.

Located between Dundas and Gerrard streets, the Hotel Ibis is part of a European economy-hotel chain. Each room has either a queen-size bed and a pull-out sofa or twin beds and is furnished with blond modern furniture. All contain the usual amenities, including clock-radios and cable and pay TV. The decor throughout is light and modern.

Dining/Entertainment: There's a restaurant, serving breakfast and lunch buffets and à la carte dinners, and a lounge.

Services: Laundry/valet.

TORONTO MARRIOTT EATON CENTRE, 525 Bay St., Toronto, ON, M5G 2L2. Tel. 416/597-9200. Fax 416/597-9211. 459 rms and suites. A/C MINIBAR TV TEL **Subway:** Dundas.

$ Rates: $118 single or double. If you book 21 days in advance a special reduced rate of $98 is available, but this rate requires prepayment and allows for no changes or cancellations. 7-day and 14-day advance purchase rates also available.

A brand-new hotel with all the hallmarks of the Marriott chain is conveniently located alongside Eaton Centre. In addition to the amenities listed above, rooms contain clock-radios and attractive furnishings. No-smoking rooms and rooms for the disabled are available, too.

Dining/Entertainment: The Parkside atrium is for all-day dining, while J.W.'s offers more intimate service. Characters bar features billiards and table games as well as music and sporting events; the lobby bar is more relaxing.

Services: 24-hour room service, concierge, babysitting.

Facilities: Indoor rooftop swimming pool, whirlpool, sauna, health club.

MODERATE

BEST WESTERN PRIMROSE HOTEL, 111 Carlton St. (between Church and Jarvis Sts.), Toronto, ON, M5B 2G3. Tel. 416/977-8000, or toll free 800/268-8082. Fax 416/977-6323. 338 rms and suites. A/C TV TEL **Subway:** College.

$ Rates: $85–$95 single; $95–$105 double. Extra person $10. Weekend packages available (except July–Sept). **Parking:** $10.

The Primrose offers spacious rooms, all with wall-to-wall carpeting and color-coordinated furnishings, color TVs, and individual climate control. About 25% contain king-size beds and sofas; the rest have two double beds.

Dining/Entertainment: The downstairs coffee shop charmingly evokes the atmosphere of a Viennese café with its painted-wood decor. For relaxing there's the One Eleven Lounge with nightly piano entertainment.

Services: Room service (available from 7am to 11pm), laundry/valet, complimentary newspaper.

Facilities: Outdoor heated pool and sauna.

BOND PLACE HOTEL, 65 Dundas St. E., Toronto, ON, M5B 2G8. Tel. 416/362-6061. Fax 416/360-6406. 286 rms and suites. A/C TV TEL **Subway:** Dundas.

$ Rates: $75–$105 single; $75–$125 double; from $125 suite. Extra person $15. Weekend packages available. **Parking:** $10.

Ideally located just a block from the Eaton Centre and adjacent to the Pantages and Elgin theatres, the Bond Place Hotel is an independently owned, medium-size modern establishment offering all the appurtenances of a first-class hotel at reasonable prices. The small triangular lobby is welcoming with its natural-oak reception desk.

The rooms, all pleasantly decorated in pastels with bamboo furniture and wall-to-wall carpeting, each contain a color TV with in-house movies available, individual climate control, and a direct-dial phone.

Dining/Entertainment: Off the lobby, the Garden Café serves from 7am to midnight daily. Downstairs, Freddy's offers a weekday buffet lunch, then turns into a piano bar at night (where you can enjoy complimentary hors d'oeuvres from 5:30 to 6:30pm).

Services: Room service (available from 7am to 10pm), laundry/valet.

HOTEL VICTORIA, 56 Yonge St., Toronto, ON, M5E 1G5. Tel. 416/363-1666. Fax 416/363-7327. 48 rms and suites. A/C TV TEL **Subway:** King.

$ Rates: $80–$105 single; $110 double. Extra person $15. Ask about special summer discounts.

In search of a small, personal hotel? Try the Hotel Victoria, with only 48 rooms spread over six floors. It's only two blocks from O'Keefe Centre. The lobby is small and elegant, and renovation has retained the marble columns, staircase, and decorative moldings of an earlier era.

The rooms are either standard or select (the latter are larger). Furnishings are modern and combined with a green-and-beige decor. Each room contains a color TV, a private bath, and a clock-radio. Some have coffeemakers and minirefrigerators. A complimentary *Globe and Mail* and free local phone calls are included in the price of a room.

Dining/Entertainment: There's an attractive restaurant and lounge, as well as a lobby bar.

Services: Room service (available from 7am to 9:30pm), laundry/valet, complimentary newspaper.

JOURNEY'S END, 111 Lombard St. (between Adelaide and Richmond Sts.), Toronto, ON, M5B 2E9. Tel. 416/367-5555. Fax 416/367-3470. 194 rms and suites. A/C TV TEL **Subway:** King or Queen.

$ Rates: $85 single; $95 double. **Parking:** $9.

Journey's End has modern rooms fully appointed with color TVs and jade-and-rose or gray-blue decor. Complimentary coffee is available in the morning.

BUDGET

AMSTERDAM GUEST HOUSE, 209 Carlton St. (at Parliament), Toronto, ON, M5A 2K9. Tel. 416/921-9797. 14 rms (none with bath).

$ Rates: $60 double for rooms upstairs from bathroom; $70 double for others. **Parking:** Free.

A brightly painted Victorian in Cabbagetown, the Amsterdam Guest House is owned by Adrian and Doreen Verpaalen, who offer 14 rooms, all with shared bath. Among these rooms are a couple of large doubles with TVs. Most of the rooms are on a different floor from the bathrooms. In summer a continental breakfast of fruits, croissants, cheese, and cold meats is served; in winter there's more likely to be a cooked breakfast. Guests have use of a comfortable living room.

NEIL WYCIK COLLEGE HOTEL, 96 Gerrard St. E. (between Church and Jarvis Sts.), Toronto, ON, M5B 1G7. Tel. 416/977-2320. Fax 416/977-2809. 190 rms. **Subway:** College.

$ **Rates:** $40 single; $45–$50 double; $50 family room (depending on number of adults). **Parking:** $8 nearby. **Closed:** Late Aug to early May.

From mid-May to late August, the Neil Wycik College Hotel has basic accommodations available to tourists and families at extremely reasonable rates. Since these are primarily student accommodations, rooms have no air conditioning and no TVs and contain only the most essential furniture—a bed, chair, and desk. Each family room has two single beds and room for two cots. Bathrooms and kitchen facilities are down the corridor. If you wish to cook, you have to furnish your own utensils. The facilities include a TV lounge, a rooftop sundeck, a sauna, a laundry room, and a cafeteria.

THE STRATHCONA, 60 York St., Toronto, ON, M5J 1S8. Tel. 416/363-3321. Fax 416/363-4679. 196 rms and suites. A/C TV TEL **Subway:** Union.

$ **Rates:** $60–$65 single; $70–$75 double.

Currently one of Toronto's best buys—if not the only good deal—the Strathcona is located right across from the Royal York Hotel, within easy reach of all downtown attractions. Although the rooms are small, they have recently been refurbished and furnished with modern blond-wood furniture, gray carpeting, and brass floor lamps. Each has a push-button phone, a color TV, and a private bath.

The coffee shop/restaurant is open daily; there's also a luncheon snack bar and a lounge with a large-screen TV for sports-watching. Room service is offered from 6am to 7pm.

TORONTO INTERNATIONAL HOSTEL, 223 Church St., Toronto, ON, M5B 1Y7. Tel. 416/368-1815. Fax 416/368-6499. 180 beds. A/C **Subway:** Dundas.

$ **Rates:** $18 per person in a dormitory; $20 per person in a semiprivate room.

Located downtown between Queen and Dundas streets, the hostel contains 180 beds in dormitory style (6 to 10 beds per room) and semiprivate accommodations. There's a comfortable lounge with a couch and TV, a kitchen, and laundry facilities. The hostel reception is open from 8am to midnight. Washrooms are on every floor.

2. MIDTOWN

The midtown area runs north from College/Carlton Street between Spadina Avenue and Jarvis Street, to where Dupont crosses Yonge Street.

VERY EXPENSIVE

THE FOUR SEASONS HOTEL, 21 Avenue Rd., Toronto, ON, M5R 2G1. Tel. 416/964-0411, or toll free 800/268-

FROMMER'S COOL FOR KIDS: HOTELS

Delta Chelsea Inn (*see p. 62*) The Chelsea Chum Club for kids aged 3 to 12 sponsors special activities in the Children's Creative Centre and throughout the hotel. When they check in at the lifesize gingerbread house they get a registration card and passport. Children under 6 eat free; there are special menus for the older set. All this goes a long way toward creating a smooth family stay.

Inn on the Park (*see p. 79*) Swings, ice skating, bicycles, and a video room make this a miniparadise for kids of all ages. The hotel operates an Inn Kids supervised recreational program for those aged 5 to 12 and even sponsors special themed weekends for them.

The Four Seasons (*see p. 66*) Free bicycles, video games, and the pool should keep them occupied. The meals served in Animal World wicker baskets or on Sesame Street plates, and the complimentary room-service cookies and milk on arrival will make them feel special.

6282. Fax 416/964-2301. 209 rms, 171 suites. A/C MINIBAR TV TEL **Subway:** Bay.

$ **Rates:** $205 single; $230–$275 double; from $300 suite. Weekend rates available. **Parking:** $15.

Located in the heart of the Bloor-Yorkville area, the Four Seasons has a well-deserved reputation for highly personal service, quiet but unimpeachable style, and total comfort. The lobby, with its marble and granite floors, Savonnerie carpets, and stunning fresh-flower arrangements, expresses the style.

The spacious rooms are furnished with king-size, queen-size, or twin beds and boast dressing rooms and marble bathrooms. The table lamps are porcelain, the furnishings elegant, and the fabrics plush. All rooms are air-conditioned and have remote-control color TVs, AM/FM radios, and terry-cloth bathrobes. Extra amenities include hairdryers, makeup and full-length mirrors, tie bars, and closet safes. Corner rooms have balconies. Four Seasons Executive Suites each have an additional seating area separated from the bedroom by french doors, two TVs, and a deluxe telephone with two lines and conference-call capacity. No-smoking rooms and special rooms for the disabled are available.

Dining/Entertainment: The hotel has two restaurants and two lounges. Truffles, on the second floor, with its antique tapestries and paintings and brocade upholstery, provides a lavish setting for continental contemporary cuisine. The main courses, priced from $24 to $35, might list lobster in a crunchy tarot-root basket with saffron broth; roast veal tenderloin with asparagus, morel cream, and natural juice; or herb-roasted chicken breast with eggplant and shallot risotto. Desserts are equally stunning. The Studio Café serves meals all day, but it's far from a typical coffee shop. The recently

TORONTO
Midtown

Brownstone Hotel 9
Four Seasons Hotel 3
Hotel Selby 11
Intercontinental 1
Journey's End 6
Park Plaza 2
Ramada Renaissance 7
Sutton Place Hotel 10
Town Inn 8
Venture Inn, Yorkville 4
Victoria University 5

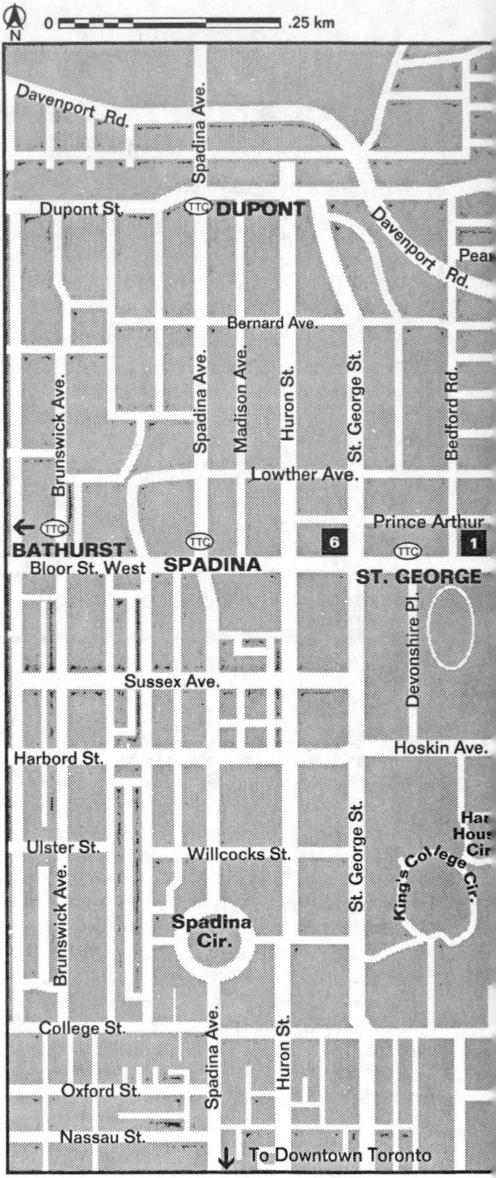
N
0
.25 km
Davenport Rd.
Spadina Ave.
Dupont St.
TTC DUPONT
Davenport Rd.
Pear
Bernard Ave.
Brunswick Ave.
Spadina Ave.
Madison Ave.
Huron St.
St. George St.
Bedford Rd.
Lowther Ave.
Prince Arthur
TTC
BATHURST
TTC
SPADINA
6
TTC
1
Bloor St. West
ST. GEORGE
Devonshire Pl.
Sussex Ave.
Hoskin Ave.
Harbord St.
Ulster St.
Willcocks St.
St. George St.
King's College Cir.
Brunswick Ave.
Spadina Cir.
College St.
Spadina Ave.
Huron St.
Oxford St.
Nassau St.
To Downtown Toronto

MIDTOWN TORONTO ACCOMMODATIONS

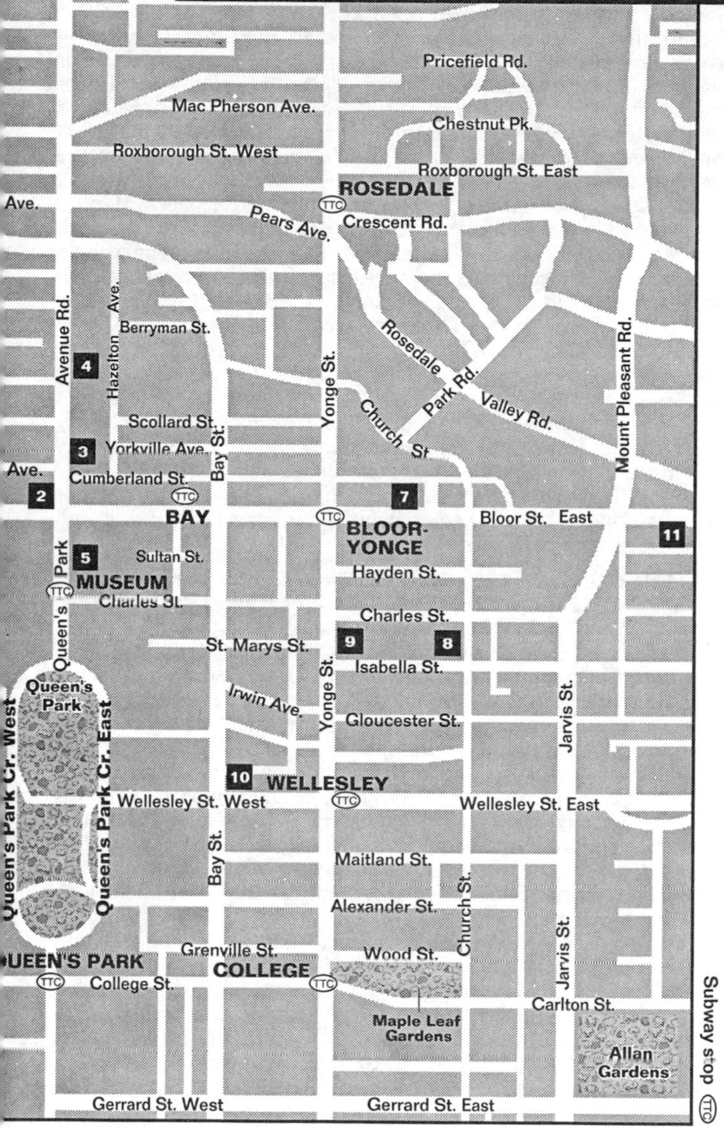

Pricefield Rd.
Mac Pherson Ave.
Chestnut Pk.
Roxborough St. West
Roxborough St. East
ROSEDALE
TTC
Ave.
Pears Ave.
Crescent Rd.
Avenue Rd.
Hazelton Ave.
Berryman St.
Rosedale
Park Rd.
Valley Rd.
Mount Pleasant Rd.
4
Yonge St.
Church St.
Scollard St.
3
Yorkville Ave.
Bay St.
Ave.
Cumberland St.
2
TTC
7
BAY
TTC
Bloor St. East
BLOOR-YONGE
11
5
Queen's Park
Sultan St.
MUSEUM
TTC
Charles St.
Hayden St.
Charles St.
St. Marys St.
9
8
Isabella St.
Queen's Park
Irwin Ave.
Yonge St.
Gloucester St.
Jarvis St.
Queen's Park Cr. West
Queen's Park Cr. East
10
WELLESLEY
Wellesley St. West
TTC
Wellesley St. East
Maitland St.
Bay St.
Alexander St.
Church St.
Jarvis St.
Grenville St.
Wood St.
QUEEN'S PARK
COLLEGE
TTC
College St.
TTC
Carlton St.
Maple Leaf Gardens
Allan Gardens
Gerrard St. West
Gerrard St. East
Subway stop
TTC

renovated room, featuring an open kitchen, is filled with light and beautifully decorated with modern Italian furnishings—including some gorgeous Gianni Versace fabrics on the tables. The decor includes display cases filled with original glass artworks, which are for sale with prices ranging from $100 (for smaller paperweights) to $4,000 (for large vases). Labels in the display cases identify the artists and where they can be contacted. The menu is inspired by the Mediterranean and offers a variety of gourmet pizzas (delicious!), pastas, salads, and light entrées—like grilled red snapper with olive oil, fennel, and sundried tomato or chicken stirfry with Shanghaianese noodles. A luncheon buffet and evening hors d'oeuvres are served in La Serre, which also features entertainment in the evenings and at Sunday brunch. The Lobby Bar serves a traditional afternoon tea. There are special kids' menus, too, with meals served either in Animal World wicker baskets or on Sesame Street plates.

Services: 24-hour concierge, 24-hour room service and valet pickup, one-hour pressing, complimentary shoeshine, twice-daily maid service, babysitting, doctor on call, children's activities, courtesy limo to downtown, complimentary coffee and newspaper.

Facilities: Business center; health club with indoor/outdoor pool, whirlpool, Universal equipment, and massage; free bicycles and video-game units for children.

INTERCONTINENTAL, 220 Bloor St. W., Toronto, ON, M5S 1T8. Tel. 416/960-5200. Fax 416/960-8269. 213 rms. A/C MINIBAR TV TEL **Subway:** St. George.

$ Rates: $185–$225 single; $200–$245 double. **Parking:** $14.

The Intercontinental, conveniently located on Bloor Street at St. George, is small enough to provide excellent, very personal service from the minute you enter the small but rich-looking marble lobby. The rooms are spacious and well furnished with comfortable French-style armchairs and love seats. The marble bathrooms, with separate showers, are large and equipped with every kind of amenity—each has a telephone; a clothesline; large fluffy towels; a bathrobe; scales; and a full range of soaps, lotions, and more. Extra-special room features include closet lights, a large desk-table, a clock-radio, a full-length mirror, and a telephone with two lines.

Dining/Entertainment: Signatures offers fine dining with dinner entrées priced from $18 to $25. It also offers one of the best brunches in town, accompanied by harp music. The attractive, comfortable Harmony Lounge, with its marble bar, fireplace, and cherry paneling, is a pleasant retreat for cocktails or afternoon tea. From here, french doors lead out to an inviting patio.

Services: 24-hour room service, laundry/valet, twice-daily maid service, nightly turndown, concierge, complimentary shoeshine and newspaper, video check-out in four languages (English, French, Spanish, and Japanese).

Facilities: Lap pool with adjacent patio; fitness room with treadmill, bikes, Stepmaster, and Paramount equipment.

THE PARK PLAZA, 4 Avenue Rd., Toronto, ON, M5R 2E8. Tel. 416/924-5471, or toll free 800/268-4927. Fax 416/924-4933. 224 rms, 40 suites. A/C MINIBAR TV TEL **Subway:** Museum.

$ Rates: Prince Arthur Tower, $160 single or double; Plaza Tower,

$255 single or double. Extra person $15. Weekend and other packages available. Children under 18 stay free in parents' room. **Parking:** $15.

The Park Plaza is currently undergoing a massive renovation to restore its former glory—it was once one of the premier hotels in the city. All 64 rooms and 20 suites in the original Plaza Tower, built in 1935, have been completely renovated and redecorated to exceptionally high standards. The rooms are very tastefully furnished in a candy-stripe style, with brass and glass accents. Each is fully equipped with the latest conveniences, including clock-radio, two push-button phones (one in the bathroom), louvered closets, and full-length mirror. The marble bathroom has hairdryer, makeup mirror, bathrobe, and full amenities. Suites have additional features: weight scales, umbrellas, and two-line telephones that can be hooked up to faxes and personal computers. The Plaza Tower rooms are more expensive than the 180 rooms in the Prince Arthur tower because they are more lavish. The latter rooms, though, are large and well furnished, with full facilities, including TVs, push-button phones, and minibars.

Dining/Entertainment: The Prince Arthur Dining room is a popular city breakfast and lunch spot. Chandeliers ring the room, and there's always a brilliant floral centerpiece. The main dining room, the Roof Restaurant, is on the 18th floor, adjacent to the lounge that has attracted so many Toronto literati. Their books are on display, and sketches of them grace the wall of this comfortable room, with inviting couches in front of the fireplace and marble-top tables. In summer the outdoor terrace affords a spectacular downtown view. Prices of main dishes in the dining room range from $20 to $28.

Services: 24-hour room service, twice-daily maid service, nightly turndown, laundry/valet, complimentary newspaper and shoeshine, concierge.

Facilities: Business center.

RAMADA RENAISSANCE, 90 Bloor St. E., Toronto, ON, M4W 1A7. Tel. 416/961-8000, or toll free 800/228-9898. Fax 416/961-9581. 238 rms, 18 suites. A/C MINIBAR TV TEL **Subway:** Bloor.

$ Rates: $175 single; from $195 double; from $250 suite. Extra person $20. Children under 18 stay free in parents' room. Weekend packages available. **Parking:** $15.

Occupying the 7th to 12th floors of a multiuse complex, the Ramada Renaissance is designed around an inner cobblestone courtyard with flowers, shrubbery, and trees. The lobby is on the street level.

All the rooms have double beds and are tastefully decorated. Appointments include the standard ones listed above as well as clock-radios, makeup mirrors, hairdryers, and in-house movies. Special Renaissance Club rooms have a concierge and private lounge.

Dining/Entertainment: Kapitals serves all day, while the piano bar overlooks Bloor Street and serves cocktails.

Services: 24-hour room service, laundry/valet, complimentary shoeshine, nightly turndown.

Facilities: Squash, pool, sauna, and whirlpool facilities in the Bloor Park Club in the building.

THE SUTTON PLACE HOTEL, 955 Bay St., Toronto, ON, M5S 2A2. Tel. 416/924-9221, or toll free 800/268-3790.

Fax 416/924-1778. 208 rms, 72 suites. A/C MINIBAR TV TEL **Subway:** Wellesley.

$ **Rates:** $180 single; $200 double. Extra person $20. Children under 18 stay free in parents' room. Weekend rates available. **Parking:** $15.

The Sutton Place is a small luxury hotel that attracts a celebrity/entertainer and business clientele. It has a luxury European flair that is exhibited in both its decor and its service. Throughout the public areas you will find authentic antiques, old-master paintings, 18th-century Gobelins, Oriental carpets, and crystal chandeliers.

The very spacious rooms are luxuriously furnished in a French style, each spacious enough for a couch and a desk. All have remote-control color TVs, two telephones (allowing hookup to a fax or PC via a modem), individual climate control, bathrobes, and hairdryers.

The Regency floor contains 10 suites that have full kitchens, living rooms, and king-size bedrooms and include two TVs and stereos among their amenities.

Dining/Entertainment: The Sanssouci is one of the city's most beautiful dining rooms, serving breakfast, lunch, dinner, and a spectacular brunch on weekends. Main courses are priced from $18 to $30 (fixed price $45), and dinner is served to piano accompaniment and candlelight. Afternoon tea is served daily from 3 to 5:30pm in the plush Lobby Salon. Alexandra's is a comfortable piano lounge where light lunches are served and you can dance in the evening. It's open from 11am to 1am daily. Stop 33 is one of the city's most romantic dining spots, too.

Services: 24-hour room service, valet pickup, complimentary newspaper and shoeshine, twice-daily maid service, concierge, beauty salon, limousine to the financial district.

Facilities: Indoor pool with sundeck, sauna, massage, fully equipped fitness center, business center.

MODERATE

JOURNEY'S END, 280 Bloor St. W. (at St. George), Toronto, ON, M5S 1T8. Tel. 416/968-0010). 214 rms. A/C TV TEL

$ **Rates:** $100 single; $110 double. Weekend and other packages available. **Parking:** $10.

Part of the budget chain, this hotel is only a few blocks west of the Intercontinental and represents a great value for the location. Rooms are modern and well equipped, with remote-control cable TVs and modern light furnishings, including useful well-lit worktables. Restaurant and coffee shop, too.

THE TOWN INN, 620 Church St. (at Charles St.), Toronto, ON, M4Y 2G2. Tel. 416/964-3311, or toll free 800/387-2755. 200 suites. A/C TV TEL **Subway:** Bloor.

$ **Rates:** $110–$120 single or double; $185–$210 two-bedroom suite accommodating up to four. Extra person $15. Children under 12 stay free in parents' room. **Parking:** $12.

Since the Town Inn was originally built as an apartment house, all units are suites, each with a bedroom, living room, dining area, kitchenette, and balcony. They also feature color TVs with in-house movies and individual climate control. Other extras include laundry/

valet service, an indoor swimming pool with a solarium roof, saunas, and an outdoor tennis court.

VENTURE INN, YORKVILLE, 89 Avenue Rd., Toronto, ON, M5R 2G3. Tel. 416/964-1220, or toll free 800/387-3933. Fax 416/964-8692. 71 rms. A/C TV TEL **Subway:** Bloor.

$ Rates (including continental breakfast): $105 single; $115 double. Extra person $10. **Parking:** $9.

The Venture Inn, with its modern rooms featuring pine accents, has a high-priced location in Yorkville, but it charges only moderate prices. Laundry and dry cleaning services are available.

BUDGET

HOTEL SELBY, 592 Sherbourne St., Toronto, ON, M4X 1L4 Tel. 416/921-3142. 67 rms (59 with bath). A/C

$ Rates (including continental breakfast): From $56–$85 single or double; $100–$125 suite. **Parking:** Limited free parking.

This hotel, located in a large heritage Victorian, represents a great downtown bargain. Downstairs at the front desk there's a comfortable lobby sitting area with a chandelier and a fireplace. The rooms are individually decorated with an eclectic mix of furniture. Ceilings are high, making the rooms airy and dramatic; many have stucco decoration and moldings. In several rooms the old bathroom fixtures have been retained. Room 303, for example, the Gooderham Suite, is very large and boasts a fireplace. Furnishings include a couch, a TV, and a push-button phone. There's a large walk-in closet, and the bathroom has a clawfoot tub and pedestal sink. The Hemingway Suite has a brass-hooded fireplace, an oak dresser, a couple of wingbacks, and a small tub with a shower in the bathroom. Room 401 has an old-fashioned burled-wood bed, angled ceilings, track lighting, and a pair of leatherette wingbacks. Facilities include a restaurant and a piano bar. Guests have access to a nearby health club for a small charge.

VICTORIA UNIVERSITY, 140 Charles St. W., Toronto, ON, M5S 1K9. Tel. 416/585-4524. 425 rms (none with bath). **Subway:** Museum.

$ Rates (including breakfast): $44 single; $62 double. Discounts available for seniors and students. **Closed:** Late Aug to early May.

Summer visitors (early May to late August) can stay at Victoria University, right across from the Royal Ontario Museum, in a 425-room university residence. Each accommodation is furnished as a study/bedroom and is supplied with fresh linen, towels, and soap. Bathrooms are down the hall. Guests enjoy free local calls and use of laundry facilities as well as access to the dining and athletic facilities, which include tennis courts.

3. UPTOWN

THE BRADGATE ARMS, 54 Foxbar Rd., Toronto, ON, M4V 2G6. Tel. 416/968-1331, or toll free 800/268-7171. Fax

416/968-3743. 110 rms and suites. A/C MINIBAR TV TEL **Subway:** St. Clair.

$ Rates: $155–$175 single; $165–$185 double. Weekend rates available. **Parking:** Free.

The Bradgate Arms, tucked away on a side street off Avenue Road at St. Clair Avenue, has a tranquil, secluded air. It was created by joining two apartment houses, which are now linked by a pink marble atrium lobby filled with trees and a fountain. The large rooms are well furnished with solid pieces and feature minibars and wet bars.

Dining/Entertainment: Avenues has a good reputation, and there's also a cozy piano lounge.

Services: Room service (available from 7am to 11:30pm), laundry/valet.

Facilities: Whirlpool at affiliated health club, library.

ROEHAMPTON HOTEL, 808 Mount Pleasant Rd., Toronto, ON, M4P 2L2. Tel. 416/487-5101, or toll free 800/387-8899. Fax 416/487-5390. 108 rms, 10 suites. A/C TV TEL **Subway:** Eglinton.

$ Rates: $100 single; $110 double. **Parking:** $6.

Situated at the center of the Eglinton Avenue business district, the Roehampton has spacious, recently renovated rooms. The corner rooms are especially large and attractive, with pleasant views. All units are well equipped with color TVs and individual climate control; some have refrigerators.

Dining/Entertainment: Bibi's Café serves an all-day menu; there are also a bar and Champs sports lounge.

Services: Room service (available from 7am to 11pm), laundry/valet.

Facilities: Outdoor pool.

4. AT THE AIRPORT

VERY EXPENSIVE

BRISTOL PLACE HOTEL, 950 Dixon Rd., Rexdale, ON, M9W 5N4. Tel. 416/675-9444. Fax 416/675-4426. 286 rms and suites. A/C MINIBAR TV TEL **Subway:** Kipling.

$ Rates: $140 single; $150 double; from $285 suite. Extra person $15. Children under 18 stay free in parents' room. Special packages available. **Parking:** Free.

For really personal service—the kind that caters to the idiosyncrasies of each guest—and ultrachic surroundings, try the Bristol Place, a select hotel where contemporary architecture and facilities blend with old-fashioned attention to detail and service. Outside, the red-brick building is striking enough, but step into the lobby and it's stunning. It soars three stories to a skylit ceiling through which the sun dances on the trees, sculptures, mosaics, and contemporary wall hangings. The sound of the waterfall alone made me want to stay.

And now the rooms. If you can't afford to stay in the Prime Minister's Suite—usually reserved only for the Aga Khan and Duke of Kent, a $3,000-a-day triplex furnished with a baby grand, antiques (many of them Chinese), a skylit bathroom with Jacuzzi whirlpool, and a private sundeck—don't despair, for the regular rooms are beautifully designed, decorated, and appointed. Each has custom-made contemporary furniture, double or king-size beds, geometric design throws, two telephones, a color TV, a bedside console, an alarm clock, individual climate control, and large parlor lights in the bathroom.

Dining/Entertainment: Le Café, raised slightly to overlook the lobby, is a plush coffee shop with comfortable banquettes and handmade ceramic tiles. Zachary's dining room is delightfully contemporary and graced with a kaleidoscopic tapestry hung over white tile. The dinner specialties cost $21 to $30 for such dishes as salmon with truffle sauce and breast of pheasant on braised green vegetables. The buffet brunch is $20.

Services: 24-hour room service, nightly turndown, laundry/valet, concierge.

Facilities: Indoor/outdoor pool with skylight dome and sundeck; flower gardens; reflecting pools; children's play area; health club with exercise room, sunroom, sauna.

SWISSOTEL, Trillium Terminal 3, Lester B. Pearson International Airport, Box 3000, Toronto AMF, ON, L5P 1C4. Tel. 416/672-7000. Fax 416/672-7100. 491 rms and suites A/C MINIBAR TV TEL

$ Rates: $160 single; $180 double. Special packages also available.

The ultimate convenience for arriving or departing passengers, this brand-new state-of-the-art hotel offers handsomely decorated rooms fully equipped with large, well-lit desks, phones with call waiting and telecommunications jacks, and comfortable furnishings.

Dining/Entertainment: Fine dining is available at Le Mistral or there's Swiss and American cuisine at the Café Suisse. There's entertainment in the Lobby Bar.

Services: 24-hour room service, complimentary shuttle to Terminals 1 and 2.

Facilities: Business center; health and fitness center with indoor swimming pool, sauna, steambath, exercise room, and massage therapy; hair salon; other boutiques.

EXPENSIVE

REGAL CONSTELLATION HOTEL, 900 Dixon Rd., Etobicoke, ON, M9W 1J7. Tel. 416/675-1500. Fax 416/675-4611. 900 rms and suites. A/C TV TEL **Subway:** Kipling.

$ Rates: $110–$130 single; $130–$150 double. Extra person $15. Children under 16 stay free in parents' room. Weekend and honeymoon packages available. **Parking:** Free.

Providing top-notch facilities and personal service, the Constellation has a certain traditional elegance—former Prime Minister Lester Pearson liked to stay here when he came to Toronto, and so do many celebrities.

Although built almost 30 years ago, the Constellation has expanded so often that its rooms offer a myriad of different styles. Color schemes run from beige-brown to green. Every room is a minisuite featuring L-shaped sofas, large desks, king-size or twin/double-bed arrangements, and a color TV with in-house movies.

Dining/Entertainment: The hotel is a veritable entertainment complex. At the Woodbine Pub you can dance to DJ entertainment or enjoy special theme nights with no cover charge. The Burgundy

Room is a popular local dining spot that offers classic grills and seafood in an elegant French-provincial setting. There's also the Atrium off the main lobby for all-day dining. At night you can sit under a spreading banyan tree overlooking a tropical garden and enjoy a cocktail or dance in the Banyan Tree bar.

Services: 24-hour room service, dry cleaning, concierge, babysitting.

Facilities: Indoor/outdoor pool (shaped like a river around a tropical island reached by small wooden footbridges), banking facilities, hair salon, amphitheater and cinema, full recreation complex with exercise room and saunas.

TORONTO AIRPORT HILTON INTERNATIONAL, 5875 Airport Rd., Mississauga, ON, L4V 1N1. Tel. 416/677-9900, or toll free 800/268-9275. Fax 416/677-7782. 413 rms, 154 minisuites. A/C MINIBAR TV TEL **Directions:** Take the Gardiner Expressway west to Hwy. 427 north, to Airport Expressway (Dixon Rd. exit).

$ Rates: $110–$135 single; $140–$160 double; minisuites from $170 single, $190 double. Extra person $25. Children stay free in parents' room. Weekend packages available. **Parking:** Free.

The Airport Hilton has all the comfort and conveniences associated with the name. A 12-story tower added to the hotel contains all minisuites, each featuring separate bedroom, bathroom, and parlor areas. Each minisuite comes fully equipped with a king-size bed, a sofa bed, two color TVs, three telephones, a table for working or dining, a minibar, a hairdryer, a bathrobe, and individually controlled air conditioning and heating. The 259 rooms contain all the expected appurtenances: queen-size beds, bedside remote-control consoles, color TVs with in-house movies, louvered closets, bathrooms with telephones, and minibars.

Dining/Entertainment: Misty's club is well known for its musically themed evenings—from country to reggae. The Harvest Restaurant/Café features international cuisine; E Ting's, a cozy intimate restaurant next door to Misty's, offers light meals and finger food.

Services: 24-hour room service, laundry/valet, babysitting.

Facilities: Outdoor heated pool with poolside deck, squash and racquetball courts, exercise room, business services.

MODERATE

BEST WESTERN CARLTON PLACE HOTEL, 33 Carlson Court, Etobicoke, ON, M9W 6H5. Tel. 416/675-1234, or toll free 800/528-1234. Fax 416/675-3436. 528 rms. A/C MINIBAR TV TEL **Subway:** Kipling.

$ Rates: $95–$105 single; $106–$122 double. Extra person $12.

Best Western's Carlton Place Hotel offers modern rooms, each equipped with two telephones, a hairdryer, and the other usual amenities listed above; some rooms have minibars. The public areas have that light-pine, wicker, and tile look.

Dining/Entertainment: Apples restaurant for all-day dining, Sundown for dancing, and a cocktail lounge.

Services: 24-hour room service.

Facilities: Hot tub and indoor swimming pool, use of nearby fitness and racquet club.

CAMBRIDGE HOTEL, 600 Dixon Rd. (at Hwy. 401), Rexdale, ON, M9W 1J1. Tel. 416/249-7671. Fax 416/249-3561. 175 rms and suites. A/C TV TEL **Subway:** Kipling.

$ Rates: $75 single; $80 double. Extra person $10. Children under 16 stay free in parents' room. Weekend packages available. **Parking:** Free.

At the city end of the airport strip, the Cambridge Hotel has spacious guest rooms and more-than-adequate facilities—but very reasonable rates! Each of the rooms has a color TV, a push-button phone, a coffeemaker and supplies, individual climate control, and modern furnishings.

Dining/Entertainment: There are two restaurants, the reasonably priced Cambridge Room and a Japanese restaurant called Ginko, plus a lounge and Studebakers Dance Club, where people dance to the hits from the 1950s and '60s.

Services: Room service, laundry/valet, complimentary newspaper, free shuttle to and from airport.

Facilities: Outdoor heated pool.

DAYS INN, 6257 Airport Rd., Mississauga, ON, L4V 1N1. Tel. 416/678-1400, or toll free 800/325-2525 in the northeastern U.S. and eastern Canada. Fax 416/678-9130. 200 rms. A/C TV TEL **Subway:** Kipling.

$ Rates: $87 single; $97 double. Extra person $10. Children under 18 stay free in parents' room. Weekend packages available. **Parking:** Free.

The Days Inn offers facilities similar to those of the larger hotels on the airport strip but at lower prices. It's a small, friendly place set in a streamlined seven-story block. The lobby has a comfy air with its natural-stone fireplace.

The rooms are bright and airy and feature natural-pine furniture, beige-and-brown color schemes, color TVs, phones, individual climate control, and a vanity outside each bathroom.

Dining/Entertainment: In the Steak and Burger, carefully tended plants and flowers are set in an actual greenhouse wall and are complemented by exposed brick and a host of Canadian artifacts—a steeple clock, Staffordshire figures, and other ceramics.

Services: Room service (available from 6am to 11pm).

Facilities: Indoor pool, fitness center and squash (available at an affiliated health club).

DELTA'S MEADOWVALE INN, 6750 Mississauga Rd. (at Hwy. 401), Mississauga, ON, L5N 2L3. Tel. 416/821-1981. Fax 416/542-4036. 374 rms, 5 suites. A/C TV TEL **Subway:** Yorkdale; then GO bus to the hotel.

$ Rates: $180 single or double. Weekend packages available. **Parking:** Free.

At Delta's, they've created a cozy rustic ambience by using a lot of wood and brass and placing a fireplace in the lobby. Here you'll find 374 fully appointed rooms with balconies. Fifteen executive rooms have special turndown service, complimentary newspapers, bathrobes, and other extra amenities.

Services: Room service, laundry/valet.

Facilities: Indoor pool; indoor tennis, racquetball, and squash courts; exercise room; creative center for children.

RAMADA AIRPORT WEST, 5444 Dixie Rd. (at Hwy. 401),

Mississauga, ON, L4W 2L2. Tel. 416/624-1144. Fax 416/624-9477. 300 rms, 8 suites. A/C TV TEL **Subway:** Kipling.
$ Rates: $100–$120 single; $112–$130 double. Extra person $10. Weekend rates are lower. **Parking:** Free.

Located on a six-acre woodland site 10 minutes from the airport, the Ramada Airport West exhibits all the current chic design modes—natural-oak walls or trim in the lobby and Seagrill's dining room, plenty of plants scattered throughout, and russet tones and modern pine furniture in the rooms and suites.

Dining/Entertainment: Meals are available in the hotel coffee shop and the Seagrill dining room. Snacks are also available in two lounges.

Services: 24-hour room service, laundry/valet, babysitting.

Facilities: Indoor/outdoor pool, saunas, exercise room, billiard room, beauty salon.

VENTURE INN AT THE AIRPORT, 925 Dixon Rd., Etobicoke, ON, M9W 1J8. Tel. 416/674-2222. Fax 416/674-5757. 283 rms. A/C TV TEL **Directions:** Take the Gardiner Expressway west to Hwy. 427 north, to Airport Expressway (Dixon Rd. exit).
$ Rates (including breakfast): $90 single; $100 double. Extra person $10. **Parking:** Free.

This hotel is part of the moderately priced Venture Inn chain, which features modern rooms furnished country style. Complimentary breakfast is available, but there is no restaurant/lounge on the premises, although Pat and Mario's is next door and plenty of others are nearby.

Facilities: Indoor pool, sauna, whirlpool.

BUDGET

COMFORT INN–AIRPORT, 240 Belfield Rd., Rexdale, ON, M9W 1H3. Tel. 416/241-8513, Fax 416/249-4203. 122 rms. A/C TV TEL **Directions:** Take Hwy. 27 north to Belfield Rd.
$ Rates: $72 single; $75 double. Extra person $8. **Parking:** Free.

Also off the airport strip but close enough to be convenient, the Comfort Inn–Airport has modern rooms with up-to-date, color-coordinated decor and pine furnishings, plus individual climate control, color TVs, and phones. There's a dining room that serves honest fare, plus a coffee shop. Room service is available from 7am to 10pm.

5. METRO WEST

Accommodations listed here are either along Hwy. 427, the route to the airport, or along Lakeshore Boulevard, once a prime motel row before new motorways lured away the business.

EXPENSIVE

VALHALLA INN, 1 Valhalla Inn Rd., Etobicoke, ON, M9B 1S9. Tel. 416/239-2391. Fax 416/239-8764. 239 rms and suites. A/C MINIBAR TV TEL **Subway:** Kipling.

$ Rates: $145 single; $155 double. Extra person $10. Children under 18 stay free in parents' room. Weekend packages available. **Parking:** Free.

If you want to experience a real smörgåsbord along with many in-the-know Torontonians, go to the Valhalla Inn, at the Burnhamthorpe Road exit of Hwy. 427. Without being obvious, the inn does have Scandinavian touches—a cedar-roofed lobby; a large dragonhead rising from the lounge bar; and, of course, those Scandinavian specialties in the Nordic dining room.

The lower rooms open out to a landscaped courtyard of trees, bushes, and flowers, while the upper ones have balconies overlooking the scene. All rooms are tastefully covered with grass-cloth wallpaper that sustains the woody effect and are decorated in rose/teal or pink/gray combinations. Phones, radios, color TVs, and individual climate control complete the room features.

Dining/Entertainment: There are two dining areas: the Terrace Café, overlooking the garden courtyard, and the Nordic, which features steak and lobster. For entertainment, you can drink and dance in the Mermaid lounge.

Services: Room service (available from 7am to midnight), laundry/valet, concierge.

Facilities: Indoor pool and sauna, exercise room, squash courts.

BUDGET

THE SILVER MOON, 2157 Lakeshore Blvd. W., Toronto, ON, M8V 1A1. Tel. 416/252-5051. 24 rms. A/C TV TEL **Directions:** Take the Queen St. streetcar (no. 501) west to the end of the line.

$ Rates: Winter, $50 single, $55 double; summer, $55 single, $70 double. **Parking:** Free.

Along Lakeshore Boulevard stretches a whole motel row's worth of accommodations that saw their heyday when Hwy. 2 was the main route into the city. Today only a few of these motels, such as the Silver Moon, deserve a mention, and these primarily for their clean but basic accommodations. Free local calls are a plus.

6. METRO EAST

The accommodations listed here are conveniently located for the Metro Zoo; the Science Centre; and Scarborough Town Centre, a vast shopping mall.

VERY EXPENSIVE

THE FOUR SEASONS' INN ON THE PARK, 1100 Eglinton Ave. E., Don Mills, ON, M3C 1H8. Tel. 416/444-2561, or toll free 800/332-3442 in the U.S., 800/268-6282 in Canada. Fax 416/446-3308. 540 rms, 28 suites. A/C MINIBAR TV TEL **Subway:** Kennedy.

$ Rates: $120–$180 single or double; from $200 suite. Extra person $20. Two children under 18 stay free in parents' room. Weekend packages available. **Parking:** Free.

The Inn on the Park is a luxury hotel/resort only 15 minutes from downtown via the Don Valley Parkway—conveniently located for the Ontario Science Centre. Set on 600 acres of parkland, the inn takes advantage of its natural setting: A lounge faces west to capture the magnificent sunsets, and a landscaped two-acre courtyard has Douglas firs, silver birches, a rock garden, and a duck pond, all crisscrossed by walkways and dotted with benches. Beautiful in summer, the courtyard walkways are flooded in winter for ice skating.

The rooms, located in a 14-story low-rise and a 21-story tower, have beautiful views (those facing west have balconies). All are superbly decorated with contemporary pieces and have those extra little features like alarm clocks, hairdryers, and bathrobes, as well as the usual color TVs with in-house movies, phones, and individual climate control.

Dining/Entertainment: The Copper Lounge, a truly comfy spot, features live entertainment and dancing nightly. The Terrace Lounge, a piano bar, features a salad-bar lunch, with wine and cheese during the cocktail hours. During the summer months the Cabana, the poolside restaurant, is open for pleasant outdoor dining. A stylish garden atmosphere is the backdrop for sophisticated continental cuisine in Seasons, the hotel's premier dining room, which serves such specialties as roast filet of red snapper with brown butter sauce or tournedos of beef in pinot noir sauce with oyster mushrooms and roast shallots, priced from $20 to $29. For casual dining, there's the Harvest Room. All the restaurants feature alternative cuisine for the health-conscious.

Services: 24-hour room service, 24-hour concierge, twice-daily maid service, complimentary shoeshine, laundry/valet, one-hour pressing.

Facilities: Indoor, outdoor, and diving pools; games room with table tennis and pinball; badminton, shuffleboard, and indoor tennis; racquet club with squash and racquetball courts; health club with saunas and gym; bicycling and cross-country skiing; Inn Kids, a supervised recreation center for children 5 to 12 (in summer the program is offered daily from 9:30am to 4:30pm; in winter, on weekends only); beauty salon, florist, and other boutiques.

PRINCE HOTEL, 900 York Mills Rd., Don Mills, ON, M3B 3H2. Tel. 416/444-2511, or toll free 800/323-7500 in the U.S., 800/268-7677 in Canada. Fax 416/444-9597. 406 rms and suites. A/C MINIBAR TV TEL **Subway:** York Mills.

$ **Rates:** $140–$160 single; $160–$180 double. Extra person $15. Children under 18 stay free in parents' room. Weekend packages available. **Parking:** Free.

The other luxury resort hotel in this area is much quieter, having an almost ethereal serenity, which may derive from its Japanese connections. The Prince Hotel, located 20 minutes from downtown, is set in 15 acres of private parkland where you can wander nature trails.

A warm and soft decor will greet you in your room, which may have a beautiful bay window or balcony. Each of the oversize rooms has a marble bathroom, a color TV with in-house movies, individual climate control, and a hairdryer.

Dining/Entertainment: Le Continental offers haute cuisine and dancing, with main courses priced from $24 to $34. Katsura, the specialty restaurant, has four separate dining areas: a tempura counter and sushi bar, tatami-style dining, teppanyaki-style cuisine, and a robata bar. Complete dinners range from $32.50 to $45. The Coffee Garden restaurant overlooks a grove of 30-foot-tall trees, as does the Brandy Tree, a sophisticated piano bar, restfully decorated in gray and plum.

Services: 24-hour room service, laundry/valet, nightly turndown, concierge, babysitting.

Facilities: Outdoor heated pool, sauna, tennis courts, fitness center, games room, putting green, nature trails.

EXPENSIVE

EMBASSY SUITES HOTEL, 8500 Warden Ave., Markham, ON, L3R 8W3. Tel. 416/470-8500, or toll free 800/668-8800. Fax 416/477-8611. 332 suites. A/C MINIBAR TV TEL **Subway:** Warden.

$ Rates: $160 single; $180 double. **Parking:** Free.

This all-suite hotel has a central section shaped like a steeple clock that is flanked by two wings. The accommodations are located around this 10-story tree-filled atrium lobby. Each suite has a separate bedroom and sitting area. Standard suites are 400 square feet, but a few large VIP units come with dining areas and Jacuzzis. Each suite has two TVs, two telephones, a hairdryer, and bathrobes.

Dining/Entertainment: The art deco Bishops' serves classic continental cuisine priced from $20 to $32; the Unionville Café offers lighter fare all day. There are also two bars (one with piano entertainment).

Services: Room service (available from 11am to midnight).

Facilities: Indoor pool; masseuse; fitness center with five squash courts, fully equipped gym with bikes, treadmills, rowing machines, aerobics studio.

HOLIDAY INN AT SCARBOROUGH, 22 Metropolitan Rd. (Hwy. 401 at Warden Ave.), Scarborough, ON, M1R 2T6. Tel. 416/293-8171. Fax 416/293-3840. 193 rms. A/C TV TEL **Subway:** Warden.

$ Rates: $100–$120 single or double. **Parking:** Free.

Located at Hwy. 401 and Warden Avenue, this hotel has rooms with contemporary furnishings.

Dining/Entertainment: There are an all-day restaurant, a pub with entertainment and dancing, and a sports bar equipped with a pool table and shuffleboard.

Services: Room service, laundry.

Facilities: Fitness club with indoor and outdoor pool and exercise room.

RADISSON—DON VALLEY, 1250 Eglinton Ave. E. (at Don Valley), Toronto, ON, M3C 1J3. Tel. 416/449-4111, or toll free 800/333-3333. 354 rms and suites. A/C MINIBAR TV TEL **Subway:** Kennedy.

$ Rates: $135 single or double. **Parking:** Free.

The standard rooms are modern and typically equipped. The Plaza Club rooms have such extra amenities as minibars and hairdryers.

Dining/Entertainment: Café Bellevue offers all-day service, and there's Antons for fine dining, plus a lobby bar, too.

Services: Room service (available from 7am to 11pm).

Facilities: Indoor pool, sauna, exercise room.

RAMADA RENAISSANCE (DON VALLEY), 185 Yorkland Blvd., North York, ON, M2J 4R2. Tel. 416/493-9000. Fax 416/493-5729. 281 rms, 16 suites. A/C TV TEL **Subway:** Sheppard; then Sheppard Ave. bus east.

$ Rates: $95 single; $110 double. Extra person $15. Weekend packages available. **Parking:** Free.

Located at Hwy. 401 and the Don Valley Parkway, the Ramada Renaissance is near the Ontario Science Centre, with public transportation one block away. All rooms, decorated in pastel colors with contemporary furnishings, have push-button phones, remote-control color TVs with in-room movies, and individual climate control.

Dining/Entertainment: Two restaurants and a lounge.

Services: Room service (available from 7am to midnight), laundry/valet, concierge.

Facilities: Indoor pool, sauna, fitness room, access to nearby racquet and fitness club.

SHERATON TORONTO EAST, 2035 Kennedy Rd. (at Hwy. 401), Scarborough, ON, M1T 3G2. Tel. 416/299-1500, or toll free 800/325-3535. Fax 416/299-8959. 385 rms and suites. A/C TV TEL **Subway:** Kennedy.

$ Rates: $150 single; $165 double. Extra person $15. **Parking:** Free.

The Sheraton offers 385 spacious, fully equipped rooms and suites.

Dining/Entertainment: Three restaurants, including Sagano, offering Japanese specialties; formal Whiteside's, for continental cuisine; Garden Café, for casual all-day dining; plus a lobby piano bar.

Services: 24-hour room service, laundry/valet, concierge, children's program.

Facilities: Indoor swimming pool, whirlpool, sauna, mini-putting green, racquetball and squash courts, exercise room.

MODERATE

RELAX INN—TORONTO EAST, 20 Milner Business Court, Scarborough, ON, M1B 3C6. Tel. 416/299-9500, or toll free 800/667-3529. Fax 416/299-6172. 160 rms. A/C TV TEL **Subway:** Scarborough Town Center.

$ Rates: $65 single; $70 double. **Parking:** Free.

The Relax Inn has rooms containing color TVs with in-room movies, individual climate control, and attractive furnishings. There are a restaurant/lounge and an indoor pool and whirlpool.

VENTURE INN, 50 Estate Dr. (Markham Rd. and Hwy. 401), Scarborough, ON, M1H 2Z1. Tel. 416/439-9666, or toll free 800/387-3933. 136 rms. A/C TV TEL **Subway:** McCowan.

$ Rates (including continental breakfast): $76 single; $86 double. Children under 19 stay free in parents' room. **Parking:** Free.

The Venture Inn has pleasantly decorated rooms with the chain's country-pine look. Facilities include a whirlpool and a sauna. Restaurants are nearby.

BUDGET

UNIVERSITY OF TORONTO IN SCARBOROUGH, STUDENT VILLAGE, Scarborough Campus, University of

Toronto, 1265 Military Trail, Scarborough, ON, M1C 1A4. Tel. 416/287-7369. Directions: Take the subway to Kennedy, then the Scarborough Rapid Transit to Ellesmere, then bus no. 95 or 95B to the college entrance.

$ Rates: $32 per person per night. Family and youth rates available. **Parking:** Free. **Open:** Mid-May to the end of Aug.

From mid-May to the end of August, the University of Toronto in Scarborough, Student Village, has accommodations available in town houses that sleep four to six people and contain equipped kitchens. None has air conditioning, a TV, or a telephone. There are a cafeteria, a pub, and a recreation center (with squash and tennis courts, a gym, and an exercise room) as well as a laundry, a bank, and a bookstore on campus.

Note: Accommodations are available for a minimum of four people for a minimum stay of two nights.

A LOVELY RURAL/CITY RETREAT

THE GUILD INN, 201 Guildwood Pkwy., Scarborough, ON, M1E 1P6. Tel. 416/261-3331, or toll free 800/877-1133. Fax 416/261-5675. 90 rms, 5 suites. A/C TV TEL **Subway:** Kennedy.

$ Rates: Main inn, $85 single or double, $10 per extra person; new wing, $120 single or double. Children under 14 stay free in parents' room. Special packages available. **Parking:** Free.

If you want to stay in a unique and beautiful setting, then try the Guild Inn, just 10 miles outside the city. Enter through the broad iron gates and follow the circular drive, which is shaded by trees and bordered with flowers. The original entrance hall retains the character of an English manor, with its broad staircase, oak beams, and wrought-iron chandeliers.

The 90-acre grounds are dotted with historic architectural fragments, remnants from the Guild of All Arts, which once occupied the property. So many visitors were attracted by the Guild's collections and workshops that dining facilities and guest rooms were added, until the Guild became a flourishing country inn. During these halcyon years many notables visited, including Queen Juliana of the Netherlands, Dorothy and Lillian Gish, Moira Shearer, Rex Harrison, Sir John Gielgud, and Lilli Palmer.

The gardens at the rear sweep down to the Scarborough Bluffs, rising 200 feet above Lake Ontario, and for a room with this view you'll pay a little extra. The original central section of the inn was built in 1914, and the rooms here have been renovated. All 90 rooms have air conditioning, AM/FM radios, color TVs, and private balconies.

Dining/Entertainment: The dining room is still a popular gathering place for Sunday brunch ($22), and it serves primarily grills, roasts, and seafood, priced from $13 to $20. In summer, tea is served outdoors in the garden, and there's a lovely veranda for cocktails.

Services: Room service (available from 7am to 10pm).

Facilities: Outdoor swimming pool, tennis court, games room, exercise room, nature trails.

CHAPTER 5

TORONTO DINING

The multicultural mosaic of the city makes dining in Toronto a delight, for you can go around the world—from Chinatown to Little Italy, from Greektown to Little Portugal—sampling all kinds of cuisine. And because the city has so many ethnic restaurants, you can experience great meals at moderate prices. Supposedly there are more than 5,000 restaurants, catering to every taste and price range, but I have enough room to select only 130 or so of my favorites, categorized according to location and price.

SOME DINING NOTES Although dining in Toronto can be expensive, it usually seems that way not so much because of the food but because of the extras—like the 8% provincial sales tax on meals and the 7% GST. In addition, wine prices are higher than those in the United States, largely because of the tax on all imported wines. So you will pay as much as $6 for a glass of house wine in the better restaurants and $17 or more for a one-liter carafe. There's also a 10% tax on all alcohol—keep in mind that the prices quoted often do not reflect that tax. Just be aware of these facts.

Prices are rather broad categories: At luxury establishments expect to pay $125 and up for dinner for two without wine; expensive, $80 to $100; moderate, $50 to $70; and budget, under $30. These, I stress, are only rough guidelines, and at many of the moderately priced and budget-priced establishments you can pay much less by choosing carefully.

Unless stated otherwise, the prices cited here are given in Canadian dollars—good news for Americans because the Canadian dollar is worth 22% less than the American dollar but buys just about as much. As we go to press, $1 Canadian is worth 82¢ U.S., which means that your $50 dinner for two will cost only $41 U.S., and your $5 breakfast will cost only $4.10 U.S.

Locations are as follows: **Downtown** refers roughly to streets from the waterfront to and including College/Carlton Street between Spadina Avenue and Jarvis Street; **midtown** refers to the area north of College/Carlton Street to Davenport and Yonge streets and also between Spadina and Jarvis; I have also further subdivided both of these sections into west and east. **Uptown** covers Yonge/Davenport Street and north.

1. DOWNTOWN WEST

There's plenty of pleasurable and reasonable dining to choose from in this area; one of the best streets on which to look for a selection of reasonably priced bistros frequented by artists and young professionals is Queen Street West. Dining in the theater district is, as in most other cities, fraught with pitfalls—high prices and poor quality—with a few exceptions, of course.

VERY EXPENSIVE

WINSTON'S, 104 Adelaide St. W. Tel. 363-1627.
Cuisine: FRENCH. **Reservations:** Required.
$ Prices: Main courses $23–$38. AE, DC, MC, V.
Open: Lunch Mon–Fri noon–2:30pm; dinner Mon–Sat 6pm–1am.

Winston's, one of the last bastions of grande cuisine, is considered Toronto's "power" dining spot. The decor is appropriately opulent—lavish murals, mirrored ceilings, oak paneling, and art nouveau and Tiffany-style lamps in excess—and the food is impeccable.

To start your dinner, you might choose the quenelles of pheasant foie gras with truffle sauce if you're in a moderate mood, or really indulge with some caviar. Even richer dishes might follow: sole with shrimp, pine nuts, and peppercorns; poached lobster; veal cutlet with glazed bananas and grapes deglazed with Cointreau and cream; or duck with papaya, mango, and rum. Top off with a Grand Marnier soufflé and don't forget to doff your hat to Winnie (who, remember, was rumored to suffer from gout) on the way out. Lunchtime offers a chance to sample the atmosphere and cuisine at lower prices—for instance, you could have a paillard of veal with mushrooms ($11) and Winston's terrine and still escape solvent.

EXPENSIVE

BANGKOK GARDEN, 18 Elm St. Tel. 977-6748.
Cuisine: THAI. **Reservations:** Recommended.
$ Prices: Main courses $17–$25; all-you-can-eat lunch buffet $15. AE, MC, V.
Open: Restaurant, lunch Mon–Fri 11:30am–2:30pm; dinner Mon–Sat 5:30–10:30pm. Brass Flamingo bar, Mon–Sat 11:30am–11pm.

Bangkok Garden offers Thai cuisine in a lush dining room fashioned out of teak. You may dine either in the tropical Garden, complete with flowing river stocked with fish, or on the Veranda, where Somerset Maugham would feel at home. A spirit house, bronze nagas, and porcelain jardinières add to the exotic ambience throughout.

Those unfamiliar with Thai food might try one of the special dinners for $37 and up, so that you can sample a selection of appetizers, shrimp soup flavored with lemon grass, three pagodas curry, stir-fried glass noodles, green beans with shrimp, rice, fruit, and Thai sweets. A la carte dishes include smooth curries made with chili, lime, and coconut milk; chicken richly flavored with tamarind; and fish steamed with ginger. Try something from the noodle bar, seasoning your choices to your own particular taste with spring onions, fresh coriander leaves, salted turnip, chili vinegar, and many other exotic flavors. For dessert, try sticky rice.

BARBERIAN'S, 7 Elm St. Tel. 597-0225 or 597-0335.
Cuisine: STEAK. **Reservations:** Required.

$ Prices: Main courses $17.50–$30. AE, DC, MC, V.
Open: Lunch Mon–Fri noon–2:30pm; dinner daily 5pm–midnight.

Steak houses, as far as I'm concerned, are usually rather dull establishments, but Barberian's is the best and brightest in town. The front half, both inside and out, remains essentially as built in 1860, and the three cozy interconnected rooms with candy-striped wallpaper house a superb collection of Canadiana that includes several originals by the Group of Seven; a bust of Canada's first prime minister, Sir John A. Macdonald; one of the original grandfather clocks made in Canada; along with pre-Confederation money, coal-oil lamps, and firearms. Despite the traditional air, Barberian's exudes friendliness and lightness of touch.

Nonchalance does not extend to the food, however, which focuses on 10 or so steak and seafood dishes, all well worth the price. After 10pm a fondue and dessert menu awaits the after-theater or late diner.

DON QUIJOTE, 300 College St. Tel. 922-7636.
Cuisine: SPANISH. **Reservations:** Recommended.
$ Prices: Appetizers around $7; main courses around $8 at lunch, $17–$36 at dinner. AE, DC, MC, V.
Open: Lunch Mon–Fri noon–3pm; dinner Mon–Sat 5pm–midnight.

At Don Quijote, a statue of this famous character stands quietly presiding over a long, narrow, beamed, and stucco-walled room hung with brilliant tapestries and paintings of windmills. There's a good selection of appetizers, primarily seafood. You can follow with one of the specialties: seafood casserole or frogs' legs cordobesa, or paella valenciana or paella marinera, both for two. Upstairs there's a tavern that features flamenco-style entertainment and dancing at 9:30 and 11:30pm (cover charge on weekends; free if you dine).

LA FENICE, 319 King St. W. Tel. 585-2377.
Cuisine: ITALIAN. **Reservations:** Recommended.
$ Prices: Main courses $14–$24. AE, DC, MC, V.
Open: Lunch Mon–Fri noon–2:30pm; dinner Mon–Sat 5:30–11pm.

Really fresh ingredients and fine authentic olive oil are the hallmarks of the cuisine at La Fenice, where a plate of assorted appetizers will include pungent roast peppers, crisp-fried zucchini, squid, and a roast veal in tuna sauce (vitello tonnato). There are 18 or more pasta dishes—tagliatelle burro and basilico with fragrant basil sauce and also seafood risotto—along with a fine selection of Provimi veal, chicken, and fresh fish dishes. Dessert offerings include a refreshing raspberry sherbet, zabaglione, tiramisu, and fresh strawberries and other fruits in season.

ORSO, 106 John St. Tel. 596-1989.
Cuisine: ITALIAN. **Reservations:** Recommended for both lunch and dinner.
$ Prices: Main courses $17–$24. AE, DC, MC, V.
Open: Mon–Sat 11:30am–midnight, Sun 5–10:30pm.

Orso, a cozy Italian bistro with an elegant small bar up front, is located in a brick town house in the theater district. Pink marble floors, low ceilings, and framed paintings make for an intimate ambience. The menu is the same at lunch and dinner. At lunch you might opt for one of the 10 or so appetizers, such as grilled smoked salmon with ginger mayonnaise, or warm spinach, arugula, and radicchio salad with roasted prosciutto, potato, and balsamic vinegar. Or try one of the half dozen delicious crisp-crusted pizzas topped variously with gorgonzola, prosciutto, and sun-dried tomato, or with onion, black olives, mushrooms, parmesan, pancetta, and tomato, to select only two. At dinner you could do the same or choose a pasta dish or a main course such as salmon with braised fennel, roasted quail with grappa and braised red cabbage, or grilled lamb chops with rosemary and polenta.

MODERATE

AVOCADO CLUB, 165 John St. Tel. 598-4656.

Cuisine: INTERNATIONAL. **Reservations:** Recommended on weekends.

$ **Prices:** Main courses $10–$14. AE, MC, V.

Open: Lunch Mon–Fri noon–2pm; dinner Mon–Sat 6–10pm.

The Avocado Club features hot flavors and hot colors—turquoise, periwinkle, coral, and mustard—while its murals evoke the Mediterranean, making it vaguely reminiscent of the south of France. The space also affords views of the CN Tower. The ingredients are fresh and seasonal, the dishes flavorful, and the prices right. To start, try the jump up and down soup, wonderfully flavored with lemon grass and filled to the brim with carrots, noodles, mushrooms, squash, and more. Follow with a roasted half chicken with mashed potatoes enhanced by thyme gravy. Other possibilities might include Shanghai noodles with seafood and tomato curry, roll-your-own tacos, or kick-ass chili. The spices and cuisines of the world are all featured here. The desserts are equally tantalizing—tropical paradise pie or angel-food cake with praline icing, for example—all made on the premises.

THE BOAT, 158 Augusta Ave. Tel. 593-9218.

Cuisine: PORTUGUESE. **Reservations:** Recommended at dinner.

$ **Prices:** Main courses $10–$21. AE, MC, V.

Open: Lunch Tues–Sat 11:30am–3pm; dinner Tues–Sat 5pm–1am, Sun 5–10pm.

In the heart of Kensington Market, The Boat serves up typical Portuguese fare and entertainment. The emphasis is on seafood—filet of sole meunière; steamed crab; cod in a casserole with green peppers, onions, and tomato sauce; and mixed seafood plate containing lobster tail, shrimp, clam, squid, and Alaskan king crab. These are supplemented by pork alentejo and barbecued chicken Portuguese style.

FILET OF SOLE, 11 Duncan St. Tel. 598-3256.

Cuisine: SEAFOOD. **Reservations:** Required two days in advance.

$ **Prices:** Main courses $10–$25. AE, DC, MC, V.

Open: Lunch Mon–Fri noon–2:30pm; dinner daily 5–11pm.

Conveniently located near the CN Tower and the theater district, this must be Toronto's favorite seafood restaurant. Here you'll find an oyster bar and an extensive seafood menu that also features daily specials. The restaurant serves everything from fish and chips to lobster with rice and vegetable. Most of the dishes are in the $12-to-$16 range for bluefish, monkfish, red snapper, salmon, swordfish, tuna, mahimahi, and many other varieties. For nonfish lovers there's sirloin steak and chicken Florentine. The dessert specialty is the frozen meringue basket filled with Grand Marnier, chocolate-pecan ice cream, fresh strawberries, and strawberry sauce—not to mention the chocolate truffle mousse and hot almond crêpes.

FRED'S NOT HERE SMOKEHOUSE AND GRILL, 321 King St. W. Tel. 971-9155.

Cuisine: CANADIAN/INTERNATIONAL. **Reservations:** Recommended.

$ Prices: Main courses $7–$14 at lunch, $14–$24 at dinner. AE, DC, MC, V.

Open: Lunch Mon–Fri noon–2pm; dinner Mon–Sat 6–10pm.

Upstairs above Red Tomato, this restaurant has a more sedate atmosphere and more formal and expensive food than its cousin below. The menu, though, is equally extensive, presenting an array of fish and meat choices—from grilled loin of lamb with a honey, rosemary, and ginger glaze to sautéed jumbo shrimp with smoked jalapeño-tequila sauce, served with black pasta. Other choices range from a pan-roasted stuffed Québec pheasant with wild rice and brandy sauce to a plain steak or lobster. The equally eclectic appetizers might include crispy Thai noodles along with pâté, coconut shrimp, and more. Favorites among the desserts are the pâté of white and dark chocolate with pistachio sauce and the banana fritters with caramel ice cream and chocolate sauce.

HSIN KUANG, 287 King St. W. Tel. 597-3838.

Cuisine: CHINESE. **Reservations:** Recommended.

$ Prices: Main courses $9–$16; Peking duck $28. AE, DC, MC, V.

Open: Daily 11am–midnight.

Hsin Kuang is Chinese deluxe, complete with huge Chinese paintings and artifacts. The food is priced to match, with such items as orange-flavor beef, shrimp in the shell with chili, pomfret with fresh-fruit mayonnaise, and moo shu pork.

JULIEN, 387 King St. W. Tel. 596-6738.

Cuisine: FRENCH. **Reservations:** Recommended.

$ Prices: Main courses $16–$20; fixed-price meal $20. AE, DC, MC, V.

Open: Lunch Mon–Fri noon–2:30pm; dinner Mon–Sat 5:30–9:30pm.

Julien, with its handsome decor of red brick and lace, is a traditional but contemporary French restaurant. Appetizers might include snails in puff pastry provençale or grilled tiger shrimp with citrus sauce. Main courses change daily depending on the freshness of the ingredients at the market. The cuisine is nouvelle/traditional, featuring confit of duck with sweet sauce, sea scallops with fresh chives, or salmon grilled with saffron. The best value is undoubtedly the fixed-price meal, which includes soup or salad and either a fish or a meat main course, like chicken with citrus sauce.

LA BODEGA, 30 Baldwin St. Tel. 977-1287.

Cuisine: FRENCH. **Reservations:** Recommended for dinner; not accepted at lunch for parties fewer than six.

$ Prices: Main courses $9–$13 at lunch, $12–$23.50 at dinner;

FROMMER'S SMART TRAVELER: RESTAURANTS

1. Go ethnic—Toronto has some great inexpensive ethnic dining.
2. Eat your main meal at lunch, when prices are lower—and you can taste the cuisine at the gourmet hot spots for a fraction of the dinner prices.
3. Picnic or grab a sandwich at a take-out spot and head for one of the parks, gardens, or plazas downtown.
4. Watch the booze—it can add greatly to the cost of any meal because it's not cheap.

fixed-price meal $19 for soup, salad, main course, and coffee. AE, DC, MC, V.

Open: Lunch Mon–Fri noon–2:30pm; dinner Mon–Sat 5–10:30pm.

Ensconced in an elegant town house, La Bodega, two blocks south of College Street and two blocks west of University Avenue, is still a favorite because it serves fine fresh food at moderate prices in a very comfortable atmosphere. The dining rooms are quite fetching, graced with French tapestries and lace curtains. French music adds a Gallic air—there's a definite glow about the place. In summer the patio, with tables covered in red gingham and bearing multicolored umbrellas, is a popular dining spot.

Specials, usually inspired by the freshest produce at the market, are written on the blackboard menu daily and include soup or salad and coffee or tea. There's usually a dozen or so interesting choices, including several fresh fish dishes. For example, on my last visit the chef was offering filet of mullet with three sauces along with a filet of cod aux St-Jacques, rabbit with wild mushrooms, veal with honey and mustard, and venison au Genievre.

LA GAMBA, 75 McCaul St. Tel. 593-4055.

Cuisine: ITALIAN. **Reservations:** Recommended, especially at lunch.

$ **Prices:** Main courses $7–$13. AE, DC, MC, V.

Open: Mon–Sat 11:30am–10pm, Sun 4–10pm.

Located in Village by the Grange, La Gamba offers classic Italian fare, from lasagne and other pastas to peppersteak. Most dishes—such as veal parmigiana; veal Valdostana; and veal della casa sautéed in brandy, mushrooms, and cream—are priced at $10.

LE BISTINGO, 349 Queen St. W. Tel. 598-3490.

Cuisine: FRENCH. **Reservations:** Recommended.

$ **Prices:** Main courses $9–$13 at lunch, $9–$16 at dinner. AE, MC, V.

Open: Lunch Mon–Fri 11am–2:30pm; dinner Mon–Sat 5:30–10:30pm.

Le Bistingo is simple and sleek, containing tables set with pristine white tablecloths. The atmosphere is intimate yet not ornate, and the food is simple, fresh, and moderately priced. The menu is the same at lunch and dinner, featuring about 10 or so dishes. You might enjoy the grilled salmon with warm saffron tomato and herbs, the breast of chicken with five spices and Chinese noodles, or the medallions of lamb with tarragon jus and crisp risotto cake. Appetizers are also appealing, like the galantine of chicken and field mushrooms and the cold black-bean soup with tomato salsa. Finish with the warm apple tart that slips down easily with the accompanying Calvados ice cream or the bitter-chocolate fondant with vanilla-and-chocolate sauce. At night the chef features and recommends a special select menu and the best wines to accompany the dishes.

LE PIGALLE, 315 King St. W. Tel. 593-0698.

Cuisine: FRENCH. **Reservations:** Recommended.

$ **Prices:** Daily lunch special $9; main courses $14–$18. AE, DC, MC, V.

Open: Lunch Mon–Fri 11:30am–2pm; dinner Mon–Thurs 5–10pm, Fri–Sat 5–11pm.

Le Pigalle is conveniently located near the CN Tower and the Royal Alexandra Theatre. The lace curtains and simple decor—and most of all, the food—will conjure up dreams of Paris and that tucked-away bistro. The prices are reasonable for such continental dishes as veal in cream-mustard sauce; grilled salmon steak with shallots, herbs, and white-wine butter; and entrecôte served with a sauce of green peppers and cognac. The desserts are also tempting: fresh fruit tarts and creamy-smooth chocolate mousse.

LE SELECT, 328 Queen St. W. Tel. 596-6406.

Cuisine: FRENCH. **Reservations:** Recommended.

$ **Prices:** Main courses average $9 at lunch, $13–$18 at dinner; fixed-price meal $19. AE, DC, MC, V.

Open: Mon–Thurs 11:30am–11:30pm, Fri–Sat 11:30am–midnight, Sun noon–10:30pm.

People throng the entrance of Le Select, a real bistro decorated in Paris Left Bank style, complete with an authentic zinc bar, breakfronts, fringed fabric lampshades over the tables, tollware, French posters, and a jazz background to set the scene.

What draws the young artistic crowd here is the chance to dine on moderately priced but good French food—from mussels steamed in white wine and shallots to pork filet with green peppercorn sauce. Most dishes, such as the filet of salmon with dill and Pernod, average under $10. The day I visited they were offering beef tongue with capers and gherkins in a warm vinaigrette and also a turkey drumstick with braised cabbage among the selections. For dessert there was fruit tart and chocolate mousse.

MASA, 205 Richmond St. Tel. 977-9519.

Cuisine: JAPANESE. **Reservations:** Recommended.

$ **Prices:** Sushi $2.20 per piece; appetizers $3.50–$5; fixed-price dinners $10–$30. AE, DC, MC, V.

Open: Lunch Mon–Fri noon–2:30pm; dinner Mon–Sat 5–11pm, Sun 5–10pm.

Masa is well known to Toronto aficionados of Japanese cuisine. Seat yourself at the sushi bar and choose from a huge assortment or dine Western or tatami style. Saké containers, Japanese prints, fans, and screens are scattered around the large room. There's a full range of appetizers—sliced fishcake, oysters in rice vinegar, and seaweed-pasted crab leg, to name only a few. Or you can preface your dinner with one of the many fascinating soups—seaweed "kobu" tea, for instance. The best deals, though, are the fixed-price dinners, which will include clear soup; a small appetizer; rice; and such main courses as salmon teriyaki, raw tuna sashimi, or garlic beef yakiniku. Don't miss the mitsu mame dessert—seaweed jelly with black peas.

MOVENPICK BELLE TERRASSE, 165 York St. Tel. 366-5234.

Cuisine: SWISS. **Reservations:** Recommended, especially at lunch.

$ **Prices:** Main courses $9–$15; buffets $16–$30. AE, MC, V.

Open: Daily 7:30am–1am.

The tiled Movenpick restaurant, filled with colorful potted plants, looks like an outdoor café and serves a variety of Swiss specialties, including rahmschnitzel (pork schnitzel covered with creamy mushroom sauce), Swiss bratwurst with Rösti, and tender veal liver sautéed in butter. Seafood, steaks, salads, curries, and various toasts complete the menu. Breakfast is served here from 7:30 to 11am. Monday and Tuesday are pasta nights, all you can eat for $18; on Wednesday and Thursday a gourmet buffet is served, while on Friday and Saturday there's a fisherman's feast (from $29).

MOVENPICK GRAPE 'N' CHEESE WINE BAR, 165 York St. Tel. 366-5234.

Cuisine: SWISS. **Reservations:** Recommended.

$ **Prices:** Main courses $7–$20. Free hors d'oeuvres 5–7pm. AE, DC, MC, V.

Open: Daily 11:30am–1am.

The Grape 'n' Cheese Wine Bar serves a complete menu, including Swiss cheese fondue and raclette.

MOVENPICK ROSSLI RESTAURANT, 165 York St. Tel. 366-5234.

Cuisine: SWISS. **Reservations:** Recommended.

$ **Prices:** Main courses $15–$22. AE, DC, MC, V.

Open: Lunch Mon–Fri 11:45am–2:30pm; dinner daily 5:45–11pm.

The wood-paneled Rossli Restaurant, decorated with horse saddlery (the name means "little horse"), is more formal than the other restaurants in the Movenpick complex. Start your meal with a Swiss barley soup with vegetables or air-dried beef and follow with one of the specialties—veal in a white-wine sauce with mushrooms, rack of lamb with flageolet beans, or sautéed beef tenderloin in mustard sauce. Seafood and steaks complete the menu. Save room for the tempting Swiss chocolate truffle cake.

OLE MALACCA, 49 Baldwin St. (between McCaul and Beverley Sts.). Tel. 340-1208.

Cuisine: MALAYSIAN. **Reservations:** Recommended.

$ **Prices:** Main courses $8–$13. AE, MC, V.

Open: Lunch Mon–Fri 11:45am–2:15pm; dinner Mon–Sat 5–11pm.

Ole Malacca is a very appealing restaurant. Comfortable, welcoming, and furnished with bamboo/rattan and paper lanterns, it's full of Southeast Asian atmosphere. So is the spicy food, such as tiger prawns with garlic, ginger, and chili with brandy; filet of sole with curry coconut; or chicken with brandy-soy sauce. Try one of the sambals (based on shrimp paste) or the satays (cooked on a hibachi at the table). Gado gado Bali (slivers of cucumber, bean sprouts, hard-boiled egg, and slivers of chicken topped with spicy peanut sauce) is enough for three. A great way to sample the cuisine is to go for the luncheon buffet, which features more than 20 dishes.

PETER PAN, 373 Queen St. W. Tel. 364-3669.
Cuisine: CONTINENTAL. **Reservations:** Recommended for parties of six or more.
$ **Prices:** Main courses $5–$9 at lunch, $11–$17.50 at dinner. AE, MC, V.
Open: Lunch Mon–Sat noon–2:30pm; dinner Sun–Wed 6pm–midnight, Thurs–Sat 6pm–1am; Sun brunch noon–4pm.

Peter Pan still remains a favorite of many who know this budget gourmet row intimately. A bare-bones 1930s look, with tin ceilings and high booths lit by art deco sconces, provides the background. On the menu you'll find about a dozen appetizers, several pastas, and about eight main courses, many of them flavored with Thai or Oriental spices. For example, you might start with Thai rolls with spicy peanut sauce or Cantonese noodle salad. Follow with salmon steak grilled with lime-butter sauce, chicken breast with orange-leek cream sauce, or scallops and shrimp with tomato-basil sauce. Desserts are always enticing, like the chocolate-pecan tart, tiramisu, and carrot cake.

RED TOMATO, 321 King St. W. Tel. 971-6626.
Cuisine: CANADIAN/INTERNATIONAL. **Reservations:** Not needed.
$ **Prices:** Main courses $5–$12 at lunch, $6–$15 at dinner. AE, DC, MC, V.
Open: Mon–Fri 11:30am–12:30am, Sat noon–1am, Sun 4:30–10pm.

This popular bar/restaurant is famous for its hot-rocks cuisine—Korean beef, Jamaican jerk chicken, chicken with mango-chili salsa—all cooked the way it sounds. At night the downstairs space with its large central bar, video screens, wild murals, and exposed plumbing is filled with the young and not-so-young feasting on an array of small dishes—like the great spicy Yucatecan shrimp; nachos; satay; and barbecued pork quesadillas with Brie, leeks, and pineapple. Afterward they can move onto something more substantial like steak or chicken fajitas, shrimp-and-scallop brochette, or a pasta or pizza dish.

SOHO BISTRO, 339 Queen St. W. Tel. 977-3362.
Cuisine: FRENCH. **Reservations:** Recommended.
$ **Prices:** Main courses $9–$15; fixed-price meal (with appetizer, main course, and dessert) $16. AE, MC, V.
Open: Lunch Mon–Sat noon–2:30pm; dinner daily 5–11pm.

Very reasonably priced fare is served at the Soho Bistro, in a pleasant atmosphere of oak and country antiques. For a mere $16 you can enjoy the table d'hôte of soup or salad and main course. Or you can choose among such à la carte items as capellini primavera, peppersteak, chicken breast with lime-and-ginger glaze, linguine with seafood and tomato sauce, or salmon in phyllo with tomato sabayon. There's a small central bar, and in summer the french doors open onto the street, creating a French country ambience.

TALL POPPIES, 326 Dundas St. W. Tel. 595-5588.
Cuisine: CONTINENTAL. **Reservations:** Recommended.

$ Prices: Main courses $6–$9 at lunch, $12–$15 at dinner. AE, MC, V.
Open: Lunch Mon–Fri 11:30am–2:30pm; dinner Mon–Sat 5:30–11pm.

Tall Poppies offers a pleasant dining experience inside or on the patio under the shade of plum and apple trees and bright hanging fuchsia. The cuisine is modern continental with Oriental and other ethnic accents—featuring such dishes as sea scallops and tiger shrimp sautéed with sugar snap peas and orange segments and served on hofan noodles with a dressing of Thai basil and lime, or lamb shanks braised in red wine with cinnamon and allspice and served with herbed orzo and cucumber-mint yogurt. As an appetizer try chevre baked in phyllo and served with sun-dried tomatoes, pesto, and pickled sweet peppers; to finish there's the crême brûlée or the chocolate-raspberry tart.

TIDAL WAVE, 100 Simcoe St. Tel. 597-0016.
Cuisine: JAPANESE. **Reservations:** Recommended.
$ Prices: Main courses $8–$11. AE, DC, MC, V.
Open: Lunch Mon–Fri noon–2:30pm; dinner Sun–Thurs 5–11pm, Fri–Sat 5pm–midnight.

The fun and focal point of Tidal Wave's dining room is the 40-seat sushi bar on which an endless procession of small barges laden with freshly made sushi and sashimi float around an oval water-filled canal. There is also a selection of udon dishes and familiar favorites like tonkatsu, tempura, and teriyaki, as well as luncheon and dinner buffets. The fun starts at 10pm, when the karaoke entertainment begins, and it goes on until 1am (1:30am on Friday and Saturday).

VASCO DA GAMA, 892 College St. Tel. 535-1555.
Cuisine: PORTUGUESE. **Reservations:** Recommended on weekends.
$ Prices: Main courses $11–$17. No credit cards (temporarily).
Open: Lunch daily noon–3pm; dinner Sun–Tues 6–11pm, Wed–Sat 6pm–1am.

Any Portuguese worth his or her salt will tell you to seek out the rather out-of-the-way Vasco da Gama, between Dovercourt Road and Delaware Avenue, for really authentic Portuguese cuisine—which means primarily seafood. Cream-of-lobster soup or jumbo shrimp with a marvelous garlic flavor make excellent previews for such dishes as charcoal-broiled squid in lemon butter or arroz marisco. For the nonbelievers, there's a selection of Portuguese-style meat dishes.

WHISTLING OYSTER, 11 Duncan St. Tel. 598-7707.
Cuisine: SEAFOOD. **Reservations:** Recommended for lunch only.
$ Prices: Main courses $10–$23. AE, MC, V.
Open: Mon–Sat 11am–1am, Sun 4–11pm.

Downstairs at the Filet of Sole, the Whistling Oyster specializes in oysters, of course, plus pasta and a raft of appetizers or dim sum. Many of the dishes have an Asian inspiration. Start with an order of fresh oysters or any one of 26 appetizers. Grilled spicy Bangkok tiger shrimp; baked oysters; or barbecued chicken quesadillas with leeks, pineapple, and Brie are good choices. Pastas include a Singapore-style noodle dish with chicken and shrimp as well as the more traditional fettuccine with four different cheeses. Besides the several fish dishes (like a blackened swordfish or baked steamed filet of sole), there's always a dozen or more specials that might include jalapeño-tequila shrimp or veal-and-shrimp curry. On Sunday from 4:30 to 10pm and Monday through Saturday from 3 to 6pm, happy hour oyster and dim sum menus are offered, featuring more than 20 items under $5.

ZAIDY'S, 275 Queen St. Tel. 977-7222.
Cuisine: CAJUN. **Reservations:** Recommended, especially at lunch.
$ **Prices:** Main courses $6–$8 at lunch, $13–$16 at dinner. AE, DC, MC, V.
Open: Lunch Mon–Fri 11:30am–2:30pm; dinner Mon–Thurs 5–10:30pm, Fri–Sat 5–11pm.

Zaidy's is a popular spot where the desserts are everyone's downfall—deep-fried ice cream, peanut-butter pie, and great sorbets, all freshly made. Start with crab cakes or a thick gumbo and follow with blackened redfish, shrimp Créole, or Cajun sirloin steak. There's always a pasta of the day, along with such dishes as veal Oscar and chicken with hot mango chutney and sautéed banana. The atmosphere is light, modern, and informal—with bricks, poster art, and a maple bar.

BUDGET

EARTHTONES VEGETARIAN RESTAURANT, 357 Queen St. W. Tel. 977-8044.
Cuisine: VEGETARIAN. **Reservations:** Not accepted.
$ **Prices:** Main courses $4–$7.50. MC, V.
Open: Mon–Sat 9am–10pm.

Earthtones consists of a small room with an outdoor patio and polished wood tables—plain and simple, like the food. You'll find piping-hot soups made daily, ratatouille, vegetarian chili, quiche, omelets, all kinds of salads, sandwiches, and hummus—all under $5. Hot dishes are sold in small, medium, and large portions.

THE EATING COUNTER, 21–23 Baldwin St. Tel. 977-7028.
Cuisine: CHINESE. **Reservations:** Accepted for parties of 4–10 only.
$ **Prices:** Main courses $7–$13. AE, DC, MC, V.
Open: Daily 11am–11pm.

Lines extend onto the street from the Eating Counter, near McCaul and Dundas streets. Many of the eager patrons here are Chinese who relish the perfectly cooked Cantonese fare—crisp fresh vegetables; noodles; barbecue specialties; and, a particular favorite, fresh lobster with ginger and green onions. Ask the waiter to recommend the freshest items of the day. The decor is nonexistent, but the food is good.

ED'S WAREHOUSE, 270 King St. W. Tel. 593-6676 or 593-6672.
Cuisine: CANADIAN. **Reservations:** Required for parties of 20 or more.
$ **Prices:** Main courses $11–$17. AE, DC, MC, V.
Open: Lunch Mon–Fri noon–2pm; dinner Mon–Sat 5–10pm, Sun 5–9pm.

A listing of Canadian restaurants would not be complete without one or two representatives from Honest Ed Mirvish's clan. Hop down the stairs past the autographed photos of Liberace, Lorne Greene, Jane Asher, and Anne Murray. In the dining area enormous fringed Tiffany-style lamps, old amusement-arcade slot machines, and huge porcelain vases (larger than you or me) join in a glorious array of Victorian kitsch. Start with Ed's French onion soup and follow with prime rib, served with rolls and butter, kosher dills, mashed potatoes, Yorkshire pudding, and green peas. Try apple pie and ice cream for dessert.

Other Ed's emporiums? They're all clustered here on King Street: **Ed's Seafood,** with prices from $10 to $30; **Ed's Chinese American,** with items from $8 to $16; **Ed's Italian Room,** with items from $10 to $17; and **Old Ed's,** featuring cabbage rolls, lasagne, veal parmigiana, and prime rib with similar prices. For reservations at any one of them, call 593-6676. Ed serves over 1.2 million meals per year using over half a million pounds of beef. After dinner, stop in at **Ed's Folly,** seat yourself in a private courting parlor, and emerge to dance only if you want to. No cover.

FREE TIMES CAFE, 320 College St. Tel. 967-1078.

Cuisine: HEALTH/VEGETARIAN/INTERNATIONAL. **Reservations:** Not needed.

$ Prices: Daily specials $7–$8. AE, MC, V.

Open: Mon–Sat 11:30am–12:45am, Sun 11:30am–10:45pm.

The Free Times Café has a casual avant-garde ambience, displays original art, and also features folk and original acoustic music nightly. The food is reasonably priced and includes such daily specials as sole with veggie stir-fry and veggie curry with couscous. Fully licensed.

GINSBERG & WONG, 71 McCaul St. Tel. 979-3458.

Cuisine: DELI/CHINESE. **Reservations:** Required for parties of eight or more.

$ Prices: Deli items less than $7; Chinese main courses $7–$12. AE, DC, MC, V.

Open: Mon–Thurs 11:30am–11pm, Fri 11:30am–12:30am, Sat noon–12:30am, Sun noon–10pm.

Ginsberg & Wong packs people in for two of the most popular food styles in the world—deli and Chinese. You can choose from the vast menu either your favorite deli-style sandwich (burgers, hot dogs, and salads also) or something from the Chinese side, which features sweet-and-sour chicken, Szechuan scallops, and more.

IL FORNELLO, 214 King St. W. Tel. 340-9329 or 977-2855.

Cuisine: ITALIAN. **Reservations:** Recommended.

$ Prices: Main courses $7.50–$13. MC, V.

Open: Mon–Fri noon–10pm, Sat–Sun 4–11pm.

Il Fornello is famous for its 50 varieties of pizza cooked in a wood-fired clay oven and for a variety of popular Italian dishes—pasta, veal, and chicken. Also featured is an alternative menu with nondairy, nonyeast, and low-cholesterol items.

KAM WAH, 149 Dundas St. W. Tel. 596-0818.

Cuisine: CHINESE. **Reservations:** Recommended.

$ Prices: Main courses $6–$17. No credit cards.

Open: Mon–Sat 11am–midnight.

Ducks hang in the window, the kitchen is up front, and so, too, is a tank containing king crab. Beyond there's a small room with Formica tables where you can sample lemon chicken, chicken with chili paste, beef with oyster sauce, and shrimp with black-bean sauce, along with such dishes as steamed chicken with spiced salt.

KENSINGTON, 51 Kensington Ave. Tel. 595-5337.
Cuisine: CONTINENTAL. **Reservations:** Recommended.
$ **Prices:** Main courses $9–$15. MC, V.
Open: Lunch Mon–Sat noon–4pm; dinner Mon–Thurs 6–10pm, Fri–Sat 6–10:30pm.

In the heart of the Kensington Market, this funky down-home hole-in-the-wall invites people to hang out comfortably, eating pizza or one of the specials that are posted daily on the blackboard—like the favorite chicken dijonnaise or the pasta with fresh scallops in white-wine cream sauce. There are a couple of tables outside; inside you'll find a narrow bar and tables with eclectic furnishings.

KENSINGTON PATTY PALACE, 172 Baldwin St. Tel. 596-6667.
Cuisine: CARIBBEAN.
$ **Prices:** Most items $1–$5. No credit cards.
Open: Mon–Wed and Sat 10am–6pm, Thurs–Fri 10am–7pm.

Folks line up here in the heart of the Kensington Market—and with good reason. For a few dollars you can secure some satisfying, tasty food that you can enjoy on the bench out front if you can find space. The beef, chicken, and goat rotis ($4.20) are famous; so, too, are the potato and chick-pea rotis, which are even cheaper. Beef, chicken, and vegetable patties are also available for $1 or less. For a real Jamaican experience try the salted codfish and callallo (a strong-flavored spinach). To round out your feast, take away some totoes (coconut cookies) or gizzadas (coconut tarts). This one's a real Toronto tradition.

KOWLOON DIM SUM, 5 Baldwin St. Tel. 977-3773.
Cuisine: CHINESE.
$ **Prices:** Combination plates less than $6. AE, MC, V.
Open: Daily 10am–11pm.

Kowloon Dim Sum is a budget diner's delight for dim sum and barbecue specialties.

LEE GARDEN, 358 Spadina Ave. Tel. 593-9524.
Cuisine: CHINESE. **Reservations:** Not accepted.
$ **Prices:** Main courses $8–$13. MC, V.
Open: Daily 4pm–midnight.

Lee Garden is known for its seafood specialties—like tiger shrimp with fresh pineapple; fresh oyster, clam, abalone, and crab cooked with green onion and ginger; or shrimp with pepper and eggplant. The menu also features such pork, beef, and chicken dishes as honey-orange back ribs, chicken in black-bean sauce, and beef with chile peppers. The duck with onion-lemon sauce is also popular.

THE MOGHUL, 33 Elm St. (between Yonge and Bay Sts.). Tel. 597-0522.
Cuisine: INDIAN. **Reservations:** Recommended, especially at dinner.
$ **Prices:** Main courses $8–$10. AE, DC, MC, V.
Open: Lunch Mon–Fri 11:30am–2:30pm; dinner Mon–Thurs 5–11pm, Fri–Sat 5pm–midnight, Sun 5–10pm.

The Moghul is a very comfortable Indian restaurant serving good curries. Try the hot vindaloo or a rogan josh or any of the other chicken, shrimp, and beef specialties. For those who prefer subtlety, the biryanis are also excellent.

There's another branch of this restaurant at 563 Bloor St. W. (tel. 535-3315).

MOVENPICK VERANDA DELICATESSEN, 165 York St. Tel. 366-5234.
Cuisine: DELI.
$ Prices: Soups, salads, and sandwiches $1–$7. AE, DC, MC, V.
Open: Mon–Fri 7:30am–6pm, Sat 10am–6pm, Sun 10am–4pm.

Located in the Movenpick complex, the Veranda is a fine place to stop for a tempting array of pastries, ice cream, truffles, cheeses, soup of the day, and sandwiches. Homemade breads, pastries, and Swiss chocolate truffles are available for take-out.

PEKING RESTAURANT, 257 College St. Tel. 979-2422.
Cuisine: CHINESE. **Reservations:** Accepted for large parties only and for Peking duck orders.
$ Prices: Main courses $8–$11. AE, MC, V.
Open: Mon–Fri 11:30am–10:30pm, Sat 11:30am–11pm, Sun noon–10pm.

Peking Restaurant specializes in Szechuan, Cantonese, and Mandarin food. Try their Peking duck, which is served in three courses—there's enough for four at a price of only $27.

QUEEN MOTHER CAFE, 208 Queen St. W. Tel. 598-4719.
Cuisine: INTERNATIONAL. **Reservations:** Recommended.
$ Prices: Most items $7–$10. MC, V.
Open: Mon–Sat 11:30am–12:30am.

A simple restaurant with polished wood tables and bentwood chairs, this is another longtime favorite on Queen Street. Food is displayed in the counter in the back, and the menu will bring forth such Asian-inspired items as pad Thai (noodles with seafood and meat), stir-fried chicken with Thai spices, and shrimp curry, as well as burgers and sandwiches.

RAJA SAHIB, 254 Adelaide St. W. Tel. 593-4756.
Cuisine: INDIAN. **Reservations:** Recommended for parties of four or more.
$ Prices: Main courses $7–$11. AE, DC, MC, V.
Open: Lunch Mon–Fri 11am–3pm; dinner Mon–Fri 5–11pm, Sat 4–11pm, Sun 5–10pm.

Raja Sahib, near Duncan, serves a variety of dishes priced under $11. Chicken tandoori, or dansak, bhuna gosht, and chicken tikka are just some of the many dishes.

RIVOLI, 332 Queen St. W. Tel. 597-0794.
Cuisine: CONTINENTAL. **Reservations:** Not accepted.
$ Prices: Main courses $9–$12. MC, V.
Open: Lunch Mon–Sat noon–4pm; dinner Mon–Sat 6pm–1am.

Rivoli attracts an avant-garde crowd. Its dinner menu features half a dozen Lao-Thai specialties, like pad Thai and Siam curry (shrimp with hot chili and fresh basil), as well as a burger and chicken pot pie, priced from $6 to $10. Three or so daily specials supplement the menu—usually one pasta, one meat, and one fish dish. The lunch menu continues the theme with special light sandwiches like the grilled cheese made with challah or the pita stuffed with crabmeat salad. In summer the sidewalk patio is jammed. There's nightly avant-garde entertainment, and the decor is appropriately basic black.

SAIGON PALACE, 454 Spadina Ave. Tel. 968-1623.
Cuisine: CHINESE/VIETNAMESE. **Reservations:** Not needed.
$ **Prices:** Main courses less than $5. No credit cards.
Open: Sun–Thurs 9am–10pm, Fri–Sat 9am–11pm.
A super-budget eatery—a Vietnamese-style café with minimal decor—Saigon Palace has hardly anything on the menu over $5. There's a fine beef with noodle soup, pork chop, and curry chicken and steamed egg, each for $4. The place is filled with Chinese and Vietnamese residents.

SAI WOO, 130 Dundas St. W. Tel. 977-4988.
Cuisine: CHINESE. **Reservations:** Not needed.
$ **Prices:** Daily specials $7–$14; main courses $6–$25. AE, DC, MC, V.
Open: Mon–Sat 11:30am–2am, Sun 11:30am–1am.
Sai Woo is a noisy, cavernous, easy-going place where you settle down at a Formica-top table to savor reasonably priced Cantonese food. (Request a tablecloth and it will be gracefully given.)

The menu runs to five pages, and there are daily specials such as baked Vancouver crab with fresh ginger, green onion, and garlic. Other dishes include diced chicken with vegetables and whole almonds, and Peking barbecued duck, with the skin, meat, and bone served separately with hoisin sauce and ginger (enough for four). Complete dinners begin at $7.

VANIPHA, 193 Augusta Ave. Tel. 340-0491.
Cuisine: THAI/LAO. **Reservations:** Accepted.
$ **Prices:** Most items $8–$10. V.
Open: Tues–Sun noon–11pm.
A Thai-Lao restaurant in a plain but comfortable step-down storefront, Vanipha serves some good cuisine. Try the pad Thai; grilled fish with tamarind sauce; chicken red curry; and, of course, the special treat—sticky rice.

WAH SING, 41 Baldwin St. Tel. 596-1628.
Cuisine: CHINESE. **Reservations:** Accepted for large parties only.
$ **Prices:** Most items $7–$10. AE, MC, V.
Open: Sun–Thurs 11:30am–10pm, Fri–Sat 11:30am–11:30pm.
People come here to enjoy terrific seafood at reasonable prices—especially the lobster special, which is two lobsters for $15.95! There's plenty of other shellfish on the menu, like the mussels with black-bean sauce or the oysters with ginger sauce, along with duck, pork, noodles, and other traditional Chinese fare, too. The decor is minimal, but the food makes for crowds. Expect to wait.

YOUNG LOK GARDENS, 122 St. Patrick St. Tel. 593-9819.
Cuisine: CHINESE. **Reservations:** Accepted for parties of six or more only.
$ **Prices:** Main courses $6–$12; lunch special $7. AE, MC, V.
Open: Mon–Fri 11:30am–10pm, Sat–Sun 11am–10pm.
One of Toronto's most highly rated and popular restaurants, Young

Lok serves good Peking and Szechuan cuisine and tasty barbecue from the Mongolian grill. The atmosphere is casual and decorous at the same time, with bamboo lanterns and kites, fans, and umbrellas adding color to the scene. The latest addition is a fresh fish market where you can select a fish and either have it steamed Chinese style in black-bean sauce or ginger and scallion or have it grilled on the barbecue. Start with one of the clear soups, like seafood chowder or Chinese peasant soup, which is filled with tofu and chicken. Follow with Szechuan shrimp sautéed with cashew nuts; vegetables in a hot chili sauce; orange-spiced duck; or the Mongolian barbecue beef marinated in mustard, chili, wine, ginger, and plenty of garlic.

2. DOWNTOWN EAST

MODERATE

BIAGIO, 157 King St. E. Tel. 366-4040.
Cuisine: ITALIAN. **Reservations:** Recommended.
$ Prices: Pasta and risotto $12–$16; main courses $16–$20. AE, DC, MC, V.
Open: Lunch Mon–Fri noon–2:30pm; dinner Mon–Sat 6–10:30pm.

This restaurant has one of the most beautiful, inviting courtyards in the whole city, as well as attractive high-ceilinged dining rooms and a separate bar inside. The menu features an array of extra-special pastas and risotto dishes. The lasagne arrives in a light-pink sauce, and the tagliolini comes with pieces of salmon, while the tortellini is crab-filled and served with green-onion sauce. Risotto can be prepared with porcini; with three peppers; with shrimp, tomato, and arugula; or several other ways. For the more robust appetite there's bistecca al barolo e funghi or a veal chop with butter and sage. To start try the carpaccio or salmon marinated in orange sauce.

BRASSERIE LES ARTISTES, 243 Carlton St. at Parliament. Tel. 963-9433.
Cuisine: FRENCH. **Reservations:** Recommended.
$ Prices: Main courses $9–$13. AE, MC, V.
Open: Lunch Mon–Fri noon–2:30pm; dinner Mon–Thurs 5–10:30pm, Fri–Sat 5:30–11pm.

For a modest bistro-style meal, try this find in Cabbagetown. The atmosphere is casual and friendly, the wall art evokes Paris in the 1890s, and the tables are marble—a suitable setting for the traditional moules marinière, steak and frites, escalope of veal aux fines herbes, and rack of lamb with fresh mint.

ENCORE, 33 Yonge St. Tel. 947-0655.
Cuisine: CONTINENTAL. **Reservations:** Recommended.
$ Prices: Pasta dishes $13–$16; main courses $9–$14 at lunch, $19–$23 at dinner. AE, MC, V.
Open: Lunch Mon–Fri 11:30am–2:30pm; dinner Mon–Sat 5:30pm–1am.

A sleek mirrored restaurant, Encore offers classic continental fare. At dinner there's a selection of pasta, fish, charcoal-grilled meats, and

Avocado Club 25
Bangkok Garden 19
Barberian's 20
Biaggio's 56
The Boat 8
The Bombay Palace 55
Brasserie les Artistes 63
Don Quijote 3
Earthtones Vegetarian Restaurant 29
The Eating Counter 11
Ed's Warehouse 38
Encore 50
Filet of Sole/Whistling Oyster 37
Florentine Court 59
Fred's Not Here/ Red Tomato 44
Free Time's Café 2
Ginsberg & Wong 22
The Groaning Board 60
Hsin Kuang 40
Ill Fornello 46
Julien 43
Kam Wah 16
Kensington 13
Kensington Patty Palace 7
Kowloon Dim Sum 12
La Bodega 9
La Fenice 42
La Gamba 21
Le Bistingo 30
Lee Garden 6
Le Papillon 57
Le Pigalle 41
Le Select 26
Maccheroni 49
Masa 33
The Moghul 18
Montréa 61
Movenpick 47
Movenpick Marche 48
Nami Japanese Seafood 56
The Old Fish Market 54
The Old Spaghetti Factory 52
Ole Malacca 10
The Organ Grinder 53
Orso 39
Peking Restaurant 4
Peter Pan 28
Queen Mother Café 36
Raja Sahib 34
Red Tomato/Fred's Not Here 44

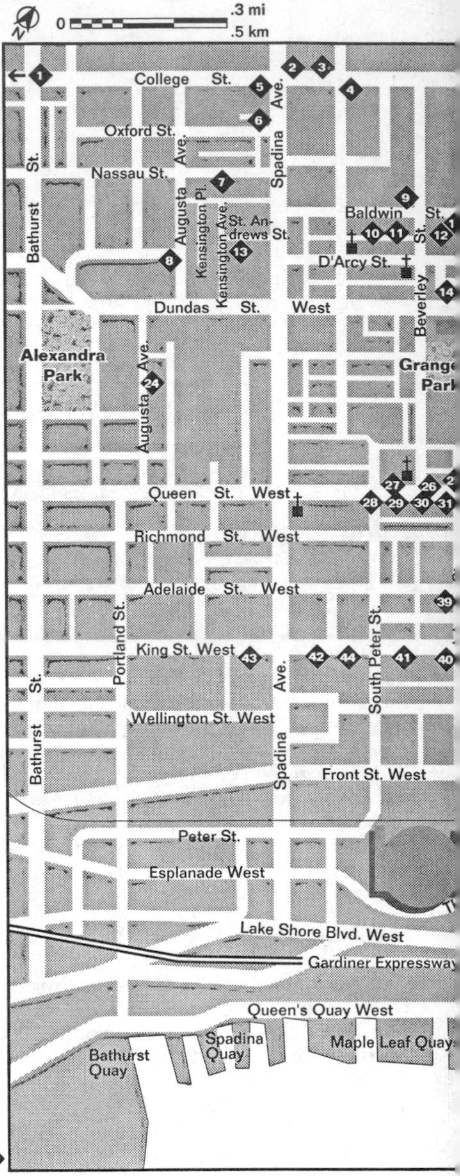

.3 mi
0
.5 km
College St.
Spadina Ave.
Oxford St.
Augusta Ave.
Bathurst St.
Nassau St.
Kensington Pl.
Kensington Ave.
St. Andrews St.
Baldwin St.
D'Arcy St.
Beverley St.
Dundas St. West
Alexandra Park
Grange Park
Queen St. West
Richmond St. West
Adelaide St. West
King St. West
Portland St.
South Peter St.
Wellington St. West
Front St. West
Peter St.
Esplanade West
Lake Shore Blvd. West
Gardiner Expressway
Queen's Quay West
Spadina Quay
Bathurst Quay
Maple Leaf Quays

Rivoli 27
Sai Woo 17
Saigon Palace 5
Soho Bistro 31
Spiaggia 62
Takesushi 51

Tall Poppies 14
Tidal Wave 35
Vanipha 24
Vasco da Gama 1
Wah Sing 15
Whistling Oyster/File of Sole 37

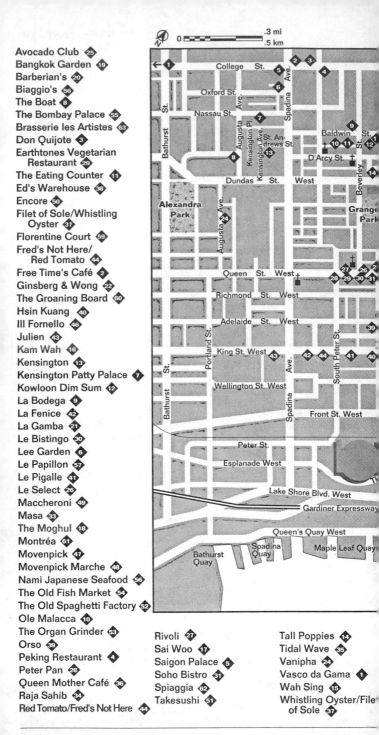

DOWNTOWN TORONTO DINING

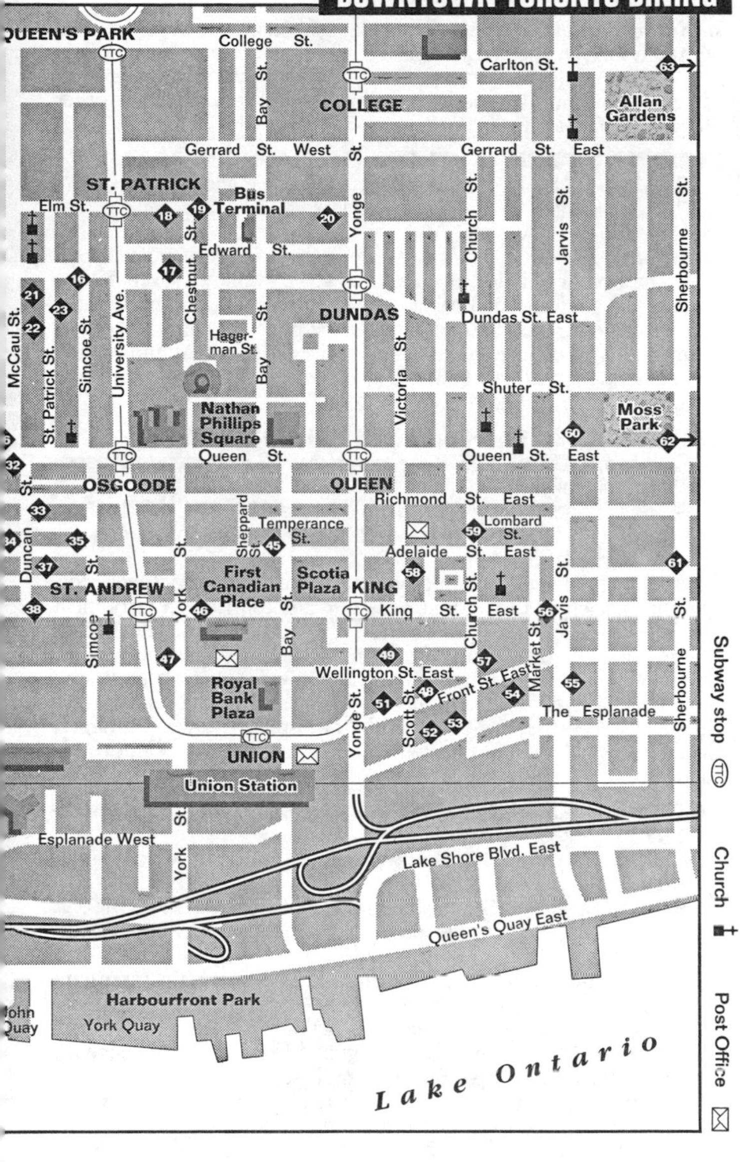

QUEEN'S PARK
College St.
Carlton St.
COLLEGE
Allan Gardens
Bay St.
Gerrard St. West
Gerrard St. East
Yonge St.
ST. PATRICK
Elm St.
Bus Terminal
Edward St.
Church St.
Jarvis St.
Sherbourne St.
Chestnut St.
University Ave.
Simcoe St.
McCaul St.
St. Patrick St.
DUNDAS
Dundas St. East
Hagerman St.
Victoria St.
Shuter St.
Nathan Phillips Square
Moss Park
Queen St.
Queen St. East
OSGOODE
QUEEN
Richmond St. East
Lombard St.
Temperance St.
Sheppard St.
Adelaide St. East
Duncan St.
York St.
First Canadian Place
Scotia Plaza
KING
ST. ANDREW
King St. East
Market St.
Wellington St. East
Front St. East
Scott St.
Royal Bank Plaza
The Esplanade
UNION
Union Station
Esplanade West
Lake Shore Blvd. East
Queen's Quay East
Harbourfront Park
York Quay
John Quay
Lake Ontario
TTC
16
17
18
19
20
21
22
23
32
33
34
35
37
38
45
46
47
48
49
51
52
53
54
55
56
57
58
59
60
61
62
63
Subway stop
Church
Post Office

Winston's 45
Young Lok Gardens 23
Zaidy's 32

such specialties as pheasant with cassis-raspberry sauce or veal flamed with Calvados and served with sliced apples and cream. Lunch offers a similar selection at reduced prices. There's a pleasant bar where you can enjoy croissants stuffed with shrimp, lamb, pheasant, or any other filling of your choice.

FLORENTINE COURT, 97 Church St. Tel. 364-3687.
Cuisine: ITALIAN. **Reservations:** Recommended.
$ Prices: Pasta $13–$15; main courses $15–$23; complete dinners $25–$33. AE, MC, V.
Open: Lunch Mon–Fri noon–2pm; dinner Mon–Sat 5:30–10pm.

In this bastion of old Toronto tradition, you can enjoy a seven-course dinner from soup through pasta, salad, main course, Florentine trifle, and beverage for just $10 more than the price of your entrée. For example, if you choose the most expensive dish—a veal-and-shrimp combination—you'll pay $33. Choose the chicken rosemary and the price goes down to $25.

MONTREAL, 65 Sherbourne St. Tel. 363-0179.
Cuisine: QUEBECOIS. **Reservations:** Recommended, especially on weekends.
$ Prices: Lunch specials $8; main courses $13–$14. AE, MC, V.
Open: Lunch Mon–Fri noon–2:30pm; dinner Mon–Thurs 6–10pm, Fri–Sat 6–11pm.

Montréal, at Adelaide and Sherbourne, is the place to try Québécois specialties, such as the famous pea soup and tourtière, a tasty meat pie. The food here is excellent and very reasonably priced. A table d'hôte lunch includes soup, brochette of beef, salad, and vegetable. At night the specialties include émincé de veau, rack of lamb, and fettuccine with seafood, with most items around $10. For dessert, try the special deep-fried ice cream with hot raspberry sauce. To the left of the entrance you'll find one of Toronto's most comfortable lounges.

NAMI JAPANESE SEAFOOD, 55 Adelaide St. E. Tel. 362-7373.
Cuisine: JAPANESE. **Reservations:** Recommended Thurs–Sat.
$ Prices: Sushi $4–$6; main courses $14–$26. AE, DC, MC, V.
Open: Lunch Mon–Fri noon–2:30pm; dinner Mon–Sat 6–10:30pm.

Nami is high-class Tokyo in Toronto. This atmospheric restaurant features sushi and such entrées as salmon teriyaki and bento. Up front there's a robata bar/sushi bar, and behind it is attractive booth seating or traditional tatami-style dining. The place attracts many Japanese, both businesspeople and families.

Start with kaki, ebi fry (oysters or shrimp), or beef sashimi—thinly sliced beef lightly coated and served with ponzu sauce. For a real treat order the tenshin bento, which provides an assortment of sushi and sashimi, or the Love Boat, which includes salad, miso, tempura, sushi, sashimi, salmon teriyaki, beef katsu, deep-fried chicken, and fruits.

SPIAGGIA, 2318 Queen St. E. Tel. 699-4656.
Cuisine: ITALIAN. **Reservations:** Recommended.
$ Prices: Pasta $10–$12; main courses $12–$14. MC, V.
Open: Dinner only, Wed–Sat 6–11pm, Sun 6–10pm.

A casual small Beaches bistro, Spiaggia is filled with tables covered in red gingham and glass. The short menu changes daily but will feature pastas, like fusilli with sausage and spicy tomato sauce or linguine with clam-and-mussel marinara, as well as more substantial dishes like veal with wild mushrooms and marsala. Desserts include tiramisu, chocolate-sambucca mousse, and a variety of gelati.

TAKESUSHI, 22 Front St. Tel. 862-1891.
Cuisine: JAPANESE. **Reservations:** Recommended.
$ Prices: Sushi combinations $13–$30; tempura and teriyaki dinners $13–$25. AE, DC, MC, V.
Open: Lunch Mon–Fri noon–2:30pm; dinner Mon–Fri 5:30–10pm, Sat–Sun 5–10pm.

This fashionable Japanese restaurant specializes in sushi—for novices there's even a beginner's sushi: salmon marinated in vinegar and salt, and ebi or cooked shrimp sushi. Otherwise, you can order combinations such as eight nigiri and one makimono or a deluxe sushi, including eight nigiri and one makimono. Other sushi thrills include uni (sea urchin gonads) and kazunoko (herring roe soaked in sake, soy, and broth). Traditional tempura and teriyaki dinners are also available.

BUDGET

THE BOMBAY PALACE, 71 Jarvis St. (between King and Adelaide Sts.). Tel. 368-8048.
Cuisine: INDIAN. **Reservations:** Recommended.
$ Prices: Main courses $9–$16. AE, DC, MC, V.
Open: Lunch daily noon–3pm; dinner daily 6–10:30pm.

The Bombay Palace is plush, with its comfortable banquettes and exotic Indian statues and idols. For the real Indian cuisine-lover, there's an 18-dish daily buffet that includes bhuna gosht, tandoori chicken, salads, and vegetable curry. At night you can select from the à la carte menu or opt for a dinner like the Palace, which includes chicken tandoor, chicken tikka, tandoori prawns, seekh kebab, beef pasanda, pulao, vegetable, naan, chutney, and pickles—all for $17.

THE GROANING BOARD, 131 Jarvis St. (at Richmond). Tel. 363-0265.
Cuisine: VEGETARIAN/CONTINENTAL. **Reservations:** Recommended on weekends.
$ Prices: Main courses $8–$10. AE, MC, V.
Open: Mon–Fri 11am–midnight; Sat–Sun 11am–1am.

One of the best entertainment buys in Toronto awaits you at the Groaning Board. Every night at 7 and 9pm (at 7, 9:30, and 11pm on weekends), a selection of international award-winning commercials is shown from the Cannes and Venice festivals. The food is 40% vegetarian, 60% meat dishes, featuring eggplant parmigiana, hummus, and spinach pie. There's a gigantic 72-item salad bar, a roast of the day, steamed vegetables, and a build-your-own sundae area. You'll find home-cooking in a plain 1960s coffeehouse atmosphere while laughing at 90-minute film reels of award-winning commercials—children love it. There's a $3 cover charge for the screenings.

LE PAPILLON, 106 Front St. Tel. 363-0838.
Cuisine: CREPES. **Reservations:** Recommended on weekends.
$ Prices: Crêpes $6–$10. AE, DC, MC, V.

Open: Tues–Wed noon–10pm, Thurs–Sat noon–midnight, Sun 11am–11pm.

There'll probably be a line of eager young folks outside Le Papillon, located just east of Jarvis Street, a pretty place to repair for a candlelit dinner and crêpes of all kinds. Exposed brick, mirrors, greenery, blue gingham tablecloths, and modern lithographs set the tone. Before you taste the imaginative crêpes, start with a vegetable cocktail or a bowl of onion soup and a salad. There are 16 savory crêpes, ranging from crêpe Marie Claude (with sausages, apples, and Cheddar cheese) to crêpe Continental (chicken, mushrooms, and peppers in béchamel). Then there are luscious dessert crêpes with sliced peaches, apples, and cinnamon.

MACCHERONI, 32 Wellington St. E. Tel. 867-9067.

Cuisine: ITALIAN. **Reservations:** Accepted for large parties only.

$ **Prices:** Main courses $5–$7. AE, MC, V.

Open: Mon–Wed and Sat 11:30am–10pm, Thurs–Fri 11:30am–midnight, Sun 11:30am–9pm.

Swathes of brilliant color—mustard yellow, periwinkle, orange, and red—will transport you to the Mediterranean, as will the faux urns, flowers, and fruit at this low-priced stage set, which serves some adequate if not exciting food. Start with the bruschetta or the crostini della casa made with gorgonzola. You can follow with a variety of pasta dishes—penne arrabiata, fettuccine Alfredo, lasagne, and manicotti—or pizza.

MOVENPICK MARCHE, in the galleria of the BCE Building, Front St. E. Tel. 366-8986.

Cuisine: CONTINENTAL. **Reservations:** Not accepted.

$ **Prices:** Main courses $5–$8. AE, DC, MC, V.

Open: Mon–Fri 11:30am–2am, Sat–Sun 7:30am–2am.

This large restaurant with a variety of seating areas is the latest innovation in food merchandising. Pick up a tab at the entrance and stroll through the bustling market, where various stands, carts, and trolleys are set up displaying fresh foods and ingredients. Stop at the rosticceria and select a meat for the chef to cook. Pause at the seafood and raw bar and pick out a fish for the grill or peruse the pasta bar. Then wander over to the bistro de vin and check out the cases of wine or enjoy a boccalino of one of the open wines. The chefs and staff are easily identifiable by their boaters as they stand behind counters heaped with fresh salads, fish, meats, and pizzas. Ask and it will be made before your very eyes—Cornish hens, rosti with salmon, steak, sausages, and more. A fun place for breakfast, lunch, or dinner.

THE OLD FISH MARKET, 12 Market St. Tel. 363-0334.

Cuisine: SEAFOOD. **Reservations:** Recommended.

$ **Prices:** Main courses $9–$28. AE, MC, V.

Open: Coasters, Mon–Sat noon–1am, Sun 1:30–10pm. Restaurant, lunch Mon–Fri noon–2pm, Sat noon–2:30pm; dinner Mon–Fri 5–10pm, Sat 4:30–11pm, Sun 1:30–10pm.

The Old Fish Market, by the St. Lawrence Market, packs 'em in. On the ground floor there's an oyster bar and a large restaurant with comfortable booths and wooden tables, decorated with photographs of old salts and fishing scenes, plus such nautical regalia as lobster traps and foghorns. Upstairs you'll find

Coasters, a black arborite shellfish bar where you can relax and eat while seated on low sofas. The decor consists of exposed brick and painted plumbing warmed by a huge fire blazing in the back during the winter. Coasters features daily specials, an oyster bar, cold and hot seafood appetizers, and imported beers.

Downstairs you'll get a selection of the freshest fish, pan-fried, broiled, or barbecued. Start with one of the chowders, then choose from the night's fresh offerings: rainbow trout, snapper, roughy, bluefish, mahimahi, or halibut, for example—all served with sourdough roll, mackerel pâté, house salad, and potatoes. Most dishes are $14 to $16, except for such items as lobster tails and surf and turf.

THE OLD SPAGHETTI FACTORY, 54 The Esplanade. Tel. 864-9761.

Cuisine: ITALIAN. **Reservations:** Required for parties of 10 or more.

$ **Prices:** Main courses $8–$12. AE, DC, MC, V.

Open: Mon–Thurs 11:30am–midnight, Fri–Sat 11:30am–1am, Sun 11:30am–11pm (winter closings an hour earlier).

The Old Spaghetti Factory turns out countless pasta favorites, such as spaghetti with tomato sauce or with meatballs, both including soup or salad, spumoni, and coffee or tea. Other dishes like veal parmigiana, chicken cacciatore, and lasagne supplement the menu. The huge space, seating 600, is cluttered with Canadiana—a good place to go with the kids.

THE ORGAN GRINDER, 58 The Esplanade. Tel. 364-6517.

Cuisine: ITALIAN. **Reservations:** Accepted only for parties of 10 or more.

$ **Prices:** Most items $7–$12. AE, DC, MC, V.

Open: Mon–Fri noon–2pm and 5–10pm, Sat 11:30am–midnight, Sun 11:30am–10pm.

The kids will love the Organ Grinder, a vast musical pizza parlor where an organist bashes out popular tunes on the theater pipe organ, which has a fascinating array of gadgets—submarine sirens, sleighbells, bird whistles, horse hooves, all kinds of drums, chimes, cymbals, and a glockenspiel—and over 1,000 pipes made of wood, zinc, lead, and tin. To the tunes of this rare monstrosity you and the kids can feast on pizza, lasagne, manicotti, veal parmigiana, and other Italian dishes.

3. MIDTOWN WEST

There's plenty of fine dining here, but note that the area includes Yorkville—and as with so many chic expensive shopping areas, dining in Yorkville is not always a pleasant experience. Here, rents are high and consequently prices are high, but the quality sometimes just doesn't match. That said, there are a few Yorkville restaurants that can be relied upon to deliver quality at a decent price.

EXPENSIVE

ACROBAT, 60 Bloor St. W. (entrance at 1221 Bay St.). Tel. 920-2323.

Cuisine: ITALIAN. **Reservations:** Recommended.
$ **Prices:** Pasta and pizza $12–$16; main courses $18–$23. AE, MC, V.
Open: Mon–Sat 4:30pm–1am.

Acrobat is dramatic indeed. To the right you'll find a sinuous bar of dark and blond wood. Behind and above it, the eye is drawn to a brilliant tile mosaic of bottles and a cascading waterfall. The dining area is equally striking, with brilliant turquoise high-back banquettes and eccentrically sculpted flower holders. The food is equally interesting, showing a definite Oriental influence—as in the spring rolls and tempura with tamarind cream and honey-mustard dipping sauce, or the Thai seafood soup, to mention but two of the 10 or so appetizers. You might be tempted to top your pizza with lamb sausage, rosemary mozzarella, roasted peppers, or Bermuda onions; if you're choosing a pasta, you may be drawn to penne with smoked salmon and vodka-tomato cream sauce. Among the main courses the Oriental touch reappears with the spicy swordfish with citrus-fruit relish and the Atlantic salmon with black-bean butter and baby bok choy.

THE CORNER HOUSE, 501 Davenport Rd. Tel. 923-2604.
Cuisine: CONTINENTAL. **Reservations:** Recommended, especially on weekends.
$ **Prices:** Main courses $27–$30. AE, DC, MC, V.
Open: Dinner only, Mon–Sat 6–10pm.

One of my favorite dining spots in the city, The Corner House also represents one of the best values going. Only minutes from Casa Loma, it looks like any other suburban single-family house, except for the discreet sign outside on the lawn. Inside, there are four dining rooms: two downstairs and two upstairs (one with only four tables), each decorated very simply with oil paintings and china plates.

Chef Peter Colberg turns out a consistently fine array of classic dishes: poached salmon with lemon-vegetable broth; lamb with herbs, mustard, and minted demiglaze; breast of chicken with shallots, orange slices, and Grand Marnier; and duckling served with mandarin-cognac sauce. Dinner will include pâté, your choice of appetizer, and a main course. Add such desserts as blueberry trifle or baked meringue at your discretion. Service is gracious, and I really can't think of a more delightful way to spend an evening.

LA SCALA, 1121 Bay St. Tel. 964-7100.
Cuisine: ITALIAN. **Reservations:** Recommended.
$ **Prices:** Main courses $22–$29. AE, DC, MC, V.
Open: Lunch Mon–Fri noon–2:30pm; dinner Mon–Sat 5–10:30pm.

You'll need a wad of banknotes to entertain at the city's plushest Italian restaurant, set in a black-and-white gabled town house with Italianate windows. Everything about the decor is opulent: the marble entrance, the chandeliers, the candlelit alcoves, the wood paneling, the antique mirrors, and the classical statues. Behind the restaurant there's an equally opulent cocktail lounge.

The menu features veal piccata, plus steak and fish dishes. During the week there's a flambé specialty—steak Diane au sherry, for example. Lunchtime prices drop substantially.

SPLENDIDO BAR AND GRILL, 88 Harbord St. Tel. 929-7788.

Cuisine: ITALIAN. **Reservations:** Recommended well in advance.

$ **Prices:** Pasta and pizza $8–$13; main courses $19–$23. AE, MC, V.

Open: Lunch Tues–Fri noon–2:30pm; dinner daily 5–11pm.

Splendido is the city's current scene-stealer—and steal the scene it does, for it's an absolutely stunning dining room. Up front there's a pink marble bar. Behind stretches the dining room, a riot of brilliant yellow that is lit by a host of tiny, almost fairylike track lights; the walls are hung with huge flower canvases by Helen Lucas.

The food is Italian with international inspirations, and the menu changes monthly. Start with the unique antipasto of bacon-wrapped shrimp, coppa, peperonata, and bocconcini, with tomatoes and tapenade crostini; or the pistachio-crust sea scallops baked in a brick oven and served with mango chutney and fermented black-bean sauce. Follow with either pasta, pizza, or a main course. For example, you might choose the pizza with goat cheese, roasted ricotta, sun-dried tomatoes, olives, eggplant and oregano or the pasta ribbons with pancetta, mushroom, and peppered-vodka cream. Among the main courses, the corn-fried salmon with mashed potatoes, sweet corn relish, and arugula with citrus dressing is a special treat; so, too, is the beef tenderloin with mushroom duxelles, artichokes, fried ravioli, and barbecue butter sauce.

MODERATE

ARLEQUIN, 134 Avenue Rd. (between Davenport and Bernard Sts.). Tel. 928-9521.

Cuisine: CONTINENTAL. **Reservations:** Recommended.

$ **Prices:** Main courses $6–$8 at lunch, $14–$18 at dinner. MC, V.

Open: Mon–Thurs 10am–10pm, Fri–Sat 10am–11pm, Sun 11am–5pm.

Arlequin is a handsome small restaurant with a counter display of fabulous pâté, cheeses, salads, and baked goods up front. The menu is keyed to market-fresh ingredients and might list brochette of quails and sausage with mushroom and juniper sauce, confit of duck, pan-fried filet of red snapper with garlic mayonnaise, or salmon with citrus salsa. Brunch also stretches to some imaginative specials. The current excitement is understandable.

BISTRO 990, 990 Bay St. Tel. 921-9990.

Cuisine: FRENCH. **Reservations:** Required.

$ **Prices:** Main courses $9–$16 at lunch, $16–$22 at dinner. AE, MC, V.

Open: Lunch Mon–Fri noon–3pm; dinner Mon–Sat 6–11pm.

Bistro 990 could have come straight from the French provinces with its french doors, lace curtains, and outdoor café tables. The chef emphasizes his use of free-range meats and organic or hydroponic produce in the typical bistro fare. Start with the chicken-liver mousse with red-onion relish or the salad of smoked trout with mixed greens and dijon dressing. To follow there will probably be about 10 or so meat and seafood dishes, like the roast pork tenderloin with prunes and red wine; a traditional cassoulet of duck confit, pork sausage, and flageolet; roast chicken with herb crust and mashed potatoes; or salmon filet with Oriental flavors, bok choy, and sesame rice cake.

CHIADO, 864 College St. (at Concord Ave.). Tel. 538-1910.

Cuisine: PORTUGUESE. **Reservations:** Recommended.
$ **Prices:** Main courses $14–$18. AE, DC, MC, V.
Open: Lunch daily noon–3pm; dinner daily 5pm–midnight.

Chiado refers to the district in Lisbon that's filled with small bistrettos like this one. Beyond the appetizing display at the front of the room you'll discover a long, narrow, elegant dining room decorated with French-style pink chairs and colorful art on the walls. In summer the storefront opens entirely onto the street, adding to the atmosphere. Among the appetizers the pinheta of salted cod and the marinated sardines with lemon and parsley will appeal to the true Portuguese; others might prefer the tiger shrimp served with sweet-pepper coulis. On the main menu a Portuguese might plump for the poached filet of cod or the bistretto-style steak with fried egg and fries, while a friend might go for the roast rack of lamb with red Douro wine sauce or the braised rabbit in Madeira sauce. To top it all off, choose the peach-coconut flan, chocolate mousse, pecan pie, or any of the other tempting desserts.

HAZELTON CLUB, 55 Avenue Rd., in Hazelton Lanes. Tel. 923-6944.

Cuisine: CONTINENTAL/LIGHT. **Reservations:** Required for Sat lunch; recommended other times.
$ **Prices:** Main courses $8–$12. AE, MC, V.
Open: Lunch only, Mon–Fri 11:30am–3pm, Sat noon–3:30pm.

The Hazelton Club is a pleasant place to have lunch, out in the courtyard in summer or inside at one of the white linen-covered tables. The menu features very light cuisine, with no cream used. Daily choices include a hot or cold soup, such appetizers as terrine or bruschetta, and salads like shrimp with wild mushroom or mixed leaves with fresh-baked goat cheese and bacon. You'll have six main-course choices, like breast of chicken with coriander-lime butter, pasta, omelets, and burgers. Desserts include chocolate terrine with crème anglais, fresh fruit, and dietetic cheesecake.

IL POSTO, 148 Yorkville Ave. Tel. 968-0469.

Cuisine: ITALIAN. **Reservations:** Recommended.
$ **Prices:** Main courses $16–$30. AE, MC, V.
Open: Lunch Mon–Sat noon–2:30pm; dinner Mon–Sat 6–10:30pm.

In the heart of high-rent Yorkville, where restaurants are constantly opening and closing, Il Posto has thrived for years and still offers a very attractive setting, both inside and out on the brick terrace under a spreading maple tree. The restaurant's beige walls, Italian prints, classical music, and handsome bouquets of fresh flowers create a serene dining atmosphere. The dessert spread at the entrance is tempting—fresh raspberry tarts with kiwi, fresh strawberry and blueberry tarts, canned oranges, and other delights.

The menu features such Italian specialties as chicken marsala, veal cooked in a spicy tomato-garlic sauce, beef with green peppercorns and brandy-flavored sauce, linguine with seafood or (even more delicious) with gorgonzola. There are also fish dishes; salads like arugula and endive; and, in summer only, a special vitello tonnato.

For dessert, besides the very special pastries, you might discover poached pears in chocolate or smooth, creamy zabaglione.

JOSO'S, 202 Davenport. Tel. 925-1903.
Cuisine: SEAFOOD. **Reservations:** Recommended.
$ Prices: Main courses $13–$30. AE, MC, V.
Open: Lunch Mon–Fri 11:30am–3pm; dinner Mon–Sat 5:30–11pm.

Yugoslav Joseph Spralja—of the duo Malka and Joso—has appeared on "The Tonight Show" and performed at Carnegie Hall, but since he gave up folk singing because of an ulcer, he has taken to combing the fish markets for his restaurant, Joso's, just east of Avenue Road. Besides having a fascinating owner, this place has some rather idiosyncratic decor (which might offend some, so I have to mention the erotic ceramic sculptures of golf-ball–bosomed females).

If you don't care a fig about such matters but you do care about fresh seafood, then stop by Joso's. At dinner you can choose your own specimen from the selection of fresh fish presented to you. Or you can have octopus steamed in garlic-and-parsley sauce; deep-fried squid with salad; or spaghetti with an octopus, clam, and squid tomato sauce. A selection of exotic coffees is available, as are French pastries for dessert.

LE RENDEZ-VOUS, 14 Prince Arthur Ave. Tel. 961-6111.
Cuisine: FRENCH. **Reservations:** Recommended.
$ Prices: Main courses $7–$9 at lunch, $18–$25 at dinner; brunch special $18. AE, CB, MC, V.
Open: Lunch Mon–Sat noon–2:30pm; dinner Mon–Sat 5:30–10pm, Sun 5:30–9:30pm; brunch Sun noon–2:30pm.

You'll find a variety of decors here in the classic French style. In summer the outdoor dining area is filled, along with the comfortable plant-filled atrium. Rattan chairs, burgundy upholstery, and classical music provide atmosphere in the interior.

Dining choices are very appealing: salmon with basil sauce, rack of lamb provençal, Dover sole, and duck with five spices. At lunch, choices might include mushrooms stuffed with crab and topped with hollandaise, plus egg and pasta dishes. For before- or after-dinner tippling, go downstairs to the wine cellar. Brunch offers a choice of juices; croissants with preserves; fresh-fruit salad with yogurt and honey, soup of the day, or Caesar salad; and then a main-course choice such as suprême of chicken with wild mushroom sauce, sautéed scallops in a garlic butter and fresh tomato, or roast beef au jus. Dessert of the day or crème caramel ice cream and sherbet will complete the meal.

LE TROU NORMAND, 90 Yorkville Ave. Tel. 967-5956.
Cuisine: FRENCH. **Reservations:** Recommended.
$ Prices: Main courses $9–$12 at lunch, $16–$21 at dinner. AE, MC, V.
Open: Lunch daily noon–3pm; dinner daily 5:30–11pm.

In Yorkville, where restaurants tend to be overpriced and touristy, Le Trou Normand is reliable, if not exciting. The atmosphere is country French, with breakfronts and tile floors inside, plus a pleasant outdoor terrace in summer.

Choose from among a dozen appetizers—leeks-and-salmon terrine or marinated beef with asparagus tips, for example—and then move on to such entrées as rack of lamb with Pommery mustard sauce, marinated rabbit with prunes and apricot, filet of pheasant with green cabbage and potato pancakes, and steamed bass with champagne. And don't forget dessert—the spreads are absolutely luscious, particularly the fresh-fruit tarts with apple, cherry, strawberry, raspberry, and more.

SHOGUN, 154 Cumberland Ave. Tel. 964-8665.
Cuisine: JAPANESE. **Reservations:** Recommended.
$ Prices: Main courses $13.50–$20; combination dinners $16.50–$30. AE, MC, V.
Open: Lunch Mon–Sat noon–2:30pm; dinner daily 5:30–11pm.

Sushi expert Mitsuhiro Kaji runs Shogun in Yorkville, where you'll find a sushi bar and several tables. The best way to explore Japanese food is to choose one of the dinners with a choice of miso or suimono soup, salad, rice, and main course. For $30 you'll also receive an appetizer, tempura, sushi, and fruit. Or you can order such à la carte dinners as beef teriyaki with soup, salad, rice, and tea.

SOUTHERN ACCENT, 595 Markham St. Tel. 536-3211.
Cuisine: CAJUN. **Reservations:** Recommended.
$ Prices: Main courses $14–$20. AE, DC, MC, V.
Open: Dinner only, daily 5–10:30pm.

This place has a real down-home Cajun feel. The background music is great, the art is interesting, and the floral tablecloths are somehow funky. There are three areas to dine in: upstairs in the dining room, downstairs on the bar level, or out on the brick patio. The menu features the goods—gumbo, jambalaya, shrimp étouffée, and blackened fish with lemon, to name only a few great dishes.

THE SULTAN'S TENT, 1280 Bay St. Tel. 961-0601.
Cuisine: MOROCCAN. **Reservations:** Required.
$ Prices: Fixed-price meals $20 Mon–Thurs, $27 Fri–Sat. AE, MC, V.
Open: Dinner only, Mon–Wed 5:30–11:30pm, Thurs–Sat 5:30pm–1am.

At the Sultan's Tent in Yorkville you'll find yourself in exotic surroundings—a tented ceiling, lavishly cushioned banquettes, leather hassocks, rugs from the Atlas Mountains and Marrakesh, and brass and copper artifacts bought by the kilo in Fez.

Weave your own fantasies while waitresses in kaftans and waiters in jalabias bring huge bowls of couscous with either lamb or chicken and vegetables and while a dancer moves to the sounds of the kanoon and oud. For $20 Monday through Thursday ($27 with live music and belly dancing other evenings), you can select a soup, an appetizer, a salad, an entrée (perhaps lamb with prunes and almonds, rabbit glazed in honey with sweet tomatoes, or couscous), a dessert, and mint tea or Moroccan coffee.

TRATTORIA GIANCARLO, 41–43 Clinton St. (at College). Tel. 533-9619.
Cuisine: ITALIAN. **Reservations:** Strongly recommended.
$ Prices: Pasta and rice $10–$12; main courses $16–$19. AE, MC, V.
Open: Dinner only, Mon–Sat 5:30–11pm.

This restaurant is one of my all-time favorite spots in Little Italy, if not in all the city, and I find myself returning here time after time. It's small and cozy and thoroughly Italian, with an outside dining area in summer. The tablecloths are covered with butcher paper, the floor is black-and-white tile, and the background music is opera or jazz.

For a real treat start with the fresh wild mushrooms brushed with herbs, garlic, and oil or the carpaccio of salmon. Follow with any one of six pasta dishes—perhaps spaghettini with shrimp and fra diavolo sauce or the risotto of the day. Good grilled fresh fish and meats are also part of the attraction, like the tender lamb brushed with lemon, rosemary, and fresh mint or the red snapper marinated in fresh thyme and bay, olive oil, and lemon. For dessert try the tiramisu, the crème caramel, or the delicious chocolate-raspberry tartufo. The evening somehow is always memorable and the welcome real.

YVES BISTRO, 36A Prince Arthur Ave. Tel. 972-1010.
Cuisine: FRENCH. **Reservations:** Recommended.
$ Prices: Prix-fixe $15 for main course and appetizer. MC, V.
Open: Lunch Mon–Fri noon–2pm; dinner Mon–Sat 6–10pm.

Comfortable, gracious, and made cozy by its mullioned windows, small serving bar, and brilliant sunflower mirrors, this bistro delivers good well-priced food. Start with the asparagus with crumbled blue cheese and raspberry vinaigrette or the mussels steamed in white wine, mushrooms, tomatoes, and tarragon. Among the 10 or so entrées you will find pasta, fish, and meat—from a fusilli with hazelnut pesto, artichokes, and black olives; to salmon steamed with leeks, tomatoes, spinach, and Pernod; to lamb chops grilled with mustard and herbs and served with mint sauce.

BUDGET

For additional budget dining, see "Light, Casual & Fast Food" and "Dining Complexes" below in "Specialty Dining."

AIDA'S FALAFEL, 553 Bloor St. W. Tel. 537-3700.
Cuisine: MIDDLE EASTERN. **Reservations:** Not needed.
$ Prices: Main courses $2–$6. No credit cards.
Open: Mon–Thurs 11am–10pm, Fri–Sat noon–midnight, Sun 11am–9pm.

Aïda's Falafel, on Bloor Street at Bathurst, is a small, unassuming restaurant with a couple of tables out front. Tabouli, falafel, and shish kebab cost $2 to $6. There's also a branch in the Beaches on Queen Street East at Woodbine.

ANNAPURNA RESTAURANT, 1085 Bathurst St. Tel. 537-8513.
Cuisine: VEGETARIAN/INDIAN. **Reservations:** Not needed.
$ Prices: Most items less than $6. No credit cards.
Open: Mon–Tues and Thurs–Sat noon–9pm, Wed noon–6:30pm.

Some 17 years ago Shivaram Trichur opened the Annapurna Restaurant, just south of Dupont. Beyond the counter, where you can purchase various goodies, including a loaf of banana bread, along with books on yoga and copies of *Meditation at the U.N.*, you'll find a room with no decor to speak of—but with some fine low-priced food. Enjoy the peaceful smoke-free atmosphere and the medieval background music along with the young, intellectual, and interesting crowd that gathers here.

Nothing on the menu is over $6, and for that amount you'll

receive a veritable vegetarian feast—raita, bonda (gingery potato-and-vegetable balls dipped in chickpea batter and deep-fried), bhajia, samosas, pappadum, sagu (spinach and mixed-vegetable curry), potato masala, and rice or puris. Salads and vegetarian sandwiches supplement the South Indian dishes.

THE BOULEVARD CAFE, 161 Harbord St. Tel. 961-7676.
Cuisine: PERUVIAN. **Reservations:** Recommended for upstairs dining.
$ Prices: Main courses $9–$14. MC, V.
Open: Lunch daily 11:30am–3:30pm; dinner daily 5:30–10:30pm.

Between Spadina Avenue and Bathurst Street is a favorite gathering spot for young creative types. Upstairs there's a dining room furnished with wooden banquettes softened by Peruvian cushions and South American wall hangings. The outside summer café is strung with colored lights and attracts an evening and late-night crowd.

The menu features Peruvian specialties—empanadas (spicy chicken or beef pastry); tangy shrimp in a spiced garlic, pimiento, and wine sauce; and tamal verde (spicy corn, coriander, and chicken pâté) to start. For the main course, try anticuchos, marinated and charbroiled brochettes of your own choosing: sea bass, shrimp, lamb, beef, or chicken. Burgers, lamb chops, and steamed mussels are some of the other selections.

CHEZ CAPPUCCINO, 3 Charles St. E. Tel. 925-6142.
Cuisine: COFFEE/LIGHT FARE.
$ Prices: Most items $2–$6. No credit cards.
Open: Daily 24 hrs.

Chez Cappuccino, just off Yonge Street, is a good way to start the day with a melt-in-the-mouth croissant, banana bread, or a bagel sandwich washed down with a smooth, frothy cappuccino. Specialty sandwiches include the half-mile-long version. Most items are around $2.

THE FARE EXCHANGE, 4 Irwin Ave. Tel. 923-5924.
Cuisine: CONTINENTAL. **Reservations:** Not needed.
$ Prices: Main courses $4–$7 at lunch, $11–$16 at dinner; fixed-price meals $13.50. AE, MC, V.
Open: Restaurant, lunch Mon–Sat 11:30am–4:30pm; dinner Mon–Sat 5–11pm. Bar, Mon–Sat 5pm–1am.

A really good downtown spot for lunch, as many shoppers and businesspeople know, is the Fare Exchange, between Wellesley and Charles streets, a small, intimate café that serves good food at fair prices. In summer there's a pleasant outdoor patio, and upstairs you'll find a comfortable bar that has a wide selection of imported beers. The cuisine is continental: chicken in pesto cream, pork tenderloin in tomato cream, and similar dishes.

GARLIC PEPPER, 578 Yonge St. (at Wellesley). Tel. 323-9819.
Cuisine: CHINESE. **Reservations:** Not needed.
$ Prices: Lunch specials $7; main courses $8–$13. AE, MC, V.
Open: Mon–Fri 11:30am–10pm, Sat 4–11pm, Sun noon–10pm.

Garlic Pepper is a good place for a budget-priced meal of Szechuan specialties. The four-course lunch changes daily and might consist of soup, shrimp rolls, and spicy beef in orange sauce, pork in Bejing bean sauce, or something similar. The decor is attractive, with gray tablecloths offset by mauve napkins.

INDIAN RICE FACTORY, 414 Dupont St. Tel. 961-3472.
Cuisine: INDIAN. **Reservations:** Not needed.
$ Prices: Main courses $7–$11. AE, MC, V.
Open: Mon–Sat 11am–11pm, Sun 4–10pm.

A friend of mine raised in India swears by the Indian Rice Factory, operated by Mrs. Patel, who was born in the Punjab. It is an elegant place, with comfortable plush booths, a light-oak bar, and Indian artifacts. The food is decent and the prices are right. All the curries—chicken, beef, shrimp—are under $11. The restaurant also serves a wide selection of Indian vegetarian dishes, including aloo gobi (a curried mixture of potato and cauliflower), matar paneer (peas and cheese cooked with spices), aloo palak (spinach with potatoes), and a complete thali for $11 that includes a meat or vegetable main course, a vegetable of the day, dal, rice, chapati, raita, pappadum, and kachumber.

JACQUES' OMELETTES, 126A Cumberland St. Tel. 961-1893.
Cuisine: CONTINENTAL. **Reservations:** Not needed.
$ Prices: Omelets $9–$12; main courses $15–$18. AE, MC, V.
Open: Lunch Mon–Sat noon–3pm; dinner Mon–Sat 5–10:30pm.

As the name suggests, the specialty here is omelets—more than 17 varieties, in fact. Everything about the small room, located above a boutique in the heart of Yorkville, is tasteful—the fresh flowers on the bar and the French prints and pictures of Paris. But the crowds come for the omelets—selections from simple fines herbes to lobster, cheese, and herbs. Salads, quiches, cheeses, and soups and a small selection of hors d'oeuvres, plus veal, chicken, and fish entrées, make this a good dining spot. You don't have to pay through the nose for well-prepared food, even in Yorkville.

KENSINGTON KITCHEN, 124 Harbord St. Tel. 961-3404.
Cuisine: MIDDLE EASTERN. **Reservations:** Not accepted.
$ Prices: Main courses $8–$11. MC, V.
Open: Mon–Sat 11:30am–11pm, Sun 11:30am–10pm.

A comfortable, casual place filled with an intellectual crowd, the Kensington Kitchen features minimal decor. A beaded-purse collection and a toy-airplane collection decorate the walls. There's a counter in the back for take-out. The menu is chalked on a board and includes felafel, shish kebab, vegetarian chili, fish of the day, vegetable kebab on hummus, and daily pasta and other specials. There are two dining rooms—one upstairs, the other downstairs—but my favorite spot is on the deck out back under the spreading trees.

MORI, 1280 Bay St. Tel. 961-1094.
Cuisine: JAPANESE. **Reservations:** Recommended at dinner.
$ Prices: Main courses $7.50–$11. AE, MC, V.
Open: Lunch Mon–Sat noon–3pm; dinner Mon–Fri 5–10pm, Sat 5–11pm.

Mori, a tiny Japanese café with wrought-iron tables and deep-blue tablecloths, is great for budget dining. The attractions here are the sushi and other Japanese dishes like salmon

TORONTO
Midtown

- Acrobat 3
- Aïda's Falafel 24
- Amelia Street Café 28
- Annapurna 19
- Arlequin 2
- Astoria 31
- Bistro 990 25
- Bloor St. Diner 18
- Boulevard Café 27
- Bumpkins 22
- Chez Cappuccino 21
- Chiado 15
- The Corner House 38
- The Fare Exchange 23
- Garlic Pepper 20
- Hazelton Club 9
- Il Posto 8
- Indian Rice Factory 39
- Jacques' Omelettes 12
- Joso's 1
- Kensington Kitchen 26
- La Scala 16
- Le Rendez-Vous 11
- Le Trou Normand 7
- Meyer's Deli 6
- Mori 5
- Omonia 33
- Ouzeria 32
- The Palace 35
- The Plume 29
- The Round Window 34
- Shogun 14
- Southern Accent 37
- Splendido 13
- The Sultan's Tent 4
- Toby's Goodeats 17
- Trattoria Giancarlo 30
- Viva 36
- Yves Bistro 10

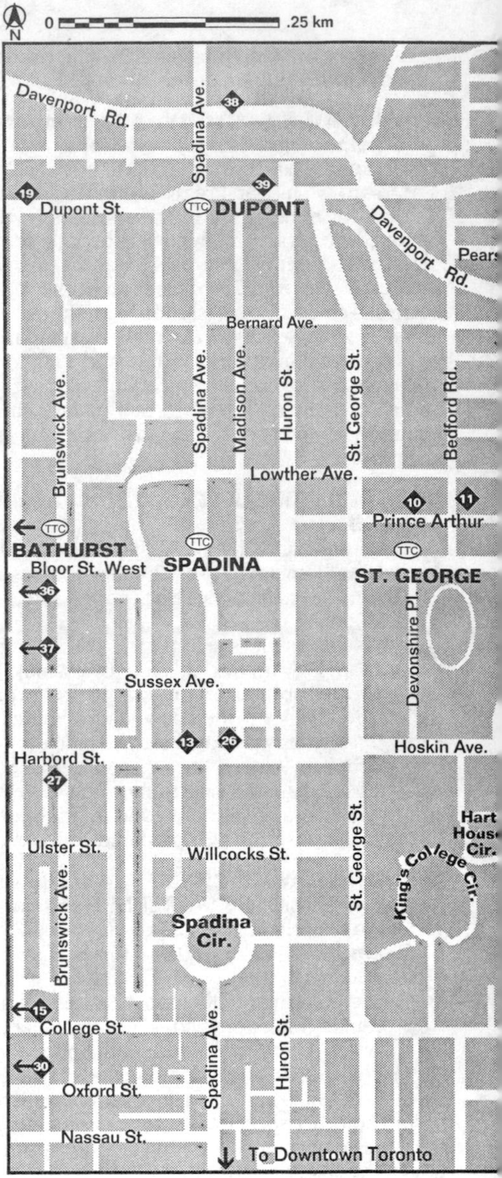
N
0
.25 km
Davenport Rd.
Spadina Ave.
38
19
39
Dupont St.
TTC
DUPONT
Davenport Rd.
Pears
Bernard Ave.
Brunswick Ave.
Spadina Ave.
Madison Ave.
Huron St.
St. George St.
Bedford Rd.
Lowther Ave.
10
11
Prince Arthur
TTC
BATHURST
TTC
SPADINA
TTC
ST. GEORGE
Bloor St. West
36
37
Devonshire Pl.
Sussex Ave.
13
26
Hoskin Ave.
Harbord St.
27
Hart House Cir.
Ulster St.
Willcocks St.
St. George St.
King's College Cir.
Brunswick Ave.
Spadina Cir.
15
College St.
Spadina Ave.
Huron St.
30
Oxford St.
Nassau St.
To Downtown Toronto

MIDTOWN TORONTO DINING

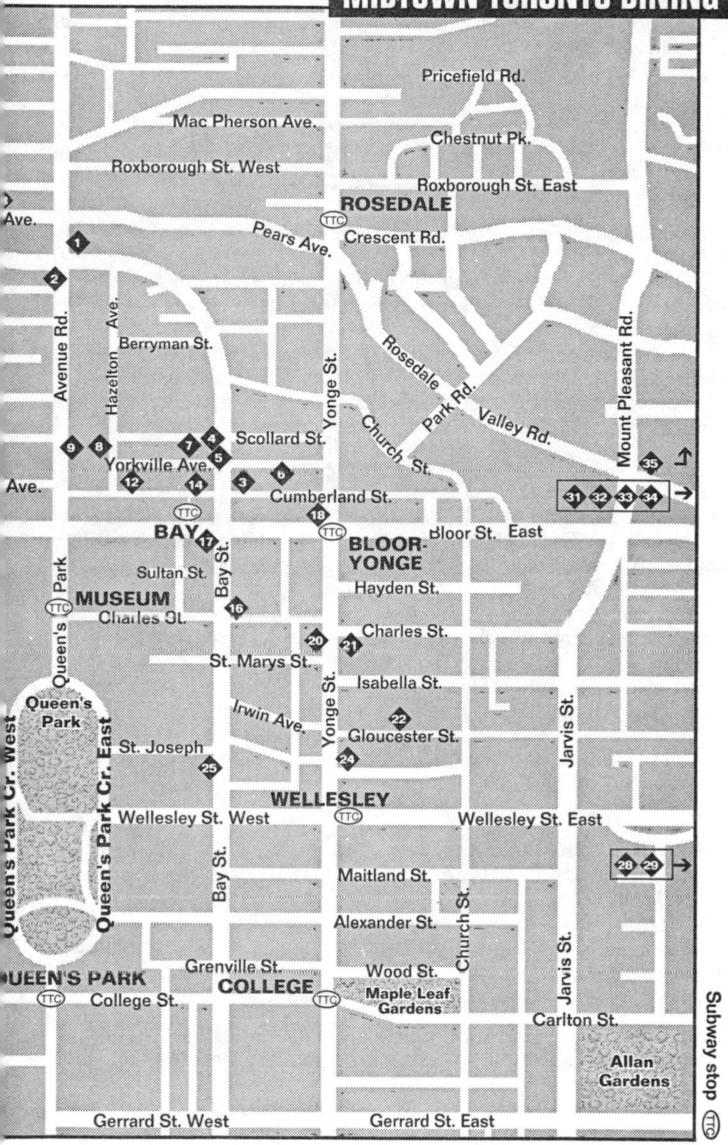
Pricefield Rd.
Mac Pherson Ave.
Chestnut Pk.
Roxborough St. West
Roxborough St. East
ROSEDALE
Ave.
Pears Ave.
Crescent Rd.
Avenue Rd.
Hazelton Ave.
Berryman St.
Rosedale Valley Rd.
Park Rd.
Yonge St.
Church St.
Mount Pleasant Rd.
Scollard St.
Yorkville Ave.
Ave.
Cumberland St.
BAY
Bloor St. East
BLOOR-YONGE
Sultan St.
Bay St.
Hayden St.
Queen's Park
MUSEUM
Charles St.
Charles St.
St. Marys St.
Isabella St.
Queen's Park
Irwin Ave.
Gloucester St.
Jarvis St.
St. Joseph
Queen's Park Cr. West
Queen's Park Cr. East
WELLESLEY
Wellesley St. West
Wellesley St. East
Maitland St.
Alexander St.
Church St.
Grenville St.
Wood St.
QUEEN'S PARK
COLLEGE
College St.
Maple Leaf Gardens
Carlton St.
Allan Gardens
Gerrard St. West
Gerrard St. East
TTC
Subway stop

teriyaki or chicken teriyaki, served with soup, oshitashi, and green tea. The variety of vegetarian sushi (spinach, carrot, and the like) is notable. So, too, is the vegetarian sukiyaki.

4. MIDTOWN EAST

Around Yonge and Bloor streets are clustered some very fine restaurants.

Like Queen Street 10 years ago, Parliament Street, the main street of Cabbagetown, is experiencing a small renaissance when it comes to restaurants.

In the east end along Danforth Avenue, you'll find yourself in a veritable Little Greece, where streets are lined with taverns and coffee places, where bouzouki music spills out onto the sidewalk and where restaurant after restaurant bears a Greek name.

MODERATE

AMELIA STREET CAFE, 12 Amelia St. Tel. 924-9901.

Cuisine: FRENCH. **Reservations:** Recommended.

$ Prices: Main courses $9–$14; three-course fixed-price meals $12. AE, MC, V.

Open: Lunch Mon–Fri 11:30am–2:30pm; dinner daily 5–10pm.

Personal recommendation led me to the Amelia Street Café, just off Parliament Street, decorated in French-provincial style with pink floral wallpaper, simple bentwood chairs, and marvelous displays of fruits and flowers. In summer you can dine outside on the terrace.

At dinner you will find daily specials, as well as favorites like confit of duck, lamb fines herbes, and steak and frites.

BUDGET

ASTORIA, 390 Danforth Ave. Tel. 463-2838.

Cuisine: GREEK. **Reservations:** Not needed.

$ Prices: Main courses $10–$13. AE, MC, V.

Open: Daily 11am–12:30am.

Astoria is a little fancier than its neighbor, Santorini, with an outdoor patio complete with fountain. Prices are moderate for dishes like shish kebab and 12-ounce New York steaks.

BUMPKINS, 21 Gloucester St. Tel. 922-8655.

Cuisine: CONTINENTAL. **Reservations:** Required for large parties only.

$ Prices: Main courses $7–$15. AE, DC, MC, V.

Open: Lunch Mon–Fri noon–2:30pm; dinner Mon–Sat 5:30–11pm.

Bumpkins was one of the first Toronto restaurants to serve interesting continental cuisine at moderate prices, and it's still around, living up to its reputation for good value. The dishes—roast leg of lamb, salmon with hollandaise, duck with cherry sauce, shrimp with garlic-lemon sauce—may not be exotic but the prices sure are: most items are priced from $7 to $15. In addition, there's a good selection of appetizers, including the avocado and crab and the oysters Rockefeller, plus a choice of desserts.

OMONIA, 426 Danforth Ave. Tel. 465-2129.

Cuisine: GREEK. **Reservations:** Required for parties of five or more.

$ **Prices:** Main courses $8–$15. AE, DC, MC, V.

Open: Daily noon–midnight.

Omonia, at Chester Street, is one of the east end's most popular Greek restaurants. It has a large outdoor dining area and up front, in the window, you can watch lamb turning on a spit. Barbecued specialties; souvlaki; chicken, pork, and steak dishes; pizza; pasta; and burgers are served. The tiles, clay oven, and blue-and-white tablecloths provide an authentic ambience.

OUZERI, 500A Danforth Ave. Tel. 778-0500.

Cuisine: GREEK/TAPAS. **Reservations:** Not accepted.

$ **Prices:** Main courses $6–$10. AE, MC, V.

Open: Mon–Fri noon–2am, Fri–Sat noon–4am. Lunch served until 4pm, dips and appetizers only 4–5pm.

This is the hot place out here. It's spirited, casual, and fun. People either jam the few small circular tables outside or occupy the tables inside, drinking one of the numerous international beers or wines by the glass. It's all *très* continental, with tile floors, sun-drenched pastel hues, and eclectic art objects.

The food is good and cheap. It runs the gamut from all kinds of seafood (oysters marinated in capers and wine, sardines, calamari, broiled octopus, and crab with lemonata) and all kinds of meat (pork, lamb, and beef kebabs) to various vegetables, rice, pasta, and phyllo pies. Various snacks, too, complete the menu, like hummus, babaganoush, taramosalata, mushrooms à la Grecque, and dolmades. At lunch Ouzeri dishes out its version of dim sum, called "meze sum"—hot and cold appetizers that are proffered on trays or wheeled by on carts. Sunday brunch here is a filling repast that begins with a buffet spread of appetizers and proceeds through cooked-to-order main courses. It's a frenetic scene, especially at night.

THE PALACE, 722 Pape Ave. Tel. 463-3393.

Cuisine: GREEK. **Reservations:** Recommended at dinner.

$ **Prices:** Main courses $13–$19. AE, DC, MC, V.

Open: Daily 11am–1am.

Around the corner from Danforth Avenue the Palace sports a more "decorated" atmosphere with whitewashed walls and Greek pictures and accents. Prices are slightly higher than those at other Greek restaurants in the area—$10 to $19 for chicken Greek style or stuffed lamb and similar items.

THE PLUME, 557 Parliament St. Tel. 921-0769.

Cuisine: CONTINENTAL. **Reservations:** Recommended.

$ **Prices:** Main courses $9–$14; daily specials around $12. MC, V.

Open: Dinner only, Mon–Thurs 5–10pm, Fri–Sat 5–11pm.

A simple but inviting restaurant, the Plume features bistro fare like grilled chicken suprême with raspberry sauce; zucchini stuffed with tomato, onion, spinach, basil, and cheese; steak au poivre; or leg of lamb with mint sauce. If you're adventurous, try their famous dessert—ice cream with crushed pineapple sautéed in Madras curry-cream sauce.

THE ROUND WINDOW, 729 Danforth Ave. Tel. 465-3892.

Cuisine: ARMENIAN. **Reservations:** Not needed.

$ Prices: Main courses $11–$22. AE, DC, MC, V.
Open: Dinner only, Tues–Sat 5:30–11pm, Sun 5–11pm.

The Round Window is a dark and intimate Armenian spot where you can feast on finely cooked fish—rainbow trout, calamari, or a seafood platter, for example.

VIVA, 459 Bloor St. W. Tel. 922-8482.
Cuisine: MEXICAN. **Reservations:** Accepted only for large parties.
$ Prices: Main courses $6–$11. AE, DC, MC, V.
Open: Daily 10am–1am.

Viva is a large restaurant filled with happy folks slurping down sangría at long family-style tables, while a Mexican music group performs in the back and the tamale machine chugs along up front, churning dough in a large bowl. Colorful paper decorations hang from the ceiling, and a few masks and other artifacts decorate the long bar area. The food can be shared or enjoyed individually. The choices are wide. You can roll your own fajitas using any of nine ingredients—from beef and chorizo to eggplant and peppers. There's a number of barbecue dishes like chicken with mole or with achiote and pineapple, and several dinners like salmon with basil, garlic, and lime or chorizo with mustard and honey. All are tasty and deserve to be washed down with a pitcher of sangría.

5. UPTOWN

EXPENSIVE

AUBERGE DU POMMIER, 4150 Yonge St. Tel. 222-2220.
Cuisine: FRENCH. **Reservations:** Required.
$ Prices: Main courses $19–$25. AE, MC, V.
Open: Lunch Mon–Fri noon–3pm; dinner Mon–Fri 5:30–10pm, Sat 5:30–11pm.

At William Carson, north of York Mills on the west side, Auberge du Pommier re-creates a corner of the French countryside in the forecourt of a corporate center. Flowers surround the house. Inside, beyond the wine display, flagstone floors and stone walls provide a cool atmosphere in the sunken dining room; in summer, seated under the striped awning, you'd swear you were in France.

The cuisine is nouvelle French. The dozen entrées might include salmon in layers of puff pastry with leek purée served on a fume of creamed fish, crispy duck with honey garlic and balsamic vinegar, or tiger shrimp and sea scallops with tangy Southeast Asian–style peanut-butter sauce. This is a pretty, romantic, atmospheric experience; the food is secondary.

CENTRO, 2472 Yonge St. Tel. 483-2211.
Cuisine: ITALIAN. **Reservations:** Recommended.
$ Prices: Main courses $19–$25. AE, DC, MC, V.
Open: Dinner only, Mon–Sat 5–11:30pm.

Just north of Eglinton Avenue, Centro exhibits grand Italian style—it's a huge space with dramatic columns, a balcony, a wine bar, brilliant murals, and ultramodern Milan-style furnishings.

The cuisine is Italian with a California accent. Among the dishes might be black tiger shrimp cooked in a wok with garlic, lemon grass, and butter and served with shiitake mushrooms, peppers, and Oriental noodles; grilled, aged Santa Fe sirloin steak with Szechuan sauce; or New Orleans–style blackened grouper with a lime, tequila, shallot, and olive-oil mignonette, accompanied by curried yams and gumbo relish. There are also several pasta dishes as well as pizza cooked in a wood-burning oven. To start, try the peppered beef carpaccio or the warm herbed and pine-nut–crusted goat cheese. The international wine list is extraordinary.

THE LOBSTER TRAP, 1962 Avenue Rd. Tel. 787-3211.
Cuisine: SEAFOOD. **Reservations:** Recommended.
$ Prices: Complete dinners $22.50–$30. AE, DC, MC, V.
Open: Dinner only, daily 5–11pm.

People wend their way north to the Lobster Trap, just north of Lawrence Avenue, for one reason only—and that really should be stressed—it's the only place in the city where you can still pick out a one- to four-pound live lobster for an honest and fair price. You may even be sitting next to a celebrity in this dining room, where the tables have brown gingham tablecloths and most are sheltered under a shingled construction to evoke a maritime atmosphere.

For a dinner with clam chowder or lobster bisque, a salad, rolls and butter, french fries or rice, and a beverage, and a one-pound lobster, steamed or broiled and served with drawn butter, you will pay $22.50. Prices rise gradually to $30 for a 1½-pound crustacean. Other fish dinners are available, but stick to the lobster.

N 44, 2537 Yonge St. Tel. 487-4897.
Cuisine: INTERNATIONAL. **Reservations:** Recommended.
$ Prices: Main courses $20–$25. AE, DC, MC, V.
Open: Dinner only, Mon–Sat 5–11pm.

Just south of Sherwood Avenue, this restaurant is housed in a dramatic space with soaring ceilings. In the back, chefs work in the glassed-in kitchen, which is etched with the compass logo (North 44° is Toronto's latitude). The atmosphere is enhanced by mirrors that sparkle and reflect the flowers displayed in the attached floral holders. The food is equally à la mode. On the dinner menu you might find rack of lamb aged in balsamic vinaigrette and cooked in honey-mustard crust; Caribbean seafood stew of simmered sea scallops with curried potato crisp and coconut-lime sauce; or noodles with hoisin chicken, peppers, shiitake mushrooms, and lemon. Pizzas and pastas are also featured. At lunch there's a nice selection of light dishes, including a tortilla spring roll with barbecue chicken and plum sauce or a lamb burger with goat cheese, onions, and peppers. Besides an extensive wine list, there's a number of wines by the glass. There's even a wine bar upstairs.

PRONTO, 692 Mount Pleasant Rd. Tel. 486-1111.
Cuisine: ITALIAN. **Reservations:** Required.
$ Prices: Main courses $18–$25. AE, DC, MC, V.
Open: Dinner only, daily 5–11:30pm.

Behind its black tile facade, Pronto, just south of Eglinton Avenue, presents a striking and lovely low-ceilinged dining room that is alive and vibrant. In the back, behind a tiled counter, you can see the chefs in their crisp white toques preparing the food. At the center of the room there's always a lavish fresh-flower arrangement. A pianist adds to the atmosphere.

The cuisine matches the decor. The menu changes monthly, but among the appetizers (any of which can be ordered as a main course), you might find lamb sausage with polenta and mushrooms, mussels in white wine and garlic, or a ceviche of sea scallops. For a main course try (if it's available) the bouillabaisse, chock-full of the fresh fish of the day; the tenderloin of pork with sweet potatoes and sun-dried sour cherries; or the grilled lamb with apples and Calvados.

SCARAMOUCHE, 1 Benvenuto Place. Tel. 961-8011.

Cuisine: CONTINENTAL. **Reservations:** Required.
$ **Prices:** Main courses $24–$30; pasta dishes $12. AE, DC, MC, V.
Open: Main room, dinner only, Tues–Sat 6–10pm. Pasta bar, dinner only, Tues–Fri 6–11pm, Sat 6pm–midnight.

Scaramouche has gained a reputation as one of Toronto's top-class restaurants. A little difficult to find (it's located in the basement of an apartment building, four blocks south of St. Clair Avenue and Avenue Road), but it's certainly worth seeking out. Try to get a window seat, which grants a view of the downtown city skyline. The decor, the flower arrangements, and the careful presentation of the food make the experience special.

Although the menu changes frequently, it may feature a selection of hot and cold appetizers, such as an herb crêpe filled with smoked salmon and served with a smoked-salmon-and-leek sauce or an organic vegetable salad with woolich goat cheese. Among the 10 or so entrées, you might enjoy pan-seared salmon on chard à la creme; lobster, sea bass, shrimp, scallops, and salmon simmered in white wine with saffron and herbs; or rack of lamb with gorgonzola and rosemary sauce. You can always select from the pasta bar menu, which offers similar appetizers and exciting variations of fettuccine, linguine, lasagne, and cannelloni.

MODERATE

BIFFI'S BISTRO, 699 Mount Pleasant Rd. Tel. 484-1142.

Cuisine: CONTINENTAL. **Reservations:** Recommended.
$ **Prices:** Pasta $7–$8; main courses less than $10 at lunch, $10–$16 at dinner. AE, MC, V.
Open: Downstairs, Mon–Fri noon–10pm, Sat 5pm–1am. Upstairs, Mon–Sat noon–1am.

A meal at Biffi's Bistro might start with the escargots en croûte or the fettuccine and follow with grilled salmon with crushed black peppercorns in a sauce of cream and fresh mint; breast of chicken braised with leeks and served with white-wine, cream, and bleu-cheese sauce; or veal with scallops and mustard-cream sauce. Among the pastas are rigatoni with porcini mushrooms or tagliatelle with clams, tomatoes, black olives, garlic, and white wine. Check out the mouth-watering desserts, especially the chocolate-raspberry tartufo filled with raspberry ice and topped with strega, the French silk pie, or the chocolate-and-amaretto pie with toasted almonds. At lunch, look for calves' liver with onion and parsley butter and also cannelloni.

BOFINGER, 1507 Yonge St. Tel. 923-2300.

Cuisine: CONTINENTAL. **Reservations:** Required at lunch; recommended at dinner.

$ Prices: Main courses $7–$13. AE, DC, MC, V.

Open: Lunch daily 11:30am–2pm; dinner Sun–Wed 5:30–10pm, Thurs–Sat 5:30–11pm. All-day menu available in the lounge.

Bofinger, at St. Clair Avenue, has been designed as a spacious, mirrored, tiled, and muraled Parisian brasserie. At the front there's a bar set with marble tables. The dining areas have tables widely spaced on tile floors and set under a stained-glass paneled ceiling.

Start with game pâté with cognac, carpaccio, or prosciutto and melon; then proceed to a brochette of prawns and scallops served on a bed of leeks with fennel-and-dill butter, rack of lamb with red cherries and juniper, or halibut with lemon-and-chive butter. Desserts are divine, like the fresh raspberries served in a tulip pastry with raspberry sabayon.

BROWNES BISTRO, 1251 Yonge St. Tel. 924-8132.

Cuisine: FRENCH/BISTRO. **Reservations:** Recommended.

$ Prices: Main courses $11–$16; pizza and pasta $8–$10. AE, MC, V.

Open: Lunch Mon–Fri noon–2:30pm; dinner Mon–Sat 6–11pm.

Just south of St. Clair Avenue is Brownes Bistro. The decor is rather nondescript, but the clientele is well-heeled and the food is well-flavored bistro fare. The menu might list fresh fish with lime coriander or lamb sausage with mashed potato and brown sauce. Pizza and pasta are also available.

CIBO, 1055 Yonge St. Tel. 921-2166.

Cuisine: ITALIAN. **Reservations:** Recommended.

$ Prices: Pastas $9–$13; main courses around $18. AE, DC, MC, V.

Open: Lunch daily noon–3pm; dinner daily 6–11pm.

Just north of Rosedale Avenue is a modish Italian restaurant with a white tile counter out front where you can see the chefs working. In summer there's an outdoor café. The chefs prepare such delights as cozze bianche (fresh steamed mussels with garlic, Pernod, scallions, tomato, and cream) and carpaccio (marinated beef thinly sliced, with a dressing of olive oil and lemon juice, sprinkled with fresh-ground pepper). Besides pastas, there are about 10 entrées to choose from, always including a fish of the day, a few veal dishes—Provimi veal sautéed with mustard, scallions, brandy, and cream, for example—and seafood delights, like grilled swordfish with fresh herbs, pearl onions, and lemon in brown-butter sauce.

GRANO, 2035 Yonge St. Tel. 440-1986.

Cuisine: ITALIAN. **Reservations:** Accepted for parties of six or more.

$ Prices: Main courses $9–$18. AE, DC, MC, V.

Open: Mon–Fri 10am–10:30pm, Sat 9:30am–11pm.

Grano is a wild Italian celebration—a celebration of down-to-earth food served in an atmosphere of washed Mediterranean pastels. It's casual and fun. The wine is served in tumblers; there's a courtyard out back; and the tables are painted in brilliant colors of mustard and cherry. The latest Italian art/posters decorate the walls, and large colorful majolica vessels abound. At the entrance the display counters are filled with a variety of antipasti, and any three (piccolo) or

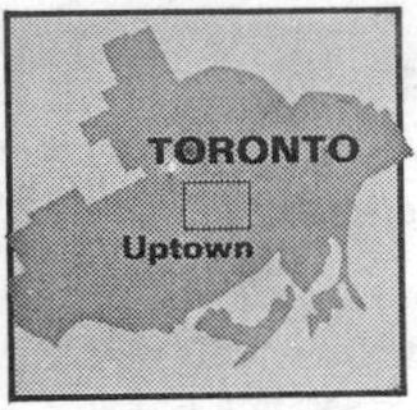

TORONTO
Uptown

ACCOMMODATIONS:

The Bradgate Arms 1
Roehampton Hotel 2

DINING:

Auberge du Pommier 14
Biffi's Bistro 10
Bofinger 8
Brownes Bistro 7
Centro 15
Cibo 5
Grano 3
Jerusalem 17
Just Deserts 4
La Grenouille 12
Le Paradis 1
The Lobster Trap 16
N44 19
Oliver's/Oliver's Bistro 11
Pronto 9
Sabatino's 18
Scaramouche 6
Thai Magic 2
Trapper's 13

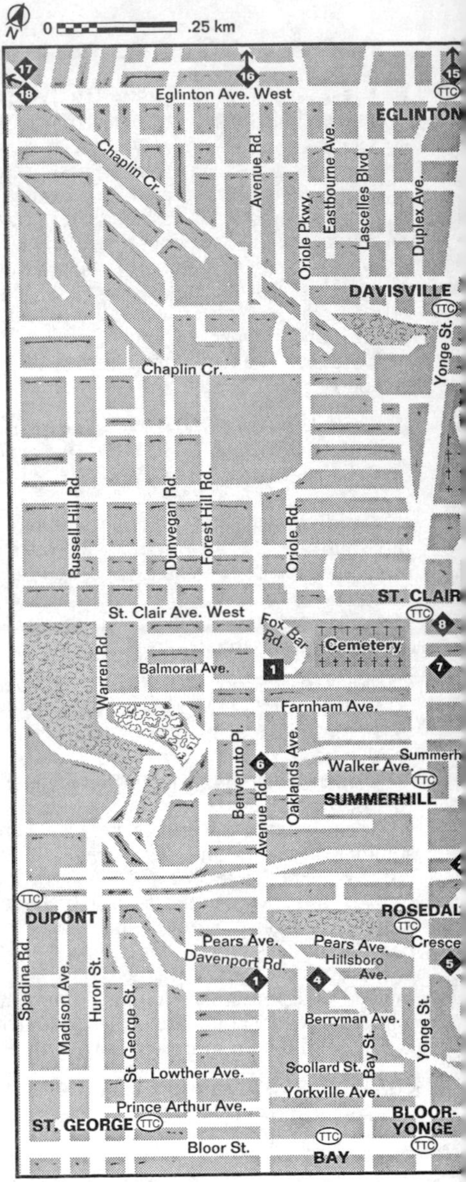

N
0
.25 km
Eglinton Ave. West
EGLINTON
Chaplin Cr.
Avenue Rd.
Oriole Pkwy.
Eastbourne Ave.
Lascelles Blvd.
Duplex Ave.
DAVISVILLE
Yonge St.
Chaplin Cr.
Russell Hill Rd.
Dunvegan Rd.
Forest Hill Rd.
Oriole Rd.
ST. CLAIR
St. Clair Ave. West
Fox Bar Rd.
Cemetery
Warren Rd.
Balmoral Ave.
Farnham Ave.
Benvenuto Pl.
Avenue Rd.
Oaklands Ave.
Walker Ave.
Summerh
SUMMERHILL
DUPONT
ROSEDAL
Cresce
Pears Ave.
Pears Ave.
Hillsboro Ave.
Davenport Rd.
Spadina Rd.
Madison Ave.
Huron St.
St. George St.
Berryman Ave.
Bay St.
Yonge St.
Lowther Ave.
Scollard St.
Yorkville Ave.
Prince Arthur Ave.
ST. GEORGE
BLOOR-YONGE
Bloor St.
BAY
TTC

UPTOWN TORONTO ACCOMMODATIONS & DINING

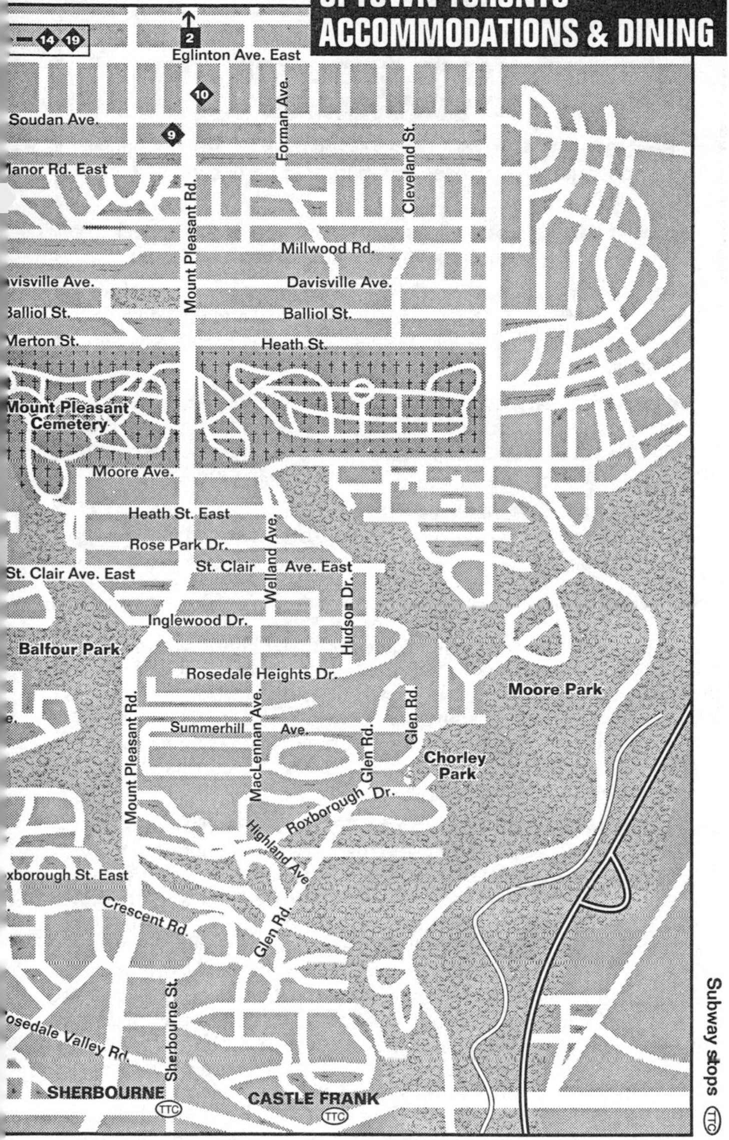

14
19
2
10
9
Eglinton Ave. East
Soudan Ave.
Manor Rd. East
Forman Ave.
Cleveland St.
Mount Pleasant Rd.
Millwood Rd.
Davisville Ave.
Davisville Ave.
Balliol St.
Balliol St.
Merton St.
Heath St.
Mount Pleasant Cemetery
Moore Ave.
Heath St. East
Rose Park Dr.
Welland Ave.
St. Clair Ave. East
St. Clair Ave. East
Hudson Dr.
Inglewood Dr.
Balfour Park
Rosedale Heights Dr.
Moore Park
Glen Rd.
MacLennan Ave.
Summerhill Ave.
Glen Rd.
Chorley Park
Mount Pleasant Rd.
Roxborough Dr.
Highland Ave.
Roxborough St. East
Crescent Rd.
Glen Rd.
Sherbourne St.
Rosedale Valley Rd.
SHERBOURNE
TTC
CASTLE FRANK
TTC
Subway stops
TTC

FROMMER'S COOL FOR KIDS: RESTAURANTS

Ginsberg & Wong *(see p. 95)* Serves the perennial junior favorites—Chinese and burgers, barbecue, and hot dogs.

Toby's Goodeats *(see p. 131)* Enough kid-appealing items to satisfy even the fussiest child. Lots of locations.

Mr. Green Jeans *(see p. 129)* Everything's somehow larger than life here. The selections are broad and include kids' favorites like barbecue and burgers and fabulous shakes and sundaes.

The Old Spaghetti Factory *(see p. 105)* The big warehouse, the carousel, the decor, the meatballs, and the spumoni should keep them happy. If not, they can wander next door and check out the sounds at The Organ Grinder.

The Organ Grinder *(see p. 105)* The organ, the pizza, and the rest of the kid crowd will keep them marvelously entertained.

seven (grande) of these can be ordered, ranging in price from $9 for a small all-vegetable plate to $18 for a large plate of salmon carpaccio. In addition there are several pasta dishes, like the rigatoni siracusa with eggplant, peppers, olives, anchovies, and capers in a spicy tomato sauce and the gnocchi with a pink sauce. The meat or fish entrées change daily. To finish there's tiramisu, biscotti, and a variety of Italian custard-cream desserts.

LA GRENOUILLE, 2387 Yonge St. Tel. 481-3093.

Cuisine: FRENCH. **Reservations:** Recommended.
$ **Prices:** Main courses $14–$20. AE, DC, MC, V.
Open: Lunch Mon–Fri noon–2:30pm; dinner Mon–Fri 5:30–10:30pm, Sat 5:30–11pm.

La Grenouille is a simple uptown French bistro serving reasonably priced, well-prepared food. The atmosphere is provided by candlelight, French music, and a sage-green neon sign reflecting against the vertical blinds at the storefront window. Select from the nine or so entrées—salmon with tomato and cucumber; rabbit with mustard sauce, and frogs' legs, of course, sautéed in garlic butter and sprinkled with fresh parsley and lemon juice. There is a selection of soups, including a Mediterranean fish soup served with Emmenthal, croutons, and rouille; or you can begin with various salads and appetizers, including deep-fried breaded cheese croquettes on a coulis of fresh raspberries or strawberries.

LE PARADIS, 166 Bedford Rd. (north of Davenport). Tel. 921-0995.

Cuisine: FRENCH. **Reservations:** Recommended.
$ **Prices:** Main courses $8–$10. AE, MC, V.
Open: Lunch Mon–Fri noon–2:30pm; dinner Mon–Sat 5:30–11pm, Sun 5:30–10pm.

At night when the french doors are flung open to the street and Le Paradis is filled with chattering diners, you could swear that you're in a residential area of Paris. The room is long and narrow; and the banquettes and tables stretch alongside one wall, facing a bar on the other. European poster and photographs only add to the atmosphere. The offerings are typical bistro fare—chicken roasted with tarragon and flank steak with fries—with some regional specialties like pork chops roasted with green peppercorns and spices or lamb and beef sausage served on couscous. Typical appetizers include mussels and pâté, along with bisque Africaine, which is a purée of peanuts, tomatoes, and coconut milk.

OLIVER'S BISTRO, 2433 Yonge St. Tel. 485-1041.

Cuisine: CONTINENTAL. **Reservations:** Recommended.
$ **Prices:** Main courses $12–$19. AE, MC, V.
Open: Mon–Thurs 11:30am–10:30pm, Fri 11:30am–midnight, Sat noon–midnight, Sun 11am–10pm.

Oliver's Bistro, just north of Eglinton Avenue and upstairs from the restaurant of the same name, is very appealing. Small and cozy with its stone fireplaces, beamed ceiling, and stucco walls, it serves good continental cuisine that might include peppered rib-eye steak with three-peppercorn sauce, frites, and grilled tomato; baked Atlantic salmon on vermouth mousseline and braised leek-and-potato galette; or the house specialty, a bistro grill consisting of a lamb chop, filet mignon, and tiger shrimp on a potato pancake and grilled California vegetables, with a Pommery-rosemary demiglaze.

SABATINO'S, 1144 Eglinton Ave. W. Tel. 783-5829.

Cuisine: ITALIAN. **Reservations:** Recommended.
$ **Prices:** Pastas $10.50–$12.50; main courses $15–$29. AE, MC, V.
Open: Dinner only, Mon–Sat 5–10pm.

Sabatino's, between Bathurst and Dufferin streets, is always crowded with Italian food fanciers dining in a low-lit romantic atmosphere. The cannelloni fiorentina, stuffed with spinach-flecked ricotta cheese and topped with nutmeg, makes a highly recommended pasta intro or main course. Main courses include scampi gratinati, and most of the veal dishes (like veal Pernod or limonc) will be served with fried green and red peppers and cubed potatoes sprinkled with rosemary. For dessert, the profiteroles al cioccolato are delicious.

THAI MAGIC, 1118 Yonge St. Tel. 968-7366.

Cuisine: THAI. **Reservations:** Recommended.
$ **Prices:** Main courses $8–$16. AE, MC, V.
Open: Dinner only, Mon–Sat 5–11pm.

Magical indeed is this long, narrow restaurant filled with orchids, Thai statuary, and artifacts. Warm mauves and greens make it even more inviting and a perfect backdrop for the sophisticated cuisine. Start with a combination plate of appetizers, tom yum kai (a really spicy soup flavored with lemon grass and containing succulent shrimp), or the familiar noodle dish pad Thai. For main courses there are stir-fries and curries (like the flavorsome green curry or shrimp red curry with okra) as well as such dishes as chicken with basil or lobster lemon grass—the last a specialty that uses a unique family recipe.

TRAPPER'S, 3479 Yonge St. Tel. 482-6211.

Cuisine: CONTINENTAL. **Reservations:** Recommended.

$ Prices: Main courses $7–$9 at lunch, $15–$20 at dinner. AE, MC, V.
Open: Lunch Mon–Fri 11:30am–2:30pm; dinner Mon–Sat 5:30–10:30pm, Sun 5:30–9:30pm.

Trapper's, between Lawrence Avenue and York Mills Road, has a seasonally changing menu that might include fettuccine with chicken, spinach, and tomatoes in mustard sauce; lamb with lemon-lime mint sauce; jump-fried duck served with the crackling; breast of chicken with lime and cilantro; and jump-fried shrimp with tomato, red onion, and coriander in a pesto-cream sauce.

BUDGET

JERUSALEM, 955 Eglinton Ave. W. Tel. 783-6494.
Cuisine: MIDDLE EASTERN. **Reservations:** Not accepted.
$ Prices: Appetizers less than $4; main courses $9–$13. AE, MC, V.
Open: Mon–Thurs noon–11pm, Fri–Sat noon–midnight, Sun noon–10pm.

At Jerusalem, just west of Bathurst Street, it's the food and prices that count. The decor is simple—just some hammered-brass tabletops on the walls—but the atmosphere is extremely warm, the service friendly and unhurried. All the appetizers are less than $4—felafel, kibbeh (a cracked-wheat roll stuffed with ground meat, onions, and pine nuts), various styles of hummus, tahina, and tabouli (a delicious blend of cracked wheat with chopped tomatoes, onions, parsley, mint, lemon, and olive oil). You can follow them with liver fried in garlic and hot-pepper sauce, siniyeh (mixed ground lamb and beef with onions, parsley, and pine nuts, oven baked with tahina sauce), and lamb or beef shish kebab.

JUST DESSERTS, 306 Davenport Rd. Tel. 922-6824.
Cuisine: DESSERTS/QUICHE.
$ Prices: Desserts $4–$6. No credit cards.
Open: Sun–Thurs 8am–3am, Fri–Sat 8am–5am.

Diet books, Optifast, and Weight Watchers may be ubiquitous, but Just Desserts, bold enough to buck the trend, is open almost around the clock on weekends for those in need of a sugar fix. Fifty-two desserts are available—as many as 14 different cheesecakes, 10 assorted pies, plus a whole array of gâteaux, tortes, meringues, and the like. I don't need to describe them—just go, order what you crave with a cappuccino or coffee, savor every bite, and feel bad afterward. Enjoy yourself in a nostalgic atmosphere created by oak swivel chairs, black-tiled tables, and the old-movie/Broadway melodies. While you're here you might like to purchase one of the many whimsical cookie jars.

OLIVER'S, 2433 Yonge St. Tel. 485-1051.
Cuisine: FRENCH/BISTRO. **Reservations:** Not needed.
$ Prices: Café main courses $7–$14. AE, MC, V.
Open: Mon–Wed 7am–11pm, Thurs 7am–midnight, Fri–Sat 7am–1am, Sun 9am–10pm.

Although Oliver's, just north of Eglinton, has expanded incredibly over the years, the bakery is still the heart of the business, turning out fresh breads, croissants, danish, muffins, pastries, tortes, flans, and pies daily. In the adjacent Food Shop you can purchase fine foods to add to the croissants—salads, pâtés, pastas, and gourmet take-out of all kinds. The café behind the bakery on the ground floor is also very popular and serves a wide range of dishes—everything from lasagne to salmon in phyllo.

6. SPECIALTY DINING

HOTEL DINING

CHANTERELLES, in L'Hôtel, 225 Front St. W. Tel. 597-1400.

Cuisine: CONTINENTAL. **Reservations:** Recommended.

$ Prices: Main courses $11–$16 at lunch, $20–$29 at dinner. AE, MC, V.

Open: Lunch Mon–Fri noon–2:30pm; dinner Mon–Sat 6–10:30pm.

Screened off by latticework and raised from the hotel lobby, this elegant dining room has won major awards for its cuisine. If you can't afford the caviar, start with the Pithivier pastry (filled with duckling and wild mushrooms and served with seasonal greens in chervil vinaigrette) or the unusual lobster bisque, flavored with ginger. Among the dozen or so entrées, which include low-salt and low-fat items, you might enjoy tiger shrimp wrapped in zucchini with pepper coulis, rack of lamb stuffed with prunes, or suprême of chicken grilled with rice vinegar and sesame oil.

CHIARO'S, in the King Edward, 37 King St. E. Tel. 863-9700.

Cuisine: FRENCH/CONTINENTAL. **Reservations:** Recommended.

$ Prices: Appetizers $6–$15; main courses $19–$36. AE, CB, DC, MC, V.

Open: Lunch Mon–Fri noon–2pm; dinner Mon–Sat 6–10:30pm.

For formal dining, Chiaro's, decorated in stunning gray lacquer with etched-glass panels and French-style chairs, specializes in fine French and continental cuisine. Start with smoked salmon carved from the trolley or a terrine of forest mushrooms with venison carpaccio. You might follow with a poached Dover sole, rack of lamb with toasted hazelnuts, or lemon- and soya-marinated swordfish.

THE ROOF RESTAURANT, in the Park Plaza, 4 Avenue Rd. Tel. 924-4571.

Cuisine: CONTINENTAL. **Reservations:** Recommended.

$ Prices: Main courses $19–$23. AE, MC, V.

Open: Dinner only, daily 5:30–10:30pm.

From this elegant room lit with brilliant chandeliers you have a splendid view of the city out over the terrace. For a luxurious start, try the lobster-and-truffle ravioli with vanilla-and-champagne beurre blanc or the crispy Stilton-and-leek fritters with port-wine sauce. Follow with the Thai chicken, the scallops simmered in tarragon-and-vermouth sauce, or the beef tenderloin with a sauce of cabernet sauvignon and horseradish. Desserts are a delight to the eye and a disaster to the diet—decadent chocolate cheesecake and maple crême brûlée are two examples.

SANSSOUCI, in the Sutton Place, 955 Bay St. Tel. 924-9221.

Cuisine: CONTINENTAL. **Reservations:** Recommended.

$ **Prices:** Appetizers $9–$11; main courses $18–$30; Sun brunch $13.95. AE, MC, V.

Open: Dinner only, daily 6–10:30pm.

The Sanssouci is one of the city's most beautiful dining rooms with its Gobelins, fresh azaleas, silver, and crystal. Breakfast, lunch, and dinner are served here, along with a spectacular weekend brunch. At dinner the menu might feature crisp duck ravioli with arugula and Thai dipping sauce or a delicious hot zucchini Rösti with thinly sliced smoked salmon and lemon to start. For main courses there are a dozen or so choices, including a couple of light dishes, like a bamboo steamer filled with vegetables. The more robust choices might include roast rack of lamb fried with garlic, red snapper grilled with thyme, or guinea fowl with tarragon reduction. Save room for a soufflé or one of the exquisite pastries and desserts. The wine list is extensive, and dinner is served to piano accompaniment enhanced by candlelight.

SEASONS, in the Inn on the Park, 1100 Eglinton Ave. E. Tel. 444-2561.

Cuisine: CONTINENTAL. **Reservations:** Recommended.

$ **Prices:** Appetizers $5–$12; main courses $20–$30. AE, DC, MC, V.

Open: Lunch Mon–Fri noon–2:30pm; dinner daily 6–10pm; brunch Sun 10:30am–3pm.

A stylish garden atmosphere is the backdrop for sophisticated continental cuisine in Seasons. Start with sautéed shrimp cakes with coriander butter or curried lobster ravioli in a fennel mango broth. Then follow with barbequed venison with clover honey glaze, crisp duckling with fried vegetable roll and hoisin sauce, beef tenderloin with pinot-noir sauce and oyster mushrooms, or fettuccine with grilled sea scallops and roast yellow-pepper sauce. Alternative cuisine is featured for the health-conscious. At brunch there's a buffet with omelets cooked to order and hot dishes served.

TRUFFLES, in the Four Seasons, 21 Avenue Rd. Tel. 964-0411.

Cuisine: CONTINENTAL. **Reservations:** Recommended.

$ **Prices:** Appetizers $7–$19; main courses $23–$35; fixed-price dinner $29. AE, DC, MC, V.

Open: Dinner only, daily 6–11pm.

This is one of the city's premier hotel dining rooms, lavishly decorated with antique tapestries and paintings and serving exquisite cuisine. The pièce de résistance among the appetizers might be the spaghettini with black truffles or the hot sautéed duck liver and sun-dried cherries. Among the outstanding specialties, which include alternative-cuisine choices, you might enjoy the crisp potato-crusted black bass; prawns with lemon grass and basil; herb-roasted chicken breast; eggplant-and-shallot risotto; or filet of beef with red-wine sauce. Top it all off with a selection of sherbets served in fruit shells with chocolate chopsticks—lime, orange, lemon, passionfruit, and pineapple.

ZACHARY'S, in the Bristol Place, 950 Dixon Rd. Tel. 675-9444.

Cuisine: NOUVELLE. **Reservations:** Recommended.
$ **Prices:** Appetizers $9.50–$13; main courses $25–$35. AE, DC, MC, V.
Open: Lunch Mon–Fri noon–2:30pm; dinner Mon–Sat 6–10:30pm; brunch Sun 11am–3pm.

Zachary's dining room is delightfully contemporary and graced with a kaleidoscopic tapestry hung over white tile. Here the specialty is the nouvelle cuisine, featuring such exciting dishes as timbale of fresh salmon tartare, julienne of leeks and truffles, thin slices of salmon sautéed in butter with sorrel sauce, and pineapple-and-mango soufflé. The hot-and-cold Sunday buffet brunch is also known for its distinguished sweets table and the chance to savor (among other things) a salmon-and-caviar omelet.

DINING COMPLEXES

Ⓢ **DRAGON CITY** In the basement of Dragon City, the Asian shopping complex on Spadina Avenue at Dundas Street, you'll find tables surrounded by a series of counters frequented by the local Chinatown residents. You could be anywhere in Asia. The food choices include Indonesian, Japanese, Chinese, Taiwanese, noodles, and seafood. A real Asian Toronto experience.

EATON CENTRE EATERIES Eaton Centre has two street-level entrances (Level 1 and Level 2). Above these, Level 3 has shopping and Level 4 houses offices. Below them, Level 0 also has shopping.

Many eating opportunities are found throughout. On Level 0 there's the North Side Food Court, consisting of a number of fast-food counters—**Thai Pearl** (curried chicken, noodles), **Bread & Bowl** (sandwiches), **Points East** (Chinese), **Aïda's Falafel;** London-style **fish and chips, Mrs. Vanellis** (Italian), **BBQ Delight,** and many more, with attractive seating in the middle. Everything is under $5, with most items less than $4.

On Level 1 there's the **Second Cup** and **Sweet Sue Pastries,** as well as the South Side Food Court featuring deli at **Druxy's,** Italian at **Sbarro,** fish at **Fins and Shells,** submarines at **Submarine Place,** noodles and teriyaki at **Made in Japan,** sandwiches at **Blend and Bowl,** burgers at **Licks,** Chinese at **Manchu-Wok,** Mexican at **Los Rios,** and Greek at **Jimmy the Greek.** In other words, it's all here. Choose your cuisine, help yourself, and take your food to the tables in the center of this food park where almost everything is less than $4 or $5.

If you prefer to sit down in a licensed restaurant, there are several on Level 2, including **Lime Rickeys** for burgers and barbecue items, as well as more expensive dishes like Cajun steak; **Elephant & Castle,** an English-style pub with good shepherd's pie and fish and chips and many other snacks, including quiche. It stocks a wide selection of beers and single-malt whiskies. **Toby's Goodeats** has burgers and a lot more at reasonable prices.

On Level 3 the options are **East Side Mario's** and **Mr. Green Jeans,** which has a huge menu featuring honey-mustard chicken, burgers, and sandwiches of all kinds priced from $5 to $8. Be prepared to wait at the latter. Also on Level 3 there are several counters along Gourmet Passage—among them **Cultures,** serving salads, sandwiches, and fresh fruit for $3.50 and up; and **Pete and Marty's,** a more formal restaurant.

Certainly, you'll not want for food as you shop Eaton Centre.

HARBOURFRONT DINING Upstairs in Queen's Quay a whole medley of counters offers everything from croûtes and pita sandwiches at **La Bouchée,** to strawberry tarts and such dishes as wienerschnitzel on a kaiser at **Sweet Gallery.** Most items cost $3 to $6. At **Sbarro's** you can choose among pizza (vegetarian even), spaghetti with all kinds of sauces, veal cutlet, lasagne, sausages, and a salad bar. All the items are less than $7.

Two more formal restaurants are also located here. The **Pink Pearl** offers good Chinese at pretty pink-clothed tables. Dishes range from $8 to $14. The **Coyote Grill** has burritos and nachos priced from $6 to $12.

Downstairs are several restaurants, each one also operating an outdoor terrace/café from which you can watch the sailboats and other craft plying the harbor. **Lakeview Fruiterie** offers soups, salads, and fresh fruits of all sorts, with most items for less than $5. **Spinnakers** has an outdoor waterfront patio and an inside dining room and a cocktail bar, too. Here you can enjoy fish and chips, baked halibut, salads, pasta, and more, priced from $10 to $17. **Baguette** has chocolate-almond croissants and makes tuna melts and other sandwiches and salads, all for less than $4. **Queen's Quay Food Shoppe** also has great baked goods and coffees.

Also on the Harbourfront on Pier 4 are **Wallymagoo's** (tel. 360-6248), a nautical-theme restaurant known for its seafood pizza and seafood luncheon buffets and afternoon jazz on Saturday and Sunday; **Pier 4 Storehouse** (tel. 863-1440), which features a raw bar and serves steak, seafood, and pasta priced from $13 to $26; and **Tony's Fish & Lobster** (tel. 360-5865), serving lobster, crab, and other shellfish. It's open Monday through Saturday from noon to 1am and from noon to 11pm on Sunday.

Outside, at Pier 4 the **Water's Edge Patio and Bar** has a cabana and serves hot dogs and other snacks.

VILLAGE BY THE GRANGE Conveniently located south of the Art Gallery, Village by the Grange, at 71 McCaul St., contains the **International Food Market,** where you'll find everything from Chinese, Middle Eastern, Japanese, and Mexican fast food to Coney Island hot dogs and a booth specializing in schnitzels. Salads, burgers, Japanese specialties, meat pies, and more are also readily available. All the fare is around $4 to $5.

LIGHT, CASUAL & FAST FOOD

THE BAGEL, 285 College St. Tel. 966-7555.

Cuisine: DELI.
$ Prices: Everything less than $9. V.
Open: Sun–Thurs 7am–10pm, Fri–Sat 7am–11pm.

You have to be a member of the "clean plate club" if you want to eat at the Bagel—otherwise the waitresses will scold you with "C'mon, eat already." Blintzes, bagels, lox, and cream cheese are the tops at this characterful spot, although special Oriental dishes are also available, along with sandwiches and dinner plates.

BLOOR STREET DINER, 50 Bloor St. W. Tel. 928-3105.

Cuisine: LIGHT FARE.
$ Prices: Most items $4–$10.
Open: Daily 11am–3am.

The Bloor Street Diner is a convenient place to stop for a wide selection of reasonably priced food—from a grilled-cheese sandwich or pizza to veal parmigiana.

HUGHIE'S BURGERS, 22 Front St. W. Tel. 364-2242.
Cuisine: BURGERS.
$ Prices: Everything less than $8.50. AE, DC, MC, V.
Open: Mon–Thurs 11:30am–11:30pm, Fri–Sat 11:30am–midnight, Sun 4:30–10pm.

Hughie's offers a variety of burgers, sandwiches, and salads. There's even a 10-ouncer for $8.50. A popular, pleasant hangout, especially in early evening.

MEYER'S DELI, 69 Yorkville St. Tel. 960-4780.
Cuisine: DELI.
$ Prices: Everything $5–$10. AE, DC, MC, V.
Open: Daily 7:30am–1am.

One place for a full-size meal at a reasonable price is Meyer's Deli. Sandwiches, burgers, and deli favorites are supplemented by familiar appetizers like chopped liver and gefilte fish, knishes, and such entrées as brisket of beef and sole amandine. Meyer's is also conveniently located for the theater and concert hall at 185 King St.

SHOPSY'S, 33 Yonge St. Tel. 365-3333.
Cuisine: DELI.
$ Prices: Sandwiches $5–$8. AE, MC, V.
Open: Mon–Wed 7am–midnight, Thurs–Fri 7am–1am, Sat 8am–1am, Sun 8am–midnight.

Right across from the O'Keefe Centre, Shopsy's occupies spiffy quarters, sporting an outdoor patio arrayed with brilliant yellow umbrellas. They serve huge stuffed deli sandwiches. Good breakfast spot, too. Look for Shopsy's carts on the streets.

TOBY'S GOODEATS, 93 Bloor St. W. Tel. 925-2171.
Cuisine: BURGERS.
$ Prices: Burgers $4–$6.50. AE, MC, V.
Open: Mon–Sat 11:30am–3am, Sun 11am–1am.

Capture those childhood dreams of milkshakes, Coke floats, and a good burger along with the rest of the crowd at Toby's Goodeats, a 1950s-style hamburger joint. The decor suits: a schizophrenic combination of Formica tables, cookie jars, and funky posters, and the traditional brick-and-plants look. It's very crowded at lunchtime. A dozen burgers are priced from $4 to $6.50 for a 10-ouncer. In addition, there are salads, sandwiches, pizza, and pasta.

Toby's Goodeats can also be found at 1502 Yonge St. (tel. 921-1062), 2293 Yonge St. (tel. 481-9183), 725 Yonge St. (tel. 925-9908), in the Eaton Centre (tel. 591-6994), 542 Church St. (tel. 929-0411), and First Canadian Place (tel. 366-3953).

FOR BRUNCH

Nearly every restaurant in Toronto offers Saturday and Sunday brunch. Here are just a few of my favorites (see the complete listings above): **Le Rendez-Vous,** 14 Prince Arthur Ave. (tel. 961-6111); **Hazelton Club,** in Hazelton Lanes, 55 Avenue Rd. (tel. 923-6944), Saturday only; **Sanssouci,** at Sutton Place, 955 Bay St. (tel. 924-9221); and the **Boulevard Café,** 161 Harbord St. (tel. 961-7676). Most major hotels also offer splendid buffet-style brunches.

CHAPTER 6

WHAT TO SEE & DO IN TORONTO

It takes five or six days to really see Toronto's highlights. Although some of the major sights are centrally located, there are also several favorites outside the downtown core, and these take extra time and effort to reach. Ideally, you should spend one day each at Ontario Place, the Ontario Science Centre, Canada's Wonderland, and Harbourfront. In fact, that's what the kids will definitely want to do. Then there's also the zoo, which could take a whole day complete with a picnic.

The Art Gallery of Ontario, Chinatown, and the Royal Ontario Museum could be combined in a pinch, but the day might be too museum-oriented for some. Ontario Place could conceivably be combined with Fort York and Exhibition Place. En route to Canada's Wonderland, you could stop in at Black Creek Pioneer Village, but I don't recommend that since it will cut into your time at Canada's Wonderland, which really requires a day.

As you can see, there are numerous major attractions in Toronto worthy of a whole day's visit. There are also many other downtown sights—the CN Tower, the Eaton Centre, Yorkville, Queen Street, City Hall, and Casa Loma—that any visitor will want to explore. Depending on your interests and whether you have children, there's enough to keep you going for several weeks in Toronto. But that said, below are a few suggestions.

SUGGESTED ITINERARIES

IF YOU HAVE TWO DAYS **Day 1** Get to the Ontario Science Centre the minute it opens and then come back into town to spend the late afternoon/early evening at Harbourfront or Ontario Place.

Day 2 Start early at the Kensington Market and from there walk up to College Street and through the university area to the Royal Ontario Museum. Leave enough time to wander through Yorkville and browse in some of the stores and galleries before they close.

IF YOU HAVE THREE DAYS **Days 1–2** Spend the first two days as outlined above.

Day 3 Explore Chinatown and stop at the Art Gallery. Then pop over to the Eaton Centre and head down to Queen Street to explore Queen Street Village in the early evening.

IF YOU HAVE FIVE DAYS Days 1–3 Spend Days 1–3 as discussed above.

Day 4 Visit either Canada's Wonderland (if the family's in tow) or the McMichael Collection in Kleinburg. Black Creek Pioneer Village could be squeezed in, too.

Day 5 Take a trip to the Toronto Islands and while away the day among the lagoons, picnicking, relaxing, or bicycling.

1. THE TOP ATTRACTIONS

ONTARIO PLACE, 955 Lakeshore Blvd. W. Tel. 314-9900 or 314-9811.

When this 96-acre recreation complex on Lake Ontario opened in 1971, it seemed futuristic—and more than 20 years later it still does (admittedly, it was renovated in 1989). From a distance you'll see five steel-and-glass pods suspended on columns 105 feet above the lake; three artificial islands; and, alongside, a huge geodesic dome. The five pods contain a multimedia theater, a live children's theater, a high-technology exhibit, and displays that tell the story of Ontario in vivid kaleidoscopic detail. The dome houses Cinesphere, where a 60- by 80-foot screen shows specially made IMAX movies—currently "Antarctica" and "Tropical Rainforest."

Under an enormous orange canopy, the Children's Village provides a well-supervised area where children under 12 can scramble over rope bridges; bounce on an enormous trampoline; slide down a twisting chute; and, most popular of all, squirt water pistols and garden hoses, swim, and generally drench one another in the water-play section. Afterward, parents can use the convenient changing room and washroom facilities before moving on to three specialty children's theaters.

A stroll around the complex will unearth two marinas full of yachts and other craft; the HMCS *Haida*, a World War II and Korean War destroyer; a miniature golf course; grassland for picnics; and a wide variety of restaurants and snack bars serving everything from Chinese, Irish, German, and Canadian food to hot dogs and hamburgers. And don't miss the wildest rides in town—the Wilderness Adventure Ride, the Water Slide, and bumper boats. For something more peaceful, there are pedal or remote-control boats.

At night the Forum, an outdoor amphitheater that accommodates 10,000, comes alive. During the summer all manner of entertainment is held here, from the Toronto Symphony and National Ballet of Canada, to concerts by Patti Labelle, Dionne Warwick, and Bruce Cockburn.

Admission: Free, except during the CNE, when it's $7.50 ($2 after 9pm) adults, $3 seniors, $2 children under 12. There is a charge for rides. Parking is $9.

Open: Mid-May to Labor Day, Mon–Sat 10:30am–1am, Sun 10am–11pm. **Subway:** Bathurst or Dufferin; then take the bus south to Exhibition. **Bus:** Call TTC Information (tel. 393-4636) for special bus service details.

HARBOURFRONT CENTRE, Queen's Quay W. Tel. 973-4000.

The federal government took over a 96-acre strip of prime waterfront land in 1972 to preserve the waterfront vista—and since then Torontonians have rediscovered their lakeshore. Abandoned warehouses, shabby depots, and crumbling factories have been refurbished, and a tremendous urban park now stretches on and around the old piers.

The resulting Harbourfront has to be one of Toronto's most exciting happenings. Sailboats, motorboats, houseboats, ferries, and other craft ply the water or sit at anchor dockside, their happy denizens dining or drinking in one of the many waterside cafés, shopping, or attending one of the entertainment events that are very much part of the waterfront scene. It's a great place to spend the whole day.

Queen's Quay, at the foot of York Street, is the closest quay to town, and it's the first point you'll encounter as you approach from the Westin Harbour Castle. From here, boats depart for tours of the harbor and islands. An old renovated warehouse now houses a dance theater, plus two floors of shops, restaurants, and waterfront cafés.

After exploring Queen's Quay, walk along the glorious waterfront promenade to **York Quay,** 235 Queen's Quay W. (tel. 364-5665), with a small pond for electric model boats and a children's play area. Here the Water's Edge Café, overlooking the pond, sells pizza, burgers, and hot dogs, and there are also outlets selling Chinese and Italian specialties, plus a bakery. You'll also find an information center, plus three art galleries, two theaters, and a craft studio where artisans blow glass, throw pots, and silk-screen. In the children's play center you might find youngsters having a jubilant time decorating one another's faces with finger paints.

From here, take the footbridge to **Pier 4,** crossing over the sailboats moored below, to the Pier 4 Sailing School, Wallymagoo's marine bar, and the Pier 4 Storehouse. There's a deck menu that offers light snacks. At the **Pier 4 Sailing School,** 283 Queen's Quay W. (tel. 366-0390), you can rent boats for $60 per day if you're a qualified sailor.

The **Harbourfront Antiques Market,** at 390 Queen's Quay W., at the foot of Spadina Avenue (tel. 340-8377), will keep antiques-lovers busy browsing for hours. More than 100 antiques dealers spread out their wares—jewelry, china, furniture, toys, and books. Indoor parking is adjacent to the market, and there's also a cafeteria serving fresh salads, sandwiches, and desserts for that oft-needed rest stop. Open May through October, Tuesday through Friday from noon to 6pm and Saturday and Sunday from 10am to 6pm; November through April, Tuesday through Friday from noon to 5pm and Saturday and Sunday from 10am to 6pm.

At the west end of the park stands **Bathurst Pier,** which resembles a park. Here you'll find a large sports field for romping around, plus two adventure playgrounds, one for older kids and the other (supervised) for three- to seven-year-olds.

More than 4,000 events take place annually at Harbourfront, including a Harbourfront Reading Festival that is held every Tuesday on York Quay, attracting some very eminent writers; Canada's largest antiques market; films; dance; theater; music; children's events; multicultural festivals; marine events; and other exciting programs. Two of the most important events are the annual Children's Festival

IMPRESSIONS

A global psychiatrist, if asked to take a look at Toronto's rather unhealthy obsession with the CN Tower, would advise the city to take a cold shower and lie down on the couch for a spell.
—ALLAN FOTHERINGHAM, *MACLEAN'S* (1975)

---

and the International Festival of Authors. Find out about Harbourfront programs by calling 973-3000. Most activities are free.

Admission: Free.

Open: Year round. **Subway:** The Light Rapid Transit (LRT) line connects Harbourfront with Union Station.

THE TORONTO ISLANDS. Tel. 392-8193 for ferry information.

A stolid little ferry will take you to 612 acres of island park crisscrossed by shady paths and quiet waterways—a glorious spot to walk, play tennis, cycle, feed the ducks, putter around in boats, picnic, or just sit.

Children will love **Centreville** (tel. 363-1112), a 19-acre old-time amusement park built and designed especially for youngsters without the usual neon signs and the aroma of greasy hot-dog stands. Instead you'll find a turn-of-the-century village complete with Main Street, tiny shops, a firehouse, and a small working farm where the kids can pet lambs and chicks and enjoy pony rides. They'll love trying out the miniature antique cars, fire engines, old-fashioned train, authentic 1890s carousel, flume ride, and aerial cars. Admission is free, but there is a charge for the rides.

Admission: Round-trip ferry, $2.75 adults, $1.50 seniors, $1 children under 14.

Open: Centreville, mid-May to Labor Day only, daily 10am–sunset. **Transportation:** Ferries operate all day, leaving from the docks at the base of Bay Street. Take the subway to Union Station, then the Bay Street bus south.

CN TOWER, 301 Front St. W. Tel. 360-8500.

As you approach the city, the first thing you'll notice is this slender needlelike structure and the tiny colored elevators that glide to the top of the 1,815-foot-high tower—the tallest free-standing structure in the world.

As you enter the base of the tower, just look up through the atrium to the top . . . yes, that's where you're going. Glass-walled elevators on the outside walls of the tower whisk you to the 1,136-foot-high seven-level sky pod in just under a minute. You can sometimes see all the way to Niagara Falls or even to Buffalo. One of the two observation levels is partially open to allow you to experience that dizzying sensation of height (vertigo sufferers beware).

The pod also contains broadcasting facilities and a revolving restaurant (for lunch, dinner, or Sunday brunch reservations at the revolving restaurant, call 362-5411). Atop the tower sits a 335-foot antenna mast that took 31 weeks to erect with the aid of a giant Sikorsky helicopter; it took 55 lifts to complete the operation. Above the sky pod is the world's highest public observation gallery, the Space Deck, 1,465 feet above the ground.

While you're up there, don't worry that the elements might sweep it into the lake: It's built of contoured reinforced concrete covered with thick glass-reinforced plastic and is designed to keep ice accumulation to a minimum. The structure can withstand high winds, snow, ice, lightning, and earth tremors, which is probably more than you can say about your own house.

Another star attraction at the tower is the futuristic "The Tour of the Universe," a simulated spaceport that will project you into the year 2019. Kids love it as they buckle up on board the Hermes Shuttle and blast off to Jupiter.

Admission: $12 adults, $8 seniors, $6 children 5–12.

Open: Summer, Mon–Sat 9am–midnight, Sun 10am–10pm; winter, daily 10am–10pm. **Subway:** Union; then walk west along Front Street.

SKYDOME, 300 Bremner Blvd., Suite 3000. Tel. 341-3663 or 341-2770 for tour information.

A gala event in 1989 was the opening of the downtown 53,000-seat SkyDome, new home to the Toronto Blue Jays baseball team and the Toronto Argonauts football team. In 1992, Skydome became the first Canadian venue to host the World Series. The stadium itself represents an engineering feat, featuring the world's first fully retractable roof spanning more than eight acres and a gigantic video scoreboard. So large is it that you could fit a 31-story building inside the complex when the roof is closed. Indeed, there's already a spectacular 11-story hotel with 70 rooms facing directly onto the field in the complex. A film is shown, and walking tours are given of the complex.

Admission: Tours, $8 adults, $5.50 students 14 and under and seniors.

Open: Tour schedule depends on events/sports schedule. **Subway:** Union.

ART GALLERY OF ONTARIO, 317 Dundas St. W. Tel. 977-0414.

The low building between McCaul and Beverley streets gives no hint of the light and openness inside its beautifully designed gallery, which is currently undergoing construction that will double its exhibition space. This massive expansion is scheduled to be completed by late January 1993, although when I was in Toronto in '92, a major financial dispute between the government and the museum had caused the facility to dismiss many staff members and close its doors for several months. The expansion will enable the museum to display much more of its permanent collection, especially Renaissance, impressionist, post-impressionist, and modernist works.

Among the museum's highlights has always been the Henry Moore Sculpture Centre, displaying over 600 pieces—original plasters, bronzes, maquettes, woodcuts, lithographs, etchings, and drawings—given to Toronto by the artist out of gratitude for the citizens' enthusiasm for his work (public donations bought his sculpture that decorates Nathan Phillips Square at City Hall). In one room, under a glass ceiling, 20 of his large works stand like silent prehistoric rock foundations. Along the walls are color photographs showing Moore's major sculptures in their natural locations, which fully reveal their magnificent dimensions.

The museum also possesses major works by Canada's greatest artists—Cornelius Krieghoff, Paul Peel, Tom Thompson, The Group of Seven, David Milne, and Emily Carr—which are now displayed in a series of new galleries. The works of more modern Canadian artists, like Harold Town, Kenneth Lochhead, John Chambers and William Kurelek, are also on display. In the new Samuel and Esther Sarrick gallery is a collection of Inuit art the museum has been amassing since the 1970s, consisting of wallhangings; drawings; prints; and sculptures made of whalebone, antler, and soapstone. Old Masters are also well represented and include Tintoretto's *Christ Washing His Disciples' Feet,* 17th-century Dutch and 18th-century Italian paintings, and French impressionist works.

Joined to the gallery by the Joey and Toby Tanenbaum Sculpture Atrium, which features such artists as Rodin and Lipchitz, is **The Grange** (tel. 977-0414). This elegant Georgian home built in 1817 by D'Arcy Boulton gives you a glimpse of the life-style of the 19th century's beautiful people (open Tuesday and Thursday through Sunday from noon to 4pm, Wednesday from noon to 4pm and 6 to 9pm, and Monday in summer from noon to 4pm).

The gallery has a comfortable restaurant, a cafeteria, and a gallery shop, plus a full program of films, concerts, and lectures.

Admission: $7.50 adults, $4 students and seniors; children under 12 free. Includes admission to the Grange.

Open: Tues and Thurs–Sun 11am–5:30pm, Wed 11am–9pm. **Closed:** Christmas Day, New Year's Day. **Subway:** St. Patrick or Dundas; then walk or take a streetcar west.

ROYAL ONTARIO MUSEUM, 100 Queen's Park Crescent. Tel. 586-5549 or 586-5551 for 24-hour information.

The ROM, as it's affectionately called, is at Avenue Road and Bloor Street. Among the ROM's highlights are the following: the Ancient Egypt and Nubia Galleries, with 2,000 artifacts, including magnificent jewelry, pottery, and the ever-popular mummies; the Samuel European Galleries, with over 2,000 objects, from armor to costumes and textiles; the popular Dinosaur Gallery, with 13 dinosaur skeletons; Outdoor Canada/The Sportsmen's Shows Gallery of Birds, with a flock of some 300 different birds from around the world; the Bat Cave, a replica of the St. Clair bat cave in Jamaica with 4,000 model bats; the Greek and Roman Galleries; the hands-on Discovery Gallery, where kids and adults can touch a few thousand authentic artifacts; and the East Asia Galleries, housing one of the best collections in the world outside China. This last includes the Bishop White Gallery, with three impressive wall paintings of Buddhist and Daoist deities (ca. 1300) and 14 monumental wooden Buddhist sculptures from the 12th to the 16th century. The Ming Tomb Gallery features a series of gateways and guardian figures arranged in typical funerary order.

Admission: $6 adults, $3.50 students and children, $13 families. Includes admission to the Gardiner Museum. Seniors admitted free on Tues.

Open: Wed and Fri–Mon 10am–6pm, Tues and Thurs 10am–8pm. **Subway:** Museum or St. George.

GARDINER MUSEUM OF CERAMIC ART, 111 Queen's Park Crescent. Tel. 593-9300, 586-8080, or 586-5549.

Across the street from the ROM, the George R. Gardiner Museum houses a diverse display of porcelain and pottery. The Pre-Columbian gallery contains fantastic Olmec and Mayan figures, plus objects from Ecuador, Colombia, and Peru. The

Majolica gallery displays modern and spectacular 16th- and 17th-century pieces from Florence, Faenza, and Venice. There's also a Delftware section displaying 17th-century chargers and other examples.

Upstairs the galleries feature 18th-century continental and English porcelain—Meissen, Sèvres, Worcester, Chelsea, Derby, and other great names. The collection includes more than 125 porcelain figurines from the commedia dell'arte as well as more than 100 porcelain scent bottles. Among other highlights are the pieces from the Swan Service—a 2,200-piece set that took four years (1737–41) to make. There's one oddity—a very prettily molded and painted bourdaloe (portable urinal).

Admission: Free with admission to the ROM.

Open: Tues–Sun 10am–5pm. **Subway:** Museum or St. George.

ONTARIO SCIENCE CENTRE, 770 Don Mills Rd., Don Mills. Tel. 429-0193.

Described as everything from the world's most technical fun fair to a hands-on museum of the 21st century, the Science Centre, at Eglinton Avenue East, holds a series of wonders for adult and child—no fewer than 700 hands-on experiments.

The building itself is another of architect Raymond Moriyama's miracles. Instead of flattening the ravine and bulldozing the trees on the site, Moriyama designed to the contours of the ravine so that a series of glass-enclosed escalators providing views of the natural surroundings take you down an escarpment to the main exhibition halls. Supposedly Moriyama built penalty clauses into the subcontractors' contracts for each and every tree destroyed!

Wherever you look there are things to touch, push, pull, or crank: Test your reflexes, balance, heart rate, and grip strength; play with computers and binary-system games and puzzles; shunt slides of butterfly wings, bed bugs, fish scales, or feathers under the microscope; tease your brain with a variety of optical illusions; land a spaceship on the moon; watch bees making honey; try to lift sponge building blocks with a mechanical grip; see how many lights you can light or how high you can elevate a balloon with your own pedal power. The fun goes on and on as you explore more than 700 participational exhibits in 10 themed exhibit halls. It's a wonder I ever made it home.

Throughout, there are small theaters showing film and slide shows, plus regular 20-minute presentations on lasers, metal casting, and high-voltage electricity (watch your friend's hair stand on end).

Facilities include a licensed restaurant and lounge, cafeteria, and science shop. By the way, with 1 million people visiting every year, the best time to get to the museum is promptly at 10am, so you can play without too much interference.

Admission: $5.50 adults, $4.50 young adults, $2 children under 12, $14 families; seniors and children under 5 free. Parking is $2.

Open: Sat–Thurs 10am–6pm, Fri 10am–9pm. **Closed:** Christmas Day. **Subway:** Eglinton; then take the Eglinton bus east to Don Mills Road.

THE METROPOLITAN ZOO, Meadowvale Rd., north of Hwy. 401, Scarborough. Tel. 392-5900.

Covering 710 acres of woodland and meadow in Scarborough, the zoo contains some 4,000 animals and thousands of plants. Many of the plants and animals are housed in eight pavilions (including Africa, Indo-Malaya, Australasia, and the Americas) or outdoors on four well-marked trails. It's a photographer's dream.

Six miles of walkways offer access to all areas of the zoo, or two modes of transportation can be used. During the warmer months the Zoo-mobile takes the zoo-goer around the major walkways, viewing the animals contained in outdoor facilities. The Monorail Ride, which runs year round, travels through the beautiful Rouge River Valley where animals native to Canada are displayed.

Facilities include restaurants, a gift shop, first aid, and a family center; strollers and wheelchairs are also available. The zoo is equipped with ramps and washrooms for the disabled. The African pavilion is also equipped with an elevator for strollers and wheelchairs. There's ample parking and plenty of picnic areas with tables.

For zoo information, contact Metro Toronto Zoo, P.O. Box 280, West Hill, ON, M1E 4R5 (tel. 392-5900). For transportation schedules, check with the TTC (tel. 393-4636).

Admission: $9 adults, $6 seniors and children 12–17, $4 children 5–11; children under 5 free.

Open: Summer, daily 9:30am–7pm; winter, daily 9:30am–4:30pm. Last admission is one hour before closing. **Closed:** Christmas Day. **Subway:** Kennedy; then take bus no. 86A north. **Directions:** By car from downtown, take the Don Valley Parkway to Hwy. 401 east and exit on Meadowvale Road.

THE McMICHAEL COLLECTION, Islington Ave., Kleinburg. Tel. 893-1121.

Located in Kleinburg, 25 miles north of the city, this collection of Canadian art is worth a visit for the setting alone.

You'll approach the gallery through quiet stands of pine trees until you reach a log-and-stone building specially designed to house the Canadian landscapes within. The lobby itself is a work of art: A pitched roof soars to a height of 27 feet on massive rafters of Douglas fir, and throughout the gallery panoramic windows look south over white pine, cedar, ash, and birch.

The gallery houses works by Canada's famous group of landscape painters, the "Group of Seven"—Arthur Lismer, Frederick Varley, and Lawren Harris, among others—as well as by Tom Thomson, David Milne, Emily Carr, and their contemporaries. These artists, inspired by the turn-of-the-century Canadian wilderness, particularly in Algonquin Park and northern Ontario, recorded its rugged landscape in highly individualistic styles.

An impressive collection of Inuit and contemporary Native Canadian art and sculpture is also on display.

Founded by Robert and Signe McMichael, the gallery began in 1965 when they donated their property, home, and collection to the Province of Ontario. Since then the collection has expanded to include over 5,000 works. Still, its unique atmosphere has been preserved—log-and-barnwood walls, fieldstone fireplaces, and homey decorative touches like hooked rugs and earthenware urns filled with flowers and dried leaves.

Admission: $5 adults, $2.50 seniors and students; children under 5 free.

Open: Apr–Oct, daily 10am–5pm; Nov–Mar, Tues–Sun 11am–4:30pm.

DID YOU KNOW . . . ?

- The first singing commercial was supposedly created by Torontonian Ernie Bushnell in 1926 for the local Jehovah's Witness radio station.
- The CN Tower has the longest concrete staircase (2,570 steps), which takes an average fit person 20 minutes to descend.
- Author Arthur Hailey (*Hotel, Airport*) worked as an assistant editor at *Bus and Truck Transport*, a MacLean-Hunter magazine.
- The Ontario Legislature sits on land that was originally occupied (appropriately, some say) by a lunatic asylum.
- Torontonian Norman Breakey invented the paint roller in 1940.
- The population of York (Toronto) was 703 in 1812.
- Canada's first postage stamp was created in Toronto by Sir Sanford Fleming in 1851.

CANADA'S WONDERLAND, 7725 Jane St., Concord. Tel. 832-7000.

Nineteen miles (30 minutes) north of Toronto, Canada now has its answer to Disney World, a splendid theme park called Canada's Wonderland. The 370-acre park is divided into eight theme areas, ranging from the Medieval Faire to Hanna-Barbera Land, and features 50 rides, including Canada's only suspended roller coaster. The newest excitement is the Splash Works, 10 acres of water activities and rides, including a water playground boasting 16 water slides, tube rides, and a separate children's water-play area. More than 10 dazzling musical shows are performed in the park, along with a special laser show. At the International Festival, daredevil divers leap from the top of 150-feet-high Wonder Mountain. The hottest names in the music industry perform at Kingswood Music Theatre (call 832-8131 for ticket information).

You'll probably need eight hours to see everything. If you picnic on the grounds and forgo buying souvenirs, a family of four can do the park for about $80. Watch out, though, for the extra attractions not included in the admission pass, particularly the many "games of skill," which the kids love but the purse hates.

Admission: Pay One Price Passport, including a day's unlimited rides and shows (excluding food, games, merchandise, and the Music Theatre), $26 adults, $13 children 3–6; children under 3 free. Grounds admission only is $17.

Open: June–Labor Day, daily 10am–10pm; May and Sept–Oct, Sat–Sun 10am–8pm. **Closed:** Nov–Apr. **Subway:** Yorkdale or York Mills; then GO Express Bus. **Directions:** By car, take Yonge Street north to Hwy. 401 and travel west to Hwy. 400. Go north on Hwy. 400 to the Rutherford Road exit and follow the signs. Exit at Major MacKenzie if you're coming south.

2. MORE ATTRACTIONS

ARCHITECTURAL HIGHLIGHTS

CITY HALL, Queen St. W. Tel. 392-7341.

An architectural spectacle, City Hall houses the Mayor's of-

FROMMER'S FAVORITE TORONTO EXPERIENCES

A Picnic on the Toronto Islands A short ferry ride will transport you to another world of lagoons and rush-lined backwaters, miles away from the urban tarmac—a world of houseboats and bicycles, a place to stroll beside the weeping willows.

A Day at Harbourfront Bring a model boat; watch artisans blowing glass; take a sailing lesson; tour the harbor; shop the Quay and the antique mart—and this is just a beginning.

A Day at the Beaches Stroll along the boardwalk, picnic in the adjacent parkland and gardens, and browse the stores one block from the beach.

An Afternoon at Kleinburg A unique Canadian and Toronto experience—the Group of Seven landscape artists' work displayed in an idyllic setting.

fice and the city's administrative offices. Daringly designed in the early 1960s by Finnish architect Viljo Revell, it consists of a low podium topped by the flying-saucer–shaped Council Chamber enfolded between two curved towers. Its interior is as dramatic as its exterior. A cafeteria and dining room are located in the basement.

In front stretches **Nathan Phillips Square** (named after the mayor who initiated the project), where in summer you can sit and contemplate the flower gardens, fountains, and reflecting pool (which doubles as a skating rink in winter), as well as listen to concerts. Here also stands Henry Moore's *Three-Way Piece No. 2,* locally referred to as *The Archer,* purchased through a public subscription fund, and the Peace Garden, commemorating Toronto's sesquicentennial in 1984. In contrast, to the east stands the **Old City Hall,** a green-copper–roofed Victorian Romanesque-style building.

Admission: Free.

Open: Free tours Mon–Fri at 3:15pm. **Subway:** Queen; then walk west to Bay or take the Queen Street streetcar west one stop.

EATON CENTRE, Dundas and Yonge Sts. Tel. 598-2322.

Buttressed at both ends by 30-story skyscrapers, this high-tech center, which cost over $250 million, stretches from Dundas Street and Yonge Street south to Queen Street and encompasses six million square feet. **Eaton's Department Store** takes up one million square feet, and the rest is filled with over 360 stores and restaurants and 2 garages. Some 20 million people shop here annually.

Inside, the structure opens into the impressive **Galleria,** an 866-foot-long glass-domed arcade dotted with benches, orchids, palm trees, and fountains; it's further adorned by Michael Snow's soaring Canada geese, entitled *Step Flight.* Three tiers rise above, reached by escalator and glass elevators, giving glorious views over this Crystal Palace and Milan-style masterpiece designed by Eb Zeidler (who also designed Ontario Place). Here, rain or shine, you can enjoy the sights, sounds, and aromas in comfort—don't be surprised by the twittering of the sparrows, some of whom have decided that this new facility is as pleasant as the outdoors.

One more amazing fact about this construction: It was built around two of Toronto's oldest landmarks—**Trinity Church** (1847) and **Scadding House** (home of Trinity's rector, Dr. Scadding)—because the public demanded that the developers allow the sun to continue to shine on the church's twin towers. It does!

Admission: Free.

Open: Mon–Fri 10am–9pm, Sat 9:30am–6pm, Sun noon–5pm. **Subway:** Dundas or Queen.

DID YOU KNOW . . . ?

- Ernest Hemingway was hired by the *Toronto Star* at age 19 and was paid $150 per year.
- Babe Ruth hit the first of his 714 major-league home runs at Hanlan's Point Stadium on the Toronto Islands in 1914. He also managed to pitch a shutout.
- 2,500 ounces of gold were used as a coloring agent in the 14,000 windows of the Royal Bank building.
- The first injection of insulin was given at Toronto General Hospital in 1922.
- Standard time was invented by Torontonian Sir Sanford Fleming.
- Yonge Street is listed in the *Guinness Book of World Records* as the longest street in the world—1,178 miles.
- When Casa Loma was built between 1911 and 1914, it was the only castle in the world that had an electrically operated elevator and an indoor swimming pool. It also had solid-gold bathroom fixtures.

METROPOLITAN TORONTO REFERENCE LIBRARY, 789 Yonge St. Tel. 393-7000.

If more libraries were built like this one, perhaps study would become more of a pastime and learning would come out of the dim and musty closets and into the world. Step inside—a pool and a waterfall gently screen out the street noise, and pine fencelike partitions, like those you find along sand dunes, undulate through the area. Step farther inside and the space opens dramatically to the sky. Every corner is flooded with light and air. I envy the citizens of Toronto their designer/architect Raymond Moriyama.

Admission: Free.

Open: Summer, Mon–Thurs 9am–8pm, Fri 9am–6pm, Sat 9am–5pm; winter, Mon–Thurs 9am–9pm, Fri 9am–6pm, Sat 9am–5pm, Sun 1:30–5pm. **Subway:** Bloor.

ONTARIO LEGISLATURE, 111 Wellesley St. W., at University Ave. Tel. 325-7500.

East of the university, at the northern end of University Avenue, lies Queen's Park, surrounding the rose-tinted sandstone-and-granite Ontario Parliament Buildings, profusely carved, with stately domes, arches, and porte-cochères. Drop in around 2pm when the legislature is in session (fall-spring) for some pithy comments during the question period, or take one of the regular tours. It's best to call ahead to check times.

Admission: Free.

Open: Tours given every half hour Mon–Fri 9–11:30am and 1–4pm, every hour Sat–Sun 9am–4pm. **Subway:** Queen's Park.

ROYAL BANK PLAZA, Front and Bay Sts.

If you want to see modern architecture at its most imaginative, then don't miss Royal Bank Plaza. It's a free visual inspiration. Shimmering in the sun on the corner of Front and Bay streets, it looks like a pillar of gold—and in a way it is. More importantly, it's a masterpiece of design and architectural drama. Two triangular towers of bronze mirrored glass flank a 130-foot-high glass-walled banking hall. The external walls of the towers are built in a serrated configuration so that they reflect a phenomenal mosaic of color from the skies and surrounding buildings.

In the banking hall, hundreds of aluminum cylinders hang from the ceiling, the work of Venezuelan sculptor Jesus Raphael Soto, while two levels below there's a waterfall and pine-tree setting naturally illuminated from the hall above.

Admission: Free.

Open: Year round. **Subway:** Union.

CEMETERIES

MOUNT PLEASANT CEMETERY, 1643 Yonge St., or 375 Mount Pleasant Rd., north of St. Clair Ave. Tel. 485-9129.

This large garden cemetery, crisscrossed by ravines and planted with foliage and flowers, was laid out from 1873 to 1876. It is the burying ground of the city's wealthy and notable, including the Massey family, and, as such, it contains some very interesting monumental sculpture. The Massey Mausoleum was built in 1894 in a Romanesque Revival style by E. J. Lennox, the architect who designed Old City Hall. The impressive mausoleum is topped by a statue of Hope. Other notable mausoleums include the Chandler mausoleum, north of the Massey on a knoll overlooking Yonge Street and the Eaton family and Cox family mausoleums. The cemetery also contains one of the finest tree collections in North America.

Admission: Free.

Open: Daily 8am–dusk.

IMPRESSIONS

It is impossible to give it anything but commendation. It is not squalid like Birmingham, or cramped like Canton, or hellish like New York or tiresome like Nice. It is all right. . . .
—Rupert Brooke, *Letters from America* (1913)

"One of the worst blue-devil haunts on the face of the earth," cried John Gaunt the Scottish immigrant poet in the days of the Family Compact. "The city has more grasping, greedy unctuous people in it than any other city in the world," shouts Ralph Maybank of Winnipeg, in the Parliament of Canada.
—Bruce Hutchinson, *The Unknown Country* (1943)

NECROPOLIS, 200 Winchester St., at Sumach St. Tel. 923-7911.

This is one of the city's oldest cemeteries (1850). Many of the remains that are buried here, though, were originally buried in Potters Field, where Yorkville stands today, and were moved from there and reinterred here.

Before strolling through the quietly affecting 15-acre cemetery, pick up a walking-tour map at the lodge. Many of the city's famous are buried or remembered here. You'll find monuments to Samuel Lount and Peter Matthews, the two rebels who were hanged after the 1837 rebellion, and also to the leader, Mackenzie himself. Among other famous Torontonians buried here are Ned Hanlan, world-champion rower; George Brown, founder of the *Globe* and a father of Confederation; and John Ross Robertson, founder of the Toronto *Telegram.*

The appealing Gothic Revival Chapel, Lodge, and porte-cochère, with their colored-slate tile roofing, were designed by Henry Langley, who is also buried here.

Admission: Free.

Open: Daily 8am–dusk.

ST. JAMES THE LESS AND ST. JAMES CEMETERY, 635 Parliament St., between Wellesley and Bloor Sts. Tel. 964-9194.

This 65-acre cemetery and its chapel, on land that stretches from Parliament Street rising to Rosedale Ravine, was laid out in 1842 and contains the tombs of several early notables, including the Austins (a miniature Italianate death residence) and the Gzowskis.

Admission: Free.

Open: Daily 8am–8pm.

COLLEGES & UNIVERSITIES

UNIVERSITY OF TORONTO, 21 King's College Circle. Tel. 978-4111 or 978-5000 for summer tours.

Just south of the Royal Ontario Museum sprawls the main campus of the University of Toronto, with its quiet wooded pathways, ivy-covered buildings, and spreading lawns. Many scientific breakthroughs have been made here. Insulin was discovered here, the first heart pacemaker was built here, and baby's pabulum was developed here.

Many famous Canadians have graduated from one or another of the colleges that make up the university, which was originally founded as King's College in 1849 and later refounded as the nonsectarian University of Toronto. Among the many Canadian notable graduates are several prime ministers, including Mackenzie King and Lester B. Pearson; politicians, such as former Ontario Premier William Davis and Sens. Keith Davey and Stephen Lewis; as well as such intellectual and literary lights as Dr. Norman Bethune, Robertson Davies, Morley Callaghan, Margaret Atwood, Northrop Frye, and Harold Innis.

Today the university has 52,000 students (36,000 full-time) and 6,200 faculty, spread over three campuses. Wander through the downtown St. George campus (see Walking Tour 4 in Chapter 7) and note the architecturally interesting buildings, such as the Gothic-inspired Hart House.

Admission: Free.

Open: June–Aug, tours leave from Hart House on Wellesley Street Mon–Fri at 10:30am and 1 and 2:30pm. **Subway:** Queen's Park or St. George.

HISTORIC BUILDINGS

CAMPBELL HOUSE, 160 Queen St. W. Tel. 597-0227.

West of City Hall and just across the street from Osgoode Hall (see below), at the corner of University Avenue, sits the 1822 mansion of Loyalist and sixth chief justice of Upper Canada Sir William Campbell. In 1829 he retired to this mansion, where he resided with his pet alligator until he died in 1834 despite a diet of snipe prescribed by his physician.

Admission: $2.50 adults; $1.25 seniors, students, and children.

Open: Mid-Oct to late May, Mon–Fri 9:30–11:30am and 2:30–4:30pm; late May to mid-Oct, Mon–Fri 9:30–11:30am and 2:30–4:30pm, Sat–Sun noon–4:30pm. **Subway:** Osgoode.

CASA LOMA, 1 Austin Terrace. Tel. 923-1171.

Every city has its folly, and Toronto has a charming one—complete with Elizabethan-style chimneys, Rhineland turrets, secret panels, underground passageways, and a mellifluous-sounding name: Casa Loma.

Sir Henry Pellatt, who built it between 1909 and 1911 at a cost of $3.5 million (plus $1.5 million for furnishings), had a lifelong and incurably romantic fascination with medieval castles—so he decided to build his own. He studied European medieval castles and gathered materials and furnishings, bringing marble, glass, and paneling from Europe, teak from Asia, and oak and walnut from prime areas of North America; and he imported Scottish stonemasons to build the massive walls that surround the six-acre site.

It's a fascinating place to explore. It has 98 rooms, including the majestic Great Hall, with its 60-foot-high hammerbeam ceiling; the Oak Room, where three artisans took three years to fashion the paneling; the Conservatory, with its elegant bronze doors, stained-glass dome, and pink-and-green marble; the battlements and tower; Peacock Alley, lined with medieval armor; Sir Henry's suite, containing a shower with an 18-inch-diameter shower head; the 1,700-bottle wine cellar; and the 800-foot tunnel to the stables (which alone cost $250,000), where horses were quartered amid the luxury of Spanish tile and mahogany. The house originally contained, by the way, 30 bathrooms, 25 fireplaces, 5,000 lights, and 3 bowling alleys. In 1923 when Pellatt was near bankruptcy, the house was auctioned for $131,600. How's that for real estate risk? As you go through the house, a tape recording in each room explains what you are seeing.

Admission: $8 adults, $4.50 seniors and children 6–16.

Open: Daily 10am–4pm. **Subway:** Dupont; then walk two blocks north.

COLBORNE LODGE, High Park. Tel. 392-6916.

When John Howard, city surveyor and architect, had this house built in 1836 to 1837, it was way out in the country and difficult to travel to in the harsh winters. It's a charming English-style Regency cottage with a three-sided veranda that was built to take advantage of the view of Lake Ontario and the Humber River. In 1873 Howard donated the house and surrounding land to the city in return for an annual salary and so created High Park—a great recreational area.

Admission: $3.25 adults, $2.50 seniors and children 13–18, $2.25 children 12 and under.

Open: Jan 7–Mar 31, Sat–Sun and holidays noon–5pm; Apr 1–May 31 and Sept 1 to mid-Nov, Mon–Fri 9:30am–4pm, Sat–Sun and holidays noon–5pm; June 1–Aug 31, Mon–Sat 9:30am–5pm, Sun and holidays noon–5pm. Call ahead for hours in other months.

FORT YORK, Garrison Rd., off Fleet St. Tel. 392-6907.

Established by Lieutenant-Governor Simcoe in 1793 to defend "little muddy York," as Toronto was then known, Fort York, between Bathurst Street and Strachan Avenue, was sacked by Americans in 1813. You can tour the soldiers' and officers' quarters and clamber over the ramparts, as well as view demonstrations and exhibits. The fort is two blocks east of Exhibition Place.

Admission: $4.75 adults, $3 teenagers 13–18 and seniors, $2.75 children 6–12.

Open: Summer (June–Oct), daily 9:30am–5pm; winter, Mon–Fri 9:30am–4pm, Sat–Sun 10am–5pm. **Subway:** Bathurst; then streetcar no. 511 south.

THE GRANGE, 317 Dundas St. W. Tel. 977-0414, ext. 237.

This is the oldest brick house in the city, and from 1910 to 1922 it was the first home of the Art Gallery. It was built in 1817 by D'Arcy Boulton, Jr., at the center of the Boulton estate, which extended from Queen Street to Bloor Street. The house passed first to D'Arcy's widow; then to her son; and then to his widow, who married Goldwin Smith, an English historian and professor at the University of Toronto, who made the Grange an intellectual and social center. He donated it to the Art Gallery. Today it has been restored to reflect the 1840s.

Admission: Included in admission fee to the Art Gallery.

Open: Tues noon–4pm, Wed noon–4pm and 6–9pm, Thurs–Sun noon–4pm. **Subway:** St. Patrick or Dundas; then take a streetcar west.

MACKENZIE HOUSE, 82 Bond St. Tel. 392-6915.

Friends and fund raisers got together to purchase this house two blocks east of Yonge Street and south of Dundas Street for William Lyon Mackenzie, leader of the 1837 rebellion, who lived here from 1859 to 1861. This typical mid-19th-century brick row house gives you some idea of what Toronto must have looked like then, when the streets were lined with similar buildings. It's furnished in 1850s style, and in the back there's a print shop designed after Mackenzie's own.

Admission: $3.25 adults, $2.50 seniors and teenagers 13–18, $2 children under 12.

Open: Mon–Sat 9:30am–5pm, Sun and holidays noon–5pm. **Subway:** Dundas.

OSGOODE HALL, 130 Queen St. W. Tel. 947-3300.

West of City Hall extends an impressive, elegant wrought-iron fence in front of an equally gracious building, Osgoode Hall, currently the home of the Law Society of Upper Canada and the superior courts of the province. (It is said that the fence was originally built to keep cows from trampling the flower beds.) Tours of the interior will show you the splendor of the grand staircase, the rotunda, the Great Library, and the fine portrait and sculpture collection. Building began in 1829 on this structure, troops were billeted here after the Rebellion of 1837, and the buildings now house the headquarters of Ontario's legal profession and several magnificent courtrooms—including one using materials from London's Old Bailey.

Admission: Free.

Open: Tours given Mon–Fri at 1 and 1:20pm in July–Aug only. Museum, year round Mon–Fri 10am–3:30pm. **Subway:** Osgoode.

INDUSTRIAL TOURS

TORONTO STOCK EXCHANGE, Exchange Tower, 2 First Canadian Place, at the northeast corner of Adelaide and York Sts. Tel. 947-4676.

This is the largest public securities market in Canada, where more than $275 million worth of stock is traded a day. Public tours, including audiovisual presentations and demonstrations of the computer system, are given at 2pm Tuesday through Friday.

Admission: Free.

Open: Mon–Fri 9am–4:30pm; tour given Tues–Fri at 2pm.

MARKETS

KENSINGTON MARKET, Kensington and Augusta Aves. and Baldwin St.

In the early 20th century Kensington Market was a thriving market in the heart of what was then the Jewish community. Today the area is part Portuguese, part Caribbean, part Jewish, and part Asian. There is no central market building but rather a number of stalls and stores that stretch along several streets—Augusta and Kensington avenues and Baldwin Street. Again, get here early for the best scene.

Open: Daily. **Subway:** College or Dundas; then take the streetcar west.

ST. LAWRENCE MARKET, 92 Front St. E. Tel. 392-7219.

This handsome food market is housed in a vast building that has been constructed around the facade of the second city hall that was built in 1850. Vendors sell fresh meat, fish, fruit, vegetables and dairy products as well as other foodstuffs. Best time to visit is early Saturday morning shortly after the farmers have brought their wares into town.

Open: Tues–Sat. **Subway:** King or Union.

MUSEUMS

THE BATA SHOE MUSEUM, The Colonnade, 131 Bloor St. W. Tel. 924-7463.

For Imelda Marcos or anyone else interested in shoes, this museum, the personal collection of the Bata family, displays decorative and functional shoes, national and international shoes, and modern and historical shoes. It makes for a fascinating history.

Admission: $3 adults, $1 students.

Open: Tues–Sun 11am–6pm.

BLACK CREEK PIONEER VILLAGE, 1000 Murray Ross Pkwy., Downsview, at Steeles Ave. and Jane St. Tel. 736-1733.

Life here moves at the gentle pace of turn-of-the-century rural

Ontario. You can watch the authentically dressed villagers going about their chores—spinning, sewing, rail splitting, sheep shearing, and threshing. Enjoy their cooking, wander through the cozily furnished homesteads, visit the working mill, shop at the general store, and rumble past the farm animals in a horse-drawn wagon. There are over 30 restored buildings to explore in a beautifully landscaped village.

Admission: $7 adults, $4.50 seniors, $3 children and students; children under 4 free.

Open: Oct–Mar, Sat–Sun 10am–4:30pm; Apr–June and Sept–Oct, Mon–Fri 9:30am–5pm, Sat–Sun 10am–6pm; July–Aug, daily 10am–6pm. **Subway:** Finch; then take bus no. 60 to Jane Street.

CANADA SPORTS HALL OF FAME, Exhibition Place. Tel. 595-1046.

Located opposite the Hockey Hall of Fame (see below), this three-floor sports hall is devoted to the country's greatest athletes in all major sports. It offers many fun interactive exhibits—computers that will tell you everything you could wish to know about particular sports personalities, famous race horses, and Canada's sport heritage.

Admission: Free.

Open: Daily 10am–4:30pm. **Subway:** Bathurst; then take streetcar no. 511 south to the end of the line.

HOCKEY HALL OF FAME, Exhibition Place. Tel. 595-1345.

A veritable shrine to Canada's game among games. Among the many trophies, ice-hockey fans can see the original Stanley Cup, donated in 1893 by Lord Stanley of Preston, plus Terry Sawchuck's goalie gear, Newsy Lalonde's skates, Max Bentley's stick, and photos of the personalities and great moments in ice-hockey history.

Admission: $4.50 adults, $3.25 children under 17 and seniors.

Open: Mid-May to Dec '92, Mon–Thurs 10am–5pm, Fri–Sat 10am–7pm, Sun noon–6pm. **Closed:** Museum will close Jan–June '93 and will reopen at Front and Yonge Sts. **Subway:** Bathurst; then take streetcar no. 511 south to the end of the line.

MARINE MUSEUM, Exhibition Place. Tel. 392-6827.

On the grounds of Exhibition Place stands the Marine Museum, which interprets the history of Toronto Harbour and its relation to the Great Lakes. Visitors can also board the fully restored 1932 *Ned Hanlan,* the last steam tugboat to sail on Lake Ontario.

Admission: $3.25 adults, $2.50 teenagers 13–18 and seniors, $2.25 children under 12.

Open: Tues–Sat 9:30am–5pm, Sun noon–5pm. **Subway:** Bathurst; then take streetcar no. 511 south to the end of the line.

MCLAUGHLIN PLANETARIUM, 100 Queen's Park Crescent. Tel. 586-5736.

Located beside the Royal Ontario Museum, the McLaughlin Planetarium offers exhibits and three or four new audiovisual presentations year round in its Theatre of the Stars. The animated Astro Centre gallery on the second floor documents the development of astronomy. One of the gallery's chief attractions is the solar telescope, which allows the visitor to observe the sun "live," as it appears at that very moment.

Admission (for Star Shows): $5 adults; $3 seniors, students, and children.

Open: Call for show times. **Subway:** Museum or St. George.

THE MUSEUM FOR TEXTILES, 55 Centre Ave. Tel. 599-5515.

This fascinating museum displays not only what you'd expect—fine Oriental rugs—but also tapestries from all over the world, including African story-telling cloth.

Admission: $2.50.

Open: Mon–Fri 11am–5pm, Sat–Sun noon–5pm. **Subway:** Osgoode or St. Patrick.

SIGMUND SAMUEL BUILDING, 14 Queen's Park Crescent W. Tel. 586-5549.

The ROM's Canadian Decorative Arts Collection, housed in the Sigmund Samuel Building, a 10-minute walk south of the museum, is a showcase for early Canadian artists and artisans. The collection displays examples of artistry from eastern Canada in thematic room settings featuring authentic 18th- and 19th-century furnishings. Glass, silver, woodenware, ceramics, toys, weathervanes, and paintings are on view. The famed McCrea models of buildings, farm implements, and tools provide a miniature representation of early rural Ontario. Plans are afoot to move the collection in late 1993, so check.

Admission: Free.

Open: Tues–Sat 10am–5pm, Sun 1–5pm. **Closed:** Christmas Day and New Year's Day. **Subway:** Queen's Park.

NEIGHBORHOODS

CHINATOWN, Dundas St. and Spadina Ave.

Stretching along Dundas Street west from Bay Street to Spadina Avenue, and north and south along Spadina Avenue, Chinatown, home to many of Toronto's 350,000 Chinese citizens, is packed with fascinating shops and restaurants. Even the street signs are in Chinese here.

In **Dragon City,** a large shopping mall on Spadina that's staffed and patronized by Chinese, you'll find all kinds of stores, some selling exotic Chinese preserves like cuttlefish, lemon ginger, whole mango, ginseng, and antler, and others specializing in Asian books, tapes, and records, as well as fashions and foods. Downstairs, a fast-food court features Korean, Indonesian, Chinese, and Japanese cuisines.

As you stroll through Chinatown, stop at the **Kim Moon Bakery** on Dundas Street West (tel. 977-1933) for Chinese pastries and a pork bun or go to one of the tea stores. A walk through Chinatown at night is especially exciting—the sidewalks are filled with people and neon lights shimmer everywhere. You'll pass windows where ducks hang gleaming, noodle houses, record stores selling the Top 10 in Chinese, and trading companies filled with all kinds of Asian produce. Another stopping place might be the **New Asia Supermarket,** around the corner from Dundas Street at 299 Spadina Ave.

For details see Walking Tour 3 in Chapter 7.

MIRVISH VILLAGE, Markham St., between Bloor and Lennox Sts.

One of Toronto's most famous characters is Honest Ed Mirvish, who started his career in the 1950s with no-frills shopping in his store at the corner of Markham Street (a block west of Bathurst Street) and Bloor Street, where the signs screaming of bargains leap at you from everywhere. Among other things, Ed Mirvish rose to save the Royal Alexandra Theatre from demolition, established a whole row of adjacent restaurants for theater patrons, and finally created this block-long complex with numerous art galleries and restaurants. His latest triumph was the purchase and renovation of London's Old Vic.

Stop by and browse and don't forget to step into Honest Ed's on the corner.

QUEEN STREET WEST VILLAGE

This is a great street for wandering—there's a marvelous collection of small avant-garde restaurants, entertainment spots, and bars along its sidewalks. A few art galleries; antiquarian and secondhand-book stores such as David Mason at no. 342; record stores selling 45s and other records from the 1950s, '60s, and '70s; junk shops; kitchen-supply stores; and all kinds of fascinating emporiums are worth a browse.

For details see Walking Tour 2 in Chapter 7.

YORKVILLE

This is the name given to the area north of Bloor Street, between Avenue Road and Bay Street. In 1853 Yorkville became a village, surrounded by trees and meadows; in the 1960s it became Toronto's Haight-Ashbury, a mecca for young suburban runaways; in the 1980s it became the focus of the chic—Hermès, Courrèges, Cartier, and Turnbull & Asser now inhabit the restored town-house boutiques, which draw well-heeled crowds to the area, which is filled with art galleries, cafés, and restaurants.

Stroll around and browse; sit outside and have an iced coffee in the sun at one of the cafés on Yorkville Avenue and watch the parade go by.

Be sure to wander through the labyrinths of **Hazelton Lanes** between Avenue Road and Hazelton Avenue, where you'll find a maze of shops and offices clustered around an outdoor court in the center of a building that is topped with apartments—some of the most sought-after in the city. In the summer the court becomes excitingly alive when the Hazelton Club erects colorful medieval-style jousting tents for one and all to relax under.

For details see Walking Tour 6 in Chapter 7.

PARKS & GARDENS

ALLAN GARDENS, stretching between Jarvis, Sherbourne, Dundas, and Gerrard Sts. Tel. 392-7259.

These gardens were given to the city by George William Allan, who was born in 1822 to wealthy merchant and banker William Allan. His father gave him a vast estate stretching from Carlton Street to Bloor Street between Jarvis and Sherbourne. George married into the Family Compact when he married John Beverley Robinson's daughter. A lawyer by training, he became a city councillor, mayor, senator, and philanthropist. The lovely old concert pavilion was demolished, but the glass-domed Palm House still stands in all its radiant Victorian glory.

Admission: Free.

Open: Daily. **Subway:** Dundas or Gerrard.

EDWARDS GARDEN, Lawrence Ave. and Leslie St. Tel. 445-5825.

This quiet formal garden with a creek cutting through it is part of a series of parks. Gracious bridges arch over the creek, rock gardens abound, and rose and other seasonal flower beds add color and scent to the landscape. The garden is famous for its rhododendrons. The Civic Garden Centre operates a gift shop and gives walking tours on Tuesday and Thursday at 11am and 1pm.

Admission: Free.

Open: Daily dawn–dusk. **Subway:** Eglinton; then take the Leslie or Lawrence bus.

HIGH PARK, in the West End, extending south of Bloor St. to the Gardiner Expressway.

This 400-acre park was John G. Howard's great gift to the city. He lived in Colbourne Lodge, which still stands in the park. The park contains a large lake called Grenadier Pond; a small zoo; a swimming pool; tennis courts; sports fields; bowling greens; and vast expanses of green for baseball, jogging, picnicking, bicycling, and more.

Admission: Free.

Open: Daily dawn–dusk. **Subway:** High Park.

TOURS

CITY TOURS One quick and easy way to see half a dozen city highlights is to take a one-hour double-decker bus tour that stops at the Eaton Centre, the CN Tower, the SkyDome, Old Fort York, the Canadian National Exhibition, and Ontario Place. It costs $10, and you're allowed on/off privileges at two places along the route. An alternate two-hour tour costing $17.65 adds City Hall, the University, and Casa Loma to the itinerary. For information contact **Grayline Tours,** 610 Bay St. (tel. 351-3311).

HARBOR & ISLAND TOURS Glass-covered boats modeled after Amsterdam's canal cruisers ply the lake and the harbor. **Gray Line Boat Tours,** 5 Queen's Quay W. (tel. 364-2412), offers one-hour cruises of the harbor and islands, leaving hourly from May to October from either the foot of Yonge Street, beside the Westin Harbour Castle Hotel, or from the foot of York Street at Queen's Quay. You can cruise in and out of the lagoons spying Canada geese and other wild fowl during the day or at night (9 and 10pm), when the twinkling skyline unfolds before you. Adults pay $9.95, and children 4 to 14 pay $6; children under 4 are free.

A similar harbor tour is given by **Toronto Tours,** 134 Jarvis St. (tel. 869-1372), which charges the same prices.

For a real thrill, board the schooner *The Challenge* for a one- or two-hour cruise weekdays at 2 and 4pm and weekends at noon, 2, 4, and 5pm. The price is $15 for adults, $12 for seniors, and $10 for children 4 to 14. For information call the **Great Lakes Schooner Company** at 601-0326.

3. COOL FOR KIDS

TOP CITY ATTRACTIONS

Look under "The Top Attractions" and "More Attractions," above, for the following Toronto-area attractions that have major appeal to kids of all ages. I've summarized them here in what I think is the most logical order, at least from a kid's point of view (the first five, though, really belong in a dead heat).

Ontario Science Centre *(see p. 138)* Kids race to be the first at this paradise of fun hands-on games, experiments, and push-button demonstrations—700 of 'em.

Canada's Wonderland *(see p. 140)* The kids love the rides in the theme park. But watch out for those video games, which they also love—an unanticipated extra cost.

Harbourfront *(see p. 134)* Kaleidoscope is an ongoing program of creative crafts, active games, and special events on weekends and holidays. There are also a summer pond, winter ice skating, and a crafts studio.

Ontario Place *(see p. 133)* Waterslides, a huge Cinesphere, a futuristic pod, and other entertainments are the big hits at this recreational/cultural park on three artificial islands on the edge of Lake Ontario.

Metro Zoo *(see p. 138)* One of the best in the world, modeled after San Diego's—the animals in this 710-acre park really do live in a natural environment.

Toronto Islands–Centreville *(see p. 135)* Riding a ferry to this turn-of-the-century amusement park is part of the fun.

CN Tower *(see p. 135)* Especially for the "Tour of the Universe."

Royal Ontario Museum *(see p. 137)* The top hit is always the dinosaurs.

McLaughlin Planetarium *(see p. 148)* For special shows and stargazing.

Fort York *(see p. 146)* For its reenactments of battle drills, musket and cannon firing, and musical marches with fife and drum.

Canada Sports Hall of Fame *(see p. 148)* Especially the interactive video displays.

Black Creek Pioneer Village *(see p. 147)* For craft and other demonstrations.

Casa Loma *(see p. 145)* For the stables and the fantasy rooms.

Art Gallery of Ontario *(see p. 136)* For its hands-on exhibit.

A ZOO & FARM

RIVERDALE FARM, 201 Winchester St., east of Parliament, north of Gerrard. Tel. 392-6794.

Idyllically situated on the edge of the Don Valley ravine, this early 19th-century farm is a favorite with small tots, who enjoy watching the cows and pigs and petting the other farm animals. Historic buildings, gardens, implement displays, and a large variety of livestock make for a surprising visit to the country in the heart of the city.

Admission: Free.

Open: Daily 9am–4, 5, or 6pm, depending on the season.

OUT-OF-TOWN ATTRACTIONS

AFRICAN LION SAFARI, R. R. No. 1, Cambridge, ON. Tel. 519/623-2620.

Kids enjoy driving through this 500-acre wildlife park, sighting lions and other game. The entrance fee entitles visitors to drive through the park, ride the *African Queen*, take the scenic railway, and see animal performances. There are playgrounds, too, for toddlers, as well as a water playground. Bring bathing suits.

Admission: $13 adults, $11 seniors and youths, $9 children 3–12.

Open: Apr 1–Labor Day, daily 10am–5:30pm; Labor Day–Mar 31, Mon–Fri 10am–4pm, Sat–Sun 10am–5pm. **Directions:** Take Hwy. 401 to Hwy. 6 south.

CHUDLEIGH'S, P.O. Box 176 (Hwy. 25 north of Hwy. 401), Milton, ON. Tel. 826-1252.

A day here will introduce the kids to life on a farm. They'll enjoy the hay rides; pony rides; sleigh rides; and, in season, the apple picking and sugaring off of the maple trees. All of the produce is on sale, too, in the bake shop and fruit-and-vegetable markets.

Admission: Free.

Open: July 1–Oct, daily 9am–7pm; Nov–June, daily 9am–5pm.

CULLEN GARDENS AND MINIATURE VILLAGE, Taunton Rd., Whitby, ON. Tel. 294-7965.

The miniature village (made to one-half scale) has great appeal. The 27 acres of gardens and the shopping and live entertainment add to the fun.

Admission: $8.50 adults, $6.95 seniors, $3.95 children.

Open: Daily 9am–8pm. **Closed:** Mid-Jan to early Apr.

WILD WATER KINGDOM, Finch Ave., 1 mile west of Hwy. 427, Brampton, ON. Tel. 794-0468 or 794-0565.

Kids love this huge water theme park complete with a 20,000-square-foot wave pool, tube slides, speed slides, giant hot tubs, and this year's thriller, the Cyclone water ride. In between they can use the batting cages or practice on the mini-golf circuit.

Admission: $16 adults, $13 children 4–9, $10 seniors.

Open: May to mid-June, Sat–Sun 10am–6:30pm; mid-June to Labor Day, daily 10am–11pm (water rides, to 8pm).

ENTERTAINMENT

THE PUPPET CENTRE, 171 Avondale Ave., Yonge St. and Hwy 401. Tel. 222-9029.

The center has more than 750 puppets from all over the world, but what gives the greatest pleasure and gets the most rapt attention are the plays that are performed Tuesday through Saturday. Call for the schedule.

Admission: $5.50.

Subway: Sheppard; then a five-minute walk south on Yonge Street.

ROY THOMSON HALL CUSHION CONCERTS, 60 Simcoe St. Tel. 593-4828.

Music is presented in the lobby of one of Toronto's premier concert halls. Kids love to settle down into the cushions and tuck into the doughnuts and meet the artists after the performance. Concerts are usually given for 4- to 6-year-olds and 9- to 11-year-olds. October to April only. Call for information.

Admission: $7.

Subway: St. Andrews.

YOUNG PEOPLE'S THEATRE, 165 Front St. E., at Sherbourne St. Tel. 864-9732 (box office) or 363-5131 (administration).

Devoted to the entertainment of young people. The season runs from November to May. Call for information.

Subway: Union.

4. SPECIAL-INTEREST SIGHTSEEING

FOR THE ARCHITECTURE LOVER

For folks interested in the architectural development of Toronto there are certain highlights that should not be missed. Most are discussed either in the attractions sections, above, or in the various walking tours in Chapter 7. Therefore only their highlights are mentioned here. Those that have not been discussed elsewhere are treated in full here.

From the early period when the city was primarily a garrison, **Fort York** stands out.

Little else remains from the early 19th-century period, except, of course, **The Grange, Campbell House,** and **Colborne Lodge** in High Park.

The highlights of the mid-Victorian period include **St. Lawrence Market** and **St. Lawrence Hall, St. James Cathedral, University College,** and **Osgoode Hall.**

Buildings from the last three decades of the 19th century are numerous. Along Front Street in the old warehousing area there are many fine cast-iron buildings. See, in particular, the **Beardmore** and the **Gooderham Building** (the Flatiron). The **Bank of Montréal** at Yonge and Front streets is an ornate gem, while in domestic architecture many of the buildings along Jarvis and Sherbourne streets that were mansions still stand today in various states of repair. See also the **George Gooderham House** (the York Club) at 135 St. George St., at Bloor Street West. The **Ontario Legislative Buildings** in Queen's Park date from this High Victorian period, as does **Old City Hall** and two emporiums, one devoted to culture and the other to retailing—**Massey Hall** on Shuter Street and **The Bay (Simpson's)** at Yonge and Richmond streets.

The Edwardian period is expressed in the homes of such magnates as **Joseph Flavelle** (Holwood) on Queen's Park Crescent and, most ostentatious of all, **Casa Loma.** The **Royal Alex** also dates from this period.

Some great skyscrapers from the 1920s and '30s can be viewed if you stroll through the financial district down Bay Street from Old City Hall. **Sunnyside** and **Exhibition Place** date from the '20s, when people flocked to the lakefront on their days off.

Highlights of the later 20th century must include the **New City Hall;** Mies van der Rohe's **Toronto Dominion Centre; Royal Bank Plaza** by Webb Zerafa Menker & Housden; **Ontario Place** by Craig, Zeidler & Strong; the **Metro Library** and **Scarborough**

IMPRESSIONS

Toronto is New York . . . run by the Swiss.
—Peter Ustinov

Lord Bessborough, later Governor-General of Canada, once described Toronto as understanding two things perfectly—"The British Empire and a good horse."
—Jan Morris, *Travels* (1976)

Civic Centre, both by Raymond Moriyama; the **Eaton Centre** by Bregman & Hamann and the Zeidler Partnership; **Roy Thomson Hall** by Arthur Erickson; **SkyDome;** and the **BCE building** on Front Street.

THE ANNEX This is a residential area containing marvelous Romanesque Revival, Queen Anne, Georgian Revival, and English Country specimens that any architecture lover will not want to miss. The area stretches west of Yorkville. Stroll down any of the streets in this neighborhood to get the flavor—Bedford, Admiral, St. George, Huron, and Madison.

On Madison, for example, stop and look at the house designed by E. J. Lennox, the **Lewis Lukes House** at no. 37, a marvelous solid Romanesque Revival residence featuring basketweave brickwork. One of the first residences located in the Annex, which set the trend to move there, was the **Gooderham House** (1889–92), at 135 St. George St., at Bloor Street. It was designed by David Roberts for George Gooderham, president of the Gooderham & Worts Distillery. This massive Richardsonian building in stone, brick, and terra cotta, with its towers and intricately patterned rounded arches, is today occupied by the York Club.

5. SPORTS & RECREATION

SPORTS

Some wag once said that there's only one really religious place in Toronto, and that's **Maple Leaf Gardens,** 60 Carlton St. (tel. 977-1641), where the city's ice-hockey team, the Maple Leafs, wield their sticks to the delight and screaming enthusiasm of fans. Tickets are nigh impossible to attain because they are sold by subscription. Your only hope is to find a scalper.

The **SkyDome,** on Front Street beside the CN Tower, is the home of the Blue Jays baseball team (World Series champs in 1992) and the Toronto Argonauts football team. For information, contact the Toronto Blue Jays, P.O. Box 7777, Adelaide St., Toronto, ON, M5C 2K7 (tel. 416/595-0077). For Blue Jays tickets, call 341-1111; for Argonauts tickets, call 872-5000.

Racing takes place at **Woodbine Racetrack,** at Rexdale Boulevard and Hwy. 427, in Etobicoke (tel. 675-6110), famous for the Queen's Plate (June) and the Rothman's International, a world classic turf race (October).

Closer to town, **Greenwood Racetrack,** 1669 Queen St. E. (tel. 698-3131), offers harness racing with thoroughbreds competing in the spring and fall.

RECREATION

For additional information on golf courses, tennis, swimming pools, beaches, and picnic areas, call **Metro Parks** (tel. 392-6641 or 392-8186 Monday through Friday).

BEACHES The most popular beaches are found on the Toronto Islands—Centre Island and Wards Island—and, of course, at the Beaches at the east end of the city. The lake is severely polluted; these are *not* swimming beaches. Call Metro Parks for the locations of the best places to swim and also for the current state of lakefront beaches.

GOLF The following 18-hole municipal golf courses are open on a first-come, first-served basis. No membership or reservations are necessary. Clubs and caddy carts can be rented. Courses are open from dawn to dusk; the season begins around mid-April.

Dentonia Park Golf Course, Victoria Park Avenue (tel. 392-2558).

Don Valley Golf Course, 4200 Yonge St. (tel. 392-2465).

Humber Valley Golf Course, Beattie Avenue, off Albion Road (tel. 392-2488).

Lakeview Golf Course, 1190 Dixie Rd., in Port Credit, 1km south of the QEW (tel. 278-4411).

Scarlett Woods Golf Course, Jane Street at Eglinton Avenue West (tel. 392-2484).

Tam O'Shanter Golf Course, Birchmount Road north of Sheppard Avenue East (tel. 392-2547).

SWIMMING For **pool information,** call either 392-7286 (east) or 392-7259 (west). There are many city indoor and outdoor pools.

The **University of Toronto Athletic Centre,** 55 Harbord St. at Spadina Avenue (tel. 978-3437), opens the swimming pool free to the public on Sunday from 12:30 to 4pm.

TENNIS The following outdoor courts are available free at any time:

Moss Park, at Sherbourne and Queen streets.

Riverdale Park, Broadview Avenue, south of Danforth.

Ryerson Community Park, Church Street, between Gerrard and Gould streets.

CHAPTER 7

STROLLING AROUND TORONTO

1. **HARBOURFRONT**
2. **THE FINANCIAL DISTRICT, CITY HALL & QUEEN STREET VILLAGE**
3. **CHINATOWN, THE ART GALLERY & KENSINGTON MARKET**
4. **QUEEN'S PARK & THE UNIVERSITY**
5. **ST. LAWRENCE & DOWNTOWN EAST**
6. **BLOOR/YORKVILLE**
7. **THE BEACHES**

Toronto is almost a distant cousin of Los Angeles: It's a huge, sprawling city, and it's difficult to imagine walking everywhere. (Fortunately, Toronto, unlike Los Angeles, is blessed with a super-efficient public transportation system.)

So the walking tours below aren't designed to give you an overview of the city; instead, they'll introduce you to the most colorful, exciting neighborhoods and areas that are packed with sights on almost every corner. We'll start with Harbourfront, which Torontonians have turned into a glorious playground opening onto the lake.

WALKING TOUR 1 — Harbourfront

Start: Union Station.
Finish: Spadina Quay.
Time: Anywhere from three to eight hours, depending on how much time you spend shopping, eating, and daydreaming.
Best Time: Sunday, when the Harbourfront Antiques Market is bustling.

As you start your tour, pause to look at the beaux arts interior of Union Station. From here, either take the LRT to York Quay or walk down York Street to Queen's Quay West. Directly ahead, across the street, is the:

1. **Queen's Quay Terminal,** a large complex that houses more than 100 shops and restaurants and, on the third floor, a theater specially designed for dance. Built in 1927 when lake and railroad trade flourished, this eight-story concrete warehouse has been attractively renovated and turned into a light and airy marketplace with garden courts, skylights, and waterfalls.

   Although you'll find few bargains here, some of my favorite fun stores on the street level are **Sportables,** for fine sportswear at not-too-outrageous prices; **Suitables,** for reasonably priced silk fashions; and **Just Kidding,** for kids' fashions.

   On the upper level there's also plenty to choose from: **Sci-Tech** for science games, clocks, globes, and all kinds of fun items associated with all the sciences; **The Nature Store,** which sells everything from bird feeders and coasters featuring birds, to carved loons, wilderness knives, compasses, and natural objects (even the T-shirts have paintings of birds on them); **Geomania,**

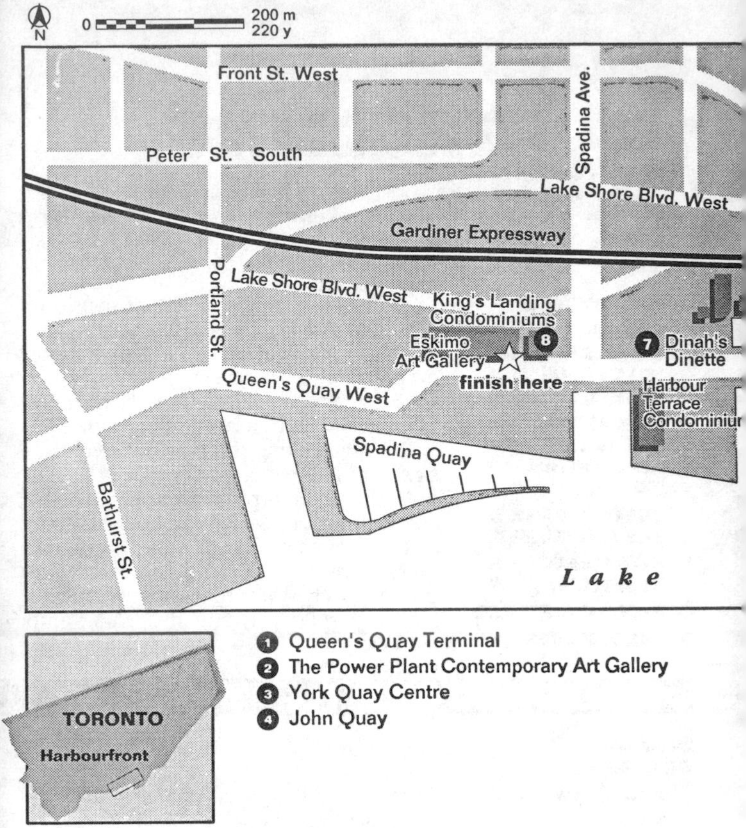
N
0
200 m
220 y
Front St. West
Peter St. South
Spadina Ave.
Lake Shore Blvd. West
Gardiner Expressway
Portland St.
Lake Shore Blvd. West
King's Landing Condominiums
Eskimo Art Gallery
8
finish here
7 Dinah's Dinette
Harbour Terrace Condominiu
Queen's Quay West
Spadina Quay
Bathurst St.
Lake
TORONTO
Harbourfront
1 Queen's Quay Terminal
2 The Power Plant Contemporary Art Gallery
3 York Quay Centre
4 John Quay

with carved, polished minerals and precious stones sculpted into images or polished into book ends; and **It's a Small World,** which has all kinds of miniatures—thimbles, carved animals, historic sites, and more.

REFUELING STOPS If you want to sit out and watch the lakefront traffic—boat and human—go to **Spinnakers,** on the ground floor of Queen's Quay. Otherwise, stay upstairs and dine at **La Bouche** and finish off with something yummy from **Sweet Temptations.**

From Queen's Quay Terminal, walk along the water to:

2. The Power Plant Contemporary Art Gallery, a former power plant that has been converted to display modern art. The same building also houses the Du Maurier Theatre Centre, which presents works in French.

Behind this building, adjacent to Queen's Quay West, is the Tent in the Park, which shelters different events during the summer season. Walk west into the:

3. York Quay Centre, another interesting complex containing a number of restaurants and galleries. Spend some time in the **Craft**

WALKING TOUR — HARBOURFRONT

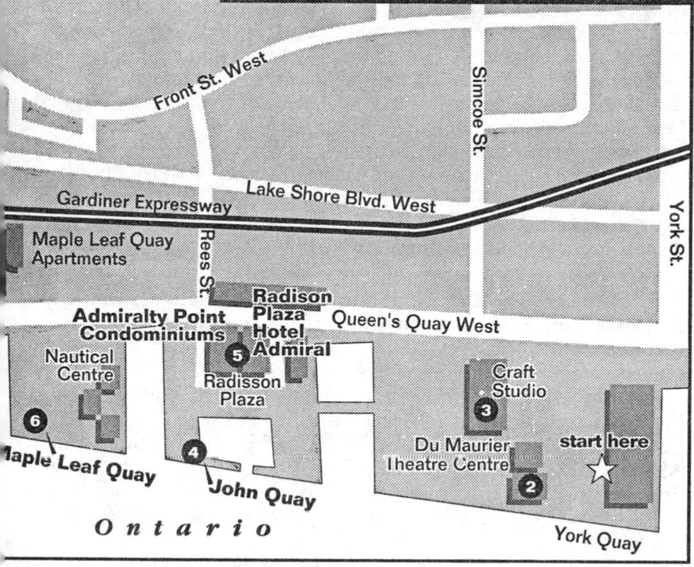
Front St. West
Simcoe St.
Lake Shore Blvd. West
Gardiner Expressway
York St.
Maple Leaf Quay Apartments
Rees St.
Radisson Plaza Hotel Admiral
Admiralty Point Condominiums
Queen's Quay West
Nautical Centre
5
Radisson Plaza
Craft Studio
3
6
4
Du Maurier Theatre Centre
start here
2
laple Leaf Quay
John Quay
Ontario
York Quay

5 Radisson Plaza Hotel Admiral and Admiralty Point Condominiums
6 Maple Leaf Quay
7 Harbourfront Antiques Market
8 Centre Francophone

Studio watching the glass-blowers, potters, jewelrymakers, and other artisans at work and browse in the store that sells their work.

On the waterfront side in front of York Quay there's a pond where kids operate model boats in summer; in winter it turns into an ice-skating rink.

From York Quay, cross the Amsterdam Bridge above Marina 4, checking out the wealth that's bobbing down below. You'll arrive on:

4. **John Quay.** The first building you'll come to contains four restaurants, beyond which you'll see the towers of the:
5. **Radisson Plaza Hotel Admiral and Admiralty Point Condominiums,** and across Queen's Quay West, the HarbourPoint Condominiums. On the ground level of the Admiralty Point Condos are a few interesting stores: The Nautical Mind Bookstore, The Dock Shoppe, and Old Firehall Sports.

REFUELING STOPS Pop into the **Radisson Plaza Hotel Admiral,** which has a couple of dining rooms, plus a pleasant poolside terrace if it's a sunny day. Or try something fresh from **Wallymagoo's Marinebar.**

Continue west along Queen's Quay West past:

6. **Maple Leaf Quay** (unless you want to stop at the Nautical Centre to sign up for sailing classes and the like). Continue west and you'll see the Maple Leaf Quay Apartments on your right and the Harbour Terrace Condominiums farther along on your left on the waterfront. Next door to the westernmost tower of the Maple Leaf Quay Apartments is the:
7. **Harbourfront Antiques Market,** a terrific market filled with more than 100 dealers selling fine furniture, jewelry, books, clocks, and art deco items. On Sunday there's also an outdoor market featuring less established dealers. Go on Sunday—few dealers are open during the week.

A REFUELING STOP In the Harbourfront Antiques Market, **Dinah's Dinette** has great fresh salads, sandwiches, quiches, and desserts.

Continue west along Queen's Quay West to Spadina Quay. First stop on your right on Lower Spadina is the:

8. **Centre Francophone** (tel. 367-1950), which hosts cultural and educational events and offers information about French life in Toronto (open Monday through Friday only). In the adjacent King's Landing Condominiums, the **Eskimo Art Gallery** is worth a stop.

At Spadina Quay board the LRT and head back to Union Station.

WALKING TOUR 2 — The Financial District, City Hall & Queen Street Village

Start: The CN Tower, near the corner of John and Front streets.
Finish: At one of Queen Street West's watering holes.
Time: Six to eight hours, depending on how long you take to browse.
Best Time: Anytime.

AROUND THE FINANCIAL DISTRICT Start by going up the:

1. **CN Tower,** which is the tallest free-standing structure in the world. Back down at the base, exit at the corner of John and Front streets. From here, look east along Front Street to see the glistening golden Royal Bank Towers. The new CBC Center stretches along the north side of Front Street for a whole long block.

   Walk north on John Street, cross Wellington, and continue up to King Street. Turn right. On the northeast corner of King Street sports fans will want to stop in at:
2. **Legends of the Game.** Doors with baseball-shaped handles open onto an emporium that features the Wall of Fame and every conceivable sports collectible.

   Continue walking along the north side of King Street, past a cluster of Ed Mirvish creations, first his restaurants (drop into one just to check out the larger-than-life decor), then a whole wall of clippings about this marvelous Torontonian who, with his great love and boostering of the city, seems a shier version of New York's Ed Koch. Then there's:

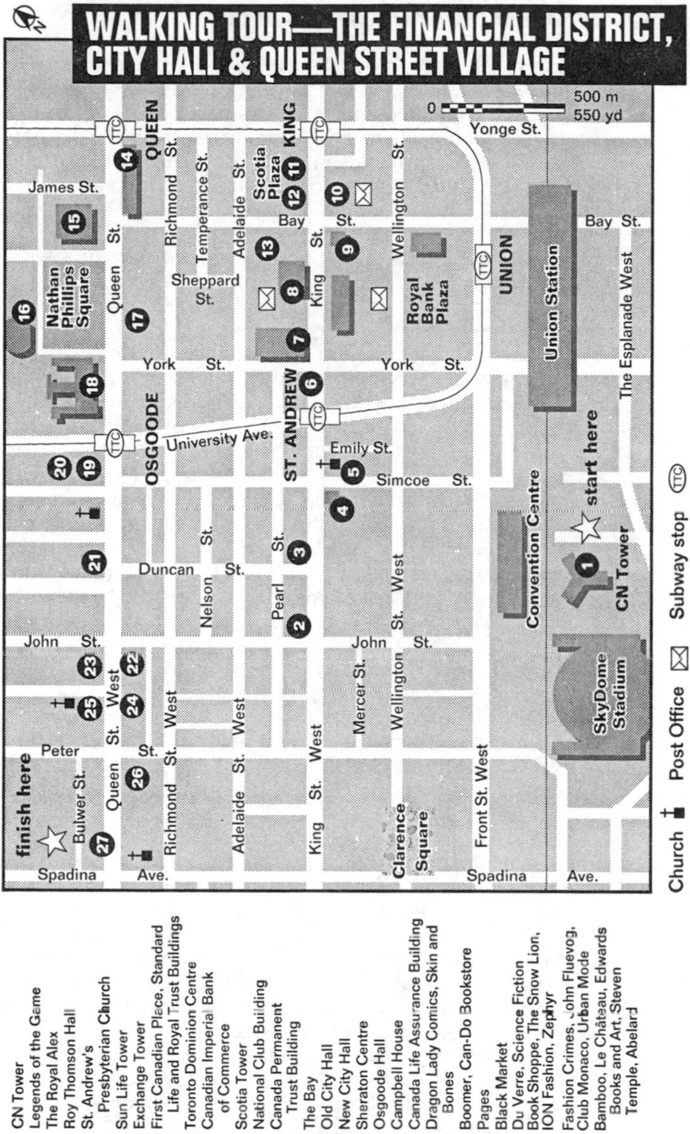
WALKING TOUR—THE FINANCIAL DISTRICT, CITY HALL & QUEEN STREET VILLAGE
0
500 m
550 yd
Yonge St.
QUEEN
KING
TTC
UNION
ST. ANDREW
OSGOODE
James St.
Queen St.
Richmond St.
Temperance St.
Adelaide St.
Scotia Plaza
Bay St.
Wellington St.
Sheppard St.
King St.
Royal Bank Plaza
Nathan Phillips Square
Union Station
The Esplanade West
York St.
University Ave.
Emily St.
Simcoe St.
Duncan St.
Nelson St.
Pearl St.
Convention Centre
start here
CN Tower
John St.
Mercer St.
Wellington St. West
SkyDome Stadium
Peter St.
Queen St. West
Richmond St. West
Adelaide St. West
King St. West
Front St. West
finish here
Bulwer St.
Clarence Square
Spadina Ave.
Church
Post Office
Subway stop
1 CN Tower
2 Legends of the Game
3 The Royal Alex
4 Roy Thomson Hall
5 St. Andrew's Presbyterian Church
6 Sun Life Tower
7 Exchange Tower
8 First Canadian Place, Standard Life and Royal Trust Buildings
9 Toronto Dominion Centre
10 Canadian Imperial Bank of Commerce
11 Scotia Tower
12 National Club Building
13 Canada Permanent Trust Building
14 The Bay
15 Old City Hall
16 New City Hall
17 Sheraton Centre
18 Osgoode Hall
19 Campbell House
20 Canada Life Assurance Building
21 Dragon Lady Comics, Skin and Bones
22 Boomer, Can-Do Bookstore
23 Pages
24 Black Market
25 Du Verre, Science Fiction Book Shoppe, The Snow Lion, ION Fashion, Zephyr
26 Fashion Crimes, John Fluevog, Club Monaco, Urban Mode
27 Bamboo, Le Château, Edwards Books and Art, Steven Temple, Abelard

3. **The Royal Alex.** This beloved theater, named after the king's consort, was built in 1906 and 1907 by John M. Lyle in a magnificent beaux arts style and was saved and refurbished by Ed Mirvish in 1963. Edwardian to a tee, it's loaded with gilt and velvet and sports an entrance foyer lined with green marble. On the south side of the street at the corner of King and Simcoe streets is:

4. **Roy Thomson Hall,** named after newspaper magnate Lord

Thomson of Fleet. Built between 1972 and 1982 and designed by Arthur Erickson, the building's exterior looks very space age, and inside, the mirrored effects are dramatic. Tours are usually given of this fabulous concert hall at 12:30pm, but call ahead at 593-4828 to confirm if you really do want to see behind the scenes. If you don't want to take a tour, at least go in for a look.

REFUELING STOPS Your best bet in this part of town is probably **Orso** for leisurely luncheons or **Meyer's Deli** on King Street for a quick-and-easy casual lunch or snack.

Continue walking east. You'll be walking through the heart of the financial district, surrounded by the many towers owned and operated by banks and brokerage, trust, and insurance companies. Cross Simcoe Street. On the northeast corner of King and Simcoe rises the Sun Life Centre; on the southeast corner stands:

5. **St. Andrew's Presbyterian Church,** a quietly inviting retreat from the city's pace and noise. Continue along the block to University Avenue. Opposite, on the northeast corner, is the:
6. **Sun Life Tower,** marked by a sculpture by Sorel Etrog. Farther along the block you'll find another sculpture, *Parent I* by Barbara Hepworth, in a courtyard setting at the northwest corner of York Street. On the northeast corner stands the:
7. **Exchange Tower,** connected to the Toronto Stock Exchange at the corner of Adelaide and York streets.

Continue along King Street past:

8. **First Canadian Place** on the north side and the **Standard Life and Royal Trust Buildings** on the south, until you reach Bay Street. Again, there are views of the magnificent Royal Bank towers from here.

The intersection of Bay and King streets was once considered the precise geographical center of Toronto's financial power, and during the mining booms in the 1920s and 1950s, Bay Street was lined with offices that were filled with commission salesmen peddling stocks to the equivalent of the little ol' lady from Dubuque. This is the hub that gave Torontonians their reputation as a voracious band of money-grubbing folks that Hugh McLennan portrayed in his marvelous novel about Québec, *Two Solitudes*. Rising at King and Bay today is the:

9. **Toronto Dominion Centre,** built between 1963 and 1969 and designed by Mies van der Rohe in his sleek trademark style. The black steel and dark-bronze–tinted glass tower rises from its gray granite base launching pad.

Cross Bay Street. On the south side of King Street, architecture buffs will want to go into the:

10. **Canadian Imperial Bank of Commerce** (1929–31) just to see the massive banking hall—145 feet long, 85 feet wide, and 65 feet high—with its coffered ceiling, gilt moldings, and decorative sculpted friezes. The main entrance is decorated, for instance, with squirrels, roosters, bees, bears, and figures representing Industry, Commerce, and Mercury. For years this 34-story building dominated the Toronto skyline. In the early 1970s I. M. Pei was asked to design a new complex while preserving the old building. He set the new stainless-steel bank

tower that glistens (thanks to its mercury lamination) back from King Street, creating Commerce Court.

Opposite, on the north side of King Street, note:

11. Scotia Tower, the red-tinted building.

Walk back to Bay Street and turn right going north. At no. 303 on the east side is the:

12. National Club Building. In 1874 the Canada First Movement, which had been started in Ottawa in 1868, became centered in Toronto. It established a weekly, *The Nation,* and entered politics as the Canadian National Association and founded the National Club. Eventually the movement's influence faded but its original ideas had lasting influence. The club moved to these premises in 1907.

Across the street on the west side at the corner of Bay and Adelaide streets stands the:

13. Canada Permanent Trust Building (1928). Go in to view the beautifully worked art deco brass and bronze, particularly the elevator doors, which are chased and engraved with foliage and flowers.

Cross Adelaide Street. As you walk up Bay Street, the magnificently solid Old City Hall is clearly in view, but first, on the east side of Bay between Richmond and Queen, look at or, if you like, stop into:

14. The Bay, one of the city's most venerable retailers, complete with an Alfred Dunhill store and an oyster bar. The Bay (formerly Simpson's), along with arch rival Eaton's, has influenced the development of the downtown areas of most major Canadian cities.

Ahead looms the:

15. Old City Hall, reflected dramatically to the right in the Cadillac Fairview Office Tower at the corner of James and Queen streets. This solid, impressive building designed by Edward James Lennox is built out of Credit River Valley sandstone in a magnificent Romanesque Revival style that is obviously influenced by H. H. Richardson. Begun in 1885, it was opened in 1899, and for years its clock tower was a familiar skyline landmark. Today the building houses the provincial criminal courts. Go in to see the impressive staircase, columns with decorative capitals, mosaic floor, and stained-glass window (1898) by Robert McCausland depicting the union of Commerce and Industry watched over by Britannia. Pause on your way out to look down the canyon of Bay Street, the city's equivalent of New York's Wall Street. Bay Street curves around, and to your left there is suddenly the:

16. New City Hall, the city's fourth, built between 1958 and 1965; in modern sculptural style, it's the symbol of Toronto's new dynamism. Designed by Finnish architect Viljo Revell, who won the competition that was entered by 510 architects from 42 countries, including I. M. Pei, it has a great square in front with fountain and pool to which office workers flock in summer to relax and then in winter to skate. The square is named after Nathan Phillips, Toronto's first Jewish mayor, who helped push the project through. The Council Chamber, supported on a two-tier podium, looks like a flying saucer, but the glass walls make it seem open and accessible. Henry Moore's sculpture *The Archer* stands in front of the building—thanks to Mayor Phil

Givens, who raised the money to buy it through public subscription after the city authorities refused to purchase it. This gesture encouraged Henry Moore to bestow a major collection of his works on the Art Gallery. The Council Chamber is flanked by two curved concrete towers that house the bureaucracy.

For the best view of City Hall, enter the:

17. **Sheraton Centre,** on the south side of Queen Street, and go up to the second-floor Long Bar, which overlooks the square.

REFUELING STOPS For some light refreshment, stop in at either the **Oyster Bar** in The Bay or any one of several dining spots in the **Sheraton Centre.**

From City Hall, walk west along Queen Street. On your right behind an ornate wrought-iron fence that once kept out the cows you'll see:

18. **Osgoode Hall,** since the 1830s headquarters of the Law Society of Upper Canada, a kind of professional trade union. Named after the first chief justice of Upper Canada, the building was constructed in stages, starting with the East Wing in 1831 to 1832, the West Wing in 1844 to 1845, and the center block in 1856 to 1860. The last, with its Palladian portico, is the most impressive. Inside, the Great Library—112 feet long, 40 feet wide, and 40 feet high—with stucco decoration and coved domed ceiling is grand. The Ontario Supreme Court is across the street on the south side of Queen Street.

Keep walking west to University Avenue. On the northwest corner you can visit the:

19. **Campbell House,** the elegant Georgian residence of Sir William Campbell, a Scot who moved to York in 1811 and rose to become chief justice of Upper Canada. A handsome piece of Georgian architecture, it was moved to this location from a few miles farther east.

Behind Campbell House, on the northwest side of University Avenue, the:

20. **Canada Life Assurance Building** stretches northward. Atop the tower a neon sign provides weather reports—white flashes for snow, red flashes for rain, green beacon for clement weather, or red beacon for cloudy weather. If the flashes move upward the temperature is headed that way, and vice versa.

At University Avenue and Queen Street you can end the tour by boarding the subway at Osgoode to your next destination, or you can continue walking west along Queen Street to explore the many delights of this thoroughfare.

AROUND QUEEN STREET VILLAGE This is one of the great "alternative" shopping and nightlife venues of the city and there are many stores that you'll want to browse in as you walk from University to Spadina and even beyond. Here are some likely ones along the route.

On the north side of the street at no. 180 there's:

21. **Skin and Bones** for Native American arts and crafts (jewelry, sculpture, and so on), avant-garde fashions, and at no. 200 there's **Dragon Lady Comics** for collectors of old and new.

REFUELING STOPS On the south side at the corner of John Street, there's **Zaidy's,** a popular restaurant specializing in Cajun cuisine and well known for its desserts. On the north side on the same block you'll find another perennial dining favorite, the **Queen Mother Café,** serving comforting bistro-style fare.

On the south side of the street:

22. Boomer stocks well-tailored men's fashions that have a youthful appeal, while at no. 311 the **Can-Do Bookstore** has books on everything from homesteading and cooking to sports and languages.

Cross to the north side of the street and at no. 256 you'll find:

23. Pages, a large, well-stocked bookstore selling hard- and softcovers and also a wide selection of magazines.

Back on the south side:

24. Black Market, upstairs, features vintage clothing.

Across the street:

25. Du Verre has a wide variety of glass vases, pitchers, and plates and proudly displays a sticker identifying it as an "alternative bridal registry." **The Science Fiction Book Shoppe,** at no. 282, amasses a vast selection of titles in the genre. **The Snow Lion,** at no. 286, sells items from Tibet and the Himalayas—rugs, jackets, hats, gongs, tankas, and more. **ION Fashion,** at no. 290, as its name would suggest, displays cool, hip clothing, including children's fashions and accessories. **Zephyr,** at no. 292, appeals to the natural world for inspiration, proferring polished rocks and minerals, pyramids, crystals, butterflies, and other natural collectibles. Soho Street cuts in here on the north.

On the south side beyond Peter Street are several funky fashion stores. Among them are these:

26. Fashion Crimes caters to the woman's sense of the outrageous; **John Fluevog** has equally wild shoes for men and women. **Club Monaco** provides a more tailored sports look. **Urban Mode** displays the latest European housewares.

Back on the north side of the street, note:

27. Bamboo, a favorite music club, with a Caribbean flavor.

REFUELING STOPS Two of the city's favorite bistros are located on the north side of Queen—the more traditional **Le Select,** with its pleasant outdoor dining area and skylit back room, and the more avant-garde **Rivoli.**

Also on the north side of Queen Street, **Le Château,** a Montréal fashion original, offers engaging fashions. **Edwards Books and Art** has some of the best prices on art books in the city and regularly advertises discounted titles in the local newspapers. Although it stocks the latest fiction and nonfiction, the store specializes in fine, illustrated books—cookbooks, gardening, art and architecture, and more.

Continue on to Spadina Avenue and board the streetcar back to the Osgoode or Queen subway stop. The unweary can continue along Queen Street beyond Spadina Avenue, discovering such wonderful rare-book dealers as **Steven Temple** and **Abelard,** along with other interesting stores.

WALKING TOUR 3 — Chinatown, the Art Gallery & Kensington Market

Start: Osgoode subway station.
Finish: College subway station.
Time: Six to eight hours, depending on whether or not you stop.
Best Time: Anytime except Monday (when the Art Gallery is closed).

AROUND CHINATOWN From the Osgoode subway station, walk west on Queen Street. Turn right onto McCaul Street. On the west side of the street (left), if you're interested in crafts, you'll want to stop at:

1. **Prime Gallery,** at no. 52, which sells ceramics, jewelry, fabrics, and other art objects crafted by contemporary artisans.

   On the right is:
2. **Village by the Grange,** an apartment/shopping complex that's laid out in a series of courtyards (one even contains a small ice-skating rink). Go into the complex at the southern end and stroll through, emerging from the food market. En route you'll come across many inviting stores, like **Bellissimo Fashions,** featuring appealing children's clothes, including Muppet-style PVC jackets and Peruvian-style sweaters with appliquéed numbers; and **18 Karat,** where the proprietors design and craft jewelry behind the counter (show them what you have in mind and they will craft it for you beautifully).

REFUELING STOPS Also in Village by the Grange are two of the city's most popular restaurants—**Ginsberg & Wong,** serving Chinese and deli, and **Young Lok,** one of Toronto's oldest Chinese restaurants. The aforementioned **Food Market** contains stalls selling everything—12 varieties of freshly brewed coffee, schnitzels, satay, Japanese noodles, salads, felafel, hot dogs, Chinese food, kebabs, pizza, and fried chicken.

Continue north along McCaul, passing the Ontario College of Art on the left side of the street, until you reach Dundas Street, where on the left you'll encounter a large Henry Moore sculpture entitled *Large Two Forms,* which is precisely what it is. Turn left. The entrance to the:

3. **Art Gallery of Ontario** is on the left (currently undergoing construction and expansion scheduled to be completed in 1993). If you don't want to go into the collections, you can browse the gallery stores without paying admission. Cross to the north side of Dundas, opposite the Art Gallery. It's worth stopping in at the:
4. **Bau-Xi,** a gallery representing modern Canadian artists. From here, walk west along Dundas, crossing Beverley Street, into the heart of Chinatown, stopping in at the grocery stores, bakeries, bookstalls, and other emporiums selling exotic foods, handcrafts, and other items from Asia.

   What follows are some of my favorite browsing stops along the stretch of Dundas Street between Beverly Street and Spadina Avenue. On the south or left side as you go west is:
5. **Tai Yan Co.,** at no. 407–09, a supermarket displaying dozens of

different mushrooms, all clearly labeled in English, as well as all kinds of fresh Chinese vegetables, meats, fish, and canned goods. **Melewa Bakery,** at no. 433, has a wide selection of pastries, like mung-bean and lotus-paste buns.

On the north side of the street:

6. **Gifts Oriental,** at no. 422, has fans, screens, china figurines, inlay tables, and small items like purses and glass cases. **J & S Arts and Crafts,** at no. 430, is a good place to pick up souvenirs, including kimonos and happy coats, kung fu suits, address books, cushion covers, and all-cotton Chinatown T-shirts for only $6. **New World Book Store,** at no. 442, has a good selection of Chinese and other Asian-language dictionaries as well as Chinese cards.

At the corner of Huron Street on the north side of Dundas:

7. **Ten Ren Tea,** no. 454, sells all kinds of teas—black, oolong, and so forth—stored in large canisters in the back of the store, as well as charming small ceramic tea pots priced from $20 to $65. A large variety of gnarled ginseng root is also displayed for sale. **W Y Trading Co., Inc.,** has a great selection of records, CDs, and tapes—everything from Chinese folk songs and cantatas to current hit albums from Hong Kong and Taiwan. This is one place a non-Chinese–speaking visitor can read what the recording contains. **Furuya,** at no. 460, stocks Japanese specialties including some really fine sushi oke, lacquer trays, bowls, boxes, and saké sets as well as food and other specialties.

REFUELING STOP Right in Chinatown, **Champion House** is a good lunch stop that offers comfortable, elegant surroundings (in contrast to the strictly functional look that prevails in Chinatown) and good Chinese cuisine. The specialty is Peking duck, and a gong is sounded when it comes out of the kitchen. They have other dishes, too, like beef with ginger and green onions and also orange chicken, priced from $9 to $13.

At Spadina, turn left and walk to no. 251, the:

8. **Great China Herbs Center,** where the friendly storekeeper welcomes curious visitors who come to look at the exotic roots and fruits that are kept in large glass jars and at other medicines like deer-tail extract and liquid-gold ginseng or royal jelly. Watch them weigh each item out on a hand-held weigh scale and total the bill with a fast-clicking abacus.

From here walk back up Spadina to Dundas and cross Spadina to:

9. **Dragon City,** an Asian-style shopping complex on the west side of Spadina at no. 280.

Spadina Avenue is the widest street in the city because the wealthy Baldwin family had a 132-foot swath cut through the forest from Queen Street to Bloor Street so that they could view the lake from their new home on the top of Spadina Hill. Later, in the early 20th century, it became Toronto's garment center, the equivalent of New York's Seventh Avenue and the focal point of the city's Jewish community.

Although it's still the garment center, with wholesale and discount fashion houses, and the fur district (farther south around Adelaide), today Spadina Avenue is more Asian than Jewish.

If you enjoy strolling through supermarkets filled with exotic Asian delights, including such fruits as durian in season, then go into the:

10. **New Asia Supermarket,** at no. 295–97, or cross the street and explore the:

11. **Tai Cheong Supermarket.** Also on the west side of the street, the **WayKing Centre** contains a number of businesses—tailors; jewelers; trading companies; and Aquarium Fantasy, where you can watch the fierce-looking black moore, the piranha, and an all-time Asian favorite, the brilliant carp.

REFUELING STOPS Here, why not join the Chinese at one of the food courts that serve all kinds of Asian cuisine. There's one downstairs at **Dragon City** and one upstairs at **WayKing Centre.** The stalls sell dim sum, noodles, curry, and all kinds of Asian fare. For the language-deficient, each of the dishes is pictured in color and assigned a number. Good food at low prices.

As the Asian community in Toronto has grown, different nationalities have opened their own specialty stores. Although many of the products are the same, there are also many products that are unique to a particular country. For example, there's the:

12. **Vientiane Trading Company,** at no. 334, and next door at no. 336 is the **Hsin Thai Market.**

    At no. 360:

13. **Tap Phong Trading** has some terrific wicker baskets of all shapes and sizes: woks and ceramic cookware; heavy, attractive mortar and pestles; and other household items.

    Continue shopping and browsing along Spadina and then double back to St. Andrews. Turn right onto St. Andrews and note the synagogue on the north side of the street.

AROUND KENSINGTON MARKET Walk along St. Andrews to Kensington Avenue and turn right. Here you'll be in the heart of the Kensington Market area, which over the years has reflected the current ethnic scene that exists in the city. Once it was primarily a Jewish market; later it became more Portuguese; and today, it is a blend of Portuguese, Jewish, Caribbean, and Asian.

Walk north on Kensington Avenue. There are several West Indian groceries on this street, like:

14. **Tropical Harvest,** on the west side of the street, selling such items as plantains. Also on the west side, **Mendel's Creamery** sells smoked fish and herring and cheeses and fine dill pickles. Next door, **Cheese from Around the World** has an enormous selection at good prices.

    Continue along Kensington Avenue to Baldwin Street. Turn right on Baldwin and browse in:

15. **Cheese Magic,** which has a small selection of cheeses and

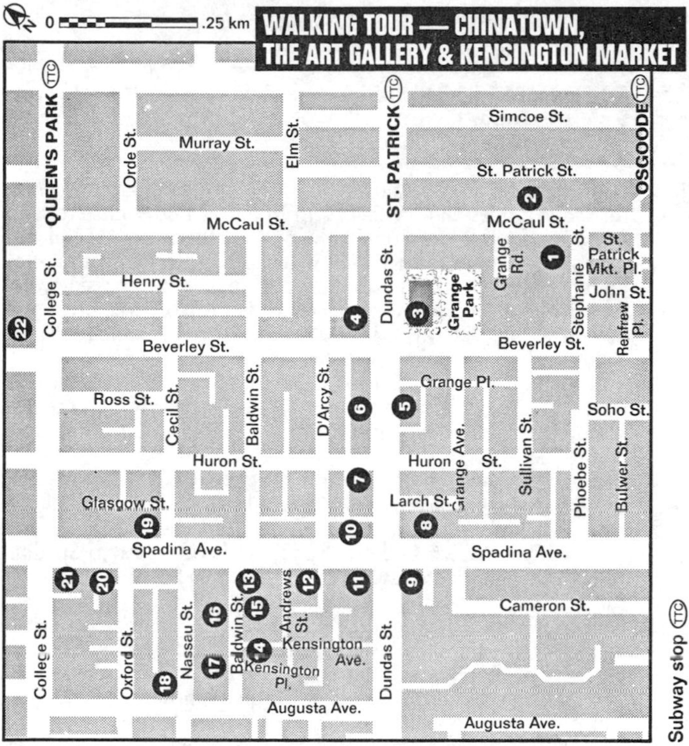

0 .25 km
WALKING TOUR — CHINATOWN, THE ART GALLERY & KENSINGTON MARKET
QUEEN'S PARK
ST. PATRICK
OSGOODE
Simcoe St.
Murray St.
Orde St.
Elm St.
St. Patrick St.
McCaul St.
McCaul St.
College St.
Henry St.
Dundas St.
Grange Park
Grange Rd.
Stephanie St.
St. Patrick Mkt. Pl.
John St.
Renfrew Pl.
Beverley St.
Beverley St.
Ross St.
Cecil St.
Baldwin St.
D'Arcy St.
Grange Pl.
Soho St.
Huron St.
Huron St.
Grange Ave.
Sullivan St.
Phoebe St.
Bulwer St.
Glasgow St.
Larch St.
Spadina Ave.
Spadina Ave.
College St.
Oxford St.
Nassau St.
Baldwin St.
Andrews St.
Kensington Ave.
Kensington Pl.
Dundas St.
Cameron St.
Augusta Ave.
Augusta Ave.
Subway stop

1. Prime Gallery
2. Village by the Grange
3. Art Gallery of Ontario
4. Baux-Xi
5. Tai Yan Co., Melewa Bakery
6. Gifts Oriental, J & S Arts and Crafts, New World Book Store
7. Ten Ren Tea, W Y Trading Co., Inc., Furuya
8. Great China Herbs Center
9. Dragon City
10. New Asia Super Market
11. Tai Cheong Supermarket, WayKing Centre
12. Vientiane Trading Company, Hsin Thai Market
13. Tap Phong Trading
14. Tropical Harvest, Mendel's Creamery, Cheese from Around the World
15. Magic Cheese
16. George Brown College
17. Salamanca, Caribbean, Saigon, Dias Fruit Market, Royal Food Centre
18. Iberica Bakery, Sagres Fish Market, Portuguese Meat Market
19. Rotman Hat Shop
20. Plaiter Place, Fortune Housewares
21. El Mocambo
22. Toronto Public Reference Library building

many gourmet items including jams. The north side of Baldwin is occupied by:

16. George Brown College, named after the founder of the *Globe and Mail.*

Now turn back and retrace your steps back along Baldwin past the junction with Kensington Avenue.

REFUELING STOP People often line up at the **Kensington Patty Palace,** on the north side of Baldwin, waiting to snack on the famous West Indian patties.

17. **Salamanca,** at 204 Baldwin St., has all kinds of grains, beans, nuts, and spices and specializes in Indian, Middle Eastern, and Mexican foods. Here on Baldwin, too, there are several fish stores, like **Caribbean** and **Saigon,** all displaying fresh fish of infinite variety, including salted cod, outside on the sidewalk. Similarly, the fruit markets, like **Dias Fruit Market,** are visual delights. The **Royal Food Centre,** on the south side of Baldwin, has Jamaican specialties, including goat meat.

At Augusta Avenue, turn right into the heart of the old Portuguese neighborhood. Many of the stores along here sell discount clothing, but there are still stores bearing Portuguese names like the:

18. **Iberica Bakery,** at no. 279; the **Sagres Fish Market;** and the **Portuguese Meat Market,** all on the east side of the street. Check out the fabric and furniture stores, too.

Turn right down Oxford Avenue and walk east to Spadina Avenue. If you're interested, turn right down Spadina to stop at the:

19. **Rotman Hat Shop,** at no. 345. Here, the Panama hats are as light as feathers and woven from the finest-quality Ecuador plants. The store, which has been in business here for over 40 years, also stocks grouser hats and other fun headgear. Or you can browse at:
20. **Plaiter Place,** at no. 384, which has a huge selection of finely crafted wicker baskets, birdcages, woven blinds, bamboo steamers, and hats and other fun items. Stop, too, at **Fortune Housewares,** no. 388, to shop for kitchen and household items—including all the good brand names—for at least 20% off prices elsewhere in the city.

Turn around and continue north up Spadina to:

21. **El Mocambo,** the rock-and-roll landmark where the Rolling Stones played on March 4 and 5, 1977, in their heyday, and hop on the trolley traveling east along College Street to the subway. Along the route, you'll pass on the left (north) side of the street what used to be the:
22. **Toronto Public Reference Library,** an attractive classical revival building now occupied by the University of Toronto bookstore and Koffler Student Centre, and on the south corner of College Street and University Avenue, the weird-looking mirrored-glass Hydro Place.

WALKING TOUR 4 — Queen's Park & the University

Start: Royal Ontario Museum.
Finish: Queen's Park.
Time: Three to four hours (more if you stop in at the museum).
Best Times: Anytime except Monday (when the museum's closed).

Take the subway to Museum to the:

1. **Royal Ontario Museum (ROM),** which is, of course, the great repository of the city's collections.

   Walk south to Queen's Park and follow its curve to the right past:
2. **Holwood,** the residence of wealthy meatpacker Sir Joseph Flavelle, which is now used by the university's School of Law. The elegant and richly decorated house was nicknamed Porker's Palace. Inside, the grand hall has decorative art nouveau features and a ceiling painted in art nouveau style by Gustav Hahn.

   Walk around to Hoskin Avenue. On the south side of the street stands:
3. **Wycliffe College,** founded in 1877 as a Low Church Anglican college and built in red brick in Romanesque Revival style. It stands across from:
4. **Trinity College,** the Anglican High Church college, founded as an independent university in 1851 by first Anglican bishop Strachan after King's College (the original university foundation) was declared nonsectarian in 1849. Trinity became part of the university in 1904. The Gothic buildings, the chapel, and the gardens are attractive sights.

   At Devonshire Place, turn right and walk north to:
5. **Massey College** (1960–63), enclosed behind modern, concertina-folded screenlike walls. It has a cloistered yet inviting air, with fountains playing in the quadrangle. Designed by Ron Thom, it has a traditional, serene yet modern quality with Frank Lloyd Wright and Japanese elements.

   Farther up Devonshire Place you'll come to:
6. **St. Hilda's,** a classic Georgian-style building housing the women's college that is part of Trinity.

   Turn around and come back to Hoskin. Turn right and walk over to St. George past St. Thomas Aquinas Chapel to see the dreadnought of a building, the:
7. **John P. Robarts Library,** the building everyone loves to hate. This huge concrete hulk houses the research library and the rare-book library.

   From here, turn back along Hoskin to Tower Road and turn right, walking toward the:
8. **Soldier's Memorial Tower** (1924), inspired by Magdalen's Big Tom, which stands between Gothic Hart House on the left and Romanesque University College on the right. Go into:
9. **Hart House** (1910–19), named after Hart Massey. It's consciously Oxford-like in style and atmosphere. Today, every U of T student belongs to Hart House, once an exclusive male domain. View the small chapel containing a memorial window created by Rosemary Kilbourn for Alice and Vincent Massey. Drift past the common rooms, where you'll probably observe a few students sleeping or lolling on couches, and proceed to the East Wing, which contains the Great Hall with its hammerbeam ceiling, stained-glass windows, and impressive fireplace. From the High Table, a staircase leads to the Senior Common Room. Under the quadrangle, the Hart House Theatre is well known for

its theatrical and other productions. The West Wing contains the Justina M. Barnicke Art Gallery, a fine collection of Canadian art.

Exit on the south side onto Hart House Circle. Proceed to your right around the circle. On the left is the:

10. **Stewart Observatory,** originally built in 1857 and reconstructed in 1908, and on the right stands:

11. **University College,** nicknamed the Godless College when it was founded in 1853 on nonsectarian lines. It was built from 1856 to 1859 by Cumberland and Storm in a fabulous Romanesque Revival style with fanciful towers and chimneys and intricately and heavily patterned round arches. Set around a quadrangle, the college has splendid East and West Halls in the south wing. The first women to enter the university were admitted to this college in 1884; there were nine at the end of that year. Go inside. The main staircase has a fantastic dragon newel post and the bottom.

Walk through into the quadrangle and around and out on the west side of the building. Turn left and walk south to King's College Circle. On your right will be:

12. **Knox College.** Go in to see the Gothic interior fan vaulting at the main entrance and the Caven Library with its hammerbeam ceiling.

Exit and continue around the circle to:

13. **Convocation Hall,** a monstrous Victorian bore. En route, you'll pass the far more elegant Simcoe Hall. Take some time to look back across the lawn at Hart House and the other university buildings across the circle.

Continue south to the:

14. **Medical Sciences Building** on the left, a concrete, brutalist building and the unimpressive classical revival **Sanford Fleming Building** on the right.

Exit onto College Avenue. If you want to, turn right to visit the:

15. **University bookstore,** at 214 College St., in the old city Reference Library, and then turn back and walk toward Queen's Park past the **Botany Building** and the lovely glass greenhouse that graces the rim of the park.

Walk into the park to the:

16. **Provincial Parliament buildings** (1886–92), an impressive example of Romanesque Revival created out of glorious pink sandstone. Beyond the entrance with its domed turrets is an impressive interior of carved wood, ornate cast and wrought iron, and a three-story legislative chamber with coved ceiling.

Exit at the northeastern rim of the circle to see:

17. **St. Michael's College,** which began in 1852 as a Roman Catholic boys' school, became affiliated with the university in 1881, and formally became a college in 1910. Nearby:

18. **Victoria College,** which was established in 1836 in Cobourg, Ontario, and moved here in 1892 when it became part of the University of Toronto. Originally a Methodist institution, it has been related to the United Church of Canada since 1925.

Note: Free tours of the university sponsored by the Alumni Association are given Monday through Friday at 10:30am and 1 and 2:30pm through the summer only. Call 978-5000.

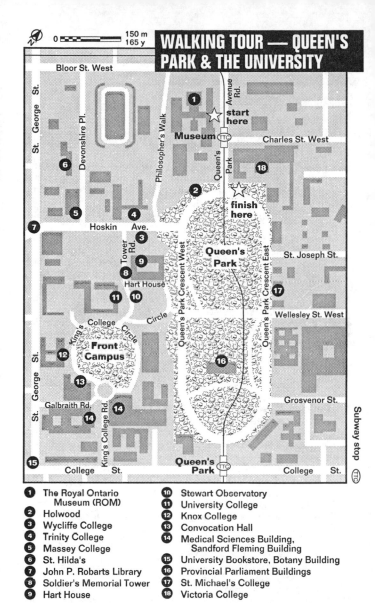

WALKING TOUR — QUEEN'S PARK & THE UNIVERSITY

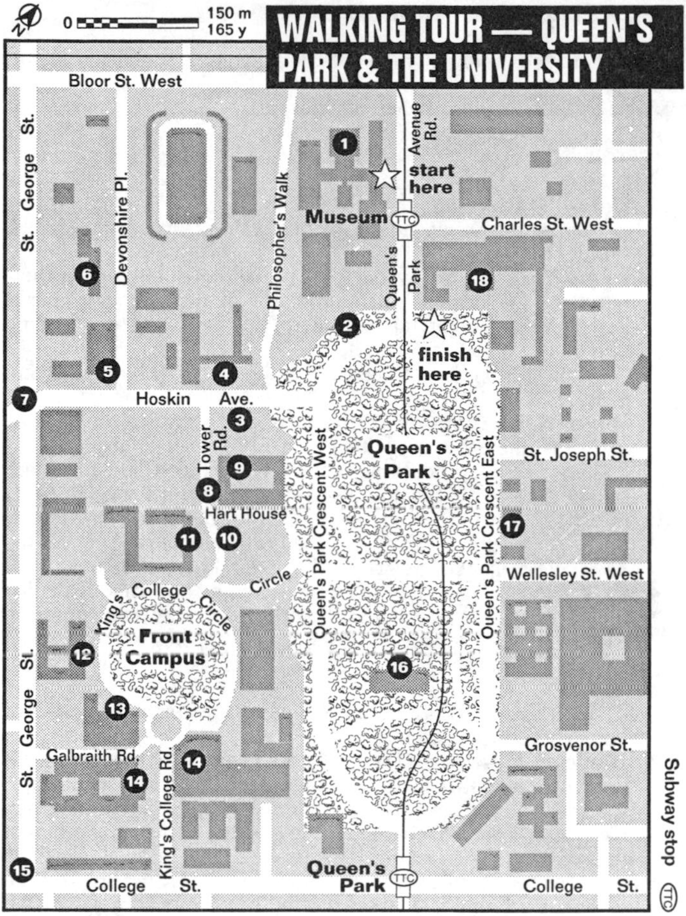

N
0
150 m
165 y
Bloor St. West
St. George St.
Devonshire Pl.
Philosopher's Walk
Avenue Rd.
start here
Museum
TTC
Charles St. West
Queen's Park
finish here
Hoskin Ave.
Tower Rd.
Queen's Park
St. Joseph St.
Hart House
Queen's Park Crescent West
Queen's Park Crescent East
College Circle
Wellesley St. West
King's College Circle
Front Campus
Grosvenor St.
Galbraith Rd.
King's College Rd.
Queen's Park
College St.
Subway stop

1. The Royal Ontario Museum (ROM)
2. Holwood
3. Wycliffe College
4. Trinity College
5. Massey College
6. St. Hilda's
7. John P. Robarts Library
8. Soldier's Memorial Tower
9. Hart House
10. Stewart Observatory
11. University College
12. Knox College
13. Convocation Hall
14. Medical Sciences Building, Sandford Fleming Building
15. University Bookstore, Botany Building
16. Provincial Parliament Buildings
17. St. Michael's College
18. Victoria College

WALKING TOUR 5 — St. Lawrence & Downtown East

Start: Union Station.
Finish: King subway station.
Time: Two to three hours, allowing for browsing time.

Best Time: Saturday (when the St. Lawrence Market is in full swing).
Worst Time: Sunday (when it's closed).

Begin at:

1. **Union Station** and check out its interior.
   Across the street, at the corner of York and Front streets, stands the:
2. **Royal York Hotel,** a venerable railroad hotel, longtime gathering place for Torontonians and home of the famous Imperial Room cabaret/nightclub (still there, but for dining and dancing only).
   Walk east on Front Street and, at the corner of Bay and Front, look up at the:
3. **Royal Bank Plaza,** two triangular gold-sheathed towers, one 41 floors, the other 26, joined by a 130-foot-high atrium.
   Cross Bay and continue east on Front Street. On the south side of the street is the impressive sweep of **One Front Street,** the Main Post Office building, which for some reason reminds me of Buckingham Palace. On the north side of the street is the city's latest financial palace, Bell Canada Enterprises's:
4. **BCE Place.** Go inside. It's impressive and you can also enjoy the Movenpick Marche and the other stores in the concourse. The twin office towers are connected by a huge glass-covered galleria five stories high spanning the block between Bay and Yonge.
   Back out on Front Street, continue to the northwest corner of Yonge and stop to admire the:
5. **Bank of Montréal** (1885–86), a suitably ornate building for the most powerful Canadian bank in the 19th century, banker to the colonial and federal governments. Inside, the banking hall rises to a beamed coffered ceiling with domed skylights of stained glass. The exterior, embellished with carvings, porthole windows, and a balustrade, is a sight in itself. From here, you can look along Front Street and see the weird mural by Derek M. Besant that adorns the famous and highly photogenic Flatiron or Gooderham Building (1892).
6. **The Gooderham Building** was built as the headquarters of George Gooderham, who had built upon his distilling business expanding into railroads, insurance, and philanthropy. It occupies a triangular site and the western tip of the five-story structure is beautifully curved—windows as well—and topped with a semicircular tower.
   Continue along Front Street, crossing Yonge to stop in at the:
7. **O'Keefe Centre** and the **St. Lawrence Centre,** next door. In the former, the National Ballet of Canada and the Canadian Opera Company perform.
   Continue along Front Street to:
8. **The Beardmore Building** (1872), at 35–39 Front St. E. This and the many other cast-iron buildings that line the street were the heart of the warehouse district in the late 19th century, close to the lakefront and rail heads. Now they're occupied by stores like **Frida Crafts,** which sells imports from Guatemala as well as jewelry, bags, candles, and other knickknacks; and **Mountain Equipment Co-op,** stocked with everything an outdoor adven-

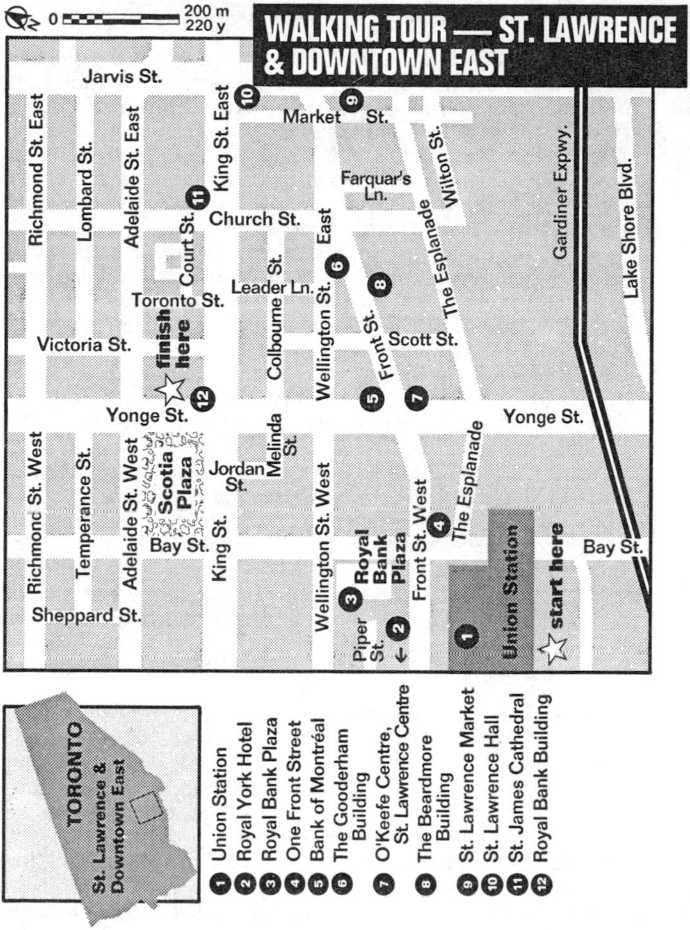
WALKING TOUR — ST. LAWRENCE & DOWNTOWN EAST
0
200 m
220 y
Jarvis St.
Market St.
Richmond St. East
Lombard St.
Adelaide St. East
King St. East
Farquar's Ln.
Wilton St.
Gardiner Expwy.
Lake Shore Blvd.
Church St.
Court St.
The Esplanade
Leader Ln.
Colbourne St.
Wellington St. East
Front St.
Toronto St.
Scott St.
Victoria St.
finish here
Yonge St.
Richmond St. West
Temperance St.
Adelaide St. West
Scotia Plaza
Jordan St.
Melinda St.
Wellington St. West
Front St. West
Bay St.
King St.
Royal Bank Plaza
Union Station
start here
Sheppard St.
Piper St.
TORONTO
St. Lawrence & Downtown East
1 Union Station
2 Royal York Hotel
3 Royal Bank Plaza
4 One Front Street
5 Bank of Montréal
6 The Gooderham Building
7 O'Keefe Centre, St. Lawrence Centre
8 The Beardmore Building
9 St. Lawrence Market
10 St. Lawrence Hall
11 St. James Cathedral
12 Royal Bank Building

turer needs. At nos. 43–45, note the handsome cast iron facades. Continue to Church Street, browsing in the stores.

Cross Church Street. More stores to browse in follow, like the **Beverley Antique Center** at no. 83, a large space filled with all kinds of large pieces of furniture as well as mirrors, lamps, pictures, and other objects.

Cross Market Street to the:

9. St. Lawrence Market, in the old market building on the right. Enter this great market hall, which was constructed around the city's second city hall (1844–45). The elegant pedimented facade that you see as you stand in the center of the hall was originally the center block of the city hall. Today the market is filled with all kinds of food vendors but is at its very best on Saturday, when the farmers bring in their fresh produce, starting at 5am.

Exit where you came in. Cross the street and cut through Market Lane Park and the shops at Market Square past the new market building. Turn right onto King Street to the:

10. **St. Lawrence Hall** (1850–51), the focal point of the community in the mid-19th century. This hall was the site of grand city occasions, political rallies, balls, and entertainment. Frederick Douglass delivered an antislavery lecture here, Jenny Lind and Adelina Patti sang here in 1851 and 1860, respectively; Gen. Tom Thumb appeared here in 1862; and George Brown campaigned for Confederation here in this most elegant Palladian-style building with its domed cupola.

    Cross the street and enter the 19th-century garden with a fountain and neatly trimmed flower beds that are filled with seasonal flowers. If you like, you can sit on a bench and rest while you admire the handsome proportions of St. Lawrence Hall and listen to the chimes of:

11. **St. James Cathedral,** which is adjacent to the garden on the north side of King Street. York's first church and first Anglican church was built here from 1803 to 1807. Originally a frame building, it was enlarged in 1818 and 1819 and replaced in 1831. The first incumbent was the Rev. George O'Kill Stuart, followed by John Strachan (pronounced Strawn), later the first bishop of Toronto, who conducted himself with great pomp from his mansion on Jarvis Street and wielded great temporal as well as spiritual power in the city. The second church was burned in 1839 and the first cathedral erected, but this, too, was destroyed by fire, in the great fire of 1849. The present building was begun in 1850 and finished in 1874. Inside, there's a Tiffany window in memory of William Jarvis at the northern end of the east aisle.

    From here you can also view one of the early retail store buildings that were built when King Street was the main commercial street. Nos. 129–35 was originally built as an Army and Navy Store, using cast iron, plate glass, and arched windows so that the shopper could see what was available in the store.

REFUELING STOPS From St. James, the venerable **King Edward Hotel** is only a block away if you need refreshment. Afternoon tea is served or you can stop for light fare or lunch in the **Café Victoria.**

From St. James, go south on Church Street and turn right onto Wellington. From Wellington you can look across to the rhythmical flow of the mansard rooflines on Front Street and also observe the Gooderham Building from another angle.

Continue walking to Yonge Street and turn right onto King Street. Note the building on the northeast corner of Yonge and King before catching the subway. It's the:

12. **Royal Bank Building** (1913–15), designed by Carrere & Hastings.

WALKING TOUR 6 — Bloor/Yorkville

Start: At the corner of Bloor and Yonge streets.
Finish: At the corner of Bloor and Yonge streets.
Time: As long as you want to make it—depends on how serious a shopper or collector you are. Just walking it will take an hour.

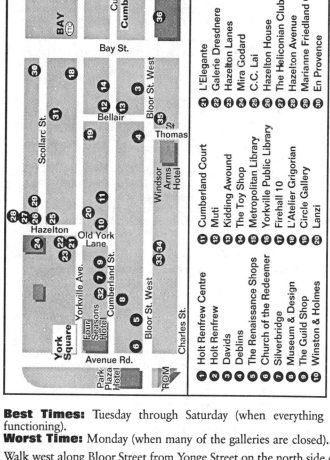

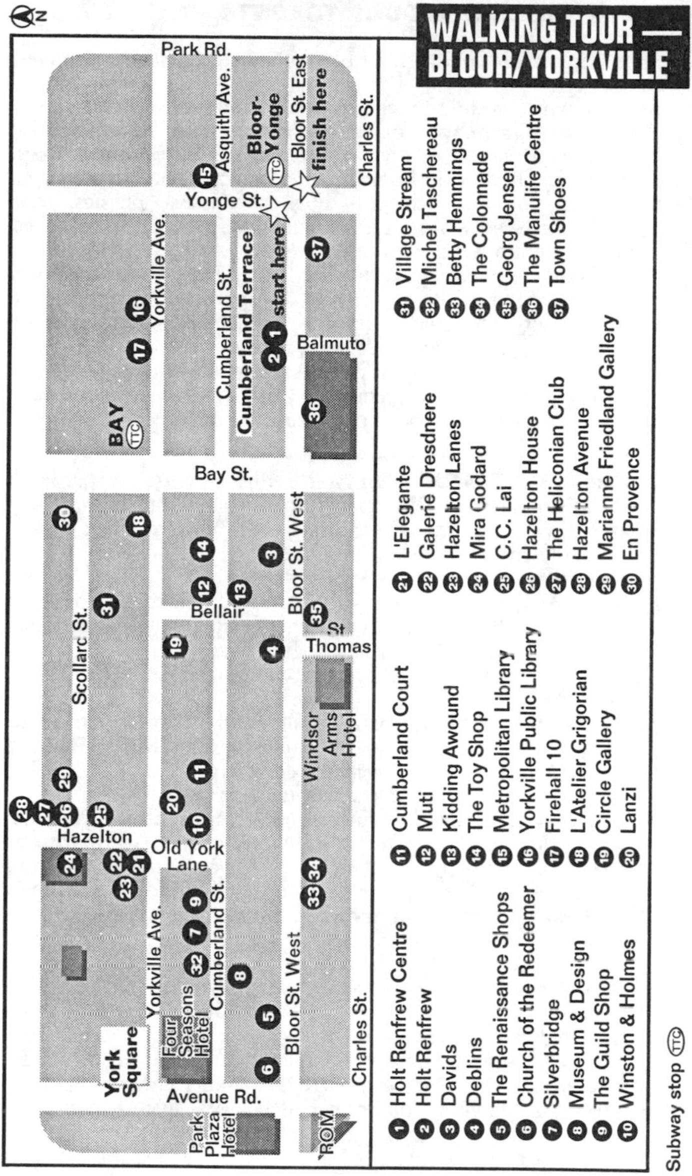
WALKING TOUR — BLOOR/YORKVILLE
Park Rd.
Asquith Ave.
Bloor-Yonge
Bloor St. East
finish here
Charles St.
Yonge St.
Yorkville Ave.
Cumberland St.
Cumberland Terrace
start here
Balmuto
BAY
Bay St.
Scollard St.
Bellair
Bloor St. West
St. Thomas
Windsor Arms Hotel
Hazelton
Old York Lane
Yorkville Ave.
Cumberland St.
Four Seasons Hotel
York Square
Avenue Rd.
Park Plaza Hotel
ROM
Charles St.
1 Holt Renfrew Centre
2 Holt Renfrew
3 Davids
4 Deblins
5 The Renaissance Shops
6 Church of the Redeemer
7 Silverbridge
8 Museum & Design
9 The Guild Shop
10 Winston & Holmes
11 Cumberland Court
12 Muti
13 Kidding Awound
14 The Toy Shop
15 Metropolitan Library
16 Yorkville Public Library
17 Firehall 10
18 L'Atelier Grigorian
19 Circle Gallery
20 Lanzi
21 L'Elegante
22 Galerie Dresdnere
23 Hazelton Lanes
24 Mira Godard
25 C.C. Lai
26 Hazelton House
27 The Heliconian Club
28 Hazelton Avenue
29 Marianne Friedland Gallery
30 En Provence
31 Village Stream
32 Michel Taschereau
33 Betty Hemmings
34 The Colonnade
35 Georg Jensen
36 The Manulife Centre
37 Town Shoes
Subway stop TTC

Best Times: Tuesday through Saturday (when everything is functioning).
Worst Time: Monday (when many of the galleries are closed).

Walk west along Bloor Street from Yonge Street on the north side of the street. The first complex you'll come to is the:

1. **Holt Renfrew Centre,** not to be confused with the Holt Renfrew store itself, which is the ultimate high-class Toronto

emporium (the equivalent of Bloomingdale's or Bergdorf in New York).

Downstairs in the center you'll find several restaurants, including **Timothy's** for coffees from around the world. Also down here is one of my favorite fun stores, **Science City,** which is filled with books, games, puzzles, and models, all relating to the sciences—life, chemistry, physics, and astronomy—as well as serious stuff like telescopes, trilobites, and hologram watches.

Another intriguing browsing experience is **Geomania,** which features all kinds of rocks and polished minerals, some worked into attractive sculptures, others into vases, and still others into plain book ends and jewelry.

At street level you'll pass **Ashley China,** the premier shopping place for fine china, crystal, and silver; and **Eddie Bauer** for casual, good-looking sportswear.

REFUELING STOP On Holt Renfrew Centre's upper level, the **Bloor Street Diner** stays open from 11am to 3am daily and offers a broad menu featuring everything from hot entrées to sandwiches.

---

2. **Holt Renfrew** itself is a delight to shop. It's filled with designer boutiques—Yves St. Laurent, Calvin Klein, Donna Karan, Anne Klein, Moschino, Ralph Lauren, and Victor Costa.

   Continue west along Bloor past Giorgio Armani to Bay Street. Cross Bay Street, eyeing:

3. **Davids** for shoes; **Capezio** for shoes and leotards; **Emporio Armani** for the less expensive Armani line; and **Harry Rosen,** one of Toronto's foremost men's designers.

   Cross Bellair Street and continue past:

4. **Deblins,** exhibiting fine linens and tableware in its windows; and the less prestigious but colorful and upbeat **Benetton;** to **The Irish Shop** for women, which has fetching fashions and accessories and books, too. More stores follow—**Louis Vuitton** and **Marc Laurent** for more avant-garde designer clothes for men and women.

   At Avenue Road you'll come to:

5. **The Renaissance Shops,** where you'll find Classico Uomo—the name says it all—and the Florentine Shop, crammed with all kinds of pretty china and gift items from Florence. This modern retail development is backdrop to the:

6. **Church of the Redeemer** (1879), a quiet enclave on Bloor Street with inviting outdoor benches set against the stone building with its slate roof and stolid belfry.

   Cut through Renaissance Shops to Cumberland, browsing as you go. Turn right onto Cumberland.

REFUELING STOPS **Il Posto** is an attractive Yorkville restaurant tucked away in a courtyard. In summer it's pleasant to lunch outside. Fine Italian cuisine and desserts. **Jacques' Omelettes** has been here for more than 10 years—a testament to the good values it offers. Omelets range from $7 to $10 and other main courses from $14 to $16—good prices for Yorkville.

Start on the north side at:

7. **Silverbridge,** at no. 162, which sells beautifully crafted modern jewelry. Move on to **Bree** for fine leathers; **Featherdown Quilts** for bedroom comforts; and **Grants of London** for brilliantly colored avant-garde ties, the ultimate robes, and spivvy suspenders.

Cross the street to:

8. **Museum + Design,** at no. 161, featuring fun and useful gadgets, all sleekly designed, many from New York's Museum of Modern Art.

Back on the north side is:

9. **The Guild Shop,** the Ontario Crafts Council store, which sells very striking ceramics, glass, baskets, jewelry, fabrics, and other craft items. Upstairs, Inuit art is on display—sculpture and paintings. You'll pay $1,500 for a soapstone bear, but it's worth coming here to see the work that is scouted and brought from the northern regions. Also on the north side, at the corner of Old York Lane, stop in at the following shops:
10. **Winston & Holmes** tobacco shop, selling Dunhill Havana and La Gloria de Cubana, among many other cigars. They will mail order. **Stephane Kelian** offers fabulous Paris shoes; and the **Papery** stocks stationery, photo albums, illustrated bags, and cards.

Continue to:

11. **Cumberland Court,** which shelters 30 shops. Cross Bellair.

REFUELING STOP The **Ballair Café** is the place to see and be seen among the young professional up-and-comers, either in the back courtyard or out front. A glass of wine will cost $6.50; main courses range from $14 to $18. Go for a drink and a snack and to watch the street scene.

Farther along the street:

12. **Muti** displays colorful Italian country furnishings, including brilliantly colored majolica urns and dinnerware, while **Ada Mackenzie** has elegant designer fashions.

On the south side:

13. **Kidding Awound** stocks hundreds of music boxes, clockwork toys, miniatures, and kids' fashions.

Cross Bay to:

14. **The Toy Shop,** on the north side—two floors filled with kids' games, toys, and books. Then it's **Dinah's Cupboard,** which has great salads and pâtés to go, as well as frozen items like vegetarian pasta to take home and pop in the oven, gourmet teas, coffees, and vinegars.

Turn left onto Bloor. Across Yonge Street stands:

15. **The Metropolitan Library** (1973–77), designed by Raymond Moriyama. It doesn't look that terrific from the outside, but go in and experience the interior. It'll make reading and studying seem a natural and wonderful part of life. Not everyone agrees, of course.

Turn left onto Yorkville Avenue and walk west. On the right stands:

16. **The Yorkville Public Library** (1906–07), at no. 22. It looks important with its porticoed entrance.

Just down the street on the same side stands:

17. Firehall 10 (1876), at no. 34, an endearing Yorkville landmark which was rebuilt, except for the tower, from 1889 to 1890. The tower where the hoses are stored bears the coat-of-arms of the Town of Yorkville, saved from the town hall when it was demolished. The images—a beer barrel, jack plane, brick mold, anvil, and bull's head—represent the vocations of the town's early councillors. Opposite is the **Omega Centre.**

Cross Bay Street to:

18. L'Atelier Grigorian, on the right, stocking a fantastic selection of CDs, but CDs only, and classical and jazz only, please note.

Walk west and cross Bellair. On the left (south) side of the street you'll find the ultracommercial:

19. Circle Gallery, which has been selling the likes of Erté and others for many years. At no. 87, cooks will want to look over the offerings at **The Compleat Kitchen.** Farther along the street, **Collection 97** has fine china and **Ulysses Bookshop** has a terrific selection of travel books.

REFUELING STOP **Le Trou Normand,** at 90 Yorkville Ave., is one of the few restaurants in Yorkville where you can secure a meal at a fairly modest price.

Still on the same (south) side of the street:

20. Lanzi of Italy has stylish items for the desk and an assortment of fine leather goods. At **Arctic,** no. 125, there's an assortment of Inuit sculpture, jewelry, clothes, fur hats, and so on. You'll need to know how to sift out the quality items here.

Across the street:

21. L'Elegante is a discount designer fashion house right here in the heart of high-rent Yorkville, while next door, at no. 124, **Maison de Presse** is the place to stop for foreign newspapers, and magazines, including the *New York Times,* the *Wall Street Journal, USA Today,* and the *Manchester Guardian.*

Turn back from the Maison and go down Hazelton Avenue. First on the left you'll come to:

22. Galerie Dresdnere, Evelyn Aimis, and **Nancy Poole's Studio,** all well-known galleries, with Aimis representing Warhol, Rauschenberg, Safdie, De Kooning, and more.

Beyond Laura Ashley, turn left into:

23. Hazelton Lanes, with **Pierre Deux,** the marvelous French country-style shop with cushions, table accessories, and more on your right. Hazelton Lanes is a difficult-to-negotiate collection of stylish boutiques and stores that is laid out on two levels around a central courtyard. The signs are poor and it's easy to get disoriented in this circular maze, where you'll find the sine qua non names of fashion and design. On the lower concourse there's **Chez Catherine,** a boutique that has dressed wealthy fashionable Toronto women for many years; **Gianni Versace Krizia,** and **Valentino; Fogal** for fashionable hose and underwear in rainbow colors; the **General Store** at several locations, featuring kitchen/housewares in one location and gifts for the person who has everything (calculators, something called a fishing mate, Newtonian puzzles, and Filofax) at another; **Classical Record Shop; Turnbull & Asser** for custom-made shirts; **Bart Furs** for furs and also leathers; **Brown's Shoes,** which besides its own label sells such well-known designers as Bruno Magli; **JJ Farmer** for casual men's sportswear; **The Palate** for kitchenware and accessories like aprons; **Timothy's Coffees of the World; Monta Bimbi,** featuring designer clothes for babies and kids; **Trussardi** for well-fashioned menswear and women's wear; and **Gianfranco Ferre** for dramatic feminine tailoring.

REFUELING STOP The **Hazelton Club,** with access to the outdoor courtyard, is the place to stop for lunch in Hazelton Lanes.

On the upper level the shopping feast continues with more great names, like **Rodier** and **Marci Lipman,** whose fun artistic designs for kids' fashions include original T-shirts and many very appealing creations. **Mark McClaine** has good-looking Oriental and Western antiques; **Hermès** and **Joan & David** are names that need no description; plus, there are **Teuscher Chocolate of Switzerland** and **Roots,** a Canadian specialty store selling leather bags as well as T-shirts, sweaters, and shorts. **Alfred Sung** is another fashion name, and so are **Polo Ralph Lauren, Issetti,** and **Il Bisonte. Aquascutum** also has a boutique here. Farther on there's **Wenger Chic,** featuring Austrian- and German-style fashions, and near the entrance to Avenue Road is **Giorgio Femme.**

You could spend the whole day shopping Hazelton Lanes. Here I ask that you do a circular browse through and exit where you entered, returning in timely fashion to Hazelton Lane.

Back on the street, art lovers will want to stop at:

24. Mira Godard, a well-known Toronto gallery that represents such famous Americans as Motherwell; Larry Rivers; Frank Stella; Lipchitz; David Hockney; and Jasper Johns; plus many Canadians, such as Lawren Harris and Clark McDougall.

Backtrack a little and cross the street to relish the offerings at:

25. C.C. Lai, selling exquisite Oriental art—furniture inlaid with mother of pearl, wonderful Oriental screens, Buddhas, jewelry, and more—and at **Bleu Nuit,** featuring such great bathroom accessories as soaps and towels, as well as tablecloths and other dining-room accessories; bedspreads and duvets are available upstairs.

Continue north along Hazelton. On the right side you'll come to:

26. Hazelton House, at no. 33, originally part of the Olivet Congregational Church (1890), which now houses several galleries including **Sable-Castelli** and the **Hollander York Gallery,** which shows many contemporary Canadian artists, like Len Gibbs and westerner Irene Klar.

Next door, look at the facade of the church housing:

27. The Heliconian Club, which was founded in 1909 as a forum for women in the arts. Since 1921 the club has occupied this

Carpenter Gothic Revival church built in 1876 as the Olivet Congregational. Note the triangular wooden lancet windows and filigree decoration. Next door in two town houses are **Robin Kay** and **Escada,** both selling women's fashions.

Continue along:

28. **Hazelton Avenue,** observing the handsome Victorian homes on either side. Nos. 49–51 and 53–55 are particularly worth noting. No. 74 has an especially attractive fan window above the entrance and decorative window bays. No. 68 has a highly decorated gable.

Continue to Berryman; retrace your steps, turn left down Scollard, and stop at the:

29. **Marianne Friedland Gallery,** at no. 122, and **Kinsman Robinson,** at no. 112, which exhibits Canadian artists, including the brilliant color-drunk Norval Morrisseau, and such contemporaries as Henri Masson, John Newman, and John Walsh. (**Gallery One** is across the street.) **Lato Design,** at no. 100, has quilts, cushions, and other antique furnishings. **Ballenford Books,** at no. 98, has a superb selection of architecture books displayed in an exquisite town house that's part of a marvelous six-house row built in 1893. Look up at the fabulous gabling of these and other beauties along Scollard.

Continuing along Scollard Street:

30. **En Provence** has fabulous country French fabrics and other household decorative items; **Kamimura** shows Japanese prints.

From Scollard, cut through Village Stream, which connects to Yorkville Avenue. Turn right and walk along the south side to:

31. **Old York Lane** and take it through to Cumberland. Turn right along Cumberland. Check into the stores that we missed earlier, like:
32. **Michel Taschereau** and **Ronald Windebanks,** both antiques dealers.

Go through Renaissance Plaza back to Bloor Street. Cross the street and "do" the south side of Bloor, walking east:

33. **Betty Hemmings** has exquisite leather goods.
34. **The Colonnade,** at no. 131, was built from 1961 to 1964, one of the first buildings to combine residence, office, and retail space. It still does so with the restaurants taking full advantage of the overhanging forecourt. Here also is the **Bata Shoe Museum.**

Cross St. Thomas Street to:

35. **Georg Jensen,** which sells finely designed Danish silver, china, and crystal. Just down the street is Canada's first branch of **Tiffany's.**

Walk east along Bloor and cross Bay Street to:

36. **The Manulife Centre,** where you'll find **Birks,** a very traditional Canadian store that offers good-priced silver, crystal, and china, including Royal Doulton, and some lovely placemats that make ideal gifts. **Brettons** is a multilevel store selling a variety of sportswear. **Calderone** specializes in shoes and leather goods. On the courtyard level there's a branch of Britain's **Marks & Spencer,** well known for reasonably priced clothes and other goods.

Cross Balmuto Street and walk to Yonge Street for a look at the merchandise at:

37. **Town Shoes** and the men's and women's fashions at **Stollery's,** located in a 1929 building at the corner of Bloor and Yonge streets. A traditional Canadian store, it has good stocks of Dacks, Aquascutum, Burberry, and other British-inspired fashions.

FINAL REFUELING STOPS For burgers and other casual fare that will please the family, there's **Toby's.** The more fashion-conscious will go to **Bemelman's,** with its polished interior and outdoor dining area.

WALKING TOUR 7 — The Beaches

Start: Queen subway station.
Finish: Queen subway station.
Time: As long as you want to make it—if it's sunny you may want to lounge a few hours.
Best Time: A weekday, unless you enjoy crowds.

Catch the Queen Street trolley going east and travel to Herbert Avenue, which is one block past Woodbine Avenue. Get off and start walking east along Queen Street. There are several shops worth browsing in along here, including, on the south side:

1. **The Pottery,** at no. 1911, which features a resident potter at work and the wares that she produces on sale. Comic collectors and sports-card collectors will want to check over the well-organized stock in **Bryan's Books,** at no. 1917. Plenty of used paperbacks here, too.

   Cross the street and you'll find:
2. **Mourguet** for attractive hand-crafted jewelry; good-looking casual clothes at **Club Monaco;** and plenty of pampering soaps and lotions and other bathroom accessories at **The Body Shop.**

   Cross Waverley Road. In this block along Queen you may want to cast your eye over the many offerings at:
3. **Pier 1 Imports,** at no. 1986.

   Continue along Queen and cross Bellefair Avenue if you're on the north side of the street. On the south side you'll see:
4. **Kew Gardens.** If you're tired of shopping you can turn right and walk down through the gardens to the boardwalk and lakefront. Turn right along the boardwalk and you can walk all the way along the lakefront past the:
5. **Olympic Pool,** at Woodbine Avenue, and around to:
6. **Ashbridge's Bay Park.** I especially love the sign on the beach that reads BIRDS ON THIS BEACH ARE PROTECTED AND IT IS ILLEGAL TO HARM THEM. That certainly says something about the citizens of this city.

REFUELING STOPS **Licks,** the now-ubiquitous burger, sloppy-joe, ice-cream/frozen-yogurt emporium, started in Toronto in the Beaches. Still delicious. Other possibilities include

Nevada for Italian specialties—pizza, pasta, and veal. Across the street from Licks.

If you want to continue strolling, then carry on. There are still a number of interesting stores to see (in fact, you can walk all the way to the end of the trolley line at Neville Park Boulevard, although the interesting browsing diminishes). **Victoria Art Gallery,** at no. 1967, displays contemporary art; there's a branch of **Edward Books & Art** at no. 2179 and also a **W. H. Smith.** Casual fun fashions can be had at **Cotton Ginny. Wacky Widdle Wearables** has "different" kids' clothes. **La Manna** has elegant fashions for men.

From here you can continue, crossing Wineva Avenue, to one or two antiques shops, some fashion boutiques, and a gallery or two, before the shops end at Willow Avenue.

Turn right for the lakefront and then walk west along the boardwalk.

WALKING TOUR — THE BEACHES

TORONTO
The Beaches

0
.25 mi
.4 km
Victoria Park Ave.
Kingston Rd.
Scarborough Rd.
Silver Birch Ave.
Willow Ave.
Beech Ave.
Glen Stewart Park
Balsam Ave.
Maclean Ave.
Pine Cr.
Glen Manor Dr.
Hubbard Blvd.
Southwood Dr.
Hammersmith Ave.
Glen Ames Rd.
Willamson Rd.
Wineva Ave.
Leuty Ave.
Alfresco Lawn
Violet Ave.
Lee Ave.
Wheeler Ave.
Belle-fair Ave.
Norway Ave.
Kew Gardens
Waverly Rd.
Kenil-worth Ave.
Kingston Rd.
Kew Beach Cr.
Kippen-davie Ave.
Elmer Ave.
Herbert Ave.
Kew Beach Ave.
Buller Ave.
Woodbine Ave.
Queen St. East
Greenwood Race Track
Eastwood Rd.
Lake Shore Blvd. East
Coxwell St.
start here
finish here
Ashbridge's Bay Yacht Club
Ashbridge's Bay Park
Lake Ontario

1. The Pottery, Bryan's Books
2. Mourguet, Club Monaco, The Body Shop
3. Pier 1 Imports
4. Kew Gardens
5. Olympic Pool
6. Ashbridge's Bay Park

CHAPTER 8

TORONTO SHOPPING A TO Z

Toronto's major shopping areas are the Bloor/Yorkville area for designer boutiques and top-name galleries; Queen Street West for a more funky mixture of fashion, antiques, and bookstores; and a number of shopping malls/centers like Queen's Quay down on the waterfront, the two-block-long Eaton Centre, and other smaller complexes like College Park, Royal Bank Plaza, and Village by the Grange.

The two great names in Toronto retailing are Eaton's and The Hudson's Bay Company (formerly Simpson's), both founded in the mid-19th century. They're still here and thriving. Canadian fashion names to look for are Alfred Sung, Cy Mann, and Norma.

The two major markets are Kensington Market and the St. Lawrence Market.

Store hours are generally Monday to Wednesday from 9:30 or 10am to 6pm and Saturday and Sunday from 10am to 5pm, with extended hours (8 to 9:30pm) on Thursday and usually Friday.

Provincial sales tax is 8%, but out-of-province visitors can reclaim it. Nonresidents can also reclaim the 7% **goods and services tax** (GST). See Chapter 3.

Best buys are mainly Canadian arts and crafts, which can be imported into the United States without duty.

ANTIQUES

You'll find the greatest concentration of good-quality antiques at the Harbourfront Antiques Market, best visited Sunday when all the dealers are in residence (during the week many are at their stores). The finest antiques can be found in the Bloor/Yorkville area, with many shops a short walk from the Four Seasons Hotel, and in the Mount Pleasant/St. Clair area along the 500-, 600-, and 700-block of Mount Pleasant Road. The more funky and often more recent collectibles can be found at various stores along Queen Street West. Markham Village also has several antiques stores.

ABACUS ANTIQUES, 6 Ripley Ave. Tel. 760-9358.

This store specializes in Canadian oak and pine furniture—rolltop desks, cabinets, tables, and chairs—and other nostalgia.

Also at Harbourfront Antiques Market.

ANTIQUERS, 517 Mount Pleasant Rd. Tel. 481-4474.

In this interesting shop, you will find antique and estate jewelry, rare Belleek pieces, silver, and other objets d'art.

ATELIER ART AND ANTIQUES, 588 Markham St. Tel. 532-9244.

The offerings at Atelier mainly consist of historical folk art from North America, although it stocks some contemporary folk pieces, too. The pieces are collector-quality and go from $50 into the thousands. Call ahead for an appointment.

BERNARDI ANTIQUES, 707 Mount Pleasant Rd., south of Eglinton Ave. Tel. 483-6471.

Look here for discontinued Doulton figurines, art glass, paintings, carpets, silver, and furniture.

BEVERLEY ANTIQUES CENTRE, 83 Front St. E. Tel. 977-2999.

A large space filled to overflowing with large furniture, plus mirrors, lamps, pictures, and more, the Beverley Antiques Centre is worth browsing through.

CAROL SOLWAY, 88 Yorkville Ave. Tel. 922-0702.

Carol specializes in late 18th- to mid-19th-century English furniture, porcelain, and glass. She also carries some French pieces as well as accessories—lamps, pillows, candlesticks, and the like. Open daily.

C. C. LAI, 9 Hazelton Ave. Tel. 928-0662.

This cluttered store has fine Chinese antiques—exquisite inlay furniture and screens, Buddhas, and jewelry—really beautiful pieces, both large and small.

CIRCA ANTIQUES, 166 Davenport Rd. Tel. 961-3744.

Circa is one of the best places to find formal and country French furniture, from Louis XIV and XV through Louis XVI and Second Empire. Buffets, tables, armoires, chairs, and desks are the main stock, along with sconces and chandeliers.

ESTATE COLLECTION, 21 Avenue Rd. Tel. 921-6443.

This store specializes in art deco, retro, and Victorian jewelry and objets d'art. It also carries silver and ormolu pieces and furniture.

FIFTY ONE ANTIQUES LTD., 21 Avenue Rd. Tel. 968-2416.

A specialist in 17th- and 18th-century furniture, as well as Empire, Biedermeier, and other later styles, Fifty One Antiques also has lots of accessories, like lamps made from old bases, carvings, European paintings, and more.

GUILDHALL ANTIQUES, 111 Jarvis St. Tel. 777-0226.

You'll find a lot of fine Canadian pine country furniture here—chests of drawers, tables, and more—along with pressed glass, goblets, and decoys.

HARBOURFRONT ANTIQUES MARKET, 390 Queen's Quay W. Tel. 340-8377.

The 100-plus dealers here sell fine-quality antiques. On summer Sundays there's also a market outside featuring less established dealers. Although it's quiet during the week, it's hopping on Sunday; you'll have to get there early. Hours are Tuesday through Friday from noon to 6pm, Saturday from 10am to 5pm, and Sunday from 7am to 6pm.

HOUSE OF DAVENPORT, 176 Davenport Rd. Tel. 921-4101.

The House of Davenport is for the collector of plates and figurines, especially Wedgwood, Doulton, and Kandler. The store also features some crystal and dinnerware.

JOURNEYS END, 612 Markham St. Tel. 536-2226.
An appropriate name for the miscellaneous assortment of estate china, jewelry, silver, and furniture that winds up here in an amorphous display. Eminently browsable.

MARK MCLAINE, Hazelton Lanes. Tel. 927-7972.
This marvelously eclectic store has unique items, like a pair of never-worn 1929 leather shoes as well as pine furniture, French sconces, costume jewelry (especially deco), carved wood and stone pieces, silver frames, perfume bottles, and blue-and-white Oriental ware. A great place to browse. Prices range from $16 to $6,000.

MICHEL TASCHEREAU, 176 Cumberland St. Tel. 923-3020.
In this fine store you'll have to thread your way through the dense collection very carefully. You'll find English and French furniture, including large 19th-century armoires and French and English china, like Coalport, Derby, Worcester, and Lalique.

MOSTLY MOVABLES, 785 Queen St. W., west of Bathurst St. Tel. 865-9716.
A large selection of furniture, mostly purchased at estate sales, is featured here, including wardrobes, dressers, couches, and dining-room sets (for as little as $950). Most of the pieces date from the 1920s on and cost $150 and up. Turn-of-the-century Canadian pine pieces are also available.

THE PAISLEY SHOP LIMITED, 889 Yonge St. Tel. 923-5830.
A specialist in 18th- and 19th-century English furniture—dining tables, chairs, sideboards, mirrors, and desks—the Paisley Shop Limited also offers such accessories as porcelain, glass, and chandeliers. Upstairs there is a selection of floral and other patterned cushions and lamps.

R. A. O'NEILL ANTIQUES, 100 Avenue Rd. Tel. 968-2806.
This is the place for country furniture from around the world—French, German, English, American, Dutch, and Irish. Along with tables, chairs, chests, and cupboards, the stock includes samplers, baskets, lamps, decoys, and brass and tin objects.

RED INDIAN AND EMPIRE ANTIQUES, 507 Queen St. W. Tel. 364-2706.
The eclectic mixture of objects here spans from the 1930s to the 1950s—fountain pens, Coke memorabilia, neon clocks, Bakelite jewelry, torche lamps, wall sconces, mirrors, figurines, and other nostalgia. It's open Monday through Saturday from 11:30am to 6pm.

RONALD WINDEBANKS, 21 Avenue Rd. Tel. 962-2862.
This store is filled with treasures found by Mr. Windebank, who has a good eye for the unique object with character and whimsy. There's an eclectic array of furniture, porcelain, crystal, glass, botanical and ornithological prints, antique garden furniture, and grand urns, plus some charming carved animal folk art.

STANLEY WAGMAN ANTIQUES, 111 Avenue Rd. Tel. 964-1047.
A major purveyor of French furniture, both country and formal, as well as art deco, Stanley Wagman also features marble fireplaces, chandeliers, and wall sconces.

ART

Most of these galleries are open Tuesday to Saturday from 10:30am to 5:30pm, so don't come around on Sunday or Monday.

ALBERT WHITE, 80 Spadina Ave., at King St. Tel. 865-1021.

This gallery has been open since 1966 and is one of the few places specializing in international art, representing such great names as Picasso, Henry Moore, Botero, Francis Bacon, and many others—oils, sculpture, and prints.

BAU-XI, 340 Dundas St. W. Tel. 977-0600.

This bilevel gallery exhibits paintings, sculptures, drawings, and prints by many contemporary Canadian artists—Ted Godwin, Jack Shadbolt, Don Jarvis, Roz Marshall, Hugh Mackenzie, Richard Bond, Gordon Smith, and David Sorensen.

CIRCLE GALLERY, 83 Yorkville Ave. Tel. 961-5806.

This is the place for the commercial and popular names in prints and lithography—Erté, Lebadang, Vasarely, and others.

DEL BELLO, 363 Queen St. W. Tel. 593-0884.

This gallery specializes in showing international contemporary artists—European, Canadian, and American. It's well known for its annual miniature art show, held in November and December, which features works of 1,500 artists from 72 countries.

ESKIMO ART GALLERY, 458 Queen's Quay W. (west of Spadina in the Condominium Building). Tel. 591-9004.

This gallery carries about 500 small and large high-quality Inuit sculptures, most of which come from Cape Dorset or Baffin Island. Prices range from $60 to $14,000. It's certainly one of the largest collections in the city.

EVELYN AIMIS GALLERY, 14 Hazelton Ave. Tel. 961-0878.

The late Andy Warhol, Rob Rauschenberg, de Kooning, and other famous names in the Canadian, European, and American contemporary art world are featured here.

FEHELEY FINE ARTS, 45 Avenue Rd. (2nd floor). Tel. 323-1373.

Mr. Feheley has been involved in collecting Inuit sculpture and art since the 1950s, and he still personally goes out looking for new artists. The gallery therefore offers a wide selection of the finest-quality sculpture and graphics from the Canadian Arctic. They range from small and primitive bone and ivory carvings to contemporary pieces.

FIRST EDITION, 491 Bloor St. W. Tel. 925-5055.

This store has many photography, art, and movie posters—about 4,000 to 5,000 images available in total—along with postcards and art note cards. It also sells Japanese craft items—vases, lanterns, teapots, saké sets, and folk art.

GALERIE DRESDNERE, 12 Hazelton Ave. Tel. 923-4662.

Another major gallery featuring contemporary Canadian artists, such as Ray Mead (Toronto) and Stephen Lack (Montréal), from coast to coast. Others include Torontonian Ronald Bloore, Jean Paul

Lemieux, and Paul-Emile Borduas. Galerie Dresdnere has long been associated with artists from Montréal's Automatistes School and other important contemporary Canadian art movements.

GALERIE HERITAGE, 137 Yorkville Ave. Tel. 967-1675.
This gallery has operated in Toronto for over 44 years. It specializes in international sculpture and also has several contemporary Gobelins tapestries commissioned from artists from 12 different countries. It features four art showcases a year and six one-artist shows.

GALLERY MOOS, 622 Richmond St. W. Tel. 777-0707.
Another longtime Toronto gallery, in business for 32 years, this establishment represents international and Canadian contemporary artists, including Jean-Paul Riopelle.

GALLERY ONE, 121 Scollard St. Tel. 929-3103.
A fixture on the Toronto scene for almost 17 years, this gallery is associated with the Abstract Expressionists—Harold Town, Jack Bush, and other Canadian artists, like Christopher Broadhurst, David Blackwood, Brian Burnett, Joseph Drapell, Harold Feist, and sculptor André Fauteux. It also represents such American artists as Helen Frankenthaler, Anthony Caro, Jules Olitski, and Stanley Boxer.

GILBERT & COLES, 160 Pears Ave., Suite 310 (in the Design Centre). Tel. 921-9145.
A specialist in antique oils, botanicals, engravings, and 19th-century English watercolors, Gilbert & Coles carries maps, too.

GLASS ART GALLERY, 21 Hazelton Ave. Tel. 968-1823.
This gallery features the work of contemporary glass artists from all over the world. When I visited, the show featured the sculptural art of nine French artists. The exhibition changes every month, and the gallery also keeps on hand samples from artists they represent.

ISAACS/INNUIT GALLERY OF ESKIMO ART, 9 Prince Arthur Ave. Tel. 921-9985.
Inuit sculpture, prints, drawings, wall hangings, and antiquities from across the Arctic are featured here, in association with the Isaacs Gallery, the oldest contemporary gallery in the city. The pieces are museum-quality. The gallery also specializes in early North American Indian art.

JANE CORKIN, 179 John St. Tel. 979-1980.
This gallery specializes in historical and contemporary photographs by international and Canadian photographers. It represents 40 Canadians as well as the estates of André Kertesz, Irving Penn, and Horst.

KAMIMURA, 1300 Bay St., at Scollard. Tel. 923-7850.
This long, narrow downstairs gallery specializes in Japanese prints. Its open hours are Tuesday through Saturday from 11am to 5pm.

KARNEY GALLERY, 11 Yorkville Ave. Tel. 964-1122.
This gallery, which has been open for seven years, represents great international names like Botero, Dufy, Picasso, Chagall, and Calder. It also exhibits Canadian contemporary artists.

KASPAR GALLERY, 27 Prince Arthur Ave. Tel. 968-2536.
Specializing in Canadian art from the 19th century to the Group

of Seven, the Kaspar Gallery features watercolors and contemporary artists, too.

KINSMAN ROBINSON, 112 Scollard St. Tel. 964-2374.

This two-room gallery exhibits such contemporary Canadian artists as the color-drunk Norval Morrisseau, Henri Masson, John Walsh, John Newman, Stanley Cosgrove, and sculptors Esther Wertheimer and Maryon Kantaroff.

LIGHT SPECTRUM, 473A Church St., at Maitland St. Tel. 921-7149.

This photograph gallery specializes in work by contemporary Canadians only. Black-and-white and color works by as many as 10 photographers are on display.

MARIANNE FRIEDLAND GALLERY, 122 Scollard St. Tel. 961-4900.

Since it opened in 1974, this gallery has shown contemporary Canadian and American artists, including Milton Avery, Phil Pearlstein, Al Held, Hans Hofmann, Margaret Priest, Karen Kulyk, Wolf Kahn, Ronald Boaks, Rafael Goldchain, and Suzanne Olivier.

MIRA GODARD, 22 Hazelton Ave. Tel. 964-8197.

Another major international player in Toronto, Mira Godard represents, among many others, such famous names as Botero, Motherwell, Frank Stella, Larry Rivers, Lipchitz, David Hockney, and Jasper Johns, as well as Canadian greats Lawren Harris and Clark McDougall.

NANCY POOLE'S STUDIO, 16 Hazelton Ave. Tel. 964-9050.

For over 20 years this gallery has been exhibiting a roster of about 25 contemporary artists. Every two weeks the gallery mounts one-artist shows, except during the summer, when group shows take over.

THE REPRODUCTION SHOP, in the Art Gallery of Toronto, 317 Dundas St. W. Tel. 979-6607.

Adjacent to the bookstore, this shop carries a great selection of reproductions of international and Canadian art, as well as posters and juvenile prints. Framing services are available.

SABLE-CASTELLI, 33 Hazelton Ave. Tel. 961-0011.

A specialist in contemporary Canadian art, with names like David Craven, Paul Hutner, Eric Fischl, and others.

BOOKS

ABBEY BOOKSHOP, 89 Harbord St. Tel. 960-9076.

This comfortable store has a very broad collection of used and rare books, with especially good concentrations in philosophy, theology, poetry, and drama.

ABELARD BOOKS, 519 Queen St. W. Tel. 366-0021.

This is one of my favorite rare-book stores in the city. It has a fabulous collection of first editions and other rare books, with every subject clearly catalogued. Armchairs invite leisurely browsing. A real book-lover's haven.

ABOUT BOOKS, 83 Harbord St. Tel. 975-2668.

Another good used-book store. The titles are all well catalogued and the selection is extensive—particularly strong in literature. Out-of-print and antiquarian volumes are available.

ALBERT BRITNELL BOOK SHOP, 765 Yonge St., north of Bloor St. Tel. 924-3321.
A Toronto tradition, this wonderful store has a great selection of hard- and softcover books displayed handsomely on wooden shelves. The staff is very knowledgeable and helpful.

ANOTHER MAN'S POISON, 29 McCaul St. Tel. 593-6451.
This store is heaven for any aspiring architect, interior designer, or graphic artist because it's filled with a large worldwide stock of books on graphics, antiques, and collectibles—all aspects of design.

ATTICUS BOOKS, 84 Harbord St. Tel. 922-6045.
The preeminent Toronto dealer in scholarly used books, it also stocks antiquarian books and illuminated manuscripts and has an art room in the back.

BAKKA SCIENCE FICTION BOOK SHOPPE, 282 Queen St. W. Tel. 596-8161.
This store is the answer to a science-fiction buff's dreams. It stocks paperback and hardcover versions of both new and used science fiction and fantasy.

BALLENFORD BOOKS, 98 Scollard St. Tel. 960-0055.
Located in an architectural Victorian gem, this store sells architecture books only.

BOB MILLER BOOK ROOM, 180 Bloor St. W. (Lower Concourse). Tel. 922-3557.
If you can't find a specific novel or literary volume—especially a Canadian one—then try here. Look for the fiction titles listed in "Recommended Books" in Chapter 1—you're likely to find them at this humanities and social sciences bookstore.

THE BOOK CELLAR—YORKVILLE, 142 Yorkville Ave. Tel. 925-9955.
This well-stocked store in Yorkville also has a large selection of domestic and foreign magazines in the back room.

BOOK CITY, 501 Bloor St. W. Tel. 961-4496.
This store offers good discounts (10%) on new books as well as a large selection of remainders. It's a well-stocked general bookstore with large philosophy and religion sections. Open late daily.

There are other branches at 348 Danforth Ave. and 2350 Bloor St. W.

CAN-DO BOOKSTORE, 311 Queen St. W., at John St. Tel. 977-2351.
This neat store has everything an active, involved person could wish for—more than 15,000 titles on homesteading, sports, languages, gardening, cooking, and more.

CHILDREN'S BOOK STORE, 604 Markham St., at Bloor and Bathurst Sts. Tel. 535-7011.
Books, cassettes, and videos for kids from birth to age 14. A staff

of librarians and teachers assist selection. The ultimate choice of book-loving kids. There are special events, too, on Sunday afternoons.

COLES THE WORLD'S BIGGEST BOOKSTORE, 20 Edward St. Tel. 977-7009.

With 17 miles of bookshelves and more than a million books categorized into more than 50 specialty departments, Coles boasts that if you can't get it here, it doesn't exist. The store also stocks videos and cassettes. Coles also has locations at 726 Yonge St. (tel. 924-1707); in Commerce Court Concourse (tel. 868-1782); in the Eaton Centre (tel. 979-9348); and at various other locations in the city and in the suburbs. Open until late.

THE COOKBOOK STORE, 850 Yonge St., at Yorkville Ave. Tel. 920-2665.

Everything's here for the cook and food lover, including international cookbooks organized by cuisine, wine books, professional books for restaurateurs, dessert books, health books, and also cooking and wine magazines and cooking videos.

DAVID MASON, 342 Queen St. W. Tel. 598-1015.

Another fine used-book store with plenty of first and collector's editions, the store has a huge selection on all subjects. Great bookish atmosphere.

DAVID MIRVISH BOOKS AND BOOKS ON ART, 596 Markham St. Tel. 531-9975.

This is a fabulous, large store specializing in current books on the visual arts—ceramics, sculpture, photography, art history, architecture, and other related subjects. Some out-of-print and rare titles are here, too. Hours are Monday through Friday from 10am to 6pm, Saturday and Sunday from 11am to 6pm.

DRAGON LADY COMIC SHOP, 200 Queen St. W. Tel. 596-1602.

Comic aficionados will find old and new comics here from 1950 to the present, as well as books related to comics. There are also posters and such collectibles as *Life* magazines (from 1915 on).

EDWARDS BOOKS AND ART, 356 Queen St. W. Tel. 593-0126.

Edwards has a complete selection of quality art books, limited editions, imported books, and bargain books. The store lists its best deals for the week in the Saturday *Globe* and *Mail;* it has probably the best discounts on art books going.

Also at 170 Bloor St. W. (tel. 961-2428), 2200 Yonge St. (tel. 487-5431), and in the Beaches.

FIRST EDITION, 491 Bloor St. W. Tel. 925-5055.

This store carries a broad range of books about Japanese subjects—origami and other crafts, folk arts, gardening, politics, and history.

GULLIVER'S TRAVEL BOOKSHOP, 609 Bloor St. W., two blocks west of Bathurst St. Tel. 537-7700.

The store carries a full range of travel guidebooks, as well as travel accessories like phrasebooks, maps, and background destination reading.

LONGHOUSE BOOKSHOP, 497 Bloor St. W., near Brunswick Ave. Tel. 921-9995.

The Canadian specialist in Toronto, it carries a large selection of books on Native Canadian subjects, as well as a full range of Canadian literature, history, political science, poetry, and drama.

OLD FAVOURITES BOOK SHOP, Hwy. 7, east of Markham. Tel. 294-3865.

This is possibly the largest collection of used books in the country—about 300,000 to 400,000 paperbacks and hardbacks. Among the rare-book specialties are equestrian titles focusing on carriages, coaches, and horses.

OPEN AIR BOOKS & MAPS, 25 Toronto St. Tel. 363-0719.

The place to go for travel guidebooks, maps, and other books relating to the outdoors and ecology.

PAGES, 256 Queen St. W. Tel. 598-1447.

This large store is a fine, well-stocked general bookstore, with an extensive selection of foreign, literary, and other magazines.

SEEKERS BOOKS, 509 Bloor St. W., at Borden. Tel. 925-1982.

This store offers an eclectic assortment of new and used books, with an emphasis on Eastern religions, the occult, meditation, and other New Age titles, as well as literature and general books.

W. H. SMITH/SMITHBOOKS, Toronto Dominion Centre. Tel. 362-5967.

This member of the famous Canadian chain is a well-stocked general bookstore, with plenty of titles on Toronto, along with bestsellers and a good selection of newspapers and magazines.

There are many locations in the Metro area, including the Eaton Centre (tel. 979-9376); Hudson's Bay Centre (tel. 967-7177); Scotia Plaza (tel. 366-7536); the Royal Bank Plaza (tel. 865-0090); Queens Quay (tel. 868-0928); and most of the airport terminals.

STEVEN TEMPLE BOOKS, 489 Queen St. W., 2nd floor. Tel. 865-9908.

This rare-book store specializes in Canadian literature, including first editions. There's also a broad selection of good-condition used volumes in various fields.

THEATREBOOKS, 25 Bloor St. W. Tel. 922-7175.

The ultimate theater bookstore has sections on opera, film, and dance. The vast number of plays is complemented by a large theater-criticism section and theater magazines.

THIS AIN'T THE ROSEDALE LIBRARY, 483 Church St. Tel. 929-9912.

You could love it for its name alone, but it also has what has to be one of the largest collections of baseball books anywhere. It also carries fiction and nonfiction on media, film, art, and design. Some first editions.

TORONTO WOMEN'S BOOKSTORE, 73 Harbord St. Tel. 922-8744.

This feminist bookstore has sections for lesbians, books by and about women of color, literary criticism, fiction, and titles that deal with violence against women and children.

ULYSSES, 101 Yorkville Ave., between Bay St. and Avenue Rd. Tel. 323-3609.
A travel-book specialist, the store is well stocked with travel guidebooks, maps, travel literature, and other travel accessories.

THE UNIVERSITY OF TORONTO BOOKSTORE, 214 College St. Tel. 978-7908.
With much more than just textbooks, this academic and general bookstore also features medical, computer, and children's books, plus U of T–crested gifts and clothes.

WRITERS & CO, 2005 Yonge St. Tel. 481-8432.
This store carries a broad selection of fiction and poetry titles as well as children's books and, strangely enough, books about baseball.

CHINA, SILVER & GLASS

ASHLEY CHINA, 50 Bloor St. W. Tel. 964-2900.
The ultimate store for china, silver, and glass, this beautiful establishment has elegant table displays of very expensive china, crystal, and flatware—all the top names at decent prices.

BIRKS, Manulife Centre. 55 Bloor St. W. Tel. 922-2266.
A quintessential, reliable Canadian store, known for its jewelry, Birks also carries the top names in china, glass, silver, and other table accessories, like handsome cork tablemats. Prices are pretty good.

Also at the Eaton Centre (tel. 979-9311), First Canadian Place (tel. 363-5663), and other in-town and suburban locations.

GEORG JENSEN, 95A Bloor St. W. Tel. 924-7707.
Georg Jensen features classical modern design in silver, china, and crystal from famous Danish designers. There's furniture, too. It's a lovely store to shop in.

CRAFTS

THE ALGONQUINS SWEET GRASS GALLERY, 668 Queen St. W., near Bathurst St. Tel. 368-1336.
This store, owned by an Ojibwa, has been in business for 20 years or so, specializing in Native American arts and crafts—Iroquois masks, porcupine quill boxes, sculpture, antler carvings, prints, Tamarack decoys, as well as mocassins and Cowichan knits that were hand-knit in British Columbia.

THE ARCTIC BEAR, 125 Yorkville Ave. Tel. 967-7885.
This store has an eclectic assortment of Inuit soapstone sculpture, fur and beaver hats, some Native Canadian clothes and jewelry. You'll need to know precisely what you're looking for.

ART ZONE, 592 Markham St., at Bloor and Bathurst Sts. Tel. 534-1892.
Here you'll find a variety of glass art—stained glass, slumped glass (bent into marvelous shapes), fused glass, in which the colors have

been melted together, as well as blown-glass vases and objects. Some glass jewelry sells for $10 to $15, but prices can rise into the thousands for custom work. The studio is adjacent.

THE CRAFT GALLERY/ONTARIO CRAFTS COUNCIL, 35 McCaul St. Tel. 977-3551.

A showcase for fine contemporary crafts from across Canada. Shows change every six to eight weeks and will feature everything from stained glass to ceramics and weaving. There's a library upstairs.

FRIDA CRAFT STORES, 39 Front St. E. Tel. 366-3169.

Canadian crafts plus items and artifacts from Africa, Asia, and Latin America are aesthetically displayed in a handsome high-ceilinged space. Everything from rugs and bags to costume jewelry, candles, and knickknacks is here. Open daily.

FIVE POTTERS STUDIO, 131A Pears Ave., between Avenue Rd. and Bedford Rd. Tel. 924-6992.

Located upstairs, this studio displays and sells the work of five women ceramicists who have worked together for many years. Their work varies: Some pieces are functional, other sculptural; some are hand-worked, other pieces fashioned on the wheel. Feel free to observe them at work but call ahead for an appointment.

GUILD SHOP, 140 Cumberland St. Tel. 921-1721.

Famous for Native Canadian crafts, it's the outlet for the Ontario Crafts Council. Wonderful selection of the best contemporary Canadian ceramics, glass, wickerwork, jewelry, textiles, and more. The upstairs gallery features Inuit sculpture and art gathered from the Northwest Territories.

PRIME CANADIAN CRAFTS, 52 McCaul St. Tel. 593-5750.

This gallery displays contemporary crafts in all materials—ceramics, clay, fabric, and metal (jewelry). Prices range anywhere from $50 for a ceramic teapot to $8,000 for a brilliantly colored ceramic sculpture by Montréaler Paul Mathieu.

SNOW LION, 286 Queen St. W. Tel. 591-6858.

If you're looking for imported crafts you'll find many Tibetan and other Himalayan objects at this store. Jewelry, clothing, jackets, hats, gongs, and tankas are all available here, along with Buddhist books.

For screens, statues, howdahs, and other furnishings, including hand-knotted Tibetan rugs, go to **Snow Lion Interiors,** 271 Queen St. E. (Tel. 861-9813).

DEPARTMENT STORES

EATON'S, Eaton Centre, 290 Yonge St. Tel. 343-3528.

There are 14 retail stores in Metro Toronto. The flagship store is in the four-level Eaton Centre, which stretches two blocks from Dundas Street to Queen Street.

THE HUDSON BAY COMPANY, Richmond and Yonge Sts. Tel. 861-9111.

Archrival to Eaton's, this downtown store has an Alfred Dunhill outlet and an oyster bar and a venerable feel to the retail space, which features a wide assortment of men's and women's fashions, including DKNY and Hugo Boss.

MARKS & SPENCER, Manulife Centre, 55 Bloor St. W. Tel. 967-7772.

This is a branch of the famous British store that's known for good-quality goods and clothes at reasonable prices.

DISCOUNT

HONEST ED'S, 581 Bloor St. W. Tel. 537-2111.

The original store that launched Ed Mirvish to fame and fortune has perhaps the biggest, most frenetic electric sign in Toronto. Check it out—as Ed says, it can't be beat, as long as you know what you're looking for. A Toronto experience.

MARILYN'S, 215 Spadina Ave. Tel. 593-0654.

In the heart of the garment center, Marilyn has been in business for over 15 years, specializing in good-value discounted Canadian fashions. Each rack here carries 200 garments organized by color. The staff are trained to sift through the vast stock and create whole looks for women, dressing them from head to toe, including accessories. In this warehouse atmosphere you'll find discounts of 20% to 80%.

The store at Yonge and Bloor streets is more sedate, but the bargains are the same.

FASHIONS

CHILDREN'S FASHIONS

BELLISSIMO FASHIONS, 122 St. Patrick St., between Queen and Dundas Sts. (in Village by the Grange). Tel. 340-6382.

Bellissimo does indeed have beautiful, but fun, clothes for kids, including Peruvian-knit sweaters with appliquéed numbers or other pictorials on them, as well as brilliantly colored Muppet-inspired PVC coats.

CRAZY MAMAS, 231 Carlton St. Tel. 969-9220.

Started by two young mothers who know their business, this store has clothes for the newborn to size 10. It stocks Bravo, Deux Par Deux, Mouse Feathers, and Lemmi from Germany, among other name brands. It even sells a bright leopard-print receiving blanket, custom-made hats, and shoes. Not a bad way to start life.

MADELEINES BOUTIQUE POUR ENFANTS, 106 Yorkville Ave. Tel. 920-0846.

A specialist in European imports—mainly French and Italian—from newborn to 12-year-olds. Madeleine's carries all the top names.

MARCI LIPMAN GRAPHICS, Hazelton Lanes. Tel. 921-1998.

This store stocks original, fun, "art" T-shirts and other kids' clothes with neat, unique designs.

MEN'S FASHIONS

In addition to the listings below, Holt Renfrew also carries men's clothing. See "Women's Clothing," below.

ALAN CHERRY, 711 Yonge St. Tel. 967-1115.

Alan Cherry carries designer wear—Valentino, Giorgio Armani, and Emanuel Ungaro—as well as his own private-label clothes made in Italy. At the clearance center in the back of the store the old inventory winds up at discount—it's worth a look. There's some women's clothing, too.

BULLOCH TAILORS, 65 Front St. E., at Church St. Tel. 367-1084.

A Toronto institution for more than 50 years, Bulloch has a reputation for outfitting the city's doctors, professionals, military men, and politicos. The emphasis is still on custom-tailoring, with suits beginning at $745, but there's also a selection of ready-to-wear, most of which is made by Bulloch.

CLASSICO UOMO, 150 Bloor St. W., in Renaissance Plaza. Tel. 961-0683.

Top-of-the-line Italian style and tailoring. This store stocks the full line of Gianfranco Ferre, Venturi, Uomo, Jean-Paul Gaultier, and Belgian designer Bikkenbergs, who sells out of Milan. The store carries the whole line—suits, shirts, and accessories. Prices average $1,500 for a suit, with Gaultier costing even more.

CY MANN CLOTHIERS, Atrium on Bay, Bay and Bloor Sts. Tel. 971-9920.

A Canadian name for custom-made suits and shirts, Cy Mann has been in business for more than 40 years. Among famous names the store has dressed are Raymond Burr, Dick Cavett, and Paul Anka. Prices are high, reflecting the quality of the workmanship, but they're still lower than you'd find in the United States. Suits are priced from $600 and they'll even custom-make one in three days.

GEORGE BOURIDIS, 193 Church St., between Dundas and Shuter Sts. Tel. 363-4868.

For almost 30 years this gentleman has been fashioning custom-made shirts and blouses as well as dressing gowns. He has 400 to 500 fabrics on hand from which to choose, from Switzerland, England, France, and Germany. Women's silk blouses cost $175 and up; men's shirts, from $85. They'd retail for much more.

HARRY ROSEN, 82 Bloor St. W. Tel. 972-0556.

Torontonians have been coming to this handsome traditional English-style store for years. The stock includes Valentino and Armani and more reasonably priced classics like Sedgwick. The upper-level Galleria features Barbera, Brioni, and D'Avenza. Accessories include a great selection of ties and shoes.

Also located at 11 Adelaide St. W. and the Eaton Centre.

IRISH SHOP FOR MEN, 110 Bloor St. W. (in the mall). Tel. 922-9400.

Best known for its jackets and linen shirts, the Irish Shop carries great sports jackets, including Donegal tweeds, plus shirts, trousers, caps, hats, and picnic blankets.

STOLLERY'S, 1 Bloor St. W. Tel. 922-6173.

This venerable store has been at this corner since 1901; it was originally a mens' store, especially well known for its vast selection of shirts (with different sleeve lengths). Today it also stocks women's wear, with such English fashion names as Burberry and Aquascutum.

THOMAS K. T. CHUI, 754 Broadview Ave. Tel. 465-8538.

For more than 20 years Mr. Chui has been dressing the wealthy and the famous, among them, Joe Clark. The custom suits take two months to make and cost from $900; there are custom-made shirts, also.

WOMEN'S FASHIONS

ADA MACKENZIE LTD., 94 Cumberland St. Tel. 922-2222.

This store specializes in European sportswear—suits, pants, golf suits, cotton skirts—all imported from England, Austria, Germany, and Switzerland, with moderate to high prices.

ASYLUM, 42 Kensington Ave. Tel. 595-7199.

Scour the racks for new and vintage clothing at this Kensington Market outlet. Dresses, reworked vintage jeans with patchwork and tattoos, men's Hawaiian shirts, belts, shoes, and skull-and-crossbone-design items—they're all here.

BENETTON, 102 Bloor St. W. Tel. 968-1611.

Stylish, colorful, well-fashioned clothes at bearable prices are available for everyone. There's another outlet in the Eaton Centre.

CHANEL, 131 Bloor St. W. Tel. 925-2577.

The name says it all—classic all the way. This boutique, one of two in Canada, carries the designer's full line.

CHEZ CATHERINE, 55 Avenue Rd. Tel. 967-5666.

A long-established doyenne of the Canadian fashion scene, this store consists of four designer boutiques—Valentino, Versace, Gianfranco Ferre, and Krizia—plus a showcase of other European designers. It's known for personalized service. There's a full line of accessories, including shoes.

CLUB MONACO, 403 Queen St. W. Tel. 979-5633.

If you're looking for casual wear and sportswear, this is a very pleasant shopping experience. There are other locations at the Eaton Centre; Hazelton Lanes; 1950 Queen St. E., in the Beaches; and the Yorkdale Shopping Centre.

GIANNI VERSACE, 55 Avenue Rd. Tel. 922-1900.

Fine Italian design is the hallmark of Gianni Versace's clothing and accessories.

HARRY ROSEN WOMEN, First Canadian Place. Tel. 586-7744.

This store caters primarily to the businesswoman seeking a classic tailored look. It carries blazers, suits, and a whole range of separates—blouses, shirts in cotton and silk, sweaters—and names like Ambience, Mr. Jacks, Tahari, Karl Lagerfeld, and Aquascutum.

HOLT RENFREW, 50 Bloor St. W. Tel. 922-2333.

This beautiful, well-laid-out store has several boutiques, including Ralph Lauren, Donna Karan, Anne Klein, Yves St. Laurent, Sonia Rykiel, and more.

IRISH SHOP, 110 Bloor St. W. Tel. 922-9400.

This is a lovely store, well-stocked with Irish fashions, lace, shawls, and accessories. Books, too.

JAEGER, 131 Bloor St. W., in the Colonnade. Tel. 966-3544.
The classic British name for fashions, Jaeger has another branch in Eaton Centre.

KRIZIA BOUTIQUE, 55 Avenue Rd. (in Hazelton Lanes). Tel. 929-0222.
Upbeat and creative as ever, this boutique stocks the full line from Milan—jackets, pants, sweaters, and dresses, as well as belts and jewelry.

NORMA, 116 Cumberland St. Tel. 923-5514.
Famous for her very expensive hand-knit jackets decorated with beads, sequins, and more, Norma makes Toronto her home base. Although the prices are still high, you'll save a little on these exquisite treasures here. She has branched out to leathers, coats, and rainwear.

SUITABLES, Queen's Quay, 207 Queen's Quay W. Tel. 367-2401
Among the many silk blouses, skirts, and suits is a full range of hand-washable silk shirts that sell three for $150. Needless to say, some folks come from far and wide every year to pick up a supply.

VALENTINO, 55 Avenue Rd. Tel. 922-5666.
The name says it all. This is Italian design at its best—dresses, blouses, and evening gowns—as well as belts and jewelry.

FOOD

ARLEQUIN RESTAURANT, 134 Avenue Rd. Tel. 928-9521.
The display up front is mouth-watering—salads, pâtés, melt-in-the-mouth croissants, pastries, and more.

DANIEL ET DANIEL, 248 Carlton St. Tel. 968-9275.
You'll find a full display of all kinds of foods and gourmet items—hot and cold salads or Chinese pasta salad plus quiches, minipizzas, and apfelstrudel and other pastries.

DAVID WOOD FOOD SHOP, 1110 Yonge St., at Roxborough St. Tel. 968-2960.
This store that serves the Rosedale set stocks an array of jams and chutneys, including the Silver Palate brands and local Catherine's antipasto, as well as cheeses, deli items, coffees, and a variety of take-out—poached salmon, vegetarian and seafood salads, soups—50 to 60 items in all.

DINAH'S CUPBOARD, 50 Cumberland St. Tel. 921-8112.
This small, cluttered store has a fine selection of gourmet items to go, as well as frozen dishes to take home and microwave. Great salads, pâtés, vegetarian pasta, and croissants, as well as teas, coffees, vinegars, oils, and herbs.

DUFFLET PASTRIES, 787 Queen St. W., near Bathurst St. Tel. 368-1812.

This specialty baker supplies many restaurants with their pastries and desserts. The special Dufflet cakes include a white-and dark-chocolate mousse, almond meringue, and many other singular creations.

GLOBAL CHEESE SHOPPE, 76 Kensington Ave. Tel. 593-9251.

More than 150 varieties of cheese are discounted here. It's worth the trip to Kensington Market.

SWEET TEMPTATIONS, 207 Queen's Quay Terminal. Tel. 861-0557.

This store is famous for offering every kind of candy available—chocolate-covered almonds and peanuts, gummy bears, and a broad selection of Canadian and imported chocolates, including handmade Belgian chocolates that sell for $1 or $1.50 apiece. Frozen yogurt and ice cream, too.

TEN REN TEA, 454 Dundas St. W., at Huron St. Tel. 598-7872.

At this fascinating Chinatown store, you can pick up some fine Chinese tea, which is stored in large canisters at the back of the store. The tiny ceramic teapots also make nice gifts in the $20-to-$30 price range. Many people are beginning to collect them.

TEUSCHER OF SWITZERLAND, 55 Avenue Rd. Tel. 961-1303.

Truffles (12 kinds) are the specialty here—the favorite being champagne. Other kinds of chocolates are also sold—containing various nuts, nougat, marzipan, and fruit. All are handmade in Zurich and flown in once a week.

There's another branch in First Canadian Place (tel. 947-9892).

FURS

Fur sales take place twice a year—in summer when business is slow (the best time to negotiate a deal) and every January right after Christmas when the dealers are anxious to get rid of their inventory.

The wholesale fur warehouse is the **Balfour Building,** at 119 Spadina Ave.; it's worth starting here and shopping all the showrooms you can find in the building.

A LA MODE FURS, 686 Bathurst St. Tel. 539-9999.

This name includes several long-time local fur wholesalers—Sable Bay Furs, Leader Furs (established 1873), Stanley Walker, S. Kuretzky (an original), and Norcan Furs. On the premises you'll find 13,000 square feet of space divided into several showrooms. Mink is the number-one item, followed by beaver, raccoon, fox, sable, and lynx. The prices are wholesale, but in summer, when business is slow, they're even better.

ATLANTIC FUR COMPANY, 263 Adelaide St. W., Suite 300. Tel. 593-0984.

Check out the factory showroom for mink, fox, raccoon, and coyote.

NORMAN ROGUL FUR COMPANY, 480 Adelaide St. W. Tel. 862-7577.

Reputed furrier to Her Majesty the Queen and other royals and celebrities.

GIFTS & MISCELLANEOUS

BLEU NUIT, 15 Hazelton Ave. Tel. 925-4593.

Terrific gifts for the bathroom include soaps, towels, and other pretty bathroom accessories. Upstairs there's a selection of duvets and other bedspreads.

GALLERY OF FINE SHOPPING AT THE ART GALLERY OF ONTARIO, 317 Dundas St. W. Tel. 977-0414.

Books, gifts, jewelry, reproductions, and rental art are all featured in this new complex in the lobby of the museum.

GENERAL STORE, 55 Avenue Rd. (in Hazelton Lanes). Tel. 323-1527.

These are three stores under the same name in Hazelton Lanes. The first carries gifts for the person who has everything—gimmicky and sophisticated calculators, Newtonian puzzles, Filofaxes, and games. The adjacent branches carry house- and kitchenwares and fun paper items.

Also located at 65 Front St. W. (tel. 363-5258).

GEOMANIA, 50 Bloor St. W. Tel. 920-1420.

Geomania is filled with highly polished, brilliantly colored pieces of minerals and stones, some fashioned into elegant jewelry, others crafted into vases, bookends, and other decorative pieces. A vision.

IRISH IMPORT HOUSE, 444 Yonge St. Tel. 595-0500.

This store sells Waterford crystal, Belleek china, Donegal tweed hats and caps, Irish linens, claddagh rings, jewelry, books, T-shirts, and more.

J & S ARTS & CRAFTS, 430 Dundas St. W. Tel. 977-2562.

In the heart of Chinatown, this store has a variety of good reasonably priced gifts and souvenirs—kimonos and happy coats, kung-fu suits, cushion covers, address books and diaries with handsome silk-embroidered covers, and all-cotton Chinatown T-shirts for only $6.

KAYA KAYA, 1104 Yonge St. Tel. 925-5292.

Named after a reed that the Japanese use for thatching houses, this store displays some beautiful and unusual objects—raku, lacquer boxes and bowls, saké sets, very useful and attractive lotus bowl sets, vases, rice-paper lamps, and kimonos. Fun to browse.

LEGENDS OF THE GAME, 322 King St. W. Tel. 971-8848.

Anyone looking for a gift for a sports lover ought to find something at this temple to sports, complete with Wall of Fame and baseball-handled entrance doors. Memorabilia of all sports are on sale, including autographed photos, old and new baseball and hockey cards, old and new comics, and jerseys that have been worn by players.

OH YES, TORONTO, 101 Yorkville Ave. Tel. 924-7198.

The ultimate souvenir store—everything in it features the Toronto name. Sweats, T-shirts, oven gloves, bags, buttons, mugs, and T-shirts range in price from $2 to $30.

There's also a branch at Queen's Quay West (tel. 862-0581).

ROTMAN HAT SHOP, 345 Spadina Ave. Tel. 977-2806.

This store has been in business here for over 40 years, and it retains the flavor of yesterday, when the area was more Jewish than it is today. Here you'll find the finest, light-as-a-feather Panama hats, as well as other fun headgear, like the grouser hats.

SCIENCE CITY, 50 Bloor St. W., in the Holt Renfrew Centre. Tel. 968-2627.

A favorite of kids and adults alike, this store has an assortment of games, models, kits, and books relating to science—physics, chemistry, and biology as well as very expensive telescopes and optics, hologram watches, trilobites, and other fossil specimens. All kinds of fun, mind-expanding stuff.

TOUCH THE SKY, 207 Queen's Quay W. Tel. 362-5983.

Kites and windsocks are the specialty here, plus wind chimes, mobiles, Frisbees, and balloons—great inexpensive gifts.

E. K. R. ZEPHYR, 292 Queen St. W. Tel. 593-0795.

Pyramids, crystals, and other natural phenomena, like rocks, butterflies, and sea creatures, are the stock-in-trade of this fascinating shop.

HOUSEWARES & KITCHENWARE

EN PROVENCE, 68 Scollard St. Tel. 975-9400.

This store has a beautiful selection of French decorative items for the home—ceramicware, table accessories, wrought-iron and wood furniture, and, in the back, the most luxurious fabrics by Les Olivades for household use. This is French country style at its best.

FORTUNE HOUSEWARES, 388 Spadina Ave. Tel. 593-6999.

This well-stocked store has a great selection of utensils and other household/kitchen items—chopping boards, aprons, Copco pots, and other brand-name items—at 20% or more off the regular prices around town.

PLAITER PLACE, 384 Spadina Ave. Tel. 593-9734.

This must be the city's wicker emporium, bar none. Every conceivable use is made of wicker: You'll find all kinds of objects made from wicker and bamboo here—birdcages, blinds, steamers, hats, and baskets galore in all shapes, sizes, and styles.

TAP PHONG TRADING, 360 Spadina Ave. Tel. 977-6364.

All kinds of utensils, woks, bamboo steamers, ceramic cookware, mortar and pestles, and terrific baskets are jammed into this small space. Fun shopping.

JEWELRY

BENI SUNG, 131 Bloor St. W. (in the Colonnade), Suite 1101. Tel. 967-1148.

This Hong Kong–born jeweler is famous for his creative unique designs. Winner of the biannual De Beers International Award for Creative Design, he is especially well known for his pearls. He travels regularly around the world from Thailand to Hawaii to select his stones. You'll pay $1,200 and up for his unique settings; for 18-karat silver and gold earrings made in molds, the price is $300.

BIRKS JEWELERS, 220 Yonge St., in the Eaton Centre. Tel. 979-9311.

A well-known Canadian retailer with stores in towns across Canada, Birks stocks fine silver and jewelry at fair prices. Also at the Manulife Centre (tel. 922-2266), First Canadian Place (tel. 363-5663), and at other in-town and suburban locations.

18 KARAT, 71 McCaul St. Tel. 593-1648.

The owners of this store will craft jewelry on the premises according to your design. They will also do repairs and redesigns of antique settings. Show them what you have in mind and they will execute it.

FIRST TORONTO JEWELLERY EXCHANGE, 215 Yonge St. Tel. 340-0008.

Thirty stores under one roof.

GOLD SHOPPE, 25 Bloor St. W. (entrance on Balmuto St.). Tel. 923-5565.

This store, which has been in business for more than 50 years, is known for its estate jewelry and silver—rings, necklaces, pins, and brooches. It also stocks new jewelry, but it's not custom-made. Prices range from $2 to $20,000.

YONGE DUNDAS JEWELLERY EXCHANGE, 295 Yonge St. Tel. 340-0008.

A complex containing more than 20 stores.

SILVERBRIDGE, 162 Cumberland St. Tel. 923-2591.

The sterling-silver jewelry here is designed by Costin Lazar and manufactured in Toronto. It's modern and reflects the talents of Mr. Lazar, who is also a sculptor. Necklaces, bracelets, and earrings, as well as cuff links, money clips, and key holders are priced from $60 to $14,000.

MAGAZINES, INTERNATIONAL NEWSPAPERS & BOOKS

LICHTMAN'S NEWS & BOOKS, Yonge and Richmond Sts. Tel. 368-7390.

Local and international newspapers and magazines, as well as hard- and softcover books are sold here and also at the Atrium on Bay, at Yonge and Bloor streets, and at Yonge and Eglinton.

MAISON DE LA PRESSE INTERNATIONALE, 124 Yorkville Ave. Tel. 928-0418.

This large store has foreign magazines and newspapers galore. It's a convenient place to pick up the *New York Times, Wall Street Journal, Financial Times,* and the like.

MALLS & SHOPPING CENTERS

ATRIUM ON BAY, Yonge and Dundas Sts. Tel. 593-1796.

Sixty stores on two floors sell fashions, shoes, jewelry, and more.

COLLEGE PARK SHOPS, 444 Yonge St. Tel. 597-1221.

More than 100 stores spread out on two floors, this is a more intimate and less harried version of the Eaton Centre.

EATON CENTRE, 220 Yonge St. Tel. 979-3300.
This glass-domed galleria has more than 360 shops and restaurants on four levels, with plenty of places to rest and eat lunch, too. This is where the real people shop.

HAZELTON LANES, 55 Avenue Rd. Tel. 968-8600.
This complex is for the wealthy and those who wish to appear so, with all the great designer fashion names and more on two levels. And it has the perfect rest stop—the Hazelton Club.

HOLT RENFREW CENTRE, Bloor St. W.
Not to be confused with the store of the same name, which is far more upscale, the center is much more down to earth. You wouldn't find Teas 'n' Tarts in Holt Renfrew. My favorite stores on the downstairs level are Science City and Geomania.

QUEEN'S QUAY TERMINAL, 207 Queen's Quay. Tel. 363-5017.
More than 100 shops and restaurants, including fashion and gift boutiques, are housed here in a converted waterfront warehouse. Remember, the rents are high. Open daily from 10am to 9pm.

ROYAL BANK PLAZA, Bay and Front Sts. Tel. 974-2880.
More than 60 shops are directly accessible from Union Station and the subway. Don't miss the building above.

VILLAGE BY THE GRANGE, 122 St. Patrick St. between Queen and Dundas Sts. Tel. 598-1414.
More than 70 shops are complemented by several major restaurants. The International Food Market is good for budget dining.

MARKETS

KENSINGTON MARKET, along Baldwin, Kensington, and Augusta Aves.
Originally a Jewish market, then a Portuguese market area, today it offers all kinds of ethnic foods from Middle Eastern to West Indian. A Toronto experience.

ST. LAWRENCE MARKET, 92 Front St. E. Tel. 392-7219.
This historic market is still favored by Torontonians for its fresh produce—from figs to fish. Best day is Saturday when the farmers come into town and the market opens at 5am. Hours are Tuesday through Thursday from 8am to 6pm, Friday from 8am to 7pm, and Saturday from 5am to 5pm.

MUSIC

A & A MUSIC & ENTERTAINMENT, 351 Yonge St. Tel. 977-4645.
This popular store has a large selection of all kinds of music.

CD BAR, 281 Queen St. W. Tel. 977-6863.

Remember the good old days when you could listen to the *records* in the store? Well, you can still do so here. Thousands of titles are in stock for your listening pleasure.

CLASSICAL RECORD SHOP, 55 Avenue Rd. (in Hazelton Lanes). Tel. 961-8999.

Listen to the melodies emanating from this store. It stocks a large selection of CDs, audio tapes, and videos for the classical music lover.

L'ATELIER GRIGORIAN, 70 Yorkville Ave. Tel. 922-6477.

This store has a fantastic selection of CDs—jazz and classical only.

RECORD PEDDLER, 621 Yonge St. Tel. 921-3566.

This specialty store stocks British imports, LPs, and CDs in rock, blues, jazz, and reggae. No classical or country.

SAM THE RECORD MAN, 347 Yonge St.

This famous Toronto record outlet is so vast and busy that the telephone number is unlisted. It has the largest laser-disc selection in the city.

TOBACCO

WINSTON & HOLMES, 138 Cumberland St. Tel. 968-1290.

Although it's not old, this store has all the appearance of tradition and age. A large selection of well-made pipes is on display behind glass; there's a broad selection of Cuban and other cigars, and all the other smoking requisites. Fine fountain pens are stocked, too, along with men's shaving accoutrements and toiletries. Mail order available.

Also at Queen's Quay (tel. 362-2878) and 2 First Canadian Place (tel. 363-7575).

TOYS

CARRIAGE TRADE DOLLS, 584 Mount Pleasant Rd. Tel. 481-1639.

A real specialty doll store, Carriage Trade carries modern vinyl and porcelain dolls, including some that are anatomically correct, dolls that you can wash, and so on. It also stocks a full range of carriages, cribs, bassinets, socks, bibs, and more—all for dolls. Also has some serious modern collector pieces.

KIDDING AWOUND, 91 Cumberland St. Tel. 926-8996.

Wind-up toys—musical boxes and clockwork toys—antique toys, and other interesting items are available here, along with kids' clothes up to size 6 or 7. Great therapy for adults.

KIDSTUFF, 738 Bathurst St., one block south of Bloor St. Tel. 535-2212.

This store does not stock video and computer games, but concentrates instead on cooperative games, Lego, Playmobile, puppets, art supplies, and other imported and educational toys.

LITTLE DOLLHOUSE COMPANY, 617 Mount Pleasant Rd. Tel. 489-7180.

This charming store carries all-wood handcrafted wooden dollhouse kits in about 12 different styles, many Victorian, complete with shingles. They also sell dollhouse furniture, wallpaper, and building supplies—wood, metal, and plastic—and display 100 room boxes. Dollhouse kits range from $125 to $600, while finished dollhouses are about twice the price.

SCIENCE CITY JR., 50 Bloor St. W. Tel. 986-2627.
A great store, it's full of games, puzzles, models, and books about science, and serious stuff like telescopes, trilobites, and hologram watches.

TOP BANANA, 583 Mount Pleasant Rd. Tel. 440-0111.
This two-floor toy store concentrates on educational and imported toys, like Brio wooden trains from Sweden, Ravensburger puzzles and games, Eduframe toys, art supplies, and plenty of products from Playmobil and Playskool. Musical tapes, art supplies, and books, too.

THE TOY SHOP, 62 Cumberland St., at Bay St. Tel. 961-4870.
The two floors of creative toys, books, and games here include videos from around the world.

WINES

You'll have to shop the LCBO outlets. Look them up in the *Yellow Pages* under "Liquor Control Board of Ontario." The most convenient downtown locations are College Park (tel. 977-3277); 2 Bloor St. E. (tel. 925-6965); 87 Front St. E. (tel. 368-0521); Manulife Centre, 55 Bloor St. W. (tel. 925-5266); the Eaton Centre (tel. 979-9978); and Union Station (tel. 368-9644). More extensive selections are found at the **Vintages** stores, like the one in Hazelton Lanes on the concourse.

CHAPTER 9

TORONTO NIGHTS

Toronto has the National Ballet of Canada, the Canadian Opera Company, the Toronto Symphony, two large arts centers, two concert halls, a special dance theater, and theaters galore (with a reputation second only to those on Broadway), plus enough bars—plush, pub, wine, jazz, casual, and otherwise—clubs, cabarets, and other entertainments to keep anyone spinning. For local happenings, check *Where Toronto* and *Toronto Life,* as well as the *Globe and Mail,* the *Toronto Star,* and the *Toronto Sun.* For the hipper scene get hold of a copy of *Eye* or *Now,* both free and available at Maison de Presse and outside many other bookstores and stores around the city.

DISCOUNT TICKETS For day-of-performance half-price tickets, go to the **Five Star Ticket Booths** at Yonge and Dundas streets outside the Eaton Centre on the southwest corner. Cash and credit cards are taken. It's open Tuesday through Saturday from noon to 7:30pm and Sunday from 11am to 3pm. For information call 596-8211.

1. THE PERFORMING ARTS

MAJOR PERFORMING-ARTS COMPANIES

In addition to the following major performing-arts companies, Toronto has many local, home-grown companies offering all sorts of concerts and performances. Check the newspapers for details.

OPERA & CLASSICAL MUSIC

CANADIAN OPERA COMPANY, 227 Front St. E. Tel. 872-2262 for tickets at the O'Keefe Centre box office, or 363-6671 for administration.

The Canadian Opera Company began its life in 1950 with 10 performances of 3 operas. It now stages eight different operas at the O'Keefe Centre, spread over the nine months from September to April.

Prices: Tickets $22–$94.

TAFELMUSIK BAROQUE ORCHESTRA, 427 Bloor St. W. Tel. 964-6337 for tickets, or 964-9562 for administration.

This group plays baroque music on authentic historic instruments, giving a series of concerts at Trinity United Church.

Prices: Call for dates, programs, and ticket prices.

TORONTO MENDELSSOHN CHOIR, 60 Simcoe St. Tel. 598-0422.

A world-renowned choir, this group first performed in Massey Hall in 1895.

Prices: Call for dates, programs, and ticket prices.

TORONTO SYMPHONY ORCHESTRA, 60 Simcoe St. Tel. 598-3375 for tickets, 593-7769 for administrative offices.

The Symphony performs at Roy Thomson Hall from September through June. The repetoire ranges from classics to pop and new Canadian works. In June and July, concerts are also given at outdoor venues throughout the city.

Prices: Call for dates, programs, and ticket prices.

THEATER COMPANIES

CANADIAN STAGE COMPANY, 26 Berkeley St. Tel. 366-7723 for tickets, or 367-8243 for administration.

The Canadian Stage Company performs comedy, drama, and musicals in the St. Lawrence Centre, and also presents free summer Shakespeare performances in High Park. Call for dates and programs.

Prices: Tickets $18–$40; discount tickets for seniors and students sometimes available 30 minutes before the performance.

THEATRE PLUS, 27 Front St. E. Tel. 366-7723.

THE MAJOR CONCERT & PERFORMANCE HALL BOX OFFICES

For TicketMaster's telecharge service, call 872-1111.

Elgin and Winter Garden Theatres, 189–191 Yonge St. (near Queen Street; tel. 872-5555).
Massey Hall, 178 Victoria St. (at Shuter Street; tel. 593-4828 or 872-4255).
O'Keefe Centre, 1 Front St. E. (tel. 872-2262).
Pantages Theatre, 244 Victoria St. (near Shuter Street; tel. 872-2222).
Premier Dance Theatre, in the York Quay Centre, 235 Queen's Quay W. (tel. 973-4000).
Royal Alexandra Theatre, 260 King St. W. (tel. 872-3333).
Roy Thomson Hall, 60 Simcoe St. (tel. 872-4255).
SkyDome, 300 The Esplanade W. (tel. 341-3663).
St. Lawrence Centre for the Arts, 27 Front St. E. (tel. 366-7723).
Young People's Theatre, 165 Front St. E. (tel. 864-9732).

Theatre Plus presents a summer season of drama, including both classics and Canadian plays, in the St. Lawrence Centre for the Arts. Call for dates and programs.

Prices: Tickets $11–$36; discount tickets for seniors and students sometimes available 30 minutes before the performance.

YOUNG PEOPLE'S THEATRE, 165 Front St. E. Tel. 864-9732.

In Toronto you'll have no problem finding kids' entertainment, for the city has taken its children's theater very seriously with the Young People's Theatre. Here, in a theater seating 468, they put on such whimsical, fun productions as *Pinocchio, Beauty and the Beast,* and *The Oracle,* plus enchanting productions of such Shakespeare plays as *A Midsummer Night's Dream.* There might be one problem: Kids have been known to weep when the show ends.

Prices: Tickets, from $25 adults, $15 seniors and children under 18.

DANCE COMPANIES

NATIONAL BALLET OF CANADA, 157 King St. E. Tel. 362-1041 or 366-4846 for information on programs and prices.

Most famous of all Toronto's cultural contributions is perhaps The National Ballet of Canada, the nation's largest classical and modern dance company. It was launched at Eaton Auditorium in Toronto on November 12, 1951, by English ballerina Celia Franca, who served initially as director, principal dancer, choreographer, and teacher. Over the years the company and stars like Karen Kain have achieved great renown. Among the highlights of its history have been the invitation to perform at Expo '70 in Osaka, Japan; its 1973 New York debut (which featured Nureyev's full-length *Sleeping Beauty*); and Baryshnikov's appearance with the company soon after his defection in 1974.

Besides its tours of Canada and its annual summer season at the Metropolitan Opera House in New York, the company performs its regular seasons in Toronto at the O'Keefe Centre in the fall, at Christmas, and in the spring, as well as making summer appearances before enormous crowds at the open-air theater at Ontario Place. Included in the repertoire are such classics as *Swan Lake, The Nutcracker,* and *The Taming of the Shrew;* and a variety of modern works, including William Forsythe's highly acclaimed *the second detail,* Glen Tetley's *Alice,* and resident choreographer John Alleyne's *Interrogating Slam.*

Prices: Tickets $10–$83.

TORONTO DANCE THEATRE, 80 Winchester St. Tel. 967-1365 for administrative offices, 973-4000 (at the Premier Dance Theatre) for tickets.

The leading contemporary dance company in Toronto performs three seasonal programs per year at the Premier Dance Theatre.

Prices: Tickets $14–$27.

MAJOR MULTIPURPOSE PERFORMANCE & CONCERT HALLS

MASSEY HALL, 178 Victoria St. Tel. 363-7301 or 872-4255 for tickets and program information.

A Canadian musical landmark, this 2,757-seat auditorium hosts a variety of programming, including classical, rock, ethnic, and theatrical presentations.

Prices: Vary with the performance.

O'KEEFE CENTRE, 1 Front St. E. Tel. 393-7469, or 872-2262 for the box office.

With its 60- by 130-foot stage and 3,223-seat auditorium, the O'Keefe Centre is home to the Canadian Opera Company and The National Ballet of Canada. It also presents the very best in live entertainment—hit Broadway musicals like *Cats* and *Grand Hotel,* variety and family shows, diverse international superstars such as Johnny Mathis and Barry Manilow, comedians, and dance companies. Tickets may be purchased at the box office or by phone (there's a service charge for phone orders).

The O'Keefe Centre Café is available for pretheater dining. Call 393-7478 for reservations. Subway: Union.

Prices: Opera and ballet tickets $11–$95; other shows $15–$55, depending on the performance.

PREMIER DANCE THEATRE, in the York Quay Centre, 207 Queen's Quay W. Tel. 973-4000.

Toronto now has a theater specifically designed for dance. For information on productions and the dance series, phone the Harbourfront box office from 11am daily. Toronto's leading contemporary dance company, the Toronto Dance Theatre, performs its season here.

Prices: Tickets $22–$35.

ROY THOMSON HALL, 60 Simcoe St. Tel. 593-4822 for administration; 872-4255 or 593-4828 for tickets and program information.

Toronto's premier concert hall presents top international performers of classical music, jazz, big-band music, and comedy. It is also home to the Toronto Symphony Orchestra.

The hall was designed to give the audience a feeling of extraordinary intimacy with every performer—none of the 2,812 seats is more than 107 feet from the stage. The exterior of the building itself is spectacular—dove-colored, petal-shaped, and enveloped in a huge glass canopy that's reflective by day and transparent by night. Subway: St. Andrews.

Prices: Vary with the performance.

ST. LAWRENCE CENTRE FOR THE ARTS, 27 Front St. E. Tel. 366-7723.

The two prime tenants are the Canadian Stage Company and Theatre Plus, both of which present a season at the St. Lawrence Centre. In addition, many classical music concerts, recitals, and chamber-music concerts featuring internationally famous artists are given here, most in the Jane Mallet Theatre.

Prices: Tickets $16–$42 for theater productions, $20–$45 for other performances; discount tickets for seniors and students sometimes available 30 minutes before the performance.

THEATERS

As the section that follows demonstrates, Toronto has become a very active theater city, with many small theater groups producing exciting offbeat drama—a slowly burgeoning Toronto equivalent of Off-Broadway. Since there are a great many of these smaller companies, I have picked out only the few whose reputations have been established. If you'd like to do some talent-scouting of your own, pick up the local newspaper or a local magazine, scan the myriad productions, and find the next Sir Laurence Olivier.

THE TOP VENUES

In addition to **O'Keefe Centre** and the **St. Lawrence Centre for the Arts** (see "Major Multipurpose Performance & Concert Halls," above), the city's big theaters include the Royal Alexandra Theatre, fondly referred to as the Royal Alex.

THE ELGIN AND WINTER GARDEN THEATRES, 189–191 Yonge St. Tel. 594-0755, or 872-5555 for the box office.

Two theater gems have been dusted off for the 1990s. This double-stacked theater opened in 1913 and cost $500,000—no mean sum in those days. Today it cost $29 million to refurbish it, restoring the stucco-and-gilt interior to its former beauty. The 1,500-seat Elgin has a domed ceiling; the upstairs Winter Garden seats 1,000 and is designed to re-create a bosky copse with real beech branches covering the ceiling. Both theaters offer everything from Broadway musicals to dramas, concerts, and opera.

Prices: Tickets $25–$75, depending on the performance.

PANTAGES THEATRE, 244 Victoria St./263 Yonge St. Tel. 872-2222 for tickets.

This magnificent old theater has been restored to host splashy Broadway shows like *The Phantom of the Opera,* which reopened the theater. It originally opened in 1920 showing silent films and hosting vaudeville performances.

Prices: Tickets $40–$91; discount seats available two hours before the performance.

ROYAL ALEXANDRA THEATRE, 260 King St. W. Tel. 593-0351, or 872-3333 for tickets.

Shows from Broadway migrate north to the Royal Alex. Tickets are often snapped up by subscription buyers, so your best bet is to write ahead to the theater (260 King St. W., Toronto, ON, M5V 1H9).

The theater itself is quite a spectacle. Constructed in 1907, it owes its current lease on life to owner Ed Mirvish, who refurbished it (as well as the surrounding area) in the 1960s. Inside it's a riot of plush reds, gold brocade, and baroque ornamentation, with a seating capacity of 1,493. Apparently, you're wise to avoid the second balcony and also the seats under the circle. Subway: St. Andrews.

Prices: Tickets $16–$84, depending on the show.

ADDITIONAL OFFERINGS

BAYVIEW PLAYHOUSE, 1605 Bayview Ave. (south of Eglinton E.). Tel. 481-6191.

The Bayview is an intimate 500-seat theater presenting a wide variety of Broadway-style entertainment—both modern dramas and musicals. Subway: Davisville; then take no. 11 bus to Manor Rd.

Prices: Tickets $15–$40.

FACTORY THEATRE, 125 Bathurst St. Tel. 864-9971.

Started in 1970, the experimental Factory Theatre is the home of Canadian playwriting, where promising new authors get the chance to develop and showcase their works. In the past it has presented festivals of Canadian plays in London and New York. The Bathurst streetcar runs nearby.

Prices: Tickets $7.50–$30.

TARRAGON THEATRE, 30 Bridgman Ave. Tel. 536-5018, or 531-1827 for tickets.

The Tarragon Theatre, near Dupont and Bathurst, opened in the early 1970s and continues to produce original works by Canadian playwrights—Michael Tremblay, David French, John Murrell, Mavis Gallant, and Judith Thompson, for example—and an occasional classic like Chekhov's *Cherry Orchard* or an Off-Broadway play like Wallace Shawn's *Aunt Dan and Lemon*. It's a small, intimate theater where you can get coffee and apple juice in the foyer.

Prices: Tickets $12–$21; on Sun, pay what you can afford.

THEATRE PASSE MURAILLE, 16 Ryerson Ave. Tel. 363-2416.

Theatre Passe Muraille started in the late 1960s when a group of actors began experimenting and improvising original Canadian material. There are two stages, the main one seating 220 and "The Backspace" seating 65. Subway: Queen; then streetcar west to Bathurst.

Prices: Tickets $5–$20.

TORONTO TRUCK THEATRE, 94 Belmont St. Tel. 922-0084.

The Toronto Truck Theatre is the home of Agatha Christie's *The Mousetrap*, now in its 16th year. It's Canada's longest-running show.

Prices: Tickets $14–$19.

COOL FOR KIDS

For enthralling theater productions designed especially for kids, check out the **Young People's Theatre** (see "Theater Companies" under "Major Performing-Arts Companies," above).

DINNER THEATER & COMEDY SHOWS

LIMELIGHT SUPPER CLUB, 2026 Yonge St. Tel. 482-5200.

Musicals, like *A Chorus Line*, are the specialty at the Limelight, where you can have dinner while enjoying the entertainment.

Prices: Dinner and show, Mon–Thurs $38, Fri $40, Sat $55. Show only, Sat $25.

THE SECOND CITY, 110 Lombard St. Tel. 863-1111.

One of Toronto's zaniest theater groups, Second City specializes in improvisational comedy. This is the company that nurtured Dan Aykroyd and Bill Murray and continues to turn out talented young comedians. The skits are always funny and topical. Its home is an old fire hall that now houses a theater seating 200 and a restaurant.

Second City has had a marked impact on Canadian entertainment with its various workshops, touring company, seasoned resident company, and internationally syndicated TV series.

Reservations are required.

Prices: Dinner-theater packages, Mon–Thurs $28, Fri $32, Sat $33. Show only, Mon–Thurs $12.50, Fri $16, Sat $17.

UKRAINIAN CARAVAN, 5245 Dundas St. W. Tel. 231-7447.

For an evening of Cossack dance, song, and comic repartee, head for the Ukrainian Caravan at Kipling Street. There are shows on Saturdays only; dinner begins at 7:30pm, the show at 9pm. Subway: Dundas; then a streetcar west.

Prices: Dinner and show, $22–$35 per person.

YUK-YUK'S KOMEDY KABARET, 1280 Bay St. Tel. 967-6425.

Situated in the heart of Yorkville, Yuk-Yuk's is an ideal location for amateur and professional stand-up comics to puncture a few contemporary social pretensions in a stream of totally unpredictable monologue. Comic Mark Breslin founded the place, following the trend of New York's Catch a Rising Star and Los Angeles's The Comedy Store. Besides the comics, other bizarre and hilariously grotesque troupes find their way to this spotlight. Monday and Tuesday are amateur nights. Reservations are needed on Saturday. Subway: Bay.

Prices: Tickets, Mon–Tues $4, Wed–Thurs $8, Fri $13, Sat $15.

2. THE CLUB & MUSIC SCENE

COUNTRY & FOLK

BIRCHMOUNT TAVERN, 462 Birchmount. Tel. 698-4115.

This is the city's longtime country venue, attracting a broad range of Canadian and American artists, including Lynn Anderson, Johnny Paycheck, and many more. The music goes on Wednesday to Sunday from 9pm to 1am.

Admission: Fri–Sat $5.

FLYING CLOUD FOLK CLUB, 292 Brunswick Ave. Tel. 533-5455.

Located in the space that serves as the headquarters for the Australian/New Zealand community, this club features local folk singers every Sunday night from mid-September to mid-June.

Admission: Free.

FREE TIMES CAFE, 320 College St. Tel. 967-1078.

The back room is one of the city's regular folk and acoustic music venues.

Admission: Free.

HORSESHOE TAVERN, 368 Queen St. W. Tel. 598-4753.

An old traditional Toronto venue that attracts a cross section of people from age 20 to 60. Live music on Thursday to Saturday attracts a hard-driving crowd; it's country on Monday to Wednesday. Bands go on at 10pm.

Admission: Thurs–Sat $7.

ROCK & REGGAE

BAMBOO, 312 Queen St. W. Tel. 593-5771.

Bamboo, decked out in Caribbean style and colors, offers an exciting assortment of reggae, calypso, salsa, and world beat sounds. The club takes up one side of the space, while a small restaurant decorated with masks from New Guinea occupies a small side area.

The menu mixes Caribbean, Indonesian, and Thai specialties. Thai spicy noodles are really popular, blending shrimp, chicken, tofu, and egg. Lamb and potato Rôti, and Caribbean curry chicken served with gado gado, banana, and steamed rice are other examples. Music starts at 10pm. Drinks run $4 to $5. Subway: Osgoode or Queen; then a streetcar west.

Admission: Mon–Thurs $5, Fri–Sat $10.

EL MOCAMBO, 464 Spadina Ave. Tel. 324-9667.

A rock-and-roll landmark where the Stones chose to take their gig in the '70s. Today international blues and rock artists perform upstairs while the downstairs room features rockabilly sounds and also folk one night a week.

Admission: Varies.

LEE'S PALACE, 529 Bloor St. W. Tel. 532-7383.

With raucous, loud rock featuring local bands downstairs every night, Lee's Palace is for the young who have poor hearing. There's alternative rock upstairs Thursday to Saturday.

Admission: Mon–Thurs $3, Fri–Sat $7–$8.

THE RIVOLI, 332 Queen St. W. Tel. 596-1908.

Currently this is the club for an eclectic mix of avant-garde performances, including blues, comedy shows, and bands—all appearing in the back room. Shows begin at 9pm and continue to 1am. There's dancing, too, plus a billiard room and espresso bar upstairs.

Admission: Mon–Thurs $3–$6, Fri–Sat $5–$8.

JAZZ & RHYTHM & BLUES

Toronto is a big jazz town—especially on Saturday afternoon, when many a hotel lounge or restaurant lays on an afternoon of rip-roaring rhythm.

In addition to the clubs listed below, **Bamboo,** listed under "Rock & Reggae," above, also offered some of the hottest jazz in town when I last visited.

ALBERT'S HALL, upstairs at the Brunswick House, 481 Bloor St. W. Tel. 964-2242.

At Albert's you'll find the funkiest blues in the city—Buddy Guy and Junior Wells, John Lee Hooker, and the like from 9pm on Monday to Saturday.

Admission: Mon–Thurs free, Fri–Sat $5–$6.

BEN WICK'S, 424 Parliament St. Tel. 961-9425.

There's jazz, usually on Saturday night only, at this comfortable English-style pub named after local cartoonist Ben Wick. The music begins at 8:30pm.

Admission: Free.

BERMUDA ONION, 131 Bloor St., in the Colonnade. Tel. 925-1470.

This restaurant/jazz club features a variety of sounds, from fusion to occasional blues, booking such international names as Oscar Peterson and Max Roach. Music begins at 9pm. There's a full menu of pasta, seafood, and meat.

Admission: Fri–Sat $8–$12.

THE CHELSEA BUN, at the Chelsea Inn, 33 Gerrard St. Tel. 595-1975.

The Chelsea Bun is another of my favorite Saturday-afternoon jazz spots, where the crowd gathers at 3pm and listens until 7pm. Six days a week there's also a piano player and a live band playing Top 40 tunes from 9pm to 1am.

Admission: Free.

CLINTON TAVERN, 693 Bloor St. W. Tel. 535-9541.

This typical down-home bar with log cabin walls features blues and rock.

Admission: $4 and up, depending on performance.

GEORGE'S SPAGHETTI HOUSE, 290 Dundas St. E. Tel. 923-9887.

George's, at Sherbourne Street, is an old Toronto favorite, featuring local jazz groups, including Moe Koffman and his quintet. The music goes from 8:30pm to 12:30am Monday to Thursday and 9pm to 1am on Friday and Saturday.

Admission: Wed–Thurs $4, Fri–Sat $5; no cover for last set or at the bar.

MEYER'S DELI, 69 Yorkville Ave. Tel. 960-4780.

Another survivor on the city's jazz scene, Meyer's features jazz on Friday and Saturday nights starting at 9pm. The sounds range from traditional to swing, fusion, or whatever reflects the age of the particular group.

Admission: Free.

MONTREAL BISTRO JAZZ CLUB, 65 Sherbourne St. Tel. 363-0179.

A cool atmosphere for an array of jazz artists. Great, too, because the bistro is next door.

Admission: Varies.

TOP O' THE SENATOR, 249 Victoria St. Tel. 364-7517.

Toronto's most atmospheric jazz club is a long, narrow room with a bar down one side and a distinct 1930s look. It's a great place to hear fine jazz, including local Moe Koffman. The atmosphere is only added to by the funky old movie theater seats set around tables, the couches alongside the performance area, and portraits of band leaders and artists on the walls. Open Tuesday to Saturday.

Admission: Fri–Sat $10, Thurs $8; may vary depending on the artist.

DANCE CLUBS

Dance clubs come and go—the hottest spot can turn into the coldest potato almost overnight—so bear with me if some of those listed below have disappeared or changed. Meanwhile, here are some of the currently crowded spots on the Toronto scene.

First, let me just remind you of those hotel clubs already

mentioned: **Misty's,** at the Toronto Airport Hilton International, 5875 Airport Rd. (tel. 677-9900), and the Woodbine Inn at the **Regal Constellation,** 900 Dixon Rd. (tel. 675-1500).

BERLIN, 2335 Yonge St. Tel. 489-7777.

This is one of the more sophisticated clubs, attracting a well-heeled crowd ranging from 25 to 55. Currently it's indulging in a Latin craze, with salsa and mambo dancing to live Latin entertainment; on Thursday there's dancing to a DJ; and on weekends there's more dancing to the house band and a DJ, too. Berlin is open Tuesday and Thursday until 2am, Friday and Saturday until 3am; it's closed other days.

Admission: Tues $7; Thurs $3; Fri–Sat $10.

BRANDY'S, 70 The Esplanade. Tel. 364-6674.

Brandy's is a singles spot that packs them in in droves. It's decorated with oak furniture, hanging plants, and lots of Tiffany-style lamps. On Thursday and Friday lines are champing at the doors to dance up a storm on the small dance floor to the DJ's Top 40 sounds. There's also karaoke fun on Thursday nights. Expect to spend $4 for a beer, $4.75 for a shot.

Admission: Free.

CHICK 'N' DELI, 744 Mount Pleasant Rd. Tel. 489-3363.

At Chick 'n' Deli, south of Eglinton Avenue, Tiffany-style lamps and oak set the background for Top 40 or rhythm and blues every night. The dance floor is always packed.

Chicken wings and barbecue are the specialties, along with nachos, salads, and a selection of sandwiches—club, corned beef, etc. On Saturday afternoon the sounds are Dixieland. Entertainment begins at 9pm on Monday to Friday (from 4pm on Sunday and from 3:45 to 7pm on Saturday).

Admission: Free.

GO GO, 250 Richmond St. W. Tel. 593-4646.

In two large rooms—one black, one white—the crowds frolic to their heart's content in Euro-disco style. Open Wednesday to Sunday.

Admission: Varies.

HARD ROCK CAFE, Gate 1, SkyDome. Tel. 341-2388.

A branch of the famous chain. There's DJ entertainment, plus food and rock-and-roll memorabilia.

Admission: $3.25 during Blue Jays games.

THE HORIZON, atop the CN Tower, 301 Front St. W. Tel. 362-5411.

What must be one of the world's highest nightclubs swings atop the CN Tower to DJ entertainment during the week and live jazz on weekends. The Horizon is open daily from 8:30pm to 1am.

Admission: $11.95.

LOOSE MOOSE, 220 Adelaide St. W. (between Simcoe and Duncan Sts.). Tel. 971-5252.

This is a crowd-pleaser for a younger set, who like the multilevel dance floors, the DJ, and the booze and schmooze. Starts every night at 9pm.

Admission: Free.

PHOENIX CONCERT THEATRE, 410 Sherborne St. Tel. 323-1251.

Rock 'n' roll, blues, and pop get the crowds dancing.
Admission: Varies; Fri–Sat $10.

RPM, 132 Queen's Quay E. Tel. 869-1462.
This large disco attracts a young crowd for the singles scene.
Admission: Varies.

ROCKIT, 120 Church St. (south of Richmond). Tel. 947-9555.
In this pizzeria and dance bar, different nights feature different sounds and attract different crowds. On Wednesday the $2 drinks and rhythm and blues attract the 20- to 25-year-olds, as does rock and dancing on Thursday. On Friday and Saturday a DJ spins the dance tunes. The proceedings begin at 9pm and go to 2am.
Admission: Fri–Sat $5–$10.

SNEAKY DEES, 431 College St. Tel. 368-5090.
The pool tables and Mexican food complement the alternative rock sounds that go on in the club upstairs until 3am weekdays, until 5am on weekends.

STILIFE, 217 Richmond St. W. Tel. 593-6116.
In this weird cavelike space, with its somewhat spooky atmosphere, the young avant-garde fashion-conscious crowd dances or gathers in the quiet back room. Thursday and Friday, according to Torontonians, are the best nights. Saturday is Scarborough night.
Admission: Wed–Thurs $7, Fri $10, Sat $12.

STUDEBAKERS, 150 Pearl St. Tel. 591-7960.
Drop in here if you want to hear the old sounds from the 1950s and '60s. It's nostalgia time.
Admission: Free.

A GAY DANCE CLUB

BADLANDS AND POWER, 9 Isabella St. Tel. 960-1200.
One of the city's most popular gay bars/dance clubs attracts a mixed crowd of men and women. Wednesday is women's night upstairs in the dance club, where the music is DJ-driven. Downstairs is country, with live shows on Monday and Thursday.
Admission: Free.

3. THE BAR SCENE

Note: Bars and pubs that serve drinks only are open Monday through Saturday from 11am to 1am. Establishments that also serve food are open Sunday, too.

PUBS & BARS

First, let me list some of my favorite hotel bars. For a really comfortable bar where you can really settle into some conversation, go to the rooftop bar atop the ✪ **Park Plaza** at 4 Avenue Rd. (tel.

924-5471). An old literary haunt, it's comfortable and the view and outdoor terrace are also splendid. The fairly formal **Chartroom,** at the Westin Harbour Castle, 1 Harbour Square (tel. 869-1600), has a good view of the lake and the island ferry. The **Consort Bar** at the King Edward Hotel, 37 King St. E. (tel. 863-9700), is also comfortable, as is **La Serre,** at the Four Seasons, 21 Avenue Rd. (tel. 964-0411). The **Chelsea Bun,** at the Chelsea Inn, 33 Gerrard St. W. (tel. 595-1975), has a fine selection of single-malt whiskeys and good musical entertainment. If you prefer a pubby atmosphere, there's **Dick Turpin's,** at the Royal York, 100 Front St. W. (tel. 368-2511), or the **Good Queen Bess,** in the Sheraton Centre, 123 Queen St. W. (tel. 361-1000). There's dancing to a trio at the **Copper Lounge** at the Inn on the Park, 1100 Eglinton Ave. E. (tel. 444-2561). At the airport, check out the **Banyan Tree** at the Regal Constellation, 900 Dixon Rd. (tel. 675-1500), a comfortable piano bar.

And now for the independents.

ALICE FAZOOLI'S, 294 Adelaide St. W. Tel. 979-1910.

Baseball art and memorabilia, including a full-scale model of an outfielder making a wall catch, fills this large bar and dining room. It's always jam-packed with an older business crowd either quaffing in the bar or feasting in the back on crabs cooked in many different styles, pizza, pasta, and raw-bar specialties.

AMSTERDAM, 133 John St. (between Richmond and Adelaide). Tel. 595-8201.

The city's first brewpub, this is *the* downtown spot where young professionals and the financial crowd make the scene at the end of the day. In winter they jam into the huge warehouse space with its exposed plumbing and in summer they cluster around the tables on the large outdoor terrace. Crowded, with a lot of networking going on. Drinks are $5 and up.

BELLAIR CAFE, 100 Cumberland St. Tel. 964-2222.

The midtown Bellair Café has a sleek suede ambience attracting a fashion-conscious and celebrity crowd. It gets really jammed every night, and on weekends, both inside at the square bar and outside on the terrace. Drinks cost from $5 to $8.

BEMELMAN'S, 83 Bloor St. W. Tel. 960-0306.

With its mirrors, marble, gleaming brass rails, and plants, Bemelman's has a certain Manhattan air about it, and the characters who inhabit it are dramatic and trendy. A long stand-up marble-top bar is the focus for the action; in the back you can get a decent meal, choosing from a large menu offering soups, salads, sandwiches, pastas, and egg dishes as well as fish, chicken, pork, and beef. Weather permitting, there's an outdoor patio open from April to October. The bar is well known for its luscious fresh-fruit daiquiris. This is also a popular place for brunch from 11am to 3pm on Sunday. Open from noon to 3am Monday through Friday, 11am to 3am Saturday, and 11am to midnight Sunday. Drinks cost anywhere from $5 to $8.

THE BRUNSWICK HOUSE, 481 Bloor St. W. Tel. 964-2242.

For a truly unique experience, go to the Brunswick House, a cross between a German beer hall and an English north-country workingmen's club. Waitresses move between the

Formica tables in this cavernous room carrying high trays of frothy suds to a largely student clientele. Impromptu dancing breaks out to the background music that drowns out the sound at least of the two large-screen TVs.

And while everyone's quaffing or playing bar shuffleboard, they're entertained by the famous Rockin' Irene who has been here years belting out three rollicking sets at the piano on Friday and Saturday nights. An inexpensive place to down some beer. Upstairs, there's a good jazz, blues, and rhythm-and-blues spot called Albert's Hall (see "Jazz & Rhythm & Blues," above).

CENTRO, 2472 Yonge St. Tel. 483-2211.

Downstairs at the restaurant, this comfortable, well-patronized bar is a relaxing place to listen to the pianist and get to know the sophisticated mid-30s-and-up crowd. Closed Sunday.

C'EST WHAT?, 67 Front St. E. Tel. 867-9499.

Downstairs in one of the historic warehouse buildings. The rough-hewn walls and cellarlike atmosphere are reminiscent of a Paris *cave*. On one side it's casual and comfortable, attracting a young, politically conscious crowd (board games are available), while on the other, live jazz, rock or folk is featured. There's a $3 to $5 cover charge on the weekends.

THE DUKE OF KENT, 2315 Yonge St. Tel. 485-9507.

On Yonge Street, one block north of Eglinton Avenue, the Duke of Kent offers Cornish pasties and shepherd's pie among the English specialties. Snacks are $5 to $9.

THE DUKE OF WESTMINSTER, First Canadian Place. Tel. 368-1555.

There's a whole series of "veddy British"-type pubs, designed in England and shipped and assembled here, where you can get as many as 16 beers and ales on tap (usually about $4 a half pint, $6 a pint, for imported premium beers). The Duke of Westminster offers a very classy English atmosphere that seems to attract those very English types for a good frothy English pint.

THE DUKE OF YORK, 39 Prince Arthur Ave. Tel. 964-2441.

The Duke of York offers plush surroundings and snacks such as steak-and-kidney pie and bangers and mash in an English country-pub atmosphere. Snacks priced from $4 to $8 available.

THE GEM, 1159 Davenport Rd. Tel. 654-1182.

A small down-to-earth, retro-style spot, the Gem attracts an artist/musician crowd. The music is 1950s and '60s, and the decor nostalgic kitsch—black, red, and vinyl in a tacky-trendy style.

HEMINGWAY'S, 142 Cumberland St. Tel. 968-2828.

A Yorkville watering hole with a definite Australian flavor, Hemingway's features piano or other entertainment daily. A pint of beer is $4.50. The rooftop patio is great in summer.

JACK RUSSELL PUB, 27 Wellesley St. E. Tel. 967-9442.

A comfortable local that attracts a mixed crowd—families, professionals, and students—it's located in an old heritage house. The main pub, complete with dart board, is warmed in winter by a fire and offers a patio in summer. Upstairs on the third floor there's a large tavern with games room. In between there's the Henley room, decked out with rowing regalia. Friendly place to go and chat. It sells 12 types of draft.

MADISON, 14 Madison Ave. Tel. 927-1722.

Madison has to be one of the city's most popular gathering places, with people jamming every floor and terrace of this town house. Everyone seems to know everyone else.

THE MORRISSEY TAVERN, 817 Yonge St. Tel. 923-6191.

Every Torontonian at some time or another has had a jar or two at this down-home, plain tile, chrome, and Formica tavern. A popular hangout for everyone—students, workers, professionals, and anyone interested in drinking a pint or two. A friendly local.

PEPINELLO, 180 Pearl St. (between Duncan and John Sts.). Tel. 599-6699.

Pepinello is currently attracting crowds to the downstairs bar, which features vino bianco and vino rosso, and the upstairs dining area, which offers separate serving counters for pizza, pasta, and risotto.

QUEEN'S HEAD, Gerrard St. E. Tel. 929-0940.

A friendly, free-wheeling bar, the Queen's Head is the kind of place where you can meet the locals, make friends, and join in the ribald discussions at the bar.

THE REAL JERK, 709 Queen St. E. Tel. 463-6906.

The original was out east and small, but it became so popular that it moved to a larger space. The hip crowd digs the moderately priced super-spiced Caribbean food—jerk chicken, curries, shrimp Créole, and Rôtis and patties—and the lively crowd and hot music background. No reservations. Open Monday through Saturday from 11:30am to 1am and Sunday from 2 to 10pm.

ROTTERDAM, 600 King St. W. (at Portland St.). Tel. 868-6882.

This brew pub is a beer-drinker's heaven, serving more than 200 different labels as well as 28 different types on draft. It's not an after-work crowd that gathers here, but by 8pm the tables in the back are filled and the long bar is jammed. In summer the patio is fun, too.

SANTA FE, 129 Peter St. Tel. 345-9345.

The Southwest hits Toronto. Snakes are painted on the walls, iguanas float down from the ceiling, and dogs bay at the moon. In the early evening the bar is jammed with financial downtown types; the crowd gets younger as the night goes on.

SCOTLAND YARD, 56 The Esplanade. Tel. 364-6572.

With its Victorian bric-a-brac and heavy bar with phony beer pumps, Scotland Yard has the flavor of a casual English local where you can stand around the bar or play a game of darts or shuffleboard in between pints. There's a mixed crowd. At night there's a small dance floor and the place has a DJ from Thursday to Sunday and Karaoke every Wednesday from 9pm. Domestic beer is $3.75; cocktails run $4.75. Open Monday to Saturday from noon to 1am and Sunday from noon to 11pm.

SQUEEZE CLUB, 817 Queen St. W. Tel. 365-9020.

This laid-back bar/restaurant and pool hall attracts a mixed crowd ranging from 18 to 50. It's the place to go on Queen for an eclectic mix of bizarre bands—from a ukelele orchestra to yodeling country-and-western or polka bands. A frequently chosen venue for rock-celebrity and other private parties.

WHEATSHEAF TAVERN, 667 King St. W. Tel. 364-3996.
Designated a historic landmark, this is the city's oldest tavern, having been in operation since 1849. Classy it ain't, but for sports mavens, it's home, with five screens showing great moments in sports.

WINE BARS

THE HOP AND GRAPE, 14 College St. Tel. 923-2715.
The Hop and Grape provides, not surprisingly, beer on one level and wine on another, and it's one of the most popular wine bars in the city. On the ground floor the pub offers 58 types of beer with 12 varieties on draft. Upstairs, the wine bar offers a selection of 100 wines, some by the glass and some by the bottle. Imported beers are $4 and up, a 5-oz. glass of wine from $3.50 and up. The wine bar is closed on Sunday.

RACLETTE, 361 Queen St. W. Tel. 593-0934.
Raclette stocks more than 150 wines, including 28 that are available by the glass; the bar also offers raclette (a round of melted cheese). Wines start at $4 a glass. Open Monday to Saturday from noon to 1am and Sunday from noon to 11pm.

VINES, 38 Wellington St. E. Tel. 869-0744.
Vines provides a pleasant atmosphere to sample a glass of champagne or any one of 36 wines, priced between $4 and $10 for a four-ounce glass. Salads, cheeses, and light meals, served with fresh french sticks, are available. Subway: King.

COCKTAILS WITH A VIEW

AQUARIUS 51 LOUNGE, 55 Bloor St. W. Tel. 967-5525.
A comfortable piano bar atop the Manulife Centre. Go for the lit skyline.

GAY BARS

THE ROSE CAFE, 547 Parliament St. Tel. 928-1495.
This is the most popular lesbian bar, with a pool table and games room downstairs, a restaurant and dance area upstairs.

WOODY'S, 467 Church St. (south of Wellesley). Tel. 972-0887.
A friendly and popular local bar, Woody's is frequented mainly by men but welcomes women. It's considered a good meeting place.

4. MORE ENTERTAINMENT

FILM

CINEPLEX, in the Eaton Centre. Tel. 593-4535.
Although it's easy enough to find a movie theater in the *Yellow Pages* or the local daily newspapers, you should know about

Toronto's exceptional film buffs' heaven. Always wary of describing any animal, vegetable, or mineral as the biggest, let me just say that the film complex houses 17 theaters with seating capacities ranging from 57 to 137.

Exterior screens over the Cineplex entrance in the Eaton Centre, display on-going slide presentations and an annunciator board in the lobby lists all movies and starting times. Recent releases are the staples. Subway: Dundas.

There's also a Cineplex Market Square at 80 Front St. E. (tel. 364-2300).

Prices: Tickets $7.

CINEMATHEQUE ONTARIO. 70 Carlton. Tel. 967-7371 or 923-3456 (box office).

This organization shows the best in contemporary cinema. The programs include directors' retrospectives, plus new films from France, Germany, Japan, Bulgaria, and other countries, not available for commercial release. There's a film research library, too.

Prices: Tickets $4 adults, $2.50 youths, $1.25 children; seniors are free.

CHAPTER 10

EXCURSIONS FROM TORONTO

1. **NIAGARA-ON-THE-LAKE**
2. **NIAGARA FALLS**
3. **STRATFORD**

For information about the area surrounding Toronto, contact the **Ontario Ministry of Tourism and Recreation,** 77 Bloor St. W., Toronto, ON, M7A 2R9 (tel. 416/314-0944, or toll free 800/668-2746 in Canada, except the Northwest Territories and Yukon, and in the U.S., except Hawaii and Alaska). The offices are open from Monday through Friday from 8am to 6pm (daily from mid-May to mid-September). Or write to **Ontario Travel,** Queen's Park, Toronto, ON, M7A 2E5.

1. NIAGARA-ON-THE-LAKE

Only 80 miles from Toronto, Niagara-on-the-Lake is one of the best-preserved and prettiest 19th-century villages in North America, with its lakeside location and tree-lined streets bordered by handsome clapboard and brick period houses. Such is the setting for one of Canada's most famous events, the Shaw Festival.

INFORMATION The **Niagara-on-the-Lake Chamber of Commerce,** 153 King St. (P.O. Box 1043), Niagara-on-the-Lake, ON, L0S 1J0 (tel. 416/468-4263), will provide information and help you find accommodations at one of 55 local bed-and-breakfasts. Open daily from 9am to 5pm.

SPECIAL EVENTS Devoted to the works of George Bernard Shaw and his contemporaries, the ✪ **Shaw Festival** plays in three theaters: the historic Court House, the exquisite Festival Theatre, and the Royal George Theatre. Ticket prices for all three theaters range from $10 (for lunchtime performances) to $49.50 on weekends.

The Shaw Festival opens in early May and runs to mid-October, offering nine plays. Some recent performances have included Shaw's *Man and Superman, Pygmalion,* and *The Doctor's Dilemma,* and *Lulu* by Frank Wedekind.

An added attraction is the free lunchtime conversations (on Saturdays in July and August).

For more information, write or phone Shaw Festival, P.O. Box 774, Niagara-on-the-Lake, ON, L0S 1J0 (tel. 416/468-2172). Or from New York, Pennsylvania, Ohio, and Michigan, call toll free 800/724-2934.

WHAT TO SEE & DO

NIAGARA HISTORICAL MUSEUM, 43 Castlereagh St., at Davy. Tel. 416/468-3912.

The Niagara Historical Museum houses over 20,000 artifacts pertaining to local history, including many possessions of United Empire Loyalists who first settled the area at the end of the American Revolution. The museum also offers guided walking tours of the area for $2.50, but they must be booked in advance.

Admission: $2.50 adults, $1 teenagers 12–18.

Open: May–Oct, daily 10am–5pm; Nov–Apr, daily 1–5pm.

FORT GEORGE NATIONAL HISTORIC PARK, Niagara Parkway. Tel. 416/468-3938.

South along the Niagara Parkway at the Fort George National Historic Park, it's easy to imagine taking shelter behind the stockade fence and watching for the enemy from across the river, even though today there are only condominiums on the opposite riverbank. The fort played a key role in the War of 1812, when the Americans invaded and destroyed it in May 1813. Although rebuilt by 1815, it was abandoned in 1828 and not reconstructed until the 1930s. View the guard room with its hard plank beds, the officers' quarters, the enlisted men's quarters, and the sentry posts. The tour includes interpretive films and performances by the Fort George Fife and Drum Corps.

Admission: $2.25 adults, $1 youths 6–18; free for seniors and children under 5; family rate, $5.50.

Open: Mid-May to June, daily 9am–5pm; July–Labor Day, daily 10am–6pm; Labor Day–Oct, daily 10am–5pm; Nov to mid-May, Mon–Fri by appointment only.

A SHOPPING & NOSTALGIA STROLL A stroll along Queen Street will take you to some entertaining shopping stops. At the 1866 **Niagara Apothecary Shop,** 5 Queen St. (tel. 416/468-3845), with its original black-walnut counters and the contents of the drawers marked in gold-leaf script, the original glass and ceramic apothecary ware is on display. **Niagara Fudge,** 29 Queen St. (tel. 416/468-7835), offers 35 varieties that you can watch being made on marble slabs. **Greaves Jam** is run by fourth-generation jam makers. **Loyalist Village,** at no. 12 (tel. 416/468-7331), has distinctively Canadian clothes and crafts, including Inuit art, Native Canadian decoys, and sheepskins. The **Shaw Shop,** next to the Royal George, has GBS memorabilia and more. There's also a Dansk outlet and several galleries selling contemporary Canadian and other ethnic crafts, and a charming toy store, **The Owl and the Pussy Cat,** at 16 Queen St. (tel. 416/468-3081).

NIAGARA-ON-THE-LAKE WINERIES If you take Hwy. 55 (Niagara Stone Road) out of Niagara-on-the-Lake, you'll come to **Hillebrand Estates Winery** (tel. 416/468-7123), just outside Virgil. It's open year round; tours are given daily at 11am and 1, 3, and 4pm.

If you turn off Hwy. 55 before reaching Hillebrand and go down Four Mile Creek Road to Line 7, you'll reach **Château des Charmes,** in St. Davids (tel. 416/262-4219). Tours are given Tuesday through Sunday at 11am and 1:30 and 3pm from May to September; by appointment at other times.

The **Konzelmann Winery,** Lakeshore Road (tel. 416/935-2866), can be reached by driving out Mary Street.

For other wineries in the region, see "Winery Tours" in the Niagara Falls section of this chapter.

WHERE TO STAY

In summer, don't despair if you're having trouble nailing down a room somewhere. Contact the chamber of commerce (see above), which provides an accommodations-reservations service. Best bet are bed-and-breakfast accommodations.

VERY EXPENSIVE

GATE HOUSE HOTEL, 142 Queen St. (P.O. Box 1364), Niagara-on-the-Lake, ON, L0S 1J0. Tel. 416/468-3263. 9 rms. A/C MINIBAR TV TEL

$ Rates: $135–$155 double.

Instead of being done in country Canadian, the rooms here are decorated in cool, up-to-the-minute Milan style. Guest rooms have a turquoise marbleized look accented with ultramodern basic black lamps, block marble tables, leatherette couches, and bathrooms with sleek Italian fitments.

PILLAR & POST INN, 48 John St. (at King St.), Niagara-on-the-Lake, ON, L0S 1J0. Tel. 416/468-2123. 91 rms. A/C MINIBAR TV TEL

$ Rates: $140–$200 double; $150 fireplace room. Extra person $15.

Rustic to every last inch of barn board, the Pillar & Post has 48 rooms with wood-burning fireplaces. Although all are slightly different, each room will certainly contain early Canadian-style furniture, Windsor-style chairs, a color TV tucked into a pine cabinet, and historical engravings, plus modern conveniences. In the back there's a secluded pool (some rooms facing the pool on the ground level have bay windows and window boxes).

Dining/Entertainment: The dining room occupies a former canning factory and basket-manufacturing plant that was converted to a restaurant in 1970. An adjoining craft shop sells country quilts, kitchenware, pine furniture, dolls, toys, and more. The menu features continental cuisine—roasted lamb with kiwi, mint, and garlic sauce, for example. Prices range from $11 to $20. There's also a comfortable lounge.

Facilities: Outdoor pool, sauna, whirlpool.

PRINCE OF WALES HOTEL, 6 Picton St., Niagara-on-the-Lake, ON, L0S 1J0. Tel. 416/468-3246. 105 rms. A/C TV TEL

$ Rates: May–Nov 1, $110–$180 single, $115–$190 double, from $240 suite; Nov–Apr, $100 single, $115 double. Extra person $12.

For a lively atmosphere that retains the elegance and charm of a Victorian inn, the Prince of Wales has it all: full recreational facilities; lounges, bars, and restaurants; and 105 rooms, some with colonial-style furniture and others with brass bedsteads—all beautifully decorated with antiques or reproductions and color-coordinated carpeting, drapes, and spreads. Most rooms have minibars.

The original section of the hotel was built in 1864. In the Prince

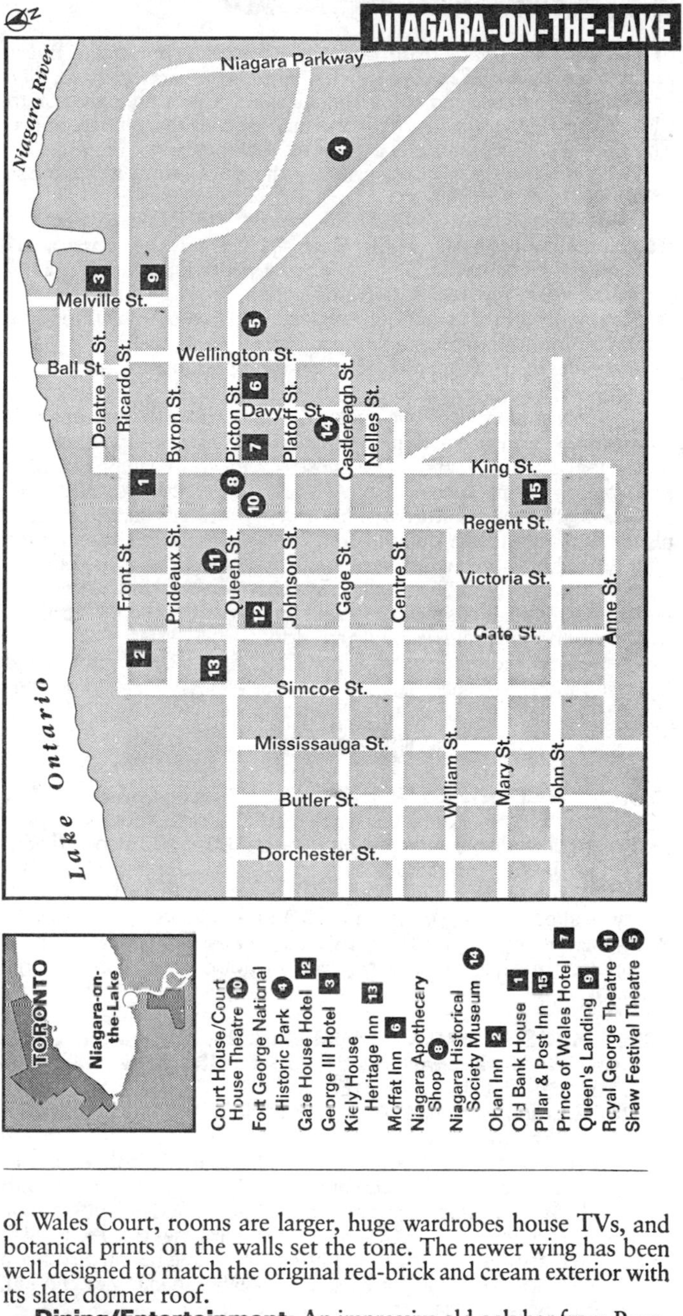
NIAGARA-ON-THE-LAKE
Niagara Parkway
Niagara River
Lake Ontario
Melville St.
Ball St.
Wellington St.
Delatre St.
Ricardo St.
Byron St.
Picton St.
Davy St.
Platoff St.
Castlereagh St.
Nelles St.
King St.
Regent St.
Victoria St.
Gate St.
Simcoe St.
Mississauga St.
Butler St.
Dorchester St.
Front St.
Prideaux St.
Queen St.
Johnson St.
Gage St.
Centre St.
William St.
Mary St.
John St.
Anne St.
TORONTO
Niagara-on-the-Lake
Court House/Court House Theatre 10
Fort George National Historic Park 4
Gate House Hotel 12
George III Hotel 3
Kiely House Heritage Inn 13
Moffat Inn 6
Niagara Apothecary Shop 8
Niagara Historical Society Museum 14
Oban Inn 2
Old Bank House 1
Pillar & Post Inn 15
Prince of Wales Hotel 7
Queen's Landing 9
Royal George Theatre 11
Shaw Festival Theatre 5

of Wales Court, rooms are larger, huge wardrobes house TVs, and botanical prints on the walls set the tone. The newer wing has been well designed to match the original red-brick and cream exterior with its slate dormer roof.

Dining/Entertainment: An impressive old oak bar from Pennsylvania dominates the quiet bar off the lobby. Royals, the elegant main dining room, serves breakfast, lunch, and dinner, offering a dozen dinner entrées, from broiled swordfish with lime-butter sauce to beef tenderloin with cream, cognac, and green peppercorns. Prices range from $18 to $24. At lunch, light dishes are featured, like ham-and-leek quiche and cold poached salmon with dill sauce ($9 to $12). Three Feathers Café is light and airy for breakfast, lunch, or tea. The Queen's Royal lounge is a pleasant drinking spot.

Facilities: Indoor pool, sauna, whirlpool, sun and exercise room, platform tennis court.

QUEEN'S LANDING, P.O. Box 1180, at the corner of Byron and Melville Sts., Niagara-on-the Lake, ON, LOS 1J0. Tel. 416/468-2195. 137 rms.

$ Rates: $155 room without fireplace; $165 room with fireplace; $205 room with fireplace and Jacuzzi.

Overlooking the river but also within walking distance of the theater, the Queen's Landing is a fine establishment where 70 rooms have fireplaces and some 32 have Jacuzzis. Each room is spacious and comfortably furnished with pine furnishings, a half-canopied or brass bed, wingback chairs, and a large desk; each is also equipped with a push-button phone, a color cable TV, and a clock-radio.

Dining/Entertainment: The lounge, with its fieldstone fireplace, is cozy; and the dining room looks out over the yacht-filled dock. At dinner about a dozen or so fish and meat dishes are offered, priced from $17 to $28 for such dishes as roasted pork tenderloin with spicy red-pepper sauce or grilled halibut with lime-butter glaze. Breakfast and lunch are served here, too.

Facilities: Indoor pool, whirlpool and sauna, exercise room and lap pool, bicycle rentals.

EXPENSIVE

THE GEORGE III, 61 Melville St., Niagara-on-the-Lake, ON, LOS 1J0. Tel. 416/468-4207. 8 rms. A/C TV

$ Rates (including continental breakfast): $90–$105 standard double; $115 double with balcony.

Down by the harbor, the George III offers attractive rooms with pretty wallpaper and quilts and flounce pillows on the beds. Amenities include clock-radios, TVs, hairdryers, and coffeemakers. A continental breakfast is delivered to your door. Room 8 has a large balcony.

KIELY HOUSE HERITAGE INN, 209 W. Queen St. (P.O. Box 1642), Niagara-on-the-Lake, ON, LOS 1J0. Tel. 416/468-4588. 13 rms. TEL

$ Rates: High season, $100 standard double; $155 double with fireplace. From $55 in winter.

Ideally situated in a stately summer home built in 1832, all the rooms here have been graciously decorated with fine antiques, some with canopy beds and fireplaces. The sitting and breakfast rooms have carved-walnut fireplaces and comfortable furnishings that make them appealing places for breakfast and afternoon tea. The inn also has a pleasant garden out back. Bicycles are available in summer and fall, cross-country skis in winter.

MOFFAT INN, 60 Picton St., Niagara-on-the-Lake, ON, LOS 1J0. Tel. 416/468-4116. 22 rms. A/C TV TEL

$ Rates: May to mid-Oct and Christmas/New Year's holidays, $85–$110 double; mid-Oct to late Apr, $65–$105 double.

Niagara-on-the-Lake has another fine accommodation at the Moffat. There are 22 comfortable rooms available (7 with fireplaces). Most are furnished with brass or cannonball beds and wicker and bamboo pieces and feature built-in closets, TVs, and hairdryers. A nice touch is the tea kettle and appropriate supplies in every room. Free coffee is available in the lobby.

OBAN INN, 160 Front St. (at Gate St.), Niagara-on-the-Lake, ON, L0S 1J0. Tel. 416/468-2165. 23 rms. A/C TV TEL

$ Rates: $85 single; $105 standard double, $150 double with lake view. Winter midweek and weekend packages available.

With a prime location overlooking the lake, the Oban Inn is probably *the* place to stay. It's located in a charming white Victorian house with a green dormer-style roof and windows, plus a large veranda. The gardens are a joy to behold and a source of the bouquets on each table in the dining room and throughout the house.

Each of the comfortable rooms is unique. Some have a chintz decor, but all have TVs, antique chests, and early Canadian-style headboards. Each is likely to have a candlewick spread on the bed, a small sofa, dressing table, and old prints or engravings on the walls—it's all very homey and comfortably old-fashioned. One or two rooms have baths only, so if you want a shower, be sure to request it.

Dining/Entertainment: Bar snacks and light lunches and dinners are available downstairs in the pubby piano bar, with its leather Windsor-style chairs and hunting prints over the blazing fireplace. The dining room has three different areas—each serving a menu priced from $18 to $21. A similar luncheon is available for $7 to $9. Meals are served only in sittings.

THE OLD BANK HOUSE, 10 Front St. (P.O. Box 1708), Niagara-on-the-Lake, ON, L0S 1J0. Tel. 416/468-7136. 4 rms (none with bath), 4 suites (all with bath). A/C

$ Rates: $90 double without bath, $100–$115 double with bath; $125 one-bedroom suite; $200 Rose Suite.

The Georgian Old Bank House, beautifully situated by the river, was built in 1817 as the first branch of the Bank of Canada. The inn is operated by Marjorie Ironmonger and her husband. It has four rooms, each with a washbasin and sharing a full bathroom plus an extra toilet. In addition, there are three suites with private baths and separate entrances and a two-bedroom suite with a sitting room and bathroom. All rooms are tastefully decorated and have air conditioning; all but one have a refrigerator and coffee or tea supplies. The sitting room, with a fireplace, is very comfortable and furnished with Sheraton and Hepplewhite pieces. The Garden Room is very appealing, with a private entrance and a trellised deck.

A SPORTS ENTHUSIAST'S PARADISE

WHITE OAKS INN AND RACQUET CLUB, Taylor Rd., Niagara-on-the-Lake, ON, L0S 1J0. Tel. 416/688-2550. 90 rms, 17 suites. A/C TV TEL

$ Rates: $100–$125 single or double; $160 Executive suite.
Not far from Niagara-on-the-Lake, the White Oaks is a fantastic facility for the fitness freak. Anyone can come here, spend the whole weekend, and not stir outside the resort. Take a break and enjoy the lounge area, the outdoor terrace café, a formal restaurant, and a pleasantly furnished café/coffee shop, or schedule a massage.

The rooms are as good as the facilities, each featuring oak furniture, gray-blue or blue-rose decor, vanity sinks, and additional niceties like a phone in the bathroom and complimentary shampoo, cologne, and toothbrush. The Executive Suites also have brick fireplaces, marble-top desks, Jacuzzis (some heart-shaped), and bidets. Deluxe suites also have sitting rooms and the ultimate in furnishings.

Facilities: Four outdoor tennis courts, eight air-conditioned indoor tennis courts, six squash courts, three racquetball courts, Nautilus room, jogging trails, sauna, suntan beds, day-care center with fully qualified staff.

WHERE TO DINE

MODERATE

THE BUTTERY, 19 Queen St. Tel. 416/468-2564.
Cuisine: CANADIAN/ENGLISH/CONTINENTAL. **Reservations:** Recommended (required for Henry VIII feast).
$ Prices: Henry VIII dinner $35; tavern menu main courses $6–$14; dinner main courses $14.50–$20. DC, MC, V.
Open: Summer, daily 11am–12:30am; other months, daily noon–8pm. Henry VIII feast, Fri at 9pm and Sat at 9:30pm; tea, daily 2–5pm.

The Buttery has been a main-street dining landmark for years, known for its weekend Henry VIII feasts, when "serving wenches" will "cosset" you with food and wine while jongleurs and musickers entertain you. You'll get broth, chicken, roast lamb, roast pig, sherry trifle, syllabub, and cheese to be washed down with a goodly amount of wine, ale, and mead.

A full tavern menu is served from 11am to 5:30pm, featuring spareribs, filet mignon, shrimp in garlic sauce, and English specialties. The dinner menu lists breast of chicken with champagne sauce or lobster Newburg (with cream and brandy). Highly recommended is the leg of lamb served with a real garden-mint sauce. Finish with key lime pie or mud pie. Take home some of the fresh baked goods—pies, strudels, dumplings, cream puffs, or scones. An after-theater menu is served from 10pm to 12:30am.

FANS, 135 Queen St. Tel. 416/468-4511.
Cuisine: CHINESE.
$ Prices: Main courses $8–$18 at dinner, $5–$8 at lunch. AE, MC, V.
Open: Daily noon–10pm. **Closed:** Mon in off-season.

Some of the best food in town can be found in this comfortable Chinese spot, decorated with fans, cushioned bamboo chairs, and round tables spread with golden tablecloths. In summer, the courtyard also has tables for outdoor dining. The cuisine ranges from Cantonese to Szechuan. Singapore beef, moo shu pork, Szechuan scallops, and lemon chicken are just a few of the dishes available. If you wish, you can order Peking duck 24 hours in advance.

THE OLD BAKERY RESTAURANT, 59 Queen St. Tel. 416/468-7217.
Cuisine: CONTINENTAL.
$ Prices: Main courses $9–$16. MC, V.
Open: Summer, daily 10am–8pm; fall, daily 11am–3pm. **Closed:** Jan–Apr 1.

The Old Bakery Restaurant features veal parmigiana, duck à l'orange, filet mignon, and filet of sole. Breakfast and lunch are served, too. The decor is plain and homey.

RISTORANTE GIARDINO, 142 Queen St. Tel. 416/468-3263.
Cuisine: ITALIAN.
$ Prices: Main courses $7–$8 at lunch, $19–$25 at dinner. AE, MC, V.
Open: Summer, lunch daily noon–2pm; dinner daily 5:30–9pm. Winter, dinner only, daily 5:30–9pm.

On the ground floor of the Gate House Hotel is this sleek, ultramodern Italian restaurant with gleaming marble-top bar and glass and brass accents throughout. The food is classic northern Italian, with a dozen or so main courses—steamed salmon with aromatic olive oil, veal tenderloin in herbed bread with balsamic vinegar sauce, and guinea fowl with juniper berries and white wine sauce. Desserts include tiramisu—lady fingers soaked in marsala and espresso, buried in sweet cream cheese, and topped with cocoa—or a terrine of white and dark chocolate with espresso sauce.

BUDGET

THE GEORGE III, 61 Melville St. Tel. 416/468-4207.
Cuisine: CANADIAN.
$ Prices: Main courses $8–$13. MC, V.
Open: Daily 11:30am–10pm. **Closed:** Mid-Nov to Apr 15.

Down by the harbor, the George III is a good budget dining choice for chicken wings, burgers, sandwiches, and stir-fries. There's a publike atmosphere and a pleasant outdoor patio.

SPECIALTY DINING

The **Niagara Home Bakery,** 66 Queen St. (tel. 416/468-3431), is the place to stop for chocolate-date squares, cherry squares, croissants, cookies, and individual quiches.

For breakfast, go to the **Stagecoach Family Restaurant,** 45 Queen St. (tel. 416/468-3133), for a down-home budget-priced meal. No credit cards are accepted.

2. NIAGARA FALLS

Niagara Falls, with its gimmicks, amusement parks, wax museums, daredevil feats, and a million motels (each with a honeymoon suite complete with heart-shaped bed), may seem rather tacky and commercial, but somehow the falls still steal the show; on the Canadian side, with its parks and gardens, nature manages to survive with grace.

Note: The area code is expected to change to 905 sometime in 1993.

ORIENTATION Park at Rapid View, several kilometers from the falls, or in Preferred Parking (overlooking the falls—it costs more), and take the **People Mover** (tel. 357-9340), an attraction in itself, making nine stops from Rapid View to the Spanish Aero Car. Shuttles to the falls also operate from downtown and Lundy's Lane; an all-day pass costs $3 for adults and $1.50 for children 12 and under in-season only.

INFORMATION Contact the **Niagara Falls Canada Visitor and Convention Bureau,** 4673 Ontario Ave., Suite 202, Niagara Falls, ON, L2E 3R1 (tel. 416/356-6061), or the **Niagara Parks Commission,** Box 150, 7400 Portage Rd. S. Niagara Falls, ON, L2E 6T2 (tel. 416/356-2241).

Summer information centers are open at Table Rock House, the *Maid of the Mist,* and Rapids View.

WHAT TO SEE & DO

VIEWING THE FALLS Aboard the ✪ ***Maid of the Mist,*** 5920 River Rd. (tel. 416/358-5781), you'll make your way through the turbulent waters around the American Falls; past the Rock of Ages; and to the foot of the Horseshoe Falls, where 34.5 million gallons fall per minute over the 176-foot-high cataract. Your sunglasses will mist, but that won't detract from the thrill of the experience. Fares are $8.30 for adults and $4.70 for children 6 to 12; children 5 and under are free.

Boats leave from the dock on the parkway just down from the Rainbow Bridge. Trips operate daily from mid-May through October 24.

Take the elevator at Table Rock House, which drops you 125 feet through solid rock to the **Table Rock Scenic Tunnels** (tel. 416/354-1551) and viewing portals. Open all year. Admission is $5 for adults and $2.50 for children 6 to 12; children under 6 are free.

Take an eight-minute spin in a chopper over the whole Niagara area. Helicopters leave from the Heliport, adjacent to the Whirlpool at the junction of Victoria Avenue and Niagara Parkway, daily from 9am to dusk, weather permitting, except in January. Contact **Niagara Helicopters,** 3731 Victoria Ave. (tel. 416/357-5672).

Or ride up in the external glass-fronted elevators 520 feet to the top of the **Skylon Tower Observation Deck** at 5200 Robinson St. (tel. 416/356-2651). The observation deck is open daily from 10am to 9pm (from 8am to 1am June through Labor Day). There's also a basement amusement park. Adults pay $6; seniors, $5; and children 12 and under, $3.50.

There's another fabulous view from the 325-foot **Minolta Tower Centre and Marine Aquarium,** 6732 Oakes Dr. (tel. 416/356-1501). On-site attractions include the *Waltzing Waters* (a computerized music, light, and water show, shown nightly from May to October for free) and the Aquarium/Reptile World. The tower is open daily year round from 9am to 11pm (closed December 24 and 25). The Aquarium is open April to November daily from 9am to

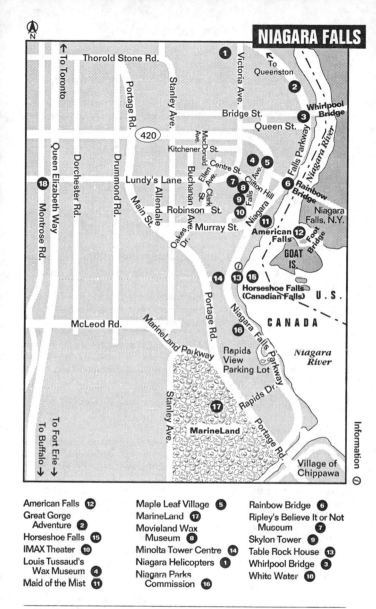

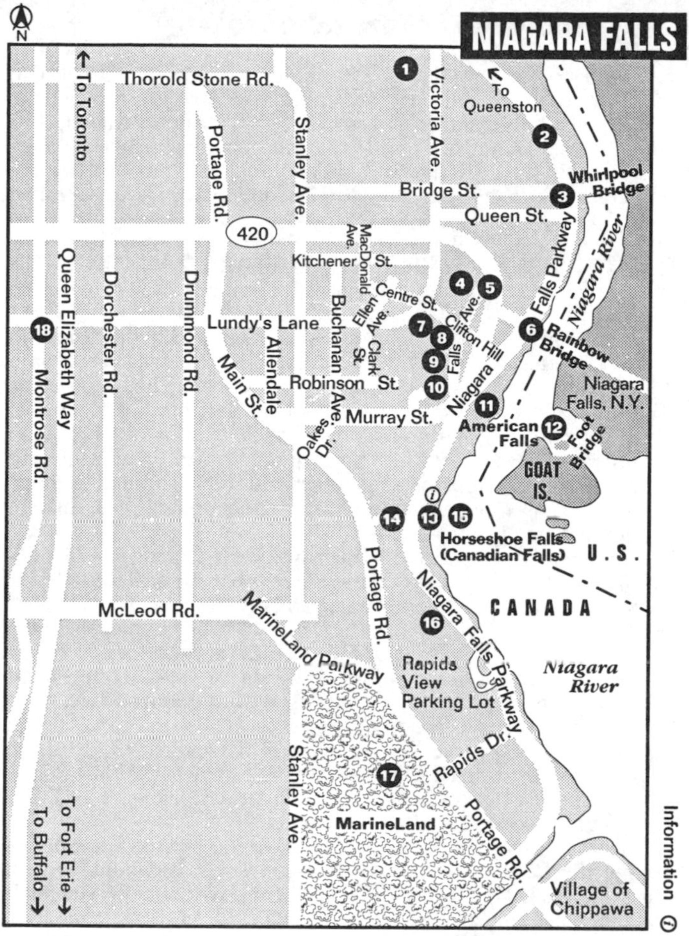
NIAGARA FALLS
N
Thorold Stone Rd.
To Toronto
Portage Rd.
Stanley Ave.
Victoria Ave.
To Queenston
Whirlpool Bridge
Bridge St.
Queen St.
420
MacDonald Ave.
Kitchener St.
Falls Parkway
Niagara River
Queen Elizabeth Way
Dorchester Rd.
Drummond Rd.
Buchanan Ave.
Centre St.
Ellen Ave.
Falls Ave.
Lundy's Lane
Clifton Hill
Rainbow Bridge
Allendale
Clark St.
Niagara
Montrose Rd.
Main St.
Robinson St.
Niagara Falls, N.Y.
Murray St.
American Falls
Oakes Dr.
Foot Bridge
GOAT IS.
Horseshoe Falls (Canadian Falls)
U.S.
CANADA
Portage Rd.
Niagara Falls Parkway
McLeod Rd.
MarineLand Parkway
Rapids View Parking Lot
Niagara River
Rapids Dr.
Stanley Ave.
MarineLand
Portage Rd.
To Fort Erie
To Buffalo
Village of Chippawa
Information

- American Falls 12
- Great Gorge Adventure 2
- Horseshoe Falls 15
- IMAX Theater 10
- Louis Tussaud's Wax Museum 4
- Maid of the Mist 11
- Maple Leaf Village 5
- MarineLand 17
- Movieland Wax Museum 8
- Minolta Tower Centre 14
- Niagara Helicopters 1
- Niagara Parks Commission 16
- Rainbow Bridge 6
- Ripley's Believe It or Not Museum 7
- Skylon Tower 9
- Table Rock House 13
- Whirlpool Bridge 3
- White Water 18

9pm. Admission to the tower is $5.50 for adults and $3.95 for students and seniors.

For a thrilling introduction to Niagara Falls, stop by the IMAX Theater and view the raging swirling waters in ***Niagara: Miracles, Myths, and Magic,*** shown on a six-story-high screen. It's at 6170 Buchanan Ave. (tel. 416/374-IMAX).

The Falls By Night Don't miss seeing the falls lit by 22 Xenon gas spotlights (each producing 250 million candlepower of light), in shades of rose pink, red magenta, amber, blue, and green. Schedules are as follows: November to February, 7 to 9:30pm; March, 7 to 10pm; April, 7:30 to 10:30pm; May, 9pm to midnight; June, 9:15pm to midnight; July, 9:15pm to 12:30am; August, 9pm to 12:30am; September 1 to Labor Day, 8pm to 12:30am; Labor Day to October, 8 to 11pm.

✪ **ATTRACTIONS ALONG THE NIAGARA PARKWAY** The Niagara Parkway provides a delightful 35-mile stretch of parkland and gardens.

Half a mile north of Niagara Falls, you'll reach the **Spanish Aero Car** (tel. 356-2241), a cable car that will whisk you on a 3,600-foot jaunt between two points in Canada, high above the whirlpool, providing excellent views of the surrounding landscape. Open daily from May through the third Sunday in October: from 9am to 6pm in May, 9am to 8pm in June, 9am to 9pm in July and August, 10am to 7:30pm in September, and 9am to 5pm in October. Admission is $4.25 for adults and $2.15 for children 6 to 12; children under 6 are free.

From here you'll pass the **Whirlpool Golf Club** (tel. 416/356-1140), an outstanding public course. Greens fees are $29 for 18 holes; from October 1 to the second Sunday in November, it costs $18 for 9 or 18 holes.

Next stop is the **School of Horticulture.** Stop for a free view of the vast gardens there before going on to look at the **Floral Clock,** containing 25,000 plants in its 40-foot-diameter face.

From here you can drive to **Queenston Heights Park,** site of a major battle during the War of 1812. On October 13, 1812, an American force invaded Canada here. Although the British forces won the Battle of Queenston Heights, General Brock was killed. You can take a walking tour of the battlefield.

Picnic or play tennis (for $5 an hour) in this shaded arbor before visiting the **Laura Secord Homestead,** on Partition Street in Queenston (tel. 416/262-4851), home of this redoubtable woman. It contains a fine collection of Upper Canadian furniture from the 1812 period as well as artifacts recovered from an archeological dig. It's open from Victoria Day weekend (late May) to Labor Day, daily 10am to 6pm. Tours are given every half hour, and admission is $1.

Next stop is the Georgian-style **McFarland House** (tel. 416/468-3322 or 356-2241), built in 1800 and home to John McFarland, "His Majesty's [George III] Boat Builder." It's open daily: Victoria Day to June 30, from 1 to 4pm; in July and August until Labor Day, from 11am to 5pm. Admission is $1.10 for adults and 60¢ for children. The last tour is at 4:30pm.

From here the parkway continues toward Niagara-on-the-Lake, lined with fruit farms and wineries, notably the **Inniskillin Winery,** Line 3, Service Road 56 (tel. 416/468-3554 or 468-2187), **Reif Winery** (tel. 416/468-7738), and **Kurtz Orchards** (tel. 416/468-2937). The first is open Monday through Saturday from 10am to 6pm from May to October and 10am to 5pm November to April. Tours are given daily at 10:30am and 2:30pm from May to October (Saturday only in May and October). At Reif Winery, tours are given on Saturday only.

A trip south along the parkway will take you by the Table Rock complex to the **Park Greenhouse,** a year-round free attraction (open daily from 9:30am to 7pm during July and August, until 4:15pm in other months).

Farther along, visit the **Dufferin Islands,** where the children can swim, rent a paddle boat, and explore the surrounding woodland areas, while you play a round of golf on the illuminated nine-hole par-three course. Open from the second Sunday in April to the last Sunday in October.

A little farther on, stop for a picnic in **King's Bridge Park** and stroll along the beaches before driving on to **Fort Erie** (tel. 416/871-0540), a reconstruction of the fort that was seized by the Americans in July 1814, besieged later by the British, and finally blown up as the Americans retreated across the river to Buffalo. Guards in period costume stand sentry duty, fire the cannons, and demonstrate drill and musket practice. Open from the first Saturday in May to Canadian Thanksgiving (U.S. Columbus Day) from 10am to 5:30pm daily. Admission is $3.50 for adults, $3.25 for seniors, and $1.75 for children 12 and under; kids under 6 are free.

THREE TOP ATTRACTIONS Opened in 1979, **Maple Leaf Village** (tel. 416/374-0735) is a large, $18 million shopping, dining, and entertainment complex modeled after San Francisco's Ghirardelli Square.

Behind the complex is the prime attraction, a theme park featuring a 175-foot-high Ferris wheel, bumper cars, and 25 other exciting rides. A laser light show, a children's theater, and the Elvis Presley Museum complete the entertainment found here. Admission to the village is free. Ride coupons cost 50¢ each; discount books are available and an all-day pass is $10 for adults and $8 for children under 12. The amusement park is open from late May to the end of September.

Everyone loves **White Water,** 7430 Lundy's Lane (tel. 416/357-3380), for its five water slides, wave pool, and hot tub. Take a picnic and spend the day (there's also a snack bar). Open spring through fall, daily from 10am to dusk. Admission is $14 per day ($11 for children aged 3 to 7), which entitles you to come back at night (or anytime) when the lights go on. The kids can also ride three small slides designed specially for them.

At **MarineLand,** 7657 Portage Rd. (tel. 416/356-8250), King Waldorf, MarineLand's sea lion mascot, presides over the performances of killer whales, dolphins, and sea lions. The indoor aquarium features a display of freshwater fish and a marine multi-species show with harbor seals as the main attraction. Visit the animal display areas where you can pet and feed the deer and see buffalo, elk, rhea, and more. There are three restaurants or you can spread your picnic lunch on one of the many tables provided.

MarineLand also has theme-park rides: The big thriller is Dragon Mountain, a roller coaster that loops, double-loops, and spirals its way through 1,000 feet of tunnels.

Open daily year round, but attractions vary according to the season. July and August hours are 9am to 6pm; other months, 10am to 4pm. The park closes at dusk. Admission in summer is $20 for adults and $17 for children 9 and under and seniors; children under 4 enter free. Check ahead for prices in other seasons. For taped information, call 416/356-9565. To get there, drive south on Stanley Street and follow the signs or from QEW take the McLeod Road exit and follow the signs.

MORE ATTRACTIONS The **Niagara Falls Museum,** 5651 River Rd. (tel. 416/356-2151), displays everything from Egyptian mummies to shells, fossils, and minerals, and the "Freaks of Nature" display. Open daily in summer from 8:30am to 11pm; in winter hours are irregular, usually weekends only, from 10am to 5pm. Admission is $5.75 for adults, $3.75 for students 12 to 18, $5 for seniors, and $2.75 for children under 12; children under 6 are free.

There's a whole slew of sideshows on **Clifton Hill**—Ripley's Believe it or Not, Castle Dracula, the Houdini Museum, Movieland Wax Museum, and Louis Tussaud's Wax Museum—all of them charging about $5 for adults and $2.50 for children. Perhaps the most entertaining for children is **Circus World,** 4848 Clifton Hill (tel. 416/356-5588), where they can walk a tightrope, have their picture taken on a tiger, and be shot out of the Whizzo Cannon (really a slide with sound and light effects). Open from 9am to 1am daily. Admission is $3 for adults and $1.50 for students and children; kids under 5 are free.

WINERY TOURS There are a number of wineries in the region: Barnes, Château Gai, Inniskillin House, Andres, and Brights. At **Brights,** 4887 Dorchester Rd. (tel. 416/357-2400), the largest winery in Canada, you can see champagne processed European style. And then comes the fun part—the wine tasting.

The best time to visit is during harvest season, from the first week in September to the end of October. At Brights, free tours are offered May through October, Monday through Saturday at 10:30am and 2 and 3:30pm, Sunday at 2 and 3:30pm; in other months, at 2pm Monday through Friday and at 2 and 3:30pm on Saturday and Sunday. Contact Brights Winery Tours, P.O. Box 510, Niagara Falls, ON, L2E 6V4 (tel. 416/357-2400).

For other winery tours and tastings, contact **Andres Wines,** Kelson Road (P.O. Box 550), Winona, ON, L0R 2L0 (tel. 416/643-TOUR).

WHERE TO STAY

In Niagara Falls it seems as though every other sign advertises a motel. In summer rates fluctuate according to what the market will bear—some prorietors won't even quote rates ahead of time. You can secure a reasonably priced room if you're lucky enough to arrive on a "down night." For example, at a very fine hotel, I was offered a room for $55 when the official rates were $89 and up. So push a little. Keep requesting a lower rate. Don't take no for an answer.

VERY EXPENSIVE

RAMADA RENAISSANCE FALLSVIEW, 6455 Buchanan Ave., Niagara Falls, ON, L2G 3V9. Tel. 416/357-5200.
187 rms. A/C MINIBAR TV TEL

$ Rates: $145–$210 single or double; $190–$230 whirlpool rooms.

The Ramada Renaissance features tastefully furnished rooms with oak furniture and TVs tucked away in cabinets. Bathrooms have double sinks and all the modern accoutrements.

Dining/Entertainment: There are a coffee shop and a cocktail lounge on the 19th floor.

Facilities: Indoor pool; whirlpool; health club featuring saunas, squash and racquetball courts, and fitness and weight room.

SKYLINE BROCK, 5685 Falls Ave., Niagara Falls, ON, L2E 6W7. Tel. 416/374-4444, or toll free 800/648-7200. 232 rms. A/C TV TEL

$ Rates: Mid-June to Sept, $109–$180 double; Oct–Dec and Apr to mid-June, $89–$140 double; winter, $70–$109 double. Children under 18 stay free in parents' room. Extra person $10. Special packages available.

For an unblemished view of the falls, try the Skyline Brock or the Skyline Foxhead. The Brock has been hosting honeymooners and falls visitors since 1929. It still has a certain air of splendor, with a huge chandelier and marble walls in the lobby. About 150 of the rooms face the falls. City-view rooms are slightly smaller and less expensive. There are minibars in rooms on the 11th floor and up.

Dining/Entertainment: The 10th-floor Rainbow Room, with a lovely view, serves a popular menu that includes half a roast chicken with cranberry sauce, salmon hollandaise, and prime rib, priced from $14 to $22. Isaac's Bar is available for drinks.

SKYLINE FOXHEAD, 5875 Falls Ave., Niagara Falls, ON, L2E 6W7. Tel. 416/357-3090, or toll free 800/648-7200. 395 rms. A/C MINIBAR TV TEL

$ Rates: Mid-June to Sept, $135–$200 double; Oct–Dec and Apr to mid-June, $115–$165 double; winter, $80–$110 double. Extra person $10. Children under 18 stay free in parents' room. Special packages available.

Built over 20 years ago, the Foxhead has 395 rooms (about half with balconies) spread over 14 floors, and it has recently undergone an extensive renovation. Each room has a private bath or shower, a color TV with in-room movies, and climate control.

Dining/Entertainment: The 14th-floor penthouse Dining Room takes fair advantage of the view with its large glass windows and serves a daily buffet for breakfast, lunch, and dinner, with nightly dancing to a live band (in season). Or there's the Steak and Burger for reasonably priced fare.

Facilities: Outdoor rooftop pool.

EXPENSIVE

THE CANUCK, 5334 Kitchener St., Niagara Falls, ON, L2G 1B5. Tel. 416/374-7666. 101 rms. A/C TV TEL

$ Rates: In season, $69 double; $79 efficiency. Off-season discounts up to 40%. Rates about $10 higher on weekends. Special packages available. **Closed:** Nov–Apr.

The Canuck has reasonably priced rooms (at least for Niagara Falls), which are pleasantly furnished and decently kept. All units have color TVs, air conditioning, phones, and contemporary furnishings. Honeymoon suites are available, and so are efficiencies with hotplates, sinks, and refrigerators. Facilities include a pleasantly landscaped pool, a restaurant that serves breakfast and dinner, laundry equipment, and a babysitting service.

CLARION OLD STONE INN, 5425 Robinson St., Niagara Falls, ON, L2G 7L6. Tel. 416/357-1234, or toll free 800/263-8967. 114 rms. A/C TV TEL

$ Rates: Mid-June to Labor Day, $95–$115 single or double; Apr to mid-June and Sept–Dec, $75–$85 single or double; winter, $55–$65 single or double. Special packages available.

The only accommodation of character at the falls, the Clarion Old Stone Inn is located across from the Skylon Tower and Pyramid Place. Built 15 years ago, it was designed to create the atmosphere of a country inn by using natural rough-hewn stone, heavy crossbeam supports, and barn-style paneling. The spacious rooms contain the usual conveniences. Three rooms have fireplaces and Jacuzzis; 36 ground-floor rooms face the outdoor heated pool. The comfortable lounge leads right out to the pool, while the dining room, with its huge fireplace, brass chandelier, and bookcases, provides a cozy atmosphere for enjoying suprême of chicken amaretto, braised rabbit in wine-and-mushroom sauce, crab Caribbean, or steaks—all priced from $14 to $20.

HOLIDAY INN BY THE FALLS, 5339 Murray St. (at Buchanan), Niagara Falls, ON, L2G 2J3. Tel. 416/356-1333. 122 rms. A/C TV TEL

$ Rates: Mid-June to Labor Day, $100–$150 single or double; Memorial Day to mid-June and Labor Day to mid-Oct. $75–$105 single or double; Apr to Memorial Day, $60–$95 single or double; winter, $55–$85 single or double. Extra person $6–$9; rollaway bed $10; crib $5.

The Holiday Inn by the Falls has a prime location right behind the Skylon Tower, only minutes from the falls. It's not part of the international hotel chain (the owner had the name first and still refuses to sell it). Each room is large, with ample closet space, an additional vanity sink, color-coordinated modern furnishings, a telephone, and a color TV. Most of the rooms have balconies. Dining facilities, a gift shop, and an indoor and an outdoor heated pool and patio are available.

THE VILLAGE INN, 5685 Falls Ave., Niagara Falls, ON, L2E 6W7. Tel. 416/374-4444, or toll free 800/648-7200. 205 rms. A/C TV TEL

$ Rates: Mid-June to Sept, $115 double; Oct–Dec and Apr to mid-June, $90 double. Special packages available. **Closed:** Jan–Mar.

Behind the two Skylines, the Village Inn is ideal for families—all its rooms are large. Some family suites have 700 square feet, which includes a bedroom with two double beds and a living room. There are an outdoor heated swimming pool and a restaurant.

MODERATE

THE AMERICANA, 8444 Lundy's Lane, Niagara Falls, ON, L2H 1H4. Tel. 416/356-8444. 120 rms. A/C TV TEL

$ Rates: Late June to late Aug, $70–$110 single or double; Sept–June, $40–$80 single or double. Extra person $5.

The Americana is one of the nicer moderately priced motels on this strip, set in 25 acres of grounds with a pleasant shady picnic area, two tennis courts, indoor and outdoor swimming pools, and a squash court. The large rooms are fully equipped with telephones, color TVs, vanity sinks, and full bathrooms. A dining room, lounge, and coffee shop are on the premises.

MICHAEL'S INN, 5599 River Rd., Niagara Falls, ON, L2E 3H3. Tel. 416/354-2727. 130 rms. A/C TV TEL

$ Rates: June 16–Sept 15, $70–$165 double; $200–$450 bridal suite. Mar 16–June 15 and Sept 16–Oct $50–$150 double; $200–$300 bridal suite. Nov–Mar 15, $45–$100 double; $100–$200 bridal suite. Rollaway bed $10; crib $5.

At this four-story white building overlooking the Niagara River gorge, the large rooms are nicely decorated, with modern conveniences. Many have heart-shaped tubs and Jacuzzis. There's a solarium pool out back. The Embers Open Hearth Dining Room is just that: The charcoal pit is enclosed behind glass so you can see all the cooking action. There's a lounge, too.

RED CARPET INN, 4943 Clifton Hill, Niagara Falls, ON, L2G 3N5. Tel. 416/357-4330. 77 rms, 6 suites. A/C TV TEL

$ Rates: Mid-May to June, $68.50 single or double; July–Sept, $86.50 single or double; Oct–Dec, $68.50 single or double; Jan to mid-May, $66.50 single or double.

Just up Clifton Hill, around the corner from the Foxhead, window boxes with geraniums draw the eye to the Red Carpet Inn. Two floors of rooms are set around a courtyard with an outdoor heated pool; the honeymoon suites have canopied beds and extra-plush decor, while the other rooms have colonial-style furniture and pink walls, clock-radios, full bathrooms, and color TVs. Rooms 54 through 58 have a direct view of the falls; 12 rooms have private balconies. Convenient facilities include a washer-dryer, a gift shop, two restaurants, and a beer garden.

BUDGET

ARKONA MOTEL, 8450 Lundy's Lane, Niagara Falls, ON, L2H 1H4. Tel. 416/356-8450. 61 rms. A/C TV TEL

$ Rates: July–Aug, $73 double; $105 family room. Winter, $35 double. Rates increase on weekends and holidays.

Rooms are located in a two-story building, arranged around a prettily kept courtyard with a pool and play area. Rooms have wall-to-wall carpeting, color-coordinated drapes and spreads, white brick walls, and plywood paneling.

FIDDLER'S GREEN, 7720 Lundy's Lane, Niagara Falls, ON, L2H 1H1. Tel. 416/358-9833. 94 rms. A/C TV

$ Rates: Late June to Labor Day, $59.50 double; $64.50–$88.50 twin; $76.50–$109 efficiency. Off-season, $29.50 double; $34.50–$56.50 twin; $42.50–$62.50 efficiency.

In this town, most rates go up and down from one week to the next. One motel that doesn't indulge in this seesaw game is Fiddler's Green—but this isn't its only recommendation. The units are all neat and clean, with color TVs, and are pleasantly decorated by owner Orest Samitz. Each efficiency contains two bedrooms plus a full-size kitchen with a refrigerator, a stove, and cooking/dining utensils. There are also two whirlpool suites. Facililties include an indoor and an attractively landscaped outdoor pool.

Fiddler's Green also offers a number of dining and sightseeing discounts, along with special savings during the off-season.

NELSON MOTEL, 10655 Niagara River Pkwy., Niagara Falls, ON, L2E 6S6. Tel. 416/295-4754. 25 rms. A/C TV
$ **Rates:** June 16–Sept 12, $55–$90 single or double; Sept 13 to mid-Nov and mid-Mar to June 15, $35–$55 single or double. Rollaways and cribs extra. **Closed:** Mid-Nov to mid-Mar.

For budget accommodations—correction: accommodations period—you can't beat the home-away-from-home feel of the Nelson, run by John and Dawn Pavlakovich, who live in the large house adjacent to the motel units. It's located a short drive from the falls, overlooking the Niagara River, away from the hustle and bustle of Niagara itself.

The units are kept spic and span, and the outdoor pool sparkles. All the units have character, especially the family units, each with a double bedroom adjoined by a twin-bedded room for the kids. These two-room units go for $90 to $110 in season. Regular units have modern furniture, some with color and some with black-and-white TVs. Singles have showers only, and all units face the neatly trimmed lawn with umbrellaed tables and shrubs.

SURFSIDE INN, 3665 Macklem St., Niagara Falls, ON, L2G 6C8. Tel. 416/295-4354. 32 rms, 8 suites. A/C TV TEL
$ **Rates:** Summer, $75.50–$120 single or double; $150 deluxe Jacuzzi suite. Off-season, $50–$70 single or double; $125 suite. **Closed:** Nov–Apr.

Another budget choice is the Surfside Inn, where the units have been redecorated in French provincial, Italian provincial, and Chinese black-lacquered style. The pastel-patterned bedspreads are color coordinated with the rugs and curtains; baths are fully tiled. A few secluded rooms in back are furnished with waterbeds and Jacuzzis with marble surround. All rooms have coffeemakers and hairdryers.

There's a public beach across the street in King's Bridge Park. To get there, follow the Niagara Parkway south.

Camping

There's a **Niagara Falls KOA** at 8625 Lundy's Lane, Niagara Falls, ON, L2H 1H5 (tel. 416/354-6472), with 340 sites (some with electricity, water, and sewage), plus three dumping stations. Facilities include water, flush toilets, showers, fireplaces, a store, ice, three pools (one indoor), a sauna, and a games room. There's a $21 minimum fee for two; each additional adult pays $5, and each additional child, $2.50; $5 for full hookup (electric, water, sewer). Open April 1 to November 1.

WHERE TO DINE

EXPENSIVE

CASA D'ORO, 5875 Victoria Ave. Tel. 416/356-5646.
Cuisine: ITALIAN. **Reservations:** Recommended.
$ **Prices:** Main courses under $9 at lunch, $12–$20 at dinner. AE, DC, MC, V.
Open: Mon–Thurs noon–midnight, Sat 4pm–1am, Sun noon–10pm.

Try Casa d'Oro for Italian dining in opulent surroundings, with gilt busts of Caesar, Venetian-style lamps, and other classical-style bric-a-brac. Specialties include saltimbocca alla romana, pollo cacciatore, or sole basilica (flavored with lime juice, paprika, and basil). If your favorite dish isn't on the menu, ask anyway. For dessert, try cherries jubilee or bananas flambé and an espresso. At lunchtime there's a shorter menu offering Canadian and Italian dishes for less than $9.

HUNGARIAN VILLAGE RESTAURANT, 5329 Ferry St. Tel. 416/356-2429.

Cuisine: HUNGARIAN/CONTINENTAL. **Reservations:** Recommended, especially on weekends.

$ Prices: Main courses $10–$18. AE, DC, MC, V.

Open: Tues–Fri 4pm–1am. Sat noon–1am, Sun noon–midnight.

Authentic Hungarian specialties are the attractions here: chicken paprikas, veal goulash, and the Transylvanian wooden platter (beef tenderloin, pork chop, veal cutlet, cabbage roll, and sausage, piled high on a bed of rice and served with french fries and sweet-and-sour cabbage; $30 for two). For dessert, there's palacsinta or Viennese pastries, of course. Continental dishes are also available.

ROLF'S, 3840 Main St., Chippewa. Tel. 416/295-3472.

Cuisine: CONTINENTAL. **Reservations:** Recommended, especially on weekends.

$ Prices: Main courses $10–$25. MC, V.

Open: Dinner only, Tues–Sun 5–9pm.

Perhaps the best dining in Niagara Falls can be found at Rolf's. Rolf hails from Germany and trained and worked in Zurich and later at several Niagara establishments before opening his own restaurant in a secluded town house complete with a front porch with room for two tables. The dining-room tables sport crisp white linen, Rosenthal china, and fresh flowers. The menu might feature beef roulade, salmon Grenoble (with caper sauce), Wienerschnitzel, chateaubriand, filet of pork (topped with Parma ham, romano cheese, and Madeira sauce), or lamb provençal.

MODERATE

HAPPY WANDERER, 6405 Stanley Ave. Tel. 416/354-9825.

Cuisine: GERMAN. **Reservations:** Not accepted.

$ Prices: Main courses $14–$25; desserts under $5. AE, MC, V.

Open: Daily 11am–11pm.

Here you can enjoy a host of schnitzels, würsts, and other German specialties in a chalet-style atmosphere with beer steins and game trophies on the walls. At lunch there are omelets, cold platters, sandwiches, and burgers. Dinner might start with goulash soup, proceed with bratwurst, knackwurst, or rauchwurst (served with sauerkraut and potato salad) or a schnitzel—wiener, Holstein, or jaeger. All entrées include potatoes, salad, and rye bread. Desserts include, naturally, Black Forest cake and apple strudel.

QUEENSTON HEIGHTS, 14276 Niagara Pkwy. Tel. 416/262-4274.

Cuisine: CANADIAN/CONTINENTAL.

$ Prices: Lunch $6–$9; dinner main courses $15–$19. AE, MC, V.

Open: Lunch Mon–Fri noon–3pm; dinner Mon–Fri 5–9pm; Sat noon–10pm, Sun noon–9pm. **Closed:** Mon in winter.

The best of the Niagara Parkway Commission's eateries stands dramatically atop Queenston Heights. Set in the park, the open-air balcony affords a magnificent view of the lower Niagara River and the rich fruit land through which it flows. There's a good selection of fish and seafood, roasts, and broiled and grilled dishes.

VICTORIA PARK RESTAURANT, 6345 Niagara Pkwy. Tel. 416/356-2217.

Cuisine: CANADIAN/CONTINENTAL.

$ Prices: Main courses $7–$11. AE, MC, V.

Open: Early May to mid-Oct, daily 11:30am–10pm. **Closed:** Late Oct to Apr.

Within a stone's throw of both the Canadian and the American falls, the Victoria Park offers a terrace for outdoor dining, a comfortable inside dining room warmed by its burnt-orange tablecloths and globe lights, a cafeteria, and a fast-food outlet pushing hot dogs and ice cream. In the dining room and terrace, you'll find an elaborate menu with a whole range of appetizers (escargots bruschetta, smoked trout, and tiger shrimp with spicy salsa and dijon mayonnaise) and main courses that include prime rib, grilled swordfish with lime-and-tequila butter, and lemon chicken breast. The main dish prices include vegetable, potato, and fresh-baked rolls. There's a children's menu featuring burgers and lasagne.

BUDGET

BETTY'S RESTAURANT & TAVERN, 8921 Sodom Rd. Tel. 416/295-4436.

Cuisine: CANADIAN.

$ Prices: Main courses $6–$12; burgers and sandwiches under $4. AE, MC, V.

Open: Mon–Sat 7am–10pm, Sun 9am–9pm.

Betty's is a local favorite for honest food at fair prices. It's a family dining room where the art and generosity surface in the food—massive platters of fish and chips, roast beef, and seafood platters, all including soup or juice, vegetable, and potato. There are burgers and sandwiches, too, all under $4. If you can, save room for enormous portions of home-baked pies. Breakfast and lunch also offer superb low-budget eating.

TABLE ROCK RESTAURANT, Canadian Horseshoe Falls. Tel. 416/354-3631.

Cuisine: CANADIAN/CONTINENTAL.

$ Prices: Main courses $8–$14; early-bird meal (served 4–6:30pm) $11. AE, MC, V.

Open: Daily 8am–10pm.

The Niagara Parkway Commission has commandeered the most spectacular scenic spots and operates on them some reasonably priced dining outlets. The Table Rock Restaurant, only a few yards from the Canadian Horseshoe Falls, offers main courses from $8 to $14, all served with vegetable of the day and french fries. Breakfast is also a good bet here, but it's served only on weekends out of season.

DINING WITH A VIEW

Besides the view from atop the 520-foot tower at the **Skylon Tower Restaurants** (tel. 416/356-2651, ext. 271), you can enjoy breakfast, lunch, or dinner buffets ($10, $16, or $27, respectively) in the Summit Suite dining room, or lunch or dinner in the Revolving Restaurant, where typical favorites like veal parmigiana, prime rib, and surf and turf are priced from $20 to $33 at dinner, $10 to $15 at lunch. It's open daily from 11:30am to 2:30pm for lunch and from 5 to 10:30pm for dinner (summer only—in other months, hours vary).

You can also dine atop the **Minolta Tower,** 6732 Oakes Dr. (tel. 416/356-1501), on typical North American favorites—steak, salmon, grilled chicken. At lunch prices range from $7 to $15; at dinner, from $14 to $29.

3. STRATFORD

Home of the world-famous Stratford Festival, this town manages to capture the prime elements of the Bard's birthplace, from the swans on the Avon River to the grass banks that sweep down to it where you can picnic under a weeping willow before attending a Shakespearean play.

INFORMATION For first-rate visitor information, go to the **information booth** by the river on York Street at Erie. It's open from May to early November, Sunday through Wednesday from 10am to 5pm and Thursday through Saturday from 10am to 8pm. At other times, contact **Tourism Stratford,** 88 Wellington St., Stratford, ON, N5A 6W1 (tel. 519/271-5140).

SPECIAL EVENTS Since its modest beginnings in 1953, when *Richard III*, starring Sir Alec Guinness, was staged in a huge tent, the artistic directors of the ✪ **Stratford Festival** have created a repertory theater with a glowing international reputation.

Stratford has three theaters: the Festival Theatre, 55 Queen St. in Queen's Park, with its dynamic thrust stage; the Avon Theatre, 99 Downie St., with a classic proscenium; and Third Stage, an intimate 500-seat theater on Lakeside Drive.

World-famous for its Shakespearean productions, the festival also offers both classic and modern theatrical masterpieces. Among the past members of the company are Maggie Smith, Sir Alec Guinness, Christopher Plummer, Irene Worth, Julie Harris, and Gordon Thompson.

The season usually begins early in May and continues through mid-November. For tickets, call 519/273-1600; or write Stratford Festival, P.O. Box 520, Stratford, ON, N5A 6V2. Tickets are also available in the United States and Canada at Ticketron outlets. Telephone orders are taken beginning in late February.

In the last week of May, **Festival City Days** celebrates the opening of the festival with marching bands, floats, and clowns.

In nearby New Hamburg in May, the annual **Mennonite Relief Sale** features some 300 quilts, an antiques auction, a large craft tent, and plenty of Mennonite food. Proceeds go to the Mennonite Central Committee to support its international relief work and service.

WHAT TO SEE & DO

Are there summer pleasures in Stratford beside the theater? Within sight of the Festival Theatre, **Queen's Park** has picnic spots beneath tall shade trees or down by the water's edge where the swans and ducks gather. To the east and west of the theater, footpaths follow the Avon River and Lake Victoria.

Past the Orr Dam and the 90-year-old stone bridge, through a rustic gate, lies a very special park, the **Shakespearean Garden.**

If you turn right onto Romeo Street North from Hwys. 7 and 8 as you come into Stratford, you'll find the **Gallery/Stratford,** 54 Romeo St. (tel. 519/271-5271), which mounts varied shows —Québec-Ontario Crafts, Twentieth-Century Canadian Drawing, and shows of individual artists. Open Sunday and Tuesday through Friday from 1 to 5pm and Saturday from 10am to 5pm from September through May; June through the first week of September, open Monday from 10am to 5pm and Tuesday through Sunday from 10am to 6pm. Admission is $3.50 for adults and $2.50 for students 12 and up and seniors.

Stratford is a historic town, and 1½-hour **guided tours of early Stratford** are given Monday through Saturday July to Labor Day, leaving at 9:30am from the visitor's booth by the river.

Boat and canoe rentals are available at the Boathouse, located behind and below the information booth. Open daily from 9am until dark in summer. Contact **Avon Boat Rentals,** 40 York St. (tel. 519/271-7739).

WHERE TO STAY

When you book your theater tickets, you can also, at no extra charge, book your accommodations. The Festival can book you into the type of accommodation and price category you prefer, from guest homes with $45 rates to first-class hotels charging over $125. Call or write the **Festival Theatre Box Office,** P.O. Box 520, Stratford, ON, N5A 6V2 (tel. 519/273-1600).

EXPENSIVE

BENTLEYS, 107 Ontario St., Stratford, ON, N5A 3H1. Tel. 519/271-1121. 13 suites. A/C TV TEL

$ Rates: May–Oct, $70 double Sun–Mon, $140 Tues–Thurs, $150 Fri–Sat. Nov–Apr, $70 double. Extra person $20.

The soundproof rooms here are in fact luxurious duplex suites, each with a bathroom, two telephones, air conditioning, a color TV, and a fully equipped efficiency kitchen. Period English furnishings and attractive drawings, paintings, and costume designs on the walls make for a pleasant ambience. Five of the suites have skylights.

FESTIVAL MOTOR INN, 1144 Ontario St. (P.O. Box 811), Stratford, ON, N5A 6W1. Tel. 519/273-1150. 152 rms. A/C TV TEL

$ Rates: Main building, $95 double; $100 twin. Outside units (with no inside access and no refrigerator), $85 single; $90 double; $95 twin. New deluxe rooms. $100 double. Extra person $10; cots $6. Winter discounts up to 40%.

The Festival Motor Inn, with its black-and-white motel-style units, is just off Hwys. 7 and 8 on 10 acres of nicely landscaped grounds. The place has an old-English air, with stucco walls and Tudor-style beams. The Tudor style is maintained throughout the large modern rooms, each with wall-to-wall carpeting, matching bedspread and drapes, reproductions of Old Masters on the walls, a direct-dial telephone, a color TV, and a full bathroom. Some of the bedrooms have charming bay windows with sheer curtains, and all rooms in the main building have refrigerators. For dining there are a dining room

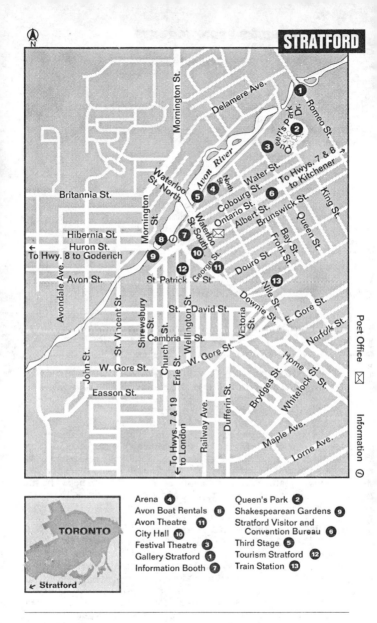

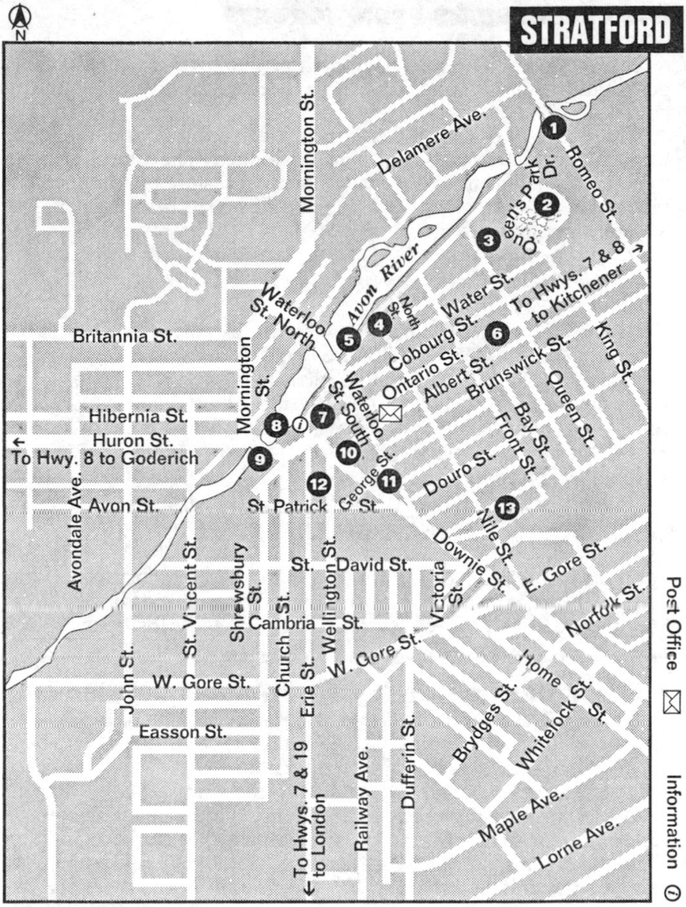
STRATFORD
N
Mornington St.
Delamere Ave.
Romeo St.
Queen's Park Dr.
Avon River
Waterloo St. North
North St.
Water St.
To Hwys. 7 & 8 to Kitchener
King St.
Cobourg St.
Ontario St.
Albert St.
Brunswick St.
Queen St.
Britannia St.
Mornington St.
Waterloo St. South
Hibernia St.
Huron St.
To Hwy. 8 to Goderich
Bay St.
Front St.
Douro St.
George St.
St. Patrick St.
Avon St.
Nile St.
Downie St.
E. Gore St.
Norfolk St.
Avondale Ave.
St. Vincent St.
Shrewsbury St.
Church St.
Wellington St.
St. David St.
Cambria St.
Victoria St.
W. Gore St.
John St.
Erie St.
Easson St.
Home St.
Brydges St.
Whitelock St.
To Hwys. 7 & 19 to London
Railway Ave.
Dufferin St.
Maple Ave.
Lorne Ave.
Post Office
Information

TORONTO
Stratford

Arena 4
Avon Boat Rentals 8
Avon Theatre 11
City Hall 10
Festival Theatre 3
Gallery Stratford 1
Information Booth 7
Queen's Park 2
Shakespearean Gardens 9
Stratford Visitor and Convention Bureau 6
Third Stage 5
Tourism Stratford 12
Train Station 13

---

and a coffee shop. Facilities include two tennis courts, shuffleboard, and an indoor pool with an outdoor patio.

THE QUEEN'S INN, 161 Ontario St., Stratford, ON, N5A 3H3. Tel. 519/271-1400. 31 rms. A/C TV TEL

$ Rates: May–Oct. $90–$160 double; Nov–Apr. $75–$100 double.

Conveniently located in the town center, the Queen's Inn has been recently restored. The rooms, all with private bath, air conditioning, push-button phones, and TVs, have been pleasantly decorated in pastels and pine.

There are two restaurants—the Queen's Table and the more formal Queen Victoria—and a piano lounge. The Queen's serves such traditional favorites as prime rib with Yorkshire pudding, stuffed sole, rack of lamb, along with roulade of bison. Prices run $11 to $20; at lunch most items are $6 to $9.

MODERATE

23 ALBERT PLACE, 23 Albert St., Stratford, ON, N5A 3K2. Tel. 519/273-5800. 34 rms. A/C TV TEL

$ Rates: $75–$85 double; $95 minisuite; from $100 suite.

Right across from the Avon Theatre, the Albert Place sports large rooms with high ceilings. Furnishings are simple and modern. Rooms have TVs, air conditioning, and push-button phones; some have separate sitting rooms.

A PICK OF THE B&Bs

For more information on the Stratford bed-and-breakfast scene, write to the **Stratford Visitor and Convention Bureau,** 38 Albert St., Stratford, ON, N5A 3K3 (tel. 519/271-5140). It's open 8:30am to 4:30pm Monday to Saturday.

ACRYLIC DREAMS, 66 Bay St., Stratford, ON, N5A 4K6. Tel. 519/271-7874. 2 rms, 1 suite (all with bath). A/C

$ Rates (including breakfast): $80 double; $95 suite. Two-night minimum on weekends. No credit cards.

In recent years, Acrylic Dreams was the "hot" B&B, drawing accolades for imaginative decor. The house is furnished with cottage-style antiques, except for the living room, which is furnished in New Wave, with transparent acrylic furniture. Upstairs there's a suite with private bath and living room. On the ground floor, there are two doubles with bath, each with an antique iron-and-brass bed. The full breakfast might feature orange juice and coffee, peaches with yogurt, scrambled eggs, and bagels.

AVONVIEW MANOR, 63 Avon St., Stratford, ON, N5A 5N5. Tel. 519/273-4603. 4 rms (none with bath).

$ Rates (including breakfast): $60 double. No credit cards.

Located on a quiet street in an Edwardian house, Avonview Manor has four rooms with fans, all attractively and individually furnished. One room has a brass bed covered with a floral-pattern quilt and flouncy pillows and is large enough for a couch and oak rocker. Another room has a cherry acorn bed, cherry dresser, and love seat. Mennonite quilts cover the beds. The rooms share two bathrooms.

A full breakfast is served in a bright dining room overlooking the garden, and a kitchen equipped with an ironing board is available on the first floor. The living room is very comfortable, particularly in winter in front of the stone fireplace. Smoking is allowed only on the porch.

BAKER HOUSE, 129 Brunswick St., Stratford, ON, N5A 3L9. Tel. 519/271-5644. 6 rms (none with bath). A/C

$ Rates (including continental breakfast): $45 single; $65 double; $75 triple.

Baker House has six rooms sharing two baths (four doubles, a triple, and a single). There are a comfy sitting room with plenty of slipcovered chairs and sofas, a small TV room, and a patio out back. An extended continental breakfast is served—fresh fruit, cereal, muffins, and croissants.

BRUNSWICK HOUSE, 109 Brunswick St., Stratford, ON, N5A 3L9. Tel. 519/271-4546. 6 rms (none with bath).

$ Rates (including breakfast): $55 and up.

If you stay here you'll enjoy the very literate surroundings created by owners Geoff Hancock and Gay Allison—portraits of Canadian authors and poetry on the walls, books everywhere, and the chance to run into a literary personality. There are six rooms, sharing two baths, all nicely decorated and with ceiling fans. One is a family room with a double and two single beds. Each room has a personal decorative touch—a Mennonite quilt, posters by an artist friend, or a parasol atop a wardrobe. A full breakfast is served. Smoking is restricted to the veranda.

CRACKERS, 433 Erie St., Stratford, ON, N5A 2N3. Tel. 519/273-1201. 5 rms (none with bath). A/C

$ Rates (including continental breakfast): $45 single; $60–$65 double.

The five rooms here are attractively and eclectically furnished. One features a four-poster bed; another has twin beds in a room with a bay window. A tiny porch with latticework is tucked away in the back—a nice retreat. A continental breakfast is served, with scones, muffins, and fresh fruit. At 5:30pm sherry and cheese and crackers are served in the sitting room.

DEACON HOUSE, 101 Brunswick St., Stratford, ON, N5A 3L9. Tel. 519/273-2052. 7 rms (3 with bath).

$ Rates (including continental breakfast): $65 double without bath, $80 double with bath. A/C

Deacon House, a shingle-style structure built in 1907, has been restored by Diane Hrysko and Mary Allen. They have seven rooms, three with bath, all decorated in country style with iron-and-brass beds, quilts, pine hutches, oak rockers, and rope-style rugs. My favorite rooms are on the top floor. The living room with fireplace, TV, wingbacks, and sofa, is comfortable. The guest kitchen is a welcome convenience; so too is the second-floor sitting/reading room. A continental breakfast is served.

FLINT'S INN, 220 Mornington St., Stratford, ON, N5A 5G5. Tel. 519/271-9579. 2 rms (none with bath), 1 suite (with bath). A/C

$ Rates (including breakfast): $60 double; $80 suite.

This steep-mansard-roofed house, built in 1862, has three air-conditioned units. One is a large suite with a sun porch, a balcony, a private bath, and a refrigerator. The iron-and-brass bed sports an old quilt, and among the decorative features are an old butter churn and a bottle collection. The other two rooms share a bathroom. The living room, with its marble fireplace and pine furnishings, is inviting. At breakfast, homemade muffins, juice, and coffee are accompanied by eggs Benedict or something similar. The garden is well kept and filled with the wonderful scent of lilac in season.

THE MAPLES, 220 Church St., Stratford, ON, N5A 2R6. Tel. 519/273-0810. 5 rms (1 with bath).

$ Rates (including breakfast): $45 single; $60 double.

The Maples is owned and run by Ruth McKeown, who keeps five nice rooms—four doubles and one single—and serves juices, fruit or cheese, and homemade breads and muffins at breakfast. The house is a red-brick Victorian with a balcony.

SHREWSBURY MANOR, 30 Shrewsbury St., Stratford, ON, N5A 2V5. Tel. 519/271-8520. 3 rms (none with bath). A/C

$ Rates: $50–$55 double.

At Shrewsbury Manor, an old Victorian built in 1872, there's a twin room and a master bedroom with a bed complete with Turkish-style canopy. Another room's bed sports a colorful log-cabin quilt made by owner Beryl Morningstar herself. The shared bathroom is large and the whole place is very comfortable.

WOODS VILLA, 62 John St. N., Stratford, ON, N5A 6K7. Tel. 519/271-4576. 5 rms (none with bath). A/C TV

$ Rates (including breakfast): $65 double.

This late 18th-century house is home to Ken Vinen, who has a passion for collecting and restoring Wurlitzers, Victrolas, and player pianos, which are found throughout the house. There are five rooms sharing two bathrooms. Four have fireplaces, and all have color TVs and air conditioning. Rooms are large and a good value. Guests are welcome to use the pool, lounges, and the TV in the living room.

Ken has other talents—at breakfast he may choose to make some doughnuts or muffins, served along with a full meal, while Barney and Fred, the macaws, add their comments.

WHERE TO DINE

EXPENSIVE

THE CHURCH, Brunswick and Waterloo Sts. Tel. 519/273-3424.

Cuisine: CONTINENTAL. **Reservations:** Required well in advance.

$ Prices: Summer fixed-price dinner $38.50–$44.50. AE, MC, V. **Open:** Tues–Sun 11:30am–1am. **Closed:** Mon, unless there's a special concert or play.

The Church must be one of the few restaurants in Canada where you have to reserve three weeks in advance. Still, it's a unique privilege because the food is so good and the decor is incredible. The organ pipes and the altar are still intact, along with the vaulted roof, carved woodwork, and stained-glass windows—you can sit in the nave or the side aisles and dine to the sounds of Bach. Fresh flowers and elegant table settings further enhance the experience.

In summer, there's a special five-course fixed-price dinner and an à la carte luncheon and after-theater menu. Appetizers might include quail marinated in lemon pepper and grilled served with parsnip, potato cake, and light curry cream; or marinated "tea" smoked salmon, with grilled sea scallops and shrimp and served in a pool of honey mustard sauce. Among the entrées might be roast lamb with couscous, candied onion, and parsnips, cooked in its natural juices with a hint of horseradish cream; or a selection of fish and shellfish in a scented stock of vegetables, herbs, and spices. There's also a short vegetarian menu. The pièce de résistance among the desserts might be an iced Grand Marnier soufflé or a trio of ices like chocolate Tía Maria and raisin, mango and coconut, and white peach sorbet. This is a very special dining experience.

The upstairs Belfry Bar is a popular pre- and posttheater gathering place for cocktails, snacks, and a full menu, priced form $15 to $24.

THE OLD PRUNE, 151 Albert St. Tel. 519/271-5052.

Cuisine: CONTINENTAL. **Reservations:** Required.

$ Prices: Fixed-price dinner $36–$45; main courses $9–$12 at lunch or after theater. MC, V.

Open: Lunch Wed–Sun 11:30am–2pm; dinner Tues–Sun 5–9pm; after-theater supper Fri–Sat 9pm–midnight. Hours change depending on the theater schedule.

Another of my Stratford favorites, the Old Prune is run by two charming, witty women—Marion Isherwood and Eleanor Kane. Set in a lovely Edwardian home, it has three dining rooms and a garden patio. The proprietors have given the place a Québec flair, which is reflected in both the decor and the menu.

At dinner the price of your entrée will determine the prix-fixe price for your appetizer, main course, and dessert. The chef uses organically grown meats and vegetables in an imaginative way that creates strong flavorsome dishes, like the medallions of rabbit with apple slices and cider-glazed onions or the warm duck confit with a mélange of organic greens topped with walnut oil and black-currant vinegar. The late-supper menu features lighter entrées, like risotto with grilled sea scallops, goat-cheese salad, or Arctic char. For dessert there are such mouth-watering combinations as rhubarb compote with fresh strawberries and Grand Marnier ice cream or chocolate cake with coffee ice cream.

RUNDLES, 9 Cobourg St. Tel. 519/271-6442.

Cuisine: CONTINENTAL. **Reservations:** Required.

$ Prices: Three-course fixed-price meal $42.50; two-course lunch $18.50. AE, MC, V.

Open: Lunch Wed and Sat–Sun; dinner Tues–Sun. Hours vary, so call ahead. **Closed:** Winter.

The large windows in this first-class restaurant take advantage of its beautiful setting overlooking Lake Victoria. There's a three-course table d'hôte, including appetizer, dessert, and coffee. The main dishes might include grilled Atlantic salmon with lentils and caramelized onions in a cumin-and-fenugreek sauce; pink roast lamb cutlets; confit of lamb shoulder; or breast of chicken with wild mushrooms and globe artichokes. Among the appetizers might be potato-wrapped duck ravioli with young green tomatoes and herbs or barbecued skewered bay scallops and vegetables, with sweet fries and salsa. Don't miss the ravishing desserts, like the delicious lemon tarts or the poached pears with chocolate mousse and butterscotch sauce. There's also an after-theater menu.

The main dining area is contemporary, with its gray tables spotlighted with brilliant colored shaded lamps, good cutlery and crystal, and contemporary art; there's also a room with a softer look.

The restaurant follows the theater schedule. For the most part it's open Wednesday through Sunday for lunch and Wednesday through Saturday for dinner. On Friday and Saturday an after-theater menu is available. During the winter the restaurant closes and functions occasionally as a cooking school until theater season comes again.

WOLFY'S, 127 Downie St. Tel. 519/271-2991.
Cuisine: INTERNATIONAL. **Reservations:** Recommended.
$ **Prices:** Main courses $12–$20. MC, V.
Open: Lunch Wed–Sun 11:30am–2pm; dinner Tues–Sat 5–8:30pm.

Wolfy's has a loyal following because it offers well-prepared cuisine. It's located in a former fish-and-chips shop and the original decor is still evident—the booths, the counter and stools, and the old fish fryer serving as a display cabinet in one corner. Yet it has a New Wave flavor. The walls are decorated with vibrant art by Kato.

On the limited menu might be found Southern-style chicken and black-bean salsa with coconut rice and grilled plantains; charred shrimp with East Asian noodles; or herb-wrapped salmon with citrus vinaigrette.

MODERATE

BENTLEY'S, 107 Ontario St. Tel. 519/271-1121.
Cuisine: CANADIAN/ENGLISH.
$ **Prices:** Appetizers and sandwiches $6–$8; main courses $12–$15. AE, MC, V.
Open: Daily 11:30am–1am.

For budget dining and fun to boot, go to Bentley's, a well-conceived reproduction of an English pub. Up front there is a bar and an area for reading the volumes in the bookcase. The dining room is at the rear, or you can sit on the garden terrace.

In this atmosphere you can savor some light fare—grilled shrimp, vegetarian wontons, and chicken fingers—along with sandwiches and salads, which are served all day. Dinner items are more substantial, like roast chicken, baked sole, sirloin, and prime rib. On one evening a week (the day varies), you can enjoy some entertainment from a pianist and double-bass player.

KEYSTONE ALLEY CAFE, 34 Brunswick St. Tel. 519/271-5645.
Cuisine: CONTINENTAL. **Reservations:** Recommended.
$ **Prices:** Main courses under $7 at lunch, $12–$18 at dinner, AE, MC, V.
Open: Lunch Mon–Sat 11am–4pm; dinner Tues–Sat 5–9pm.

Actors often stop in for lunch at the Keystone Alley Café. There are butcher-block tables as well as a counter where you can order a light lunch—soups, salads, burgers, sandwiches, New York cheesecake, and a daily selection of muffins.

At night the atmosphere changes, and there's a full dinner menu featuring eight or so items, such as calves' liver with apple-and-shallot compote and pink-peppercorn sauce; pork loin in sauce of honey, lime, ginger, and Calvados with caramelized apricots and water chestnuts; and grain-fed chicken with mango, ginger, and coriander cream sauce. Wine and beer are available.

OLDE ENGLISH PARLOUR, 101 Wellington St. Tel. 519/271-2772.

Cuisine: ENGLISH.
$ **Prices:** Appetizers under $5; main courses $9–$20. AE, MC, V.
Open: Mon 11:30am–11pm, Tues–Sat 11:30am–1am, Sun 11:30am–9pm.

For medium-priced fare, head for the Olde English Parlour. In this pubby atmosphere, you can select sandwiches, steak-and-kidney pie, fish and chips, and other British fare, along with burgers, seafood, and steaks.

BUDGET

CAFE MEDITERRANEAN, in the Festival Square Building. Tel. 519/271-9590.
Cuisine: LIGHT FARE.
$ **Prices:** Most items under $6. No credit cards.
Open: Summer, Mon–Tues 8am–6pm, Wed–Sat 8am–7pm, Sun 10am–2pm; winter, Mon–Sat 9am–5pm.

In the Festival Square Building, the Café Mediterranean is great for fruit flans, croissants (cheese, almond, and chocolate), quiches, salads, pastries, and crêpes. You can take them out or dine there while seated on director's chairs.

LET THEM EAT CAKE, 82 Wellington St. Tel. 519/273-4774.
Cuisine: DESSERTS.
$ **Prices:** Breakfast and lunch items under $8; desserts $1–$4. MC, V.
Open: Mon 7:30am–6pm, Tues–Fri 7:30am–12:30pm, Sat 9am–12:30pm, Sun 11am–6pm.

Let Them Eat Cake is great for breakfast (bagels, scones, and croissants), and lunch (soups, salads, sandwiches, quiche, and chicken pot pie), but best of all for dessert. There are about 30 items to choose from—pecan pie, orange Bavarian cream, lemon bars, carrot cake, Black Forest cake, and chocolate cheesecake among them.

PICNIC FARE & WHERE TO EAT IT

Stratford is really a picnicking place. Take a hamper down to the banks of the river or into the parks: Plenty of places cater to this business. **Rundles** will make you a super-sophisticated hamper; **Café Mediterranean** has salads, quiches, crêpes, and flaky meat pies and pastries. Or go to **Tastes,** 40 Wellington St. (tel. 519/273-6000), which offers all kinds of salads—pasta, grains, and vegetables—pâtés; fish, chicken, and meat dishes; soups; and breads and pastries. The shop also sells imported specialty foods. Open in summer Monday through Friday from 10am to 6pm, Saturday from 9am to 5pm, and Sunday from 11am to 2pm.

APPENDIX

METRIC CONVERSIONS

LENGTH

1 millimeter	=	0.04 inches (*or* less than 1/16 inch)
1 centimeter	=	0.39 inches (*or* just under 1/2 inch)
1 meter	=	1.09 yards (*or* about 39 inches)
1 kilometer	=	0.62 mile (*or* about 2/3 mile)

To convert **kilometers to miles,** take the number of kilometers and multiply by .62 (for example, 25km × .62 = 15.5 miles). To convert **miles to kilometers,** take the number of miles and multiply by 1.61 (for example, 50 miles × 1.61 = 80.5 km).

CAPACITY

1 liter	=	33.92 ounces
	=	1.06 quarts
	=	0.26 gallons

To convert **liters to gallons,** take the number of liters and multiply by .26 (for example, 50 l × .26 = 13 gal). To convert **gallons to liters,** take the number of gallons and multiply by 3.79 (for example, 10 gal × 3.79 = 37.9 l).

WEIGHT

1 gram	=	0.04 ounce (*or* about a paperclip's weight)
1 kilogram	=	2.2 pounds

To convert **kilograms to pounds,** take the number of kilos and multiply by 2.2 (for example, 75kg × 2.2 = 165 lbs). To convert **pounds to kilograms,** take the number of pounds and multiply by .45 (for example, 90 lb × .45 = 40.5kg).

TEMPERATURE

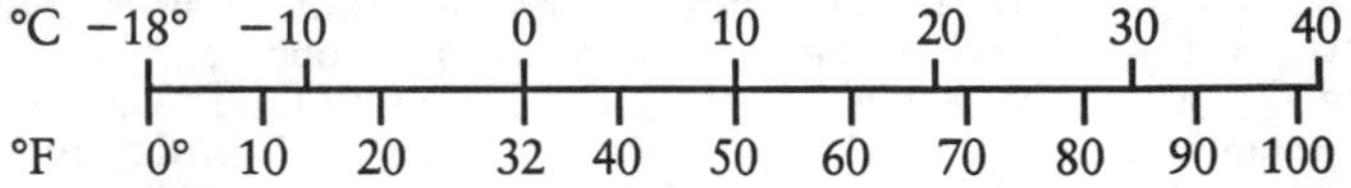
°C −18° −10 0 10 20 30 40
°F 0° 10 20 32 40 50 60 70 80 90 100

To convert **degrees C to degrees F,** multiply degrees C by 9, divide by 5, and add 32 (for example 9/5 × 20°C + 32 = 68°F). To convert **degrees F to degrees C,** subtract 32 from degrees F, multiply by 5, and divide by 9 (for example: 85°F − 32 × 5/9 = 29°C).

INDEX

GENERAL INFORMATION

SIGHTS & ATTRACTIONS

TORONTO & ENVIRONS

Note: *indicates an author's favorite.

EXCURSION AREAS

ACCOMMODATIONS

TORONTO & ENVIRONS

AT THE AIRPORT

DOWNTOWN

Key to Abbreviations: *B* = Budget; *E* = Expensive; *M* = Moderate; *VE* = Very expensive; *B&B* = Bed & Breakfast; *CG* = Campground; *Hs* = Hostel; * = Author's favorite; *$* = Super-value choice

EXCURSION AREAS

RESTAURANTS

TORONTO & ENVIRONS

BY CUISINE

Key to Abbreviations: *B* = Budget; *E* = Expensive; *M* = Moderate; *VE* = Very expensive; * = Author's favorite; *$* = Super-value choice

BY LOCATION

EXCURSION AREAS

Please Send Me the Books Checked Below

FROMMER'S COMPREHENSIVE GUIDES

(Guides listing facilities from budget to deluxe, with emphasis on the medium-priced)

	Retail Price	Code
☐ Acapulco/Ixtapa/Taxco 1993–94	$15.00	C120
☐ Alaska 1990–91	$15.00	C001
☐ Arizona 1993–94	$18.00	C101
☐ Australia 1992–93	$18.00	C002
☐ Austria 1993–94	$19.00	C119
☐ Austria/Hungary 1991–92	$15.00	C003
☐ Belgium/Holland/ Luxembourg 1993–94	$18.00	C106
☐ Bermuda/Bahamas 1992–93	$17.00	C005
☐ Brazil, 3rd Edition	$20.00	C111
☐ California 1993	$18.00	C112
☐ Canada 1992–93	$18.00	C009
☐ Caribbean 1993	$18.00	C102
☐ Carolinas/Georgia 1992–93	$17.00	C034
☐ Colorado 1993–94	$16.00	C100
☐ Cruises 1993–94	$19.00	C107
☐ DE/MD/PA & NJ Shore 1992–93	$19.00	C012
☐ Egypt 1990–91	$15.00	C013
☐ England 1993	$18.00	C109
☐ Florida 1993	$18.00	C104
☐ France 1992–93	$20.00	C017
☐ Germany 1993	$19.00	C108
☐ Italy 1993	$19.00	C113
☐ Jamaica/Barbados 1993–94	$15.00	C105
☐ Japan 1992–93	$19.00	C020
☐ Morocco 1992–93	$18.00	C021
☐ Nepal 1992–93	$18.00	C038
☐ New England 1993	$17.00	C114
☐ New Mexico 1993–94	$15.00	C117
☐ New York State 1992–93	$19.00	C025
☐ Northwest 1991–92	$17.00	C026
☐ Portugal 1992–93	$16.00	C027
☐ Puerto Rico 1993–94	$15.00	C103
☐ Puerto Vallarta/ Manzanillo/ Guadalajara 1992–93	$14.00	C028
☐ Scandinavia 1993–94	$19.00	C118
☐ Scotland 1992–93	$16.00	C040
☐ Skiing Europe 1989–90	$15.00	C030
☐ South Pacific 1992–93	$20.00	C031
☐ Spain 1993–94	$19.00	C115
☐ Switzerland/ Liechtenstein 1992–93	$19.00	C032
☐ Thailand 1992–93	$20.00	C033
☐ U.S.A. 1993–94	$19.00	C116
☐ Virgin Islands 1992–93	$13.00	C036
☐ Virginia 1992–93	$14.00	C037
☐ Yucatán 1993–94	$18.00	C110

FROMMER'S $-A-DAY GUIDES

(Guides to low-cost tourist accommodations and facilities)

	Retail Price	Code
☐ Australia on $45 1993–94	$18.00	D102
☐ Costa Rica/ Guatemala/Belize on $35 1993–94	$17.00	D108
☐ Eastern Europe on $25 1991–92	$17.00	D005
☐ England on $60 1993	$18.00	D107
☐ Europe on $45 1993	$19.00	D106
☐ Greece on $45 1993–94	$19.00	D100
☐ Hawaii on $75 1993	$19.00	D104
☐ India on $40 1992–93	$20.00	D010
☐ Ireland on $40 1992–93	$17.00	D011
☐ Israel on $45 1993–94	$18.00	D101
☐ Mexico on $50 1993	$19.00	D105
☐ New York on $70 1992–93	$16.00	D016
☐ New Zealand on $45 1993–94	$18.00	D103
☐ Scotland/Wales on $50 1992–93	$18.00	D019
☐ South America on $40 1993–94	$19.00	D109
☐ Turkey on $40 1992–93	$22.00	D023
☐ Washington, D.C. on $40 1992–93	$17.00	D024

FROMMER'S CITY $-A-DAY GUIDES

(Pocket-size guides with an emphasis on low-cost tourist accommodations and facilities)

	Retail Price	Code
☐ Berlin on $40 1992–93	$12.00	D002
☐ Copenhagen on $50 1992–93	$12.00	D003
☐ London on $45 1992–93	$12.00	D013
☐ Madrid on $50 1992–93	$13.00	D014
☐ Paris on $45 1992–93	$12.00	D018
☐ Stockholm on $50 1992–93	$13.00	D022

FROMMER'S TOURING GUIDES

(Color-illustrated guides that include walking tours, cultural and historic sights, and practical information)

	Retail Price	Code
☐ Amsterdam	$11.00	T001
☐ Barcelona	$14.00	T015
☐ Brazil	$11.00	T003
☐ Florence	$ 9.00	T005
☐ Hong Kong/Singapore/Macau	$11.00	T006
☐ Kenya	$14.00	T018
☐ London	$13.00	T007
☐ New York	$11.00	T008
☐ Rome	$11.00	T010
☐ Scotland	$10.00	T011
☐ Sicily	$15.00	T017
☐ Thailand	$13.00	T012
☐ Tokyo	$15.00	T016
☐ Venice	$ 9.00	T014

FROMMER'S FAMILY GUIDES

	Retail Price	Code
☐ California with Kids	$17.00	F001
☐ Los Angeles with Kids	$17.00	F002
☐ New York City with Kids	$18.00	F003
☐ San Francisco with Kids	$17.00	F004
☐ Washington, D.C. with Kids	$17.00	F005

FROMMER'S CITY GUIDES

(Pocket-size guides to sightseeing and tourist accommodations and facilities in all price ranges)

	Retail Price	Code
☐ Amsterdam 1993–94	$13.00	S110
☐ Athens, *9th* Edition	$13.00	S114
☐ Atlanta 1993–94	$13.00	S112
☐ Atlantic City/Cape May 1991–92	$ 9.00	S004
☐ Bangkok 1992–93	$13.00	S005
☐ Barcelona/Majorca/Minorca/Ibiza 1993–94	$13.00	S115
☐ Berlin 1993–94	$13.00	S116
☐ Boston 1993–94	$13.00	S117
☐ Cancún/Cozumel/Yucatán 1991–92	$ 9.00	S010
☐ Chicago 1993–94	$13.00	S122
☐ Denver/Boulder/Colorado Springs 1990–91	$ 8.00	S012
☐ Dublin 1993–94	$13.00	S128
☐ Hawaii 1992	$12.00	S014
☐ Hong Kong 1992–93	$12.00	S015
☐ Honolulu/Oahu 1993	$13.00	S106
☐ Las Vegas 1993–94	$13.00	S121
☐ Lisbon/Madrid/Costa del Sol 1991–92	$ 9.00	S017
☐ London 1993	$13.00	S100
☐ Los Angeles 1993–94	$13.00	S123
☐ Madrid/Costa del Sol 1993–94	$13.00	S124
☐ Mexico City/Acapulco 1991–92	$ 9.00	S020
☐ Miami 1993–94	$13.00	S118
☐ Minneapolis/St. Paul, 3rd Edition	$13.00	S119
☐ Montréal/Québec City 1993–94	$13.00	S125
☐ New Orleans 1993–94	$13.00	S103
☐ New York 1993	$13.00	S120
☐ Orlando 1993	$13.00	S101
☐ Paris 1993–94	$13.00	S109
☐ Philadelphia 1993–94	$13.00	S113
☐ Rio 1991–92	$ 9.00	S029
☐ Rome 1993–94	$13.00	S111
☐ Salt Lake City 1991–92	$ 9.00	S031
☐ San Diego 1993–94	$13.00	S107
☐ San Francisco 1993	$13.00	S104
☐ Santa Fe/Taos/Albuquerque 1993–94	$13.00	S108
☐ Seattle/Portland 1992–93	$12.00	S035
☐ St. Louis/Kansas City 1993–94	$13.00	S127
☐ Sydney 1993–94	$13.00	S129
☐ Tampa/St. Petersburg 1993–94	$13.00	S105
☐ Tokyo 1992–93	$13.00	S039
☐ Toronto 1993–94	$13.00	S126
☐ Vancouver/Victoria 1990–91	$ 8.00	S041
☐ Washington, D.C. 1993	$13.00	S102

Other Titles Available at Membership Prices

SPECIAL EDITIONS

	Retail Price	Code		Retail Price	Code
☐ Bed & Breakfast North America	$15.00	P002	☐ Where to Stay U.S.A.	$14.00	P015
☐ Caribbean Hideaways	$16.00	P005			
☐ Marilyn Wood's Wonderful Weekends (within a 250-mile radius of NYC)	$12.00	P017			

GAULT MILLAU'S "BEST OF" GUIDES

(The only guides that distinguish the truly superlative from the merely overrated)

	Retail Price	Code		Retail Price	Code
☐ Chicago	$16.00	G002	☐ New England	$16.00	G010
☐ Florida	$17.00	G003	☐ New Orleans	$17.00	G011
☐ France	$17.00	G004	☐ New York	$17.00	G012
☐ Germany	$18.00	G018	☐ Paris	$17.00	G013
☐ Hawaii	$17.00	G006	☐ San Francisco	$17.00	G014
☐ Hong Kong	$17.00	G007	☐ Thailand	$18.00	G019
☐ London	$17.00	G009	☐ Toronto	$17.00	G020
☐ Los Angeles	$17.00	G005	☐ Washington, D.C.	$17.00	G017

THE REAL GUIDES

(Opinionated, politically aware guides for youthful budget-minded travelers)

	Retail Price	Code		Retail Price	Code
☐ Able to Travel	$20.00	R112	☐ Kenya	$12.95	R015
☐ Amsterdam	$13.00	R100	☐ Mexico	$11.95	R016
☐ Barcelona	$13.00	R101	☐ Morocco	$14.00	R017
☐ Belgium/Holland/Luxembourg	$16.00	R031	☐ Nepal	$14.00	R018
			☐ New York	$13.00	R019
☐ Berlin	$11.95	R002	☐ Paris	$13.00	R020
☐ Brazil	$13.95	R003	☐ Peru	$12.95	R021
☐ California & the West Coast	$17.00	R121	☐ Poland	$13.95	R022
			☐ Portugal	$15.00	R023
☐ Canada	$15.00	R103	☐ Prague	$15.00	R113
☐ Czechoslovakia	$14.00	R005	☐ San Francisco & the Bay Area	$11.95	R024
☐ Egypt	$19.00	R105			
☐ Europe	$18.00	R122	☐ Scandinavia	$14.95	R025
☐ Florida	$14.00	R006	☐ Spain	$16.00	R026
☐ France	$18.00	R106	☐ Thailand	$17.00	R119
☐ Germany	$18.00	R107	☐ Tunisia	$17.00	R115
☐ Greece	$18.00	R108	☐ Turkey	$13.95	R027
☐ Guatemala/Belize	$14.00	R010	☐ U.S.A.	$18.00	R117
☐ Hong Kong/Macau	$11.95	R011	☐ Venice	$11.95	R028
☐ Hungary	$14.00	R118	☐ Women Travel	$12.95	R029
☐ Ireland	$17.00	R120	☐ Yugoslavia	$12.95	R030
☐ Italy	$13.95	R014			